Elizabeth Buchner
April 2011.

LAW FOR THE PROTECTION OF GERMAN BLOOD AND GERMAN HONOR

Special legislation for Jews in the National Socialist State:

1. Marriage between Jews and German Citizens is forbidden. Existing marriages of this kind are nullified.

2. Sexual relationships between such persons are forbidden.

3. Only persons of German blood are German citizens.

4. Jews cannot be German citizens, cannot vote, and cannot have an official occupation.

5. Children from mixed marriages are *Mischlinge*, "halfbreeds." Such marriages [that have produced children] are "privileged mixed marriages."

From the Nuremburg Laws, 1935

Berlin, 1933

A PRIVILEGED MARRIAGE

*The Autobiography of
Elizabeth Pschorr*

"Grau, teurer Freund, ist alle Theory."
"Gray, dear friend, is all theory."

—Johann Wolfgang von Goethe, *Faust*

Elizabeth Pschorr

Library of Congress Cataloging-in-Publication Data: 2007901101

Pschorr, Elizabeth, 1911-
    A privileged marriage: the autobiography of Elizabeth Pschorr/
        p.   cm.
    ISBN: Hardcover   978-1-4257-5259-0
               Softcover   978-1-4257-5258-3

    1. Pschorr, Elizabeth, 1911- . 2. Jews-Germany-Biography.
    3. Children of interfaith marriage-Germany-Biography.
    4. Holocaust, Jewish (1939-1945)-Germany-Personal narratives.
    I. Title.
    DS 135. G5P756   1994
    943'. 004924'092-dc20
    [B]   94-15618
                                                        CIP

FIRST PRINTING
Printed in the United States of America

To order additional copies of this book, contact:
Xlibris Corporation
1-888-795-4274
www.Xlibris.com
Orders@Xlibris.com
35362

CONTENTS

PREFACE

It built up inside like the fire of a volcano, surging then receding—the urge to take a closer look at my life could not be denied. This excitement, this inner turmoil, had nothing to do with the ocean before me or the white beach with its tropical vegetation, exotic and foreign to me. Nor was the cause of my emotion the happy circumstance of seeing in the distance my grandchildren—Michelle Brody, six years old, and Jason, in his eighth year—running back and forth in the foaming waves under the watchful eye of Irene, my tanned and beautiful daughter. A ship moved almost imperceptibly in the glittering sun, its contours visible against the horizon. There was no sound but the steady beat of the surf.

I had wondered why this, my first visit to Hawaii, didn't stir the same feeling I had experienced in younger years when I stood on the beach of the North Sea, when the wind brushed my body, cooled my skin, and blew my hair, and my naked feet felt the soft, warm sand. That was long ago, when I was young and full of expectations. With a deep breath, I had greeted the wide, limitless ocean and had felt its eternity. This surge of joy I had always cherished so much; mysteriously it would well up when least expected, and I did not know then how to summon it. But as my life unfolded, this unidentified part of me could be called upon as an ever-present friend.

But now, suddenly, on a quiet afternoon in Hawaii, in the summer of 1977, the almost forgotten excitement overcame me and erupted: the past would come forth. The joy was a signal that I was ready to explore the world of my past.

Once, I remembered having the same experience when I was seventeen years old. I described it in my diary as being in touch with the sublime. Sitting alone in my room I had tried to identify the longing, the almost painful feeling that filled my heart. Some years later I wrote to Friedel, my beloved friend and future husband, about this indescribable emotion, which had overcome me in the church during my confirmation ceremony:

Long afterwards I sensed the solemnity of this special moment,
a juncture in my life. This feeling of elation overcomes me

unexpectedly and involuntarily. I cannot define it and I wonder if every person can experience this the same way.

And now, much later, I was going to see from a bird's eye view the history I had witnessed and lived. I felt the reason for unlocking this seemingly closed door was a need to speak about myself. It was a victory over imposed rules that were integrated almost permanently into my personality. The social code of my time had been self-reliance and discipline, and to talk and act freely according to one's inner, personal condition—as we are urged to do today—was simply not the custom. Aside from this, my own experience of persecution in Nazi Germany had taught me to shut out thoughts and feelings which did not serve mere survival. Twelve years under Hitler's regime forced me to trust myself and my husband only. Sharing fears and opinions with others would have endangered them and myself, so we learned then to keep to ourselves. My father had formulated this doctrine after he returned from six months in a concentration camp: never expect another person to risk his or her life for your sake.

All this had caused me to shut myself off in the very real sense. This was going to change now. Would I be able to communicate with the past, with myself and others? And what would I find out? Was it the first years of my life, protected, happy and also blissfully ignorant, or was it later experiences that had formed me? Visions of those early, peaceful years float as happy memories through my mind, and change slowly, almost reluctantly approaching the dark time of my middle age. I felt myself clinging to the scenes of my childhood, I wanted to hold on to them, dreaming of their return. It hurts to realize that my early world was a dream world, that a tiger lurked unnoticed in the shadows. I needed to tear myself away from illusions.

Where is the true beginning of life? Pictures of my early childhood, recalled through my parents' and grandparents' tales, are succeeded by those remembered of my awakening, the years darkened by Hitler's regime and World War II. I was faced with problems that, surprisingly, gave me strength, awareness, faith, and humility. Looking back, I realized the effect of these tribulations on my development and never regretted them. This, then, is the story of my life and also of my birth as the person I am today.

CHAPTER ONE

The Family Blum

On the twenty-third of September, 1911, I was born into a Hamburg family that consisted of my parents, Marcel and Gertrud Holzer; my brother, Erich, then three years old; and my grandparents, Adolf and Elise Blum. I remember my childhood as beautifully enriched by the presence and the compassionate and loving care of my grandparents; I cannot imagine what my life would have been without them. Their example and the influence of their traditions still live in my heart.

Adolf Blum, my grandfather, was born in 1849; his hometown, Gross Meseritsch, was situated in Moravia which, one year after his birth, became part of the Austro-Hungarian Empire ruled by Emperor Franz-Joseph I. Europe at that time was shaken by revolutions and wars; unrest between European monarchies and various small and larger principalities would continue for decades and, over sixty years later, culminate in World War I.

My Opi (that was my pet name for my grandfather) told us many stories, but nothing about his childhood. I know that he was the fourth child of Mina and Jonas Blum, and that he grew up in Vienna. He left his family as a youth and went to Germany where he settled in Hamburg, one of the ancient, free city-states on the North Sea. He founded his own freight-forwarding business in 1875 when he was only twenty-six years old and named it Adolf Blum, Transportation. A little later he took a partner, Ludwig Popper, and the firm became Adolf Blum & Popper. Business was booming in Hamburg; both the Austro-Hungarian Empire and the newly formed German Empire profited in the aftermath of the Franco-Prussian War which had ended just four years earlier. Merchandise and raw materials flowed through the seaport of Hamburg from England and elsewhere, and the small firm grew steadily. Although Adolf Blum & Popper was known for its reliability, it suffered a setback when Ludwig Popper was caught in some impropriety. He was given a choice: go to prison or leave the country; and, not surprisingly, he chose the latter. He emigrated to the United States. In those days, it was not unusual for criminals and other so-called black sheep to seek their fortunes in America.

Although Adolf now headed the firm alone and never again took a partner, the name remained Adolf Blum & Popper. He must have accumulated capital quite rapidly in the first years of business, for he soon thought of marriage, and not to just anyone. He decided that Elise Goetz would be his wife. It was quite daring of him to ask for her hand and quite an honor when his offer was accepted. She was the eldest daughter of a well-to-do widow, Rosette Goetz, who surely never would have consented to a marriage of her Elise to so young a suitor as Adolf, had not her advisors approved of this honorable, exceptional, and successful young man.

Elise's mother had been born in Copenhagen in 1824. She married well and had eight children, but her husband, Leopold Goetz, died in 1868 when he was only forty-eight years old. She raised the children by herself, fortunately, without financial worries. Leopold had been a prosperous merchant, but it is not known whether it was he who provided for his family so well or if Rosette had inherited money from her father, who was Minister of Finance at the Danish Royal Court. Not only did Rosette live comfortably, but at her death, she left quite a bit of money. To be sure, she lived simply enough; apparently she did not hire much domestic help for her large household. Her eldest daughter, Elise, was in charge of the younger children.

When my great-grandmother Rosette died in 1908, she left a handwritten will, a document that has been passed down from generation to generation. It shows her to be a good-hearted, clear-minded person who included not only her family in her loving thoughts but social organizations as well. Her will specified 500 crowns each to the Society for the Elderly, the Society for Old Maids and Widows, the Food Cooperative, a public meal distribution for the needy, a public school, and the Society for Cremation. In straight German letters she wrote:

> Beloved children, all of you,
>
> Herewith I let you know my wishes to be executed after my death: A capital of 15,000 crowns for Mihval in case she does not marry; if she dies the sum should go to my heirs. Furthermore I wish that my niece Aurelia, as long as she is not married, should be paid 125 crowns per year. Bertha Fraenkel in Copenhagen should get the sum of 125 crowns per year. Furthermore, I wish that the sum of 15,000 crowns should be invested and that on the due dates my granddaughter Elly Goetz, daughter of my son Theodor, should

be paid the interest thereof, either until her marriage or her death. She should use the money for her personal benefit.

These, my wishes, I wrote and I made not other arrangements. My silverware should be divided among my three daughters, all other things my children should divide according to their wishes and with each other's consent in such a way that nobody is forgotten.

Finally, I take my farewell of all of you, my beloved children and grandchildren. I thank you for all your love and care by which you have brightened my old age. Uphold the loving bond between you, which was my joy and pride during my lifetime. Do not mourn my departure. Although I weathered several storms I had a long and beautiful life with you and because of you. I give you at the end of my life my motherly blessings.

Your mother, Rosette Goetz, nee Simonson.

January, 1908

Great-grandmother's spirit of caring for children, grandchildren, and others beyond her own death set an example that became a tradition in our family, whereby parents and grandparents took direct responsibility for the next generation. There was a strong bond between members of the close and wider family, always renewed at family gatherings and holidays. Nobody was forgotten, and relatives knew there was always a haven in my grandparent's home in the *Alsterchaussee* in Hamburg.

In those days it was perhaps easier for families to remain close, geographically and spiritually, than it is today. There was more time to meet and talk, problems were discussed around the dinner table, and sharing of ideas and feelings was a natural everyday process. Activities that today send family members in different directions were centered then in the home. The group where one found understanding and advice was the family. My grandmother saw to it that family members kept in touch with one another. She would remind me of birthdays and other family occasions with a gentle admonition to write a word or two to the relative in question. After her death, these anniversary dates faded from my memory. Women like my great-grandmother and my grandmother may not have made history, but their meritorious way of life keeps them alive in the memory of succeeding generations.

After I was grown and had read Rosette Goetz's will, I understood how proud Adolf Blum must have been to have won Elise. It was customary then, and legally required, that a man take complete responsibility for his bride.

Parents truly "gave away" their daughter: they expected the husband to vouch for her security and support. In wedding ceremonies today when the father escorts the bride down the aisle to her husband-to-be, it is a mere gesture by comparison. Women have gained equality with men in some ways, but they have also lost something which is very natural to their femininity, the enjoyment and inner security of being protected.

Elise Blum, my grandmother, was born on August 18, 1854. She seldom spoke about her youth. I feel she knew few pleasures outside the home, where she had many duties. She put her motherly instincts to use and gained joy from them.

Adolf and Elise established their first home in Hamburg on the *Bahnhofstrasse*. Adolf's office was in that same house until it was transferred to the *Mönkebergstrasse*, where it remained until Hitler's time. Later the family moved to the suburb of *Harvestehude*, or, in the local jargot, "*Poeseldorf*." Thirty years later, by the time I was born, this section of Hamburg had become engulfed by the expanded city.

My grandparents raised four children: Edgar, their first son, was born in 1880, followed by Hans in 1882. After that two daughters appeared—Gertrud Therese, my mother, in 1885, and the youngest, Mina, in 1890.

I have the impression of tranquility and stability flowing around my grandparents' life although a closer look reveals that their world changed considerably during their lifetime. I think the atmosphere in which my mother grew up seems peaceful to me because she told us so much of her happy youth, of her lifelong friendships with men and women who were almost like family members, and of sharing so many hours of fun and laughter with them. I tend to forget about World War I and the poverty and death that also characterized that era; but my impression of my mother's carefree youth was not mere illusion. Hamburg, although one of Germany's biggest cities at the time, was considerably smaller than it is today. Townsfolk lived close to each other and they also seldom changed their domiciles. They walked to and from their work or to meet their friends, or used public transportation—horse-drawn streetcars, or, later, electric trolleys. Shopping for daily supplies was done in one's street. The farmers, a large part of Germany's population, came to town and sold their goods directly from their horse-drawn wagons or on stands in street markets. Since travel, even within Germany, was expensive and cumbersome, only businessmen and rich people undertook such ventures. The majority of working-class citizens stayed in the same place year after year.

Life gave them little time for leisure or reflection if they were so inclined. Local news was spread by word of mouth. National news and current events were communicated through the press, but only a fraction of the male population took an interest in it. And it was not a free press as we know it. International news traveled slowly, in step with the technology of the time. Ordinary citizens were much less informed than the leading personalities of the day who made foreign affairs, politics, and government their lives' purpose. The ordinary worker or farmer had little access to information about things that directly affected his life. He was dependant on scholars, doctors, and trained leaders. This vacuum of knowledge often perpetrated superstitions and fears, especially when illness and death threatened. The "great unknown" often caused more harm than the illness itself. The welfare of one's fellow citizen was not the ordinary person's responsibility. This centralization of activity and interest contributed heavily to the quiet life of the time and to the importance of family life. It was such a different world.

Although we might consider the former way of life limited—not yet influenced by radio and television—I doubt that one thought as critically as we do now about one's personal situation. Only in later years, after the works of Freud and Jung became better known, self-awareness and questions of consciousness came into play, which made the following generations' lives apparently more problematic.

Indeed, life in those days remained simple, perhaps even primitive, by today's standards, in spite of a considerable evolution in industry brought on by a burst of fundamental inventions in science and technology. The electric light, for instance, had not yet replaced the gas light. The telephone was a rare novelty, used only by a few. Daily life then, with its slower pace, was conducive to human contact and created what seemed to be a more peaceful time.

World War I changed all that. Although the war was not fought within Germany as was World War II, the years from 1914 to 1918 left deep, permanent marks on the country. Feelings of well-being and prosperity gave way to insecurity. The tragic loss of fathers and brothers reversed the patriotic enthusiasm that almost always grips a nation at the beginning of a war. Personal bereavement carried a bitter reality into many families' lives.

I was three years old when my mother's eldest brother, Edgar, was killed in action on November 14, 1914, in Wytschaete, Flanders, in the Netherlands. I remember the atmosphere of mourning—the family in shock and adults crying. The old photographs, now fading in the album, show the family clad head to toe in black, my mother in her black taffeta dress, and me with long, black woolen stockings under my dress with even a black ribbon in my hair. Although I have few personal recollections of my uncle Edgar, he remains fixed in my memory as being a very special person, my mother's adored brother who shared her confidences. He had always stood by her. To him she could confide secrets she would never have dared mention to her mother.

When my father-to-be, Marcel Holzer, went to work for Adolf Blum and Popper, Edgar became his friend long before he fell in love with Gertrud, Edgar's charming and jolly sister. Edgar, his brother Hans, and Marcel passed many good times together. One evening, while the young men were seated at a table at an outdoor cafe, laughing and joking, Marcel had taken Edgar's hand and examined the lines in his palm. Although he was a rather stiff and serious young man, Marcel had made chiromancy his special interest. Palm reading was a semi science, which gypsies were known to practice. Although conservative men like these never admitted believing in such a thing, they curiously bent over Edgar's outstretched hand and listened to Marcel: "Edgar, what are you up to? You'd better watch out, with that short life line." One can imagine my father's shock when, a short time later, Edgar was killed during one of the first battles of the war. He wondered if his friend had had a premonition of an early death in mind when he faced the enemy. Did Edgar believe as firmly as my father that fate and character are written into the palms of our hands? After this my father never said aloud what he saw in a person's palm. He would take my hand frequently and examine it, then close his large, well-shaped hand over mine and smile mysteriously.

CHAPTER TWO

HAMBURG

My grandparents lived in Hamburg almost all their lives. Adolf Blum was a typical Hamburg merchant, which, in those days, implied qualities like honesty, integrity, and pride in his profession and its traditions. Although from a Jewish family, he didn't practice the religion of his forefathers. Like most German Jews, he was assimilated and did not consider himself different from other Germans. He never spoke about religion. I think, however, that he was aware of social barriers that separated Jewish from Christian society.

The history of Jews settling in Hamburg goes back to the sixteenth century. At that time, escaping persecution in their homelands, they came to the German states from Portugal, Spain, and Holland. Some earned their living in commerce and banking, and they soon earned a fine reputation by dealings which were advantageous for both their clients and themselves. Among the famous and still existing German banks founded by Jews are the Dresdener, the Darmstaedter, the Warburg, and the Rothschild banks. The founders became wealthy and their families became leaders of Hamburg society. By the seventeenth century, Hamburg was the second largest German city, with about 50,000 inhabitants. Of this population, 20,000 were Jews, who had a relatively comfortable existence. Over the next century, stable living conditions fostered a firm social structure and religious liberalism in Hamburg. Within the next one hundred years, Jews became deeply rooted in German culture and contributed immeasurably to all fields of human knowledge. By the time my grandfather was born, the majority of Germany's Jews were well educated and of the merchant class and lived their private lives far from political ambitions. My grandfather was no exception.

Although mixed marriages had furthered Jewish assimilation to a great extent, Jews were often subject to certain social prejudices that were not based solely on anti-Semitism. It is difficult to determine the rules that govern the formation of cliques. Old families were like clans; one belonged to one of them and was a "born so-and-so" or else one was not one of them. If one was a member of a well-known family, one was automatically accepted by the group to which that family belonged. This was true of both Jewish and Christian families.

There was a lot of gossip and quick judgement among the clans. If a young man from one group wished to be invited to the home of a member of a different social group, he had to earn a place in the hostess's social register. On a Sunday morning, his first step would be to drop off a visiting card, which one of the servants would place on a silver tray in the entrance hall. When the master and mistress, respectfully called *die Herrschaft* by the servants, returned home, they would pick up the calling cards and notice the visitor's name. Then, after a certain polite interval of a few days, a bouquet of flowers with a few formal words on a card to the lady of the house would follow. Even if the young man meant to direct his attentions to the daughter, it was the mother who received the flowers first, since her approval had to be earned. Then, one day, the prospective visitor might find a printed invitation in his mail. He had to be careful to respond in the style in which the invitation was formulated; for instance, with the name on the first line and the text written in the third person. By observing such formalities, one became eligible for high society.

In Hamburg, high society consisted of members of the government, ship owners, and bankers. The names of these respected and honored citizens were engraved on commemorative plaques mounted in the *Rathaus*, or city hall, and thus preserved as part of Hamburg's proud past. As one of the free German city-states and, therefore, a customs-free enclave, Hamburg had its own government in the form of a senate and a *Buergerschaft* that made important political and other decisions.

The *Rathaus*, built in the late nineteenth century, is the seat of Hamburg's government and the pride of every citizen, although its eclectic, neo-Gothic, neo-baroque architecture is not especially beautiful. This civic pride is common even today in old European cities. For example, when Munich's opera house, completely destroyed during World War II, was rebuilt, even the man and woman on the street, people who perhaps never had or would enter the building, beamed joyously over its rebirth. The same was true of Hamburg, where the *Rathaus* symbolizes the spirit that fills the hearts of true Hamburg citizens who still call it "*our Rathaus.*"

Connected to the *Rathaus* is the stock exchange, which used to be not only the place where stocks and bonds were traded, but also where merchants and shipping agents conducted business, all during one very special half hour, from one forty-five to two fifteen in the afternoon. These gentlemen therefore always spoke of their business day as either "before" or "after" the "*Börse*, the stock-market session. My uncle Hans described the very narrow entrance doors, which were closed exactly at one forty-five. After this, the doorman would open one door just enough for one person at a time to enter: the latecomer had to pay a fine of 35 *Pfennig* and drop it into a metal box. The click was heard distinctly. Bankers and merchants, who during the session would be trading millions, rushed and pushed to avoid the latecomer's penalty. All rushed except two—the banker Max Warburg and Albert Ballin, general manager of the *HAPAG* shipping line—who were known to deliberately approach the doors slowly and to drop their coins leisurely into the box, a grand gesture noticed by many.

Hamburg is famous world-wide as a seaport, its ideal harbor is situated at the mouth of the Elbe, where that mighty river flows into the North Sea. A great center of shipping and shipbuilding, its merchants brought goods from overseas and transported them to the heart of Europe by rivers and waterways. In my grandfather's time, the most important shipping line was the Hamburg-America Line, originally the *Hamburg Amerikanische Paketfahrt Aktien Gesselschaft* or *HAPAG*. It achieved its prominent position under the brilliant leadership of Albert Ballin. At that time, the name was changed to *Hamburg-Amerika Linie* and the sea routes that connected Hamburg to the United States were extended to South America. The second largest shipping line was the *Hamburg Sued*; the third was the *Woerman Linie*. All of these, as well as great shipbuilding companies like *Blohm und Voss*, were founded by and run by Hamburg families. Hamburg was, thus, an ideal place for shipping agents such as my grandfather, who acted as a link between dealers and consumers; they handled freight via ship or railroad.

Hamburg's port, aside from its commercial importance, was also a favorite destination for sightseers. Visitors were proudly shown around on small steam-puffing launches and ferries that toured among the anchored ocean liners and freighters heavy laden with fruit from warmer countries, wood and coal, and every imaginable cargo. Foreign flags and foreign crews brought an exotic tropical atmosphere into the often cold and rainy northern world. The noise of the agitated water splashing against the launches and the tooting whistles of open coal barges mixed with the ear-shattering sound of the launch's diesel engine so that the visitor could hardly hear his own words. As he shouted his comments against the wind, they were carried towards the open ocean. If the tour included a visit aboard one of the oceangoing passenger ships in the harbor, the launch would be secured alongside the giant vessel and the visitors invited to climb a rope ladder hanging from the ship's rail.

With the launch rising and falling in the swell, this climb was a daring feat. Once aboard, however, the visitor was rewarded for his courage. He could vicariously experience the excitement of an ocean voyage, of leaving the land to see distant parts of the world.

Young sons of families living in such port cities have often realized this dream by seeking work on the steamers; and, as often, they have ended up shoveling coal in the company of rough sailors from different countries, many of whom were social outcasts with little alternative to suffering in the stifling heat and grime in the belly of a steamship. Or the seafaring boys would find that life on the high seas with the fishing fleet was equally trying. To take up the seaman's life might rob them of their ideals, but at least they escaped their hometown routine and had good prospects for adventure.

My grandfather took my brother and me regularly on Sunday excursions. The harbor was one of his favorite destinations. Erich and Opi were fascinated by the ships; I was probably more concerned about my Sunday coat with its large cape-like collar and my wide-brimmed straw hat. But I do remember the sense of adventure, the excitement of sniffing the air of foreign countries that seemed to linger in the long passageways and staterooms, in the beautifully decorated dining halls and the carpeted staircases. How impressive the stewards were in their white uniforms—the more so because some were black men, a rare sight in Hamburg at that time. How thrilling, in spite of my fears, to clamber down the narrow, metal stairs to the vast and noisy engine room, or up to the captain's bridge, where one of the officers might hold me high in the air so that I could peer out to see Hamburg's contours across the harbor.

I still see my grandfather so clearly, with his shining blue eyes, his alabaster skin, white hair, and pointed beard (in retrospect, the picture of a perfect Aryan and such an exception in our olive-skinned family that we called him the "alabaster uncle"). He had never taken an ocean trip himself, and I could feel his excitement as he held me by the hand and explained everything he knew about the steamers. Wind or rain never prevented him from wandering about the decks. Indeed, it was on a particularly stormy, unfriendly Sunday in 1928 that he took us aboard the *Corona*, the newest and most modern ship in the harbor. That was our last excursion with him; he caught a cold that day which led to his sudden death. He was seventy-nine years old. My first personal encounter with death prompted me to write in my diary:

> The last day of this year, 1928, was not the kind we felt like celebrating in the usual way, with laughter and merriment. While Hamburg's five beautiful cathedrals announced the arrival of the

new year with the sonorous sounds of their bells, two people, my beloved grandparents were suddenly separated after fifty years of marriage. My Opi, who in my mind's eye I see radiating light, the head of the family, passed away during the night. The days which followed will remain unforgotten.

Die Alte (the dear "old one," my grandmother) does not live in the *Alsterchaussee* anymore; I cannot visualize her in the new home in the *Maria-Louisenstrasse*, because I have not visited her yet. The sad event, Opi's death, brought another proof of what an admirable woman *die Alte* is. My highest goal is to become like her, to lead a life as she does; to consider life a permanent school in which we are trained and which enables us to meet the challenges of fate with dignity, to uphold courage as she does when suddenly life's substance disappears; not to look back, but think: this is the way it has to be. Her attitude recalls Pfarrer Priebe's words: "Do not ask why, but for what purpose did this happen to me?" Even if my grandmother's answer might be different, this is mine: fateful events are tests of strength; they should make us feel as if called by a higher power and bring out the best in us; so that we may serve as an example, a guiding light for others on the path we have must follow.

Die Alte's own words, simple and beautiful are the best indication of her complete love for her husband: "If I lost courage to go on living and the joy of life left me now, I would not be worthy to have lived fifty years by his side."

But in spite of this grief, the memory of many other happy excursions with Opi has always stayed with me. Several times, for example, we went to the Elbe by train. The majestic river and its white beaches attracted many people on Sundays, in those days the only work-free day. They spread their blankets for picnics, or to watch the lively traffic on the river—the small pleasure boats floating by, big steamers heading for the sea, and open coal barges on which the captains' wives hung their laundry in the sun and wind. The people on the beach wore their Sunday best; the women, with long skirts down to the ankles and huge hats pinned on their voluminous hairstyles, watched their children build sand castles while the men rolled up their trousers just enough to safely dip their bare feet into the water. The men wore their hats and smoked cigars, chatted, and enjoyed their leisure time.

Sometimes we went on one of the small excursion steamers on the river. Leaning over the railing, we watched the broad stream of foaming water the boat left in its wake and the graceful flight of the seagulls as they circled about us trying to snatch some morsel of food thrown overboard. The boat took us past the fertile countryside called *Vierlanden*. The peaceful sight of the fishing villages, with their low, straw-covered houses, the surrounding gardens populated with chicken and geese, the fields with grazing cows and sheep, added to the languid scene. We didn't give much thought to the fate of the *Vierlanden* goose that would grace our Christmas dinner table in traditional German fashion. These geese were force-fed to produce the enlarged liver out of which goose-liver pâté is made. The farmer's wife would take the struggling bird between her knees and stuff the helpless bird with grain. But on summer Sundays, we saw none of that. The farmer and his wife would sit contentedly on the bench in front of their house, enjoying their rest and watching the children. In the morning, they had joined the other villagers on a slow walk to church and exchanged greetings, wishes about the weather and the harvest, news of a child to be born and of sickness or death of a member of the community. Clutching their hymn books, they had humbly entered the church while the bells were calling the faithful to fulfill their duty. Then, after hearing their preacher's warnings and admonitions, they had left again feeling perhaps more conscious of their sins than consoled.

Fruits and vegetables grown in *Vierlanden* flooded the markets and stores in Hamburg and nearby towns. As in all of Germany and the rest of Europe, the open markets were usually on a centrally located square surrounded by old houses with beautiful facades. Many narrow streets led to the marketplace. They brightened the aspect of villages and most cities when, once a week, the farmers set up their tables, protected against the sun and rain by colorful umbrellas and awnings. The farmers spread their goods and sold them with the pride of the grower who is certain of their quality. The merchandise was carefully weighed on the kind of scale sold as an antique today. While the produce was wrapped in newspaper, the housewife exchanged good-natured remarks with the farmer and his family; the atmosphere was very jovial. The ladies were accompanied by their maids dressed in blue-and-white-striped uniforms with large sparkling white aprons tied around their waists. The maids carried the abundance home in big baskets that hung on their arms.

The women knew each farmer's specialties, the vegetables or meats in which they excelled. White asparagus, for example, was preferred in Germany and France. To produce asparagus stalks as delicate and delicious as the gourmet buyers expected them to be, they are planted in long rows of sandy soil, and as soon as the points appeared, they are covered with mounds of earth so they never grew above the surface. This procedure preserves the whiteness of the stalks. They must be cut at exactly the right time, and that very morning brought to market. The first asparagus usually appeared just in time for my mother's birthday, the eighteenth of May. When the fresh-cut spears reached the kitchen they were wrapped in a damp towel and placed in bundles in a cool place. Before being cooked in salt water, they were always very carefully peeled by my mother, who, supposedly, was the only one who could remove all of the harder outer skin. The precious stalks were arranged on the rack of a special silver platter, allowing the water to drip off, then they were served with Westfalian ham and new potatoes with melted butter, on which the cook had spread diced hard-boiled eggs. Asparagus was one of the exceptional vegetables that even in the most elegant circles one might hold on one end with the fingers, while supporting the other end with a silver fork. The birthday meal was topped off with the first strawberries from our garden.

The farmers living in the Hamburg area played another important role for the city population: their daughters flocked to the city to serve the bourgeoisie and tend to their children. Along the well-raked paths of Hamburg's parks, these country girls could be seen pushing high-wheeled perambulators, their plump figures squeezed into tightly fitting uniforms. The babies were done up in starched, lacy clothes; older children tripped alongside holding on tightly to the carriages. Little boys, their hair long and curly, wore wide-brimmed straw hats held by elastic bands under the chin and often wore dresses as frilly as those of the girls. There was a distinctive Hamburg fashion for children: the dresses were smocked, a type of decorative stitch that gathers the material and gives it a shirred effect. The coats were usually light grey and double-breasted with large, mother-of-pearl buttons. Girls' coats had a large, cape-like collar overlaid with a smaller, starched white collar and cuffs. The bonnets were made of shirred silk, usually lined in another color, and held with a large ribbon under the chin. I suppose that the windy, chilly Hamburg climate favored this children's fashion, which was traditional for many generations. Walking in the parks was part of a daily routine, but the children were required to stay close to an adult. Held by the hand, they had little freedom and were not allowed to move at their own pace. The nursemaids were just as restricted as their charges. They lived under the rigorous discipline of their employers and, though entrusted with the children, had no freedom or authority. They addressed their masters respectfully in the third person, never answered back, and carefully followed rules of politeness appropriate to their social standing. It is hard to imagine why a child sensing this would obey a nursemaid, or how the young girls managed their charges when away from home.

When the children were not taken to the parks, they could walk on the *Harvestehuder Weg*, a tree-and-garden-lined street leading along the *Aussenalster*, Hamburg's central waterway, to the heart of the city. Here were elegant villas—homes of the upper class—later, for the most part destroyed. Wrought-iron fences enclosed the gardens and elaborately decorated gates allowed carriages to be driven up to the front portal of each villa. The inhabitants had an unmatched view of the Alster, glittering in the sun, and of the steeples of the cathedrals of Saint Nikolai, Saint Petri, Saint Jakobi, Saint Katharinen, and Saint Michaelis.

The Alster typifies Hamburg as much as its five church steeples, since the city is built around it. Though easily mistaken for a lake, it actually is a river whose course has been diverted twice over the centuries by dams and is now much like two lakes separated by a strip of land. The *Lombards Brücke*, a wide bridge, was constructed on the site of the fortification wall that protected the city from enemies and pirates during the Thirty Years War, a safeguard that enabled Hamburg to experience an economic boom after that war while much of Germany was laid waste. By the Second World War, vital railroad tracks ran across the bridge. To protect the bridge and the tracks from air raids, a second decoy bridge was built next to it. Including the Alster, there are altogether sixty-two kilometers of waterways in this amphibious city and now more than two thousand bridges.

The Alster gives Hamburg a romantic and pleasant quality. Like my parents, many people enjoyed their leisure time in small canoes or sailboats, gliding soundlessly through the picturesque, narrow waterways, passing swans and ducks that floated quietly in the slight current and boats that were tied up here and there in the cooling shade of weeping willows. These canoes were given individual names and painted in gay colors and were furnished with soft pillows, which invited romance. A nosy photographer once even caught my mother—known for her absolute fidelity—in the arms of her handsome brother-in-law Leon Holzer in their canoe, the *Zitravelli*.

Even today, Hamburg has a certain attractive, small-town atmosphere. For instance, one can still walk from the *Harvestehuder Weg* to the center of the city and enjoy the Alster or one can use the ferryboats. These small, white boats, a peaceful means of transportation, exist as if new technology had not reached these shores. Along the river the boats stop at small piers. The ship's bell rings, and down comes the wooden plank, and the uniformed mate throws a rope around the mooring post so that the passengers can comfortably disembark. Today, just as in my grandfather's time, the small fleet adds to the comfort of circulating in this town.

In my childhood, there was such a ferryboat station at the bottom of the *Alsterchaussee*, the street where my grandparents lived. I remember one particular Sunday—I was perhaps four or five years old—when my grandfather was going to take us on the ferryboat to the *Ulenhorster Fährhaus*, a restaurant just across from the *Alsterchaussee*. It was a white, castle like structure, reminiscent of a French chateau with little towers and stucco decorations, in the middle of a park. The garden bordered the water in which ducks and swans floated around waiting to be fed. Inside the restaurant the gold-trimmed walls, the glittering chandeliers, and the chairs covered with red velvet impressed us greatly. This place attracted thousands of people over the years, was famous for good food and the customary coffeehouse music. Unfortunately, the building was destined to be destroyed by bombs during World War II in the disastrous air attacks on the residential section of Hamburg. The Sunday long ago I have in mind was in fact marred by an airplane accident, for me the first of many unfortunate experiences with airplanes. A small sports plane appeared suddenly, dangerously low and right in front of us, and crashed into the lake. Although my little hand rested so securely in my grandfather's strong one, I panicked. Nobody, least of all me, imagined then the role that airplanes would continue to play in my life.

Recalling these Sunday excursions, I search my memory in vain for my grandmother. Instead, I see her small, well-rounded figure, hidden under a long, dark dress, bent over her laundry basket, counting the linens on Sundays in preparation for the Monday wash day, or supervising the preparations for Sunday dinner. To me she was always a very old lady, although she was only around sixty at the time. Her appearance never changed. Photographs of her younger years show her with the same hairstyle, grey for so many years that nobody recalls the original color. It was done every morning by a *coiffeuse*, who would come to the bedroom, wrap a short cape around my grandmother's shoulders, brush and pin up her rather thin hair over a hairpiece, which we called the *Matraze* (literally the mattress). A hairnet was fastened over the finished hairdo; my grandmother would hold the edge of the fine net with her lips and stretch it over her outspread fingers, pull it over her head, and fasten it with tiny, silver hairpins.

The *coiffeuse* provided the only personal service my grandmother required. During her entire life, she took care of her family and many other people, but she, herself, was never in need of help. Her responsibilities were the children, her Adolf's health and clothing, and the household which required two maids, the cook and housemaid and a seamstress for mending. Her strict and scheduled life left her little private time. The main reason was that she did not delegate responsibility. It was the affirmation of her position of power within the household. After all, this was the *Hausfrau*'s domain; here she organized, commanded, and supervised, just as the master did in the rest of life's endeavors. Although the maids and servants often spent their entire life with one family, they were never actually entrusted with responsibility. The class difference between them and their masters required that the *Hausfrau* was the keeper of the keys. It was not that she thought the servants might steal from the household, it was her duty to be in control. It would have been unfair, improper, and unthinkable to place the burden of responsibility for the family silver and linen on a member of the servant class.

In any event, in my grandmother's household everything was locked up. Linen, silver, and china were sorted and counted, and she "gave it out" as needed. The maids had to ask for everything and made no decisions on their own. The grocer, the butcher, the milkman, and the baker made their deliveries every morning under her scrutiny. The iceman, wearing a leather apron and wielding ice tongs, carried big slabs of ice into the cellar and put it in heavily insulated storage bins. The household expenses were accounted for to the last penny; the mistress of the house kept little, blue books for all orders and paid the tradesmen weekly in cash at the door. Checks were not used at all for private commerce, and credit cards were, of course, unknown.

Some of these little account books have survived; they tell a great deal about the simplicity of life in those days. Life was so regulated that one wonders if it was not also boring. The week was planned so that every day of every week the same chores were done at the same time. Every day, for example, the bed linens were aired by laying them over the sills of open windows. After a lengthy exposure to fresh air and sunlight, the mattresses were turned and the beds made up for the day. This custom, which survives today in many places, was a rule, and anybody who omitted this process and made the bed without airing the linen was looked upon as slovenly. Every fourth week the bed linens were changed.

In my childhood, the Monday following the change of linen was wash day. This event affected the whole family—imagining the work involved, one understands the importance of this event. Since there were no washing machines, no running hot water, or modern soap powders available, linens were boiled. A huge copper tub was filled with water—in the cities this tub was in the cellar; in the country, in a separate wash house. Thus the family would not be disturbed by the steam and heat, the clatter of the washerwomen's wooden shoes mixed with their chatter and singing, and the splattering of the water. Early in the morning, the fire under the tub had to be started to bring the water to a boil; the fire had to be replenished with wood or coal all day long. The heavy, often homespun, linens had been soaked overnight together with towels, underwear, and shirts. Then, each piece was spread over a washboard made of ribbed metal and scrubbed with a bristle brush and soap, called *Kernseife*, before being boiled.

By midday the laundry had to be hung on the line so that air and sun would dry and bleach it to a sparkling white by nightfall. The clothesline was strung between trees or, in winter, in the attic or cellar. It was heavy work to wring out the water and needed the strong hands of two women to twist and roll the sheets between them, and, then, to throw the large pieces over the line and fasten them with wooden pins. Before the heavy irons did their work, one more task had to be done: after the sheets were dry, two people grabbed each end and pulled with all their might so that the woven threads were straightened out. After that, the pieces were folded, sprinkled lightly with water, and placed in the linen basket. The irons—one can find them today in antique shops—were made of heavy cast iron, with wooden handles and a hollow belly into which a glowing hot piece of iron was placed that had been heated on the coals. On a large, wooden table the irons were passed back and forth over the sheets until the linen had no wrinkles. Folded meticulously, the pressed linen pieces were placed with the rest of their kind and kept together with a shiny ribbon, which held a card indicating the number of pieces in the bundle. This way, the precious trousseau was kept intact.

On those well-remembered wash days of my childhood, it was the custom that family and staff shared the same simple meal: usually potato soup with sausages and slices of bread. Since many families needed extra help on those days, the "profession" of washer woman helped provide sustenance for many females of poor families.

These women who served the rich were often factotums, part of the family and its tradition, although of a distinctly lower class. With the rise of mechanization and time-saving methods society has lost a well of warm, human relationships such as the ones between master and servants. Today, the status of servants has changed in the mind of society. In former days, the servants felt protected in their station and in their dependency and were even proud of their masters. "Serving" was more than carrying out orders or doing lowly work; it was honest employment, usually gratefully accepted, and it evoked fidelity in both parties, the family and the servants. I considered my grandparents' and my parents' servants friends to whom I could, and did, turn without restraint. They could rely on us as we could count on them.

A large part of the population served the bourgeoisie within a class system that today, in large measure, has disappeared. Today in Germany, it is possible for children of poor families to get a higher education and compete with children from more fortunate homes. But in those days, the children of the middle and lower classes left school at the age of fourteen. Girls did not learn a trade but became apprentices in households and, if they did not marry, stayed with the same family into their old age.

An employer took full responsibility for a girl he employed. There would be a first encounter when the girl's father, as bashful as his daughter, came to talk to the man of the house about the employment. He would stand apologetically by the door, turning his cap nervously in his rough hands, and would hesitantly respond to the invitation to step closer. His wife would follow in her Sunday best, one step behind him. Both were neatly but simply groomed, their hair brushed, and their heavy shoes polished. She might send a discreet but curious look around the living room, her eye would rest a moment on the brightly polished silver tray with the tea and coffee set, a status symbol for a refined family of that time. The thought would cross her mind that it would probably be some time before her own daughter would be given the honor to polish such a set.

The conversation between the prospective employer and the girl's parents would be more or less one-sided. Since the parents considered it a privilege for their daughter to serve in such a distinguished family, they humbly accepted the terms of agreement, which put the servant entirely at the mercy of the master. But he would most likely maintain a fair relationship with his charges, at least according to the ideas of the day. A place to work and live was the reward for work, not the meager pocket money. The girl's father was happy to have one less mouth to feed, which did not mean he did not love his children. But training and discipline was considered a sign of concern for the well-being of a young person. The submissive young girl would generally become attached to the family and responded with warm feelings despite the hard work, long hours, simple quarters, and lack of freedom.

In my lifetime, I have known a number of these women who served my grandparents and my parents. At the time, they were better off in service than they would have been with their own family, where there were sometimes ten children or more. Mimi, my grandmother's maid, told me how glad her parents were when the interview with the Blums was over and the door closed softly behind them. She was frightened suddenly to be left to cope with the unfamiliar surroundings and the strange behavior of city people. Never before had she left her village. Never had she known running water, toilets, and electricity. But, she told me, my grandmother and my mother, who was then a mere child, won her confidence quickly and that their easygoing manners were soon a great comfort to her. My mother as a young girl had a sort of conspiracy with the maids and would suggest ways to cover up for their, and her, innocent adventures. For the servant girls, these escapades consisted of meetings with the delivery boy from the corner store or staying outside a few minutes longer than my grandmother permitted. In spite of the rules and strict supervision, they, thus, managed to have some girlish fun from time to time.

The work conditions were hard, with little time for recreation. Only on Sunday after the midday meal was cleared were the girls allowed to leave the house, and then only until dusk. If they returned late, the house was locked: they had to ring the doorbell and my grandfather would be standing there, his gold watch in his hand. My mother sometimes went to the basement kitchen when her parents had their after-dinner snooze, my grandmother curled up behind my grandfather on the living room sofa, her head resting on his rear end, which she called "Mount Ararat." Meanwhile, my mother would be in the kitchen, polishing the brass border of the large, free-standing kitchen stove for Mimi, so that the maid could have a longer afternoon off. The polishing had to be done every day; one used a wine cork dipped in a salt-ammoniac solution and scrubbed the metal until it gleamed. On other occasions, Mimi helped my mother to sneak out secretly.

My grandmother was a fun-and laughter-loving woman when I knew her, but in her younger years she was apparently strict and serious. I often teased her, talking about her attitude when my mother was young, and the old lady would shake with laughter till the tears ran down her cheeks. We recalled her custom of inspecting the maids early each morning when they had to parade at her bedside. She would check to see if they were fully dressed or if they had just thrown their uniforms over their nightgowns. Women wore corsets reinforced with whalebone stays and over that underwear, a shirt; a bodice; petticoats; and heavy, black woolen, hand-knit stockings. Until midday the maids wore blue-and-white striped cotton dresses and large, white, starched aprons to protect the dresses. In the afternoon they changed into black dresses with white, lacy collars and cuffs. On their heads they wore matching bonnets.

Understandably, the household was in need of a seamstress to do the mending. My grandmother's factotum was Fräulein Schaf, a pale, elderly virgin, who seemed forgotten by fate. She would sit in a small back room, her rattling sewing machine restlessly spurred on by her foot, which rocked the pedal back and forth all day long. The laundry basket next to her seemed never to get emptier. In addition to clothing to be mended, it held bedsheets to be "turned" when the centers got thin from use. She would cut the sheets lengthwise and sew the outside edges together to form a center seam. Comfort for the sleeper was of little consideration to the ever-frugal *Hausfrau*; after all, the dowry was precious, every piece embroidered with initials and supposed to last a lifetime. Actually most brides had so much in their linen closets that several generations could inherit it. Fräulein Schaf was not troubled by these thoughts. She seemed content never to leave the room and even to take her meager meals from a tray that was brought to her. She was in a class somewhere between the maids and *die Herrschaft*.

For Sunday meals we were numerous. My grandfather sat at the head of the table in an armchair—the rest of the chairs had no armrests. This distinction was one of many bestowed on the master only. The meat platter was placed in front of him, and he would stand up—with a large linen napkin tucked into his vest thus serving as apron—and with a horn-handled carving set, he would commence carving the roast. When my mother was a child, my grandfather often ate veal with new potatoes in season, while the rest of the family had less expensive pork or beef with old, winter potatoes. Nobody knew whether this was on account of economy or Adolf's sensitive stomach. Or was it perhaps a symbol of rank?

Actually, there was no doubt in anybody's mind who was the master of the house, but since Adolf Blum was such a quiet, soft-spoken, and good-natured man, I think it was Elise Blum who had created this autocratic image. She referred to her husband when speaking to the staff in the third person as "*der Herr*", equivalent to "the master." My grandmother would tell the cook that the master would come for dinner at one o'clock and meant that the tureen of steaming soup had to be on the table at that time, with the silver soup ladle and the soup plates next to it. My grandmother believed that a father should exercise complete authority, and she tried hard to impress that concept of discipline on the four children; but they were not impressed very much. They knew that when their father came home and she complained about Trudel's pranks and Hans's careless writing, he would quietly hang up his coat and hat and tell her, "*Lass das Kind zufrieden und stoer es nicht*" ("leave the child alone and don't disturb it").

When my brother and I were allowed to sleep weekends in my grandparents' home in the *Alsterchaussee*, we would creep in the morning into the large beds and watch Opi as he stood in his long-legged underwear, brushing his short, white hair with two small, round brushes, one in each hand. If we woke up early enough to catch him in bed, he would take us each in one arm and tell us a story. It always started with "once upon a time there was a little boy . . . ." Erich, his favorite grandson would perk up and ask: "*Dieses Bubi hier?*" ("This little boy?"). One day my grandfather was seen on the *Jungfernstieg*, Hamburg's most elegant shopping street, and, with a radiant smile pointing his finger to his chest, murmuring "*Dieses Bubi hier?*" He was well dressed as always, the pearl in the tie and the bowler hat pushed just slightly back, indicating this happy mood. Most probably he was coming from one of the lunches which he took from time to time after the stock market in one of Hamburg's famous gourmet restaurants.

These *Schlemmerlokale*, as they are called, are small, intimate places along the old streets and canals, usually dimly lit because of the narrow streets and the often overcast sky. They were simply furnished, but, at the tables with their white tablecloths, one ate Hamburg's delicacies served by diligent waiters in tailcoats and big, white aprons. When the respected clientele arrived, the waiter would bow deeply, a napkin squeezed under his arm, pull out a chair, whisk it once with the napkin, and push it gently under the honored guest. The guest was king: he could and did demand the greatest possible attention from staff and kitchen. The manager would emerge personally and take the order or make suggestions; he would mention the special dish of the day in a whisper as if this guest were the only one so privileged, as if the dish in question would be prepared for him alone. It might be eel, fresh from the sea, or smoked fish, nowhere as good as in Hamburg. The gentlemen would indulge in food and drink and the jokes might even be a little risqué in the absence of ladies. One has the impression that their absence made the meal somewhat festive and that these honorable family fathers did not report every detail of their pleasurable outings to their beloved, but homebound, wives. Thus was my grandfather's mood when he ventured alone on the *Jungfernstieg*, a radiant gleam in his blue eyes.

The *Jungfernstieg* was also the scene of family promenades on those rare Sundays when the clouds lifted on the northern sky and the sun emerged. Gentlemen and ladies walked ahead of their children, women proudly displaying their huge, feathered and flowered hats, which were fastened to their towering hairdos with long, fancy hatpins, indispensable in a windy town like Hamburg. The hatpins stuck out so far that the public vehicles were posted with warnings like: "Ladies with unprotected hatpins are excluded from riding on this vehicle."

I remember excursions to the city with our grandfather holding Erich and me by the hand, wandering along the *Jungfernstieg* and the Inner Alster, its boats and steamships on one side, and the elegant shops on the other. The brilliant glare of the sun on the water, the passing horse-drawn carriages with their coachmen on high seats, balancing top hats on their heads and cracking their whips in the air—all that left a lasting impression on me. My dear grandfather, a respected and well-known citizen, returned greetings, lifting his bowler hat and bowing slightly. Each time he lifted his hat, he let go of my hand; the moment I could slip mine again into his, I felt a twinge of pride and security. I loved him, that was certain.

We were as much at home in the *Alsterchaussee* as my mother had been. In fact, we had two homes. I believe that my father's frequent absences on business trips made us regard my grandfather as his equal. I was told that the only time the family saw him upset was when I got spanked. I remember that event quite distinctly; it happened when the first air-raid alarm frightened everyone just at the beginning of World War I in 1914. We were sitting in the bathtub when Marie, our maid, grabbed me and my mother grabbed Erich and hurriedly wrapped us in large towels and somehow brought us to my grandparents' home in the *Alsterchaussee*. I guess our sixth-floor apartment seemed less safe than the Blums' ground-floor one. We considered this an exciting adventure and did not understand the implications. It turned out to be a false alarm and everyone went to sleep. That night, my brother and I came down with the measles, and my mother stayed with us in the *Alsterchaussee*; my father was already working for the government in Berlin. I was a spoiled child and I tyrannized my mother. Because I was ill, I expected her to stay near my bed all the time, and when she left the room I screamed as loud as a three-year-old can scream so that my grandparents heard me in the living room. Suddenly the door opened quietly, my grandfather came in, threw back the covers, lifted my nightgown, and, with a firm hand, left a red mark on my backside. He told me calmly that now I had a reason to scream. This brought me involuntary fame in the family.

One day my grandmother answered the doorbell and was confronted with a poor man begging for clothes. She went to the bedroom to examine Adolf's wardrobe. She found his tuxedo, and, since the tailor had just delivered a new one, she decided to give away the old trousers. Weeks later, when Opi was invited to a formal men's dinner, he discovered that his wife had given away his new tuxedo trousers. Instead of scolding her, he patted her on the cheeks tenderly and consoled her saying that the poor man certainly needed the trousers more than he did. He was never impatient with my grandmother. It seems as if this unusual couple shed forth rays of peacefulness on my childhood and marked my life with their presence.

CHAPTER THREE

THE FAMILY HOLZER

Gertrud Therese Blum, called Trudel, was born in 1885, in Hamburg, the third child of Adolf and Elise Blum. Photographs of her as a young girl show her to be chubby, dark haired, and olive skinned. She teased and laughed her way into everyone's heart; she had immediate concerns, like her growing breasts. She tried to hide this sign of womanhood by pinning her petticoat together with a safety pin. She wondered about the mysteries of nature and the changes in her body but, because she did not dare to speak to her mother about her worries, she turned to her grandmother to ask how babies came into a woman's belly. The embarrassed answer left her even more puzzled: "Where they go in they come out."

Her vivaciousness made her the life of the party and everyone loved to be with her. She made friends easily and many of these friendships were long lasting. A favorable fate even reunited her much later with some of the girls from her kindergarten, and they became the companions of her old age. Two of her childhood acquaintances who became lifelong friends provided me, in later years, with glimpses into my mother's childhood. They told me about the light-hearted days they had spent together in private school around the turn of the century.

At that time, there were social and political changes in Germany that made life more urban. Bismarck, chancellor under Kaiser Wilhelm I, was forced to retire to make way for social reforms, including a changing role for women in German society. Up to the turn of the century, women were without civil rights. Actually, they were not considered legal persons. Married women could not hold jobs or sign contracts without their husbands' permission. They even had no rights over their children. The Kaiser had said emphatically that women should be educated merely to raise their children for the good of the fatherland and teach them obedience and respect for their elders. In school, girls should be taught to cook, clean, and sew, and should never be trained to participate in the men's world.

After 1894, the first *Gymnasiums* (equivalent to American high schools) were opened to girls, but it was not until seven years later that women were admitted to universities.

Thus, Trudel and her friends attended private school, where girls did not learn much at all. Trudel made up naughty verses about her teachers instead, and was often punished by having to spend time in the hallway. But neither she or her parents worried too much about education because girls were supposed to become housewives and mothers. While sister Mini enjoyed a higher education, Trudel later was sent to a secretarial school where she learned typing and shorthand. Her parents thought her well equipped to face the storms of life. As a matter of fact, this proved to be true since her secretarial skills enabled her to enter the men's world and escape her mother's apron strings. Many years later, she was able to be helpful to my father and could function as his secretary when he started a new career in a foreign country.

Marcel

Marcel, my father, was born in 1879 in Graz, Austria, the first son of Karl Holzer and his wife, Karoline. My paternal grandfather, Karl Holzer, came from the small village of Kobersdorf in the *Burgenland*. The area was at that time part of Hungary but became Austrian at the end of World War I. This strip of land was only fifteen kilometers from Vienna and the population was German speaking, which explains why my father's birth certificate was written in two languages, Hungarian and German.

According to this and other documents, my grandfather, Karl Holzer, was of "Mosaic" religion but I don't have the impression that the family practiced Judaism. Karl Holzer attended a Catholic teachers' college in 1860, and received a teaching certificate in 1866 and that same year moved to Vienna. After he married the "virgin Karoline Preiss" (as it was stated in the marriage certificate) on April 25, 1875, the couple settled in the *Gumpendorfer Strasse* in Vienna, where they still lived when I visited them in my childhood.

Karl and Karoline Holzer, my paternal grandparents, had six more children after my father was born, three daughters and three sons. After leaving home at the age of sixteen, my father seldom returned to visit, but he never forgot his family: even during the first years of his apprenticeship, he sent money faithfully from his meager earnings. He never talked much about his youth. His ardent goal was to rise above his family's middle class standard of living. His father ran a small tobacco shop, and the crowded, dark house proved to be a stifling environment for a youth with my father's ambitions. He never was close to his parents. Because of this we, his children, did not know our uncles (except Leon), aunts, and cousins well on that side of the family.

His youngest sister, Flora, lived in Vienna and never married and died in a concentration camp during the Nazi years. Over the years, my father had helped support her financially.

Marcel, with only a basic elementary school education, knew that he had to start at the bottom of the ladder to success. He was determined to acquire enough knowledge in the field of shipping and freight forwarding to make this a career. How he made his way to the Austrian port of Trieste I don't know, but it was there that he started at a simple job. He kept his eyes and ears open, absorbing with his eager mind every detail of freight forwarding, spotting problems in the small firm's functioning, and thinking of ways to reform and improve the system, to make transport more efficient. He soon was rewarded with his first promotion and given a more interesting assignment, a better outlet for his ever-increasing energy. The drive to expand and modify established methods of transportation by land and sea, in fact, marked my father's entire life and the way he started out—young, poor, unassisted, and without friends or advice—formed him at the root. He applied himself at his fullest capacity even after he reached levels of achievement which few of his peers ever did. Thus, he laid the foundation for his family's and future generations' well-being.

Shortly after 1900, Marcel came to Hamburg to live and became a clerk in my grandfather's firm, Adolf Blum & Popper. My mother-to-be was assigned to him as his secretary—an event which would determine their future lives and mine. Marcel Holzer, a serious young man, was a diligent worker. One found him usually bent over his rate calculations with a stern face, and he stayed after office hours almost every evening. Trudel wondered if he had any interests in life other than the firm; she had noticed that he did not smoke or drink or look at the girls. Although only in his late twenties, he was almost bald, but, she had to admit, he was impeccably well-dressed; yet he seemed poor. Annoyed by his refusal to notice her, she told her friends and her mother that she hated him. This was her way of dealing with people who, in her estimation, showed her too little attention. Even in later life she felt that people who paid no attention to her, even salesclerks, were "unfriendly," and she did not like them, she used to say.

To Marcel's great surprise, one day Trudel asked him to take her ice skating. This was one of the few pastimes that allowed young men and women to meet freely and unchaperoned, although to skate as a couple was a little risqué. Accompanied by her brothers, Trudel often enjoyed evenings waltzing around the ice. Arriving home that particular night, with flushed cheeks and sparkling eyes, her hand in her muff and her feet ice cold in her pretty, buttoned boots, she told her mother frankly, and somewhat triumphantly, that she had warmed her hands in Marcel Holzer's coat pockets. Her mother was shocked and forbade Trudel to ever repeat such frivolous behavior.

My grandparents did not realize that the young man for whom Trudel worked had taken a fancy to their daughter. It would have been hard for anyone to imagine what was happening behind Marcel's silent and serious facade, or the true feelings Trudel had for Marcel. Mocking him, she demonstrated for her parents his way of taking off his pince-nez eyeglasses and cleaning them with his spotless handkerchief, then carefully folding the handkerchief and returning it to his jacket breast pocket, leaving one corner visible.

If Marcel noticed Trudel's interest in him, he was careful not to let her know it. In the office there was no time for such distractions: work had to be the first consideration, and private talk would definitely be a waste of time. Besides, he was almost sick with shyness and it would not have occurred to him that he, the poor young clerk, could merit the boss's daughter's attention. How could she know that he already had a lifetime goal? He wanted more than anything to lift himself out of the masses and become a useful member of society, an important part of the wheel that turns the economy. He had never spoken about this to anyone; only much later, when we children were old enough to appreciate these ideas, did he disclose them. His ardent wish to be in the mainstream of life in order to help other people advance along with him spurred him ever onward. Those who might have criticized his ambitions never understood the fire which guided this man throughout his life. And there was another invisible part in him: only his letters and poems reveal how deeply sentimental and romantic this outwardly stiff man became when passion took hold of him.

Courtship

Who knows when the wind changed? The small notes that suddenly flew onto my mother's typewriter and their letters reveal a flaring romance, a previously unknown fire that seized them both and which would engulf them the rest of their lives. I imagine my mother's merriment and humor breaking into the quiet of my father's life like a flash of lightning. The shy, tender words written on scraps of paper, exchanged in secret, virtually under the desk or left in hidden places, are a touching testimony to their budding love. Marcel's messages were usually in the form of poetry. And beautiful poems they were; he found the sweetest words and the most tender expressions in the depth of his heart, buried for so long they sprang from his pen like the water of a clear mountain spring.

He wrote his first real letter to her in January 1906, telling Trudel he had noticed her interest in him but that he would not permit himself to address her privately. Trudel was caught by surprise, and, after all her talk behind his back, she was truly embarrassed to discover that she did not hate this man after all. She wrote that a stupid and rather plain girl like herself could only wonder what someone so superior and so different could possibly see in her. Likewise, Marcel considered himself too insignificant and poor, too low in standing, to be of any interest to her. Anyway, he felt that he had no right to speak to her privately because "feelings are forbidden if one cannot openly discuss them" as he said in one of his letters.

But forbidden or not, they eventually expressed their mutual love regularly in their letters, and, although Trudel sat opposite him all day long to take dictation, they kept the unwritten rule not to speak of their love in public or in private. At home, Trudel continued to pretend that Marcel Holzer did not interest her in any way and she enjoyed the "trick" she was playing on her parents. Romance had to be an adventure, for she enjoyed drama and acting and, in fact, continued all her life to create scenes in which she was the main actress. My grandmother used to say, after my parents were married, that one need not visit a theater if one was in the Holzer house.

It was difficult for Marcel to keep his little secretary happy without being distracted from work. He warned her that he was in no financial position to take care of her. But Trudel was convinced that poverty was no hindrance to enjoy life and marriage. "I need so little to live," she wrote in her naive way, "just love and sunshine." And another time, "I will teach you to love life and I will give it purpose." And finally, "Speak to my parents about us, so that I can openly confess my love for you. Mama won't be surprised because lately I have spoken often about you, obviously in a negative way, which she took for joking."

Trudel wanted to *hear* him say at long last that he loved her. Driven by her desire and her temperament, she raced ahead like a young colt, disregarding Marcel's stern and solemn attitude and trying to break down the barriers of the social code. This code required that she address her boss with the formal "*Sie*" and forbade her to speak to him in the way she felt. In a letter, one could safely speak about emotions; letters and diaries seem, indeed, to have been the only suitable place for expressing thoughts and feelings.

Passionate as his writing was at this time, he was depressed, almost a pessimist, without hope for personal happiness. I ask myself why he worked so furiously from early youth on if he saw no purpose in living, as he claimed to Trudel on several occasions. Even as first love stirred his entire being, even after experiencing the reassurance of success in business, he never ceased to search for satisfaction in hard work and continued to strive for excellence in everything he did. Had I not heard my mother talk about their romance and engagement, had I not read his poems and letters, I never really would have known him. To my brother and me, he was optimistic, daring in his enterprise, and always calm, strong, and sure of his talents and capabilities.

As he aimed to reach the top and give his best, so were we expected to do the same. He regarded leadership as a responsibility, a code he instilled in us. To do one's duty was the obvious and was no reason for praise, whereas negligence or failure were punished with his or my mother's sadness, which for us was punishment enough.

Trudel and Marcel pledged to stay "strong and honest" at the very beginning of their relationship, and from then on they supported each other in every situation throughout their life together. In their early letters, Trudel appealed to him, "Help me to stay strong and honest to Mama and Papa," and Marcel responded, "Help me Trudel, to hide my passion in the presence of your parents and friends." This was the sort of "honesty" in which behavior counts more than disclosure of a true inner condition. They genuinely felt that honesty in this case meant concealing their true feelings.

> My dearest, dearest Trudel,
>
> It is a great pleasure that I am able to address you this way. I read and reread your wonderful words, which came from your heart; they comfort me. If you only knew how often in the past I was tempted to open my heart to release the pain and desolation.
>
> But now I am just sitting here, every one of your words vibrates in my soul, and I cannot believe that you really speak to me that way, you, the proud, pure creature. I thank you for revealing your feelings: you have made me rich. Thank you for the pure, quiet joy of these last nights, they can never be forgotten.
>
> If only I could speak to you the way I write, holding your soft hand and looking into your bewildering eyes. Is it true that you will actually stand by me in all my future struggles? Will you try

to build a deep happiness with me—even if your life should have to be modest?

Oh, if only I could hear the answer from your lips and read it in your eyes . . . .

Days after Marcel and Trudel had declared their love for each other, Trudel went to Krefeld in the Rhineland to join her cousins for the Carnival. The Rhinelanders, famous not only for their wine, but for their lightheartedness and good humor, celebrate the Carnival in the right spirit. During the week-long event, everyone shelves his problems and, clad in costumes and masks, makes merry in the streets, restaurants, and homes.

The Carnival then was little different than it is now. Whoever could stand up long enough danced, kissed, and drank, and forgot about sleep and work. Strangers became friends and sometimes lovers, girls and boys, men and women, enjoyed the incognito guaranteed by their masks. Girls let boys kiss them, which was an exception to the rigid rules common in my mother's day; but Trudel went along with the others, all in good fun. This was my mother's idea of a farewell to maidenhood. I can imagine my father's feelings of jealousy when his "gypsy" bride-to-be fluttered away to the Carnival.

As much as Trudel loved dancing and flirting and the wild amusement of the Carnival, she had not anticipated her state of involvement with Marci, as she called Marcel, or how it would affect her. She wrote to him from Krefeld on January 31, 1907:

> The entire evening I thought of you. Although it was fun to dance as wildly as my heart desired, so wildly that I could hardly breathe, I was glad to get home to be able to concentrate on my thoughts of you, my beloved. I would not have dared to hope that you will speak to Papa so soon. I know you told me a long time ago that you love Papa as if he was your father. Now your friends, Edgar and Hans will become your brothers; now you will have a home and you belong to us. But foremost you belong to me, your bride-to-be. What bliss! I embrace you and hold you close forever . . . .

Pages and pages are filled with such words of love, the eternally beautiful theme: lovers expressing their feelings which they think of as something no one before them has ever experienced. They wrote many such letters and used them as a means of avoiding personal contact in the name of decency.

My only beloved Trudel,

I thank you again for letting me know what is in your heart. Thank you for letting me be close and intimate with you. But do not worry. Although I am thrown into a wildly tumultuous emotion when I read your letters, I will stand by our vows.

So far, my love, I have not shed my shyness; I hardly dare to look into your eyes. I fear to get lost in them, not to be able to return from their depth. Perhaps I even blush? My thoughts are circling around you all the time. If my dream castle becomes too lofty, a nervous conductor quickly taps the baton to stop me.

So think of me tomorrow night, beloved, when I confess everything to your brother Hans. Will he approve? Later on when he sees that I will do my utmost to make you happy, he will be pleased.

Reading my mother and father's letters and witnessing their life together gave me a deep understanding of them—of Trudel, an energetic, loving woman, and of Marcel, her strong but loving and devoted husband. Their love lasted in all its beauty for more than half a century and was the rock on which my, and my brother's, life was built. Their union was of such a quality that no quarrel, no jealousy could ever really shake it, so perfectly were these two people suited to each other.

My mother had the kind of feminine traits which enabled her to be happy and fulfilled next to a powerful husband. Her dependance on him was not a sign of weakness, but evidence of complete trust and devotion. However, despite his determination, he was actually putty in her hands. She was a bundle of emotions and feelings who rose to become a person of authority before him when the situation called for a decision concerning the children or other family matters. Indeed, he observed certain "off-limits" areas, so they did not quarrel or discuss disagreements in front of the children or the staff. My father usually proclaimed the outcome starting with, "Your mother said . . . ." He seldom called his wife by her name in front of us or other people; it was usually "my wife" or "your mother." "*Wozu hast du mich entschlossen?*" he often said: "What did you decide for me?" But it really meant, "You decide for me." Then the big man would bend down and kiss his little wife meekly.

We had their example of a harmonious relationship and strove to live up to it. Divorce would have been completely foreign to my parents' ethical standards, and separation unthinkable. Parents were a unit, the idea of their splitting up was impossible. I think that it was my parents' marriage that taught me dependability, faithfulness, and the beautiful ability to trust another human being.

Much is said about personal rights and freedom, the pursuit of which can lead to the break-up of a marriage. I have the impression that my grandparents and my parents didn't linger much on these ideas; they had enough self-esteem and love to carry them past egotism. I don't believe that they planned or directed their conduct according to psychological considerations. These philosophies were integrated parts of their personalities and, in my opinion, provided strong support and a beneficial restraint in moments of doubt and indecision. My parents' fundamental happiness proved that the social rules of the time were no hindrance to their individual development.

Engagement

Letting my imagination drift back in time, I see a shy, young man filled with anguish typical for young suitors, a man so different from the father I knew. He, Marcel Holzer, was struggling for the courage to assert himself before Adolf Blum, his respected boss—a man of authority. It is hard to understand how anyone could be afraid of such a soft-spoken, mild man as my grandfather. But, actually, Adolf had felt the same way when he had proposed to Elise. And just like Adolf, Marcel was conscious of the responsibility and, perhaps, not quite ready for it. But in this, as in all such cases, love helped overcome these unpleasant doubts.

On that certain Sunday in 1907, he mustered his courage and let his love for Trudel carry him to the doorstep of Adolf Blum. He had prepared himself for this visit like a general going into battle. But he was painfully aware of his poverty and his unimportant position in Adolf Blum & Popper. Forgetting his diligence and his other outstanding qualities, he felt self-critical and was downright sick with fear. To anyone who knew my father, this seems unimaginable, and it is certainly hard for me to visualize since I knew him as proud and self-assured. But then, he was at the bottom of the ladder and was tortured by qualms about not being able to offer his bride the comfort she was used to; he dreamed of providing royally for her. If he could have looked into a crystal ball and seen her twenty years hence as mistress of the Grunewald villa, how much better he would have felt.

And so, on that fateful day, Marcel put on his striped, black trousers and long, narrowly cut jacket, a stiffly starched collar buttoned to his white shirt, a black tie, and black shoes polished to a high gloss, as usual. He strung his silver key chain through the third buttonhole of his tightly fitted vest. Before placing the gold watch into the vest pocket, he pushed the small, gold button, the lid sprang open, and he threw a quick glance at the time, because punctuality was an important feature of his life. He picked up his black leather gloves and silver-knobbed cane, the carefully brushed bowler hat—and he was ready to go.

On the way he stopped at a flower shop; on this special day, the flowers were intended for the mother of his beloved. In the years to come I will bring her flowers often, he thought. And on her birthdays, she will always get as many red carnations as she counts years. After once more checking the time in order to arrive precisely at the assigned hour, straight and firm steps took him to the house in the *Alsterchaussee*. He found the apartment door on the ground floor, paused a moment, and cleared his throat, which was strangely dry. He cleaned his pince-nez with the familiar gesture, replaced the handkerchief carefully into the jacket breast pocket so that only one corner was showing, then, with a deep sigh, he rang the doorbell. He waited, his heart beating. The door opened, and there was Madame Blum herself in her Sunday best. Her welcoming words were dryly spoken: "Until now, we were happy."

I don't know what happened for certain behind the closed doors in that living room; even Trudel was excluded while her future was discussed, but she was confident that her parents would give their blessings, and that was the result. My grandmother's harsh words later became a laughing matter, for there never was a happier relationship than theirs with their son-in-law.

Trudel Blum and Marcel Holzer celebrated their engagement in February 1907 surrounded by 200 guests, including Trudel's family and unmarried friends. Uncle Robert Goetz, Elise's youngest brother and the poet of the family, had composed and staged hilarious scenes from Trudel's life for the occasion. He had plenty of material to draw from and no one was spared. Each guest placed his gift on a table, which was soon covered with engraved silver, crystal, and china objects, lace, and flowers. The guests admired this exhibition, noting, at times a little maliciously, who had given less than they. On the third of September, 1907, bride and groom were united in marriage in the *Ulenhorster Faehrhaus*, the delightful restaurant in the park across from the *Alsterchaussee*. There Trudel said farewell to her carefree youth; she placed her tiny hand in his and turned her eyes, shining with love, up to him. Fortunately, most of her expectations were to be fulfilled, although she had to learn to abandon some illusions which did not correspond with life's realities. The couple fled the noisy party to the Black Forest resort of St. Blasien to enjoy their first days as a married couple, the fulfillment so anxiously and patiently awaited. The carefully preserved photographs of their honeymoon show Trudel in a lacy blouse and a long, white skirt, her long black hair pinned up in a flattering upswing, her radiant face turned up to Marci, who towers with straight posture above her small form.

Among the yellowing souveniers of their wedding, there is a telegram imprinted with the Imperial Eagle of the German Empire, addressed thus: "Blumolf (the cable address of Adolf Blum & Popper) for Holzer, Hamburg." It was from Vienna, and read: "Kindest regards to you and your bride," and was signed: "Johanna, Karl, Regina, Fritz, Hugo, Arthur, Flora, Leon." A second telegram read "Very pleased with the happy choice of a life companion; we congratulate you and your bride; affectionately, your parents."

This rather cool response to their eldest son's marriage exemplified the kind of relation the Holzer grandparents maintained with us. Used as I was to the warm familiarity of my mother's family, this estranged attitude of my father's family would always bother me. The bond with my other grandparents filled me with confidence and trust beyond time and space, especially during long separations, and the contrast was inexplicable to me until, decades later, I saw these telegrams. The change from my father's obvious coolness towards his own family to a warm closeness with wife's became more comprehensible. My mother offered Marcel a wealth of love and feelings he had never known before, her heart was in her hand, so to speak, and filled a gap in his life. He never mentioned it, but we knew that he had no real love for his family in Vienna. There was a world, a deep chasm between them—the boy who left at sixteen could not return the same as the man he had become. His letters to Trudel would appear exaggerated if one were unaware of the shock he must have experienced in discovering his slumbering capacity for love.

Marriage did not change their romantic relationship, but it deepened and matured the understanding for each other. My father learned to deal with Trudel's temperament and her exaggerated need for constant confirmation of affection, and to share her joys and exaltations. Indeed, we children knew we must admire the objects of her delight or our "lack of enthusiasm for beauty" would make her unhappy. Everybody had to join in exclamation about some sight; little things like that made her happy, happier, I dare say, than all the beautiful jewels my father gave her.

After their honeymoon, the young couple moved into their little flat on the fifth floor of a grey apartment building on *Abendrots Weg* 25 in a quarter of Hamburg called *Ependorf.* Here my mother gave birth on July 10, 1908, to their first child. They named him Erich Karl Adolf after his two grandfathers.

Frau Doering, the midwife, had moved in with them some days before the event. And so began in this small apartment what my mother always described as her happiest years, often recalling with a sigh the days when she was concerned only with the welfare of her little son and Marci's contentment. She described how she would pack Marci's lunch in *Butterbrot Papier*, and walk him to the trolley-car stop. I have a photograph of them—Trudel wearing a cute hat and Marcel in his business suit and straw hat standing with his back to the camera, the sandwich package in his hands behind his back. Later on, Erich and I would go along and watch him jump up on the steps of the trolley with a last wave to us. The bell would gaily chime and off it would go on its shiny tracks down the *Mittelweg*.

My parents lived on a tight budget; every penny was accounted for in a small blue book, and the only way Trudel could put aside a little money from the household funds was by walking instead of taking the trolley when she visited her parents. Pennies thus saved she placed in a box to be used for the layette. When they asked friends to supper, everyone brought his own food. In Germany, the evening meal consisted of simple sandwiches and was called *Abendbrot* (evening bread). The main meal was taken at midday and usually was hot soup, meat, vegetables and potatoes, and desserts—which varied in different parts of the country. In northern Germany, for example, people liked cold fruit soups or puddings. In the south, a meal without pastry was unthinkable. And everywhere, afternoon coffees with whipped cream, or tea with pastry, was enjoyed around four o'clock—the time to meet friends in tearooms and coffeehouses or to have a romantic rendezvous. Women were not at all self-conscious about their figures and ate sweets to their hearts' delight. Diets were for sick people.

My brother Erich was a fat baby, photographs show him squeezed in the high chair in lacy clothes and his dark curls surrounding his happy, smiling face. After being nursed for nine months, he was fed, as most babies were in those days, with great quantities of cream of wheat made with whole milk and sugar. One held the baby tightly on one's lap, both his arms tucked away, and the spoon was relentlessly stuffed into his little mouth. Erich, his grandfather's special darling, was a smart little fellow; his intelligence was detected at an early age by his teacher who came one afternoon to observe Erich at play. He claimed that the intensity with which a child plays is an indication of his learning ability. Indeed, he was certainly right, for Erich grew up to be an excellent student, with a gift for languages.

When Erich was three, his small world on the *Abendrots Weg* 25 was changed by the arrival of a sister.

CHAPTER FOUR

LIESEL

On the twenty-third of September, 1911, my mother decided that it was time she gave birth. With the intention of inducing labor, she had jumped around and had even climbed a fence while walking home with her Marci through Hamburg's dimly lit streets from a night of celebrating at her father's birthday party. Everything was prepared: Frau Doering, the same midwife who had assisted at Erich's birth, had returned, and the doctor was on alert.

A birth in the home was routine, but it could last several days because there were no drugs to speed labor or, for that matter, to relieve pain. Also, the women knew little, if anything, about the physical events taking place in their bodies or about techniques to ease the pain. They were, depending on their nature, prepared to endure the dreadful suffering with more or less fortitude. The mother-to-be was practically isolated in her confinement and thrown into the darkness of her hour without help.

Moral support was about the only relief a husband could have given had he been present. But it was customary to send him away to spare him his wife's cries and his consequent guilt over having caused her suffering. He usually tried to overcome his fears by drinking or celebrating in his office and offering cigars to his friends in hopes of a son. To fathers, it was of the utmost importance that the firstborn was a son, a "name-carrier," and heir. If the firstborn was a girl, she was just tolerated.

There was also the specter of childbed fever, an infection that killed many young mothers. Although fifty years before I was born, the famous scientist Dr. Semmelweiss, had found the bacillus which caused the killing disease, the danger was still ever present and on everyone's mind until sulfonamides were found.

Infections were a constant danger, and it so happened that days after I was born, my mother contracted a breast infection. My mother was so ill after my birth that she shook with fever and Frau Doering was worried enough to call for help. She summoned my father and bade him to undress and hold

Gertrud close in his arms. She figured that the human warmth would be the best remedy. In spite of the infection, nursing was not interrupted, although the sucking baby and the pressure of the milk flow increased the pain. But mother's milk was life sustaining and there was no substitute, except for goat's or cow's milk. The dangers in unpasteurized milk from farm animals was great, so there was little choice but to continue nursing. Some women of the upper classes who could not, or would not, nurse were able to hire a "wet-nurse," usually a poorer women who had given birth recently. She would move into the house of the wealthier family and nurse her own and the other baby at the same time. But my mother nursed my brother and me for many months. That was what a mother was supposed to do.

The midwife, or a nurse, stayed with the household for six weeks while the new mother, a *Wöchnerin* ("a lying-in woman"), was considered a convalescent. She had to stay in bed for at least four weeks, and, even after that, she was treated as if she were recovering from a serious illness. When she finally got her legs on the ground, they were weak and stiff and her body was heavy, her muscles attenuated. After my mother's midwife, Frau Doering, left our family, Marie came to take her place as an *Allein Mädchen*, a "maid for everything." Marie came from a little village in Schleswig-Holstein called Lågerdorf. My grandmother had traveled there in search of a maid. It was customary to check the prospective maid's background and meet her family. My grandmother had visited Marie and her family and found her to be satisfactory. But it seems that *Grossmama* had not looked too closely, for a little while later my mother found out why Marie, although very efficient and hard-working, cried when she cuddled me. The girl confessed, very embarrassed, that she was the mother of an illegitimate baby exactly my age. Her baby was left with her grandmother so that Marie could earn money for the child's support. My parents did not scorn her as she had feared and they provided clothing for her baby, who was called Lieschen. They asked Marie to send Lieschen to us when she reached sixteen and they would train her for domestic service. And since there was no social assistance from the government in such cases, my grandparents also supported the widowed grandmother in every way they could. Lieschen did actually come to us later when we lived in Berlin and stayed with us until her marriage. She and I became good friends and shared many experiences during the hard years of World War II, when I often needed support and help.

In 1911, when I was a baby and Erich was three years old, Marie had her hands full. But nothing seemed to have been too hard or too heavy for her. We lived on the sixth floor, and it was understood that it was the servants' job to carry household items and all other supplies, like coal and food (and baby carriages), up the stairs. In addition to her other cooking and scullery duties, Marie washed everything from bed linens and tablecloths and napkins to the master's shirts. She also had to care for the baby clothes, made from fine batiste with ruffles that had to be boiled and starched, and Erich's garments with frilly collars and cuffs that had to be worked with heated "crimping irons."

Nobody gave a thought to the fact that Marie was in the same physical condition as my mother, since both her baby and I were the same age. The difference between Marie and my mother was social standing, the class. One was the master and the other was the servant. No matter how considerate the employer was, and I am sure that my parents were just that, a servant did not expect to be treated otherwise. My mother told me about Marie, who loved to go out and dance. She would slip back into the apartment at dawn, then, without a wink of sleep, stand singing and humming, bent over the wooden washtub ready for a full day's work. But whenever her work was done, Marie would shower me with all the tender love that her Lieschen missed. A little later, my mother tried to break me from the habit of sucking my thumb; but whenever my mother was away from the apartment, I would cuddle up in Marie's lap and suck my thumb as she sang a nursery rhyme, her kind face nodding at me.

Some people claim to remember the first years of their lives and others think that they can even evoke memories from before their birth. Fortunately for me, since I can do neither, my mother described these scenes so vividly that I can look back at them as if they were memories. But my own impressions, although blurred, began in my third year, the time of the Great War.

In the summer of 1914, when I was three years old, Germany declared war against France, Great Britain declared war against Germany, and the Austro-Hungarian Empire declared war against Russia. The war, triggered by the assassination of the Austrian Crown Prince, Franz Ferdinand, in Sarajevo, spread across central Europe and into Russia and Africa, with Germany fighting on all fronts. The Kaiser had acted on a long-prepared plan by General Count Alfred von Schliefen to fulfill Germany's desire for world domination. This plan called for a short war, six weeks at most, followed by a clear, decisive victory. The German government convinced the German people that it would succeed. Men all over Germany were eager to fight and rushed to enlist by the thousands. Among the early volunteers was Adolf Hitler, a young Austrian who had left his homeland to join the German army in Bavaria. This generation of soldiers was too young to remember the last major European conflict, the Franco-Prussian War of 1870, and thus had no idea of the reality of war. Filled with feelings of superiority and trained with militaristic Prussian discipline, they dreamt of heroic times.

The war was not over in six weeks. It continued into 1915 and into 1916. The great land battles had been inconclusive and trench warfare with its attendant horrors, had shattered hopes of a quick victory. The British naval blockade of German ports had begun in 1915 following German submarine attacks on British ships. By 1916, the problem of feeding not only Germany's civilian population, but hundreds of thousands of soldiers at the front, had become immense.

My father was called to the War Ministry in Berlin to help direct the transportation of food and clothing to the German army. Leaving us was painful for him, but a call to the War Ministry was not only an honor, it was a lot safer than a call to the army would have been. He took a leave of absence from Adolf Blum & Popper and went to Berlin, which would be his home for the duration of the war. Erich and I stayed with our mother and grandparents in Hamburg.

By 1917, conditions within Germany had grown steadily worse. Farmers had become soldiers and their fields lay neglected. Food from neutral nations was prevented from reaching Germany due to Britain's blockade, and, anyway, most of Germany's merchant ships were interned in foreign ports. Food became scarce. Families faced the grim realities of a nation at war. But the clouds, which hung so heavily over Germany, did not darken our childhood.

In our small world in the *Abendrots Weg*, my brother and I were unaware of the consequences of the war; but we knew about the eternally reappearing turnips on our table. In the winter of 1916-17, there was a critical shortage of food, due, in a large part, to a disastrous potato harvest. We were fed with turnips, the only available vegetable, in every imaginable form; as bread or cake and even as a bitter-tasting brew. My mother was rather proud of her desserts and puddings made from turnips, but we greeted them with a sour grimace. Our reaction prompted her to "punish" us by sending her desert over to the Schlesingers, a neighboring family with three boys, our playmates. While we blessed our fate to have escaped the pudding, my mother considered it a gift to our neighbors.

In the afternoons, Erich often persuaded Grete, Marie's successor, to take us to the city to watch the railroad trains pass over the *Lombards Bruecke*. At home, Erich had a Marklin toy train set which occupied him for many years. But real locomotives and railway cars fascinated him, too. Because of our train-watching, we had become accustomed to seeing the soldiers leaving Hamburg in their mouse-grey uniforms on their way to the front. They would lean out of the windows for a last look back at their loved ones, waving handkerchiefs and small, black-white-and red-striped German flags. They shouted and sang joyously, so it seemed, to the crowd of mothers, wives, and sweethearts, who didn't know if they would ever see their men again. The soldiers acted as if they were unaware that they were going into battle and, perhaps, to their death. In the first months and years of the war, many very young boys just out of school had volunteered. Enthusiastic and filled with patriotism, they were ready to die for their fatherland, and many of them did. Among those who fell in the first weeks of the war was my mother's oldest brother, Edgar, whose fate had been foretold by my father's palm reading. My mother's cousin Oswald Goetz was just sixteen when he lost a leg early in the war. Years later, after Hitler became Germany's dictator, Oswald left the country along with many other Jews who had served the fatherland during the First World War.

Later experience taught me that military music arouses enthusiasm regardless of the flag's color. No matter which medals decorate the uniforms or what leader is in power, the magic rhythm of drums and trumpets seems to inspire people. When the troops marched by on their way to battle, the women rushed to windows and doorways, spilled into the street, and often fell into step with the marchers. They didn't realize that the trains would return with the maimed, the wounded, the suffering. But the day inevitably came when the trains did return. Hospitals in Hamburg and other cities filled up, so that public buildings had to be used as substitute Red Cross shelters. Many women were trained as nurse's aides. We observed them at the stations, giving out hot soup and bread to the exhausted soldiers, who passed in long trains through Hamburg.

My mother and grandmother, like most women, were busily knitting. The endless task of manufacturing thousands of badly needed field-green wristlets, shawls, socks, and sweaters for the men in the trenches fell to the able hands of volunteers. Good will and enthusiasm drove most citizens to participate and to give of themselves. All usable scrap fabric was turned in for recycling by volunteers into bandages, which were then rolled and wrapped for shipment to hospitals. People donated silver, gold, and bronze items and received medals in exchange engraved with the words "*Gold gab ich zur Wehr, Eisen nahm ich zur Ehr*" ("I gave gold for defense and took iron for honor"). This patriotic gesture became quite another thing under Hitler's regime when such action was turned into a discriminatory command performance by the government, for Jews only.

As the war dragged on, life in Hamburg changed. Where busy men had gone about their daily tasks and peaceful work, and streets and shops had been alive with shoppers and sightseers, gloom settled in. Instead of casual friendly greetings, people exchanged remarks about the mutual worries which, in a way, united them. Men and women stood around in small groups discussing their fears and the war's latest developments, food shortages, and mounting prices. Worse still, one family after another received the laconic, formal message from the Ministry of War: "We are sorry to inform you that your son is missing in action." The postman, formerly welcomed, became a dreaded messenger. In contrast to the early months of the war when young sons were called or joined the army, now the older generation, husbands and fathers, were sent into battle.

Our mother was often away from home, busy with war work. I would awaken from my afternoon nap and cry bitterly for her. I was used to having her by my side at all times. But now she worked regularly in one of the, "*Volksküchen*", or public kitchens, installed for the needy, mostly elderly people who lived in unheated rooms. These kitchens were scattered all over town, and women volunteers, like my mother, cooked and served food out of huge copper kettles. On one occasion, Grete, who had succeeded Marie, took us there and I saw my mother—a large, white apron tied around her small figure and a white cap covering her dark hair—as she was stirring a steaming soup with a large ladle.

The production of food in large quantities was quite artless. The army used the same kind of copper kettles, but mounted on wheels. Those horse-drawn, rolling kitchens called *Gulasch Kanonen*, or "stew cannons," accompanied the troops as they moved along.

While my mother helped to feed civilians in *Volksküchen*, my father continued to apply his skills to help supply food to the army. It is not surprising that Marcel Holzer had come to the attention of the War Ministry. He had established his reputation in the transportation business through his inventiveness and creative solutions to difficult problems. Shipping beer, for instance, presented a special problem in the early years of the century because of the lack of adequate refrigeration. Once, long before the war, when my father was staying in Leipzig, he happened to read in an American newspaper a list of ship arrivals and departures. He was amazed to see the amount of beer shipped from Hamburg to New York, especially *Pilsner Urquell* and the Munich beer, *Löwenbräu*. He then insisted that Adolf Blum & Popper engage an agent to go after the business in New York. Up to that time, beer en route to steamships was kept cool in railway cars with ice. In summer, the ice melted quickly and had to be replaced often. The delays often meant that the trains were late and missed the departing ships. My father mobilized a fleet of *Elbkähne*, "Elbe river barges." He persuaded their owners to install cooling devices in the barges and arranged for the barges, loaded with beer, to be towed directly to the waiting steamships in the harbor by fast vessels. The *HAPAG* agreed to take on cargo this way, and my father thus shipped the beer through import agents, such as August Lüchow, to the United States.

In 1916, when my father had first been called to Berlin, he joined the *Lagerhaus und Speditions Gesellschaft*, the "Warehouse and Transportation Agency," in Berlin. Later, the name of this firm was changed to *Zentral Einkaufs Gesellschaft*, the "Central Purchasing Agency," or *ZEG*, as it was called. His responsibilities, and his salary, were greatly increased from his pre-war work with Adolf Blum & Popper.

It was during his wartime work in Berlin that my father first came to the attention of Schenker & Company of Vienna. Schenker was at that time not only Europe's largest shipping company, they also had the job to supply the Austrian army. The *Zentral Einkaufs Gesellschaft* had become so efficient, in part due to my father's efforts, that Schenker & Company patterned its operations after those of *ZEG*. In one of his letters, my father told my mother that through his assignment of shipments to the front, he had made the acquaintance of Emil Karpeles, the owner of Schenker & Company.

The general staff of the War Ministry had called Marcel to discuss railroad shipments from the Balkans. He wrote in March 1916: "I can report with satisfaction that I mastered the subject better than the professional railroad staff." He obtained permission to use Adolf Blum & Popper as a distributor for the produce coming into Germany from various neutral countries. Trainload after trainload of all kinds of raw material and food was thus shipped into Germany under Hans Blum's supervision. Marcel hoped that Adolf Blum and Popper would appreciate that, on one occasion, he managed to get them a contract to handle three trainloads of sugar, while Karpeles, in spite of his powerful connections, was allotted only two trainloads. Emil Karpeles kept a watchful eye on my father's activities and noticed the remarkable vitality and effectiveness of this young man in Berlin. Consequently, Karpeles offered Marcel Holzer a partnership in Schenker & Company as soon as he would be released from his wartime responsibilities. My father received other offers as well, but in March 1917, he accepted Schenker's.

The negotiations and the agreement were kept very confidential by my father since he was still working with the War Ministry and, after all, the nation was still at war. However, a rumor went through the ministry that

Marcel Holzer had signed a contract with the Austrian firm. He believed the source of the rumor was Emil Karpeles himself, who was perhaps overeager to announce the new partnership. My father had only recently become a German citizen and felt that his confidential agreement with an Austrian company might be seen as disloyal. He had no choice but to deny it. He wrote to Trudel: "It was a dangerous moment and a vision of the trenches flashed before my eyes." Later he was able to laugh about it since it turned out that *ZEG* was concerned only that they would lose him. The *Hamburg Amerika Linie*, who had hoped to recruit my father, also regretted losing "the ablest man in the field" to an Austrian firm like Schenker.

Under the terms of his agreement with Schenker, my father agreed to open an independent office with himself as president, called Schenker & Company, Berlin, after the war. He saw this opportunity not only as a tremendous increase in salary, but as a beginning of an important career, a chance to develop his far-reaching ideas for transportation systems in Europe. He realized, however, the problems of transplanting his Trudel and us children away from our beloved grandparents. My mother had to summon the courage and trust which springs from love to overcome her ever-mounting fear of losing her Marci to his increasing fascination for business.

Their letters, written during their wartime separation, tell the whole story of Trudel's romantic longing, her need for reassurance, her pleading for expressions of love, and his attempts to pacify her. He told her that he was overwhelmed with work and had little time to write long letters, but he assured her that his love for her was unchanged. Once, out of loneliness and desperation, she visited him and tried to persuade him to look for an apartment for us in Berlin. But he insisted the time was not right. They could not be together as she wished anyway because he was frequently away from Berlin and spent many nights on trains between Germany and Austria and the Balkans, even the Ukraine and the Netherlands. His important work did not allow him to surrender to her wishes. The struggle between his infatuation for his work and his love for wife and children was one that would continue all his life, but Marcel's love for Trudel was always victorious.

On his foreign travels, Marcel was able to purchase certain items for personal use, such as soap, rice, coffee, and tea, which he would then send to us in Hamburg. Other items that were strictly rationed or unavailable in Germany, like sugar, butter, and ham, he could also occasionally purchase. These he would send to us with instructions that Trudel register the items with the police, as required. She would openly share these unexpected gifts with friends. Apparently, on one occasion, someone who witnessed her generosity concluded that the food was illegally obtained and denounced her to the police.

The police investigated and found that the foodstuffs were legally purchased abroad, but reprimanded her for not paying import duties and threatened to confiscate the food items. Marcel wrote to Trudel to calm her worries, saying that he had consulted with a lawyer and that the items in question had come from a duty-free country and could not legally be taken from her. Marcel's main concern was that his family would not suffer, and he regretted the trouble his gifts to us had caused.

The years of separation during the war had been difficult for both of them, and he was anxious to have the family together again. Later on, my mother would recall those years, especially when she was angry with us, how hard it had been for her to stay in Hamburg and care for my brother and me instead of being with her Marci.

In time Marcel's foreign contract negotiations were successfully concluded and he was not required to travel as much. In late 1917, he wrote to Trudel that "perhaps in four or five months it will be over and the bells of peace will ring." The time had come for us to join him in Berlin. He rented an apartment in the *Badenschestrasse* in the Berlin suburb of Schoeneberg and began to plan for our move. My parent's difficult time of separation during the important early years of their marriage was over. The young couple soon found consolation in each other's arms.

CHAPTER FIVE

BERLIN

Much has been written about Berlin as it was before the rise of Hitler, and I feel fortunate to have lived there at that time. Berlin's favorable star, shining for many centuries upon her, and her unmatched development as a world center sank away during Hitler's regime. He condemned her to fall to ashes. Now, after enduring decades of division and struggle, Berlin has begun a new epoch in her long history. As time passes, the number of those who witnessed the glamorous cultural and social life of Berlin before World War II grows steadily smaller. When I look at a faded and worn 1926 edition of the Baedeker guidebook that describes the Berlin of my youth, I unfold maps that show streets and parks, entire sections of the city once familiar to me, but which no longer exist. Bombs and fire changed the face of Berlin, as they did so many other European cities. The old Berlin is no more.

When Berlin first appeared in recorded history in the thirteenth century, it was a simple village on the Rivers Havel and Spree in the province of Brandenburg in an unusually beautiful district of forests, lakes, and streams, and favored by a moderate climate. When, in the seventeenth century, a canal was built linking the River Spree to the River Oder, giving Berlin access to the sea, the former village became a major trading center and blossomed into a city. In 1701, Berlin became a royal residence for Frederick III of Brandenburg, who crowned himself and was known as King Frederick I of Prussia. Eleven years later, his grandson Frederick II, called Frederick the Great, transformed the kingdom into a powerful nation. He led his well-trained army successfully through the Seven Years' War (1756-1763) winning for Prussia an entirely new position of power and prestige in Europe. When peace finally returned to his troubled land, the king rebuilt the destroyed towns and farms and resettled homeless families. He introduced freedom of the press and of worship in Prussia, and he founded village schools for the rural population. Previously, education had been the exclusive privilege of the aristocracy and especially, the members of the royal court.

The king was a great lover of music. He played the flute and composed occasionally. He engaged a court composer for his favorite residence, the beautiful castle *Sans-Souci*. The castle interior was created by the architect von Knobelsdorf in delicate rococo style, the new school of architecture which had come from France and was spreading all over Europe. The rococo style influenced all the arts as well as popular manners and fashion. The king and his court were models for Prussian life. Many drawings and paintings show Frederick in his blue, red, and gold uniform playing the flute surrounded by other musicians, his litter of nervous whippets at his feet. The mirrored halls, the glittering chandeliers, and the ladies and gentlemen with their white wigs and richly embroidered costumes add to the impression of well-being and luxury.

The king commissioned famous architects to build bridges over the Rivers Spree and Havel. The grand edifices he built for the government, the university, and museums, moved Berlin into the focus of artistic and intellectual life and attracted famous men in the course of its history. Leibniz, Planck, Helmholtz, Mommsen, and Hegel and many others made Berlin's Academy of Art and Science, its hospitals and institutes world famous. During Frederick's reign, from 1740 to 1786, Berlin acquired the face which would make it the glorious city it remained during the following two hundred years.

Shortly after Frederick the Great's death, the *Brandenburger Tor* was built to commemorate his many victories. The wide boulevards leading to the gateway allowed the victorious army thereafter to enter the capital under its arches, displaying the glittering pomp of kings and emperors who ruled Prussia and Germany. They passed along *Unter den Linden* and entered the *Tiergarten*, Berlin's biggest park.

In 1871, after the Franco-Prussian War, Berlin became the capital of a united Germany under Kaiser Wilhelm I. The industrial revolution had begun to transform city life. Berlin grew rapidly as people from all parts of Germany and elsewhere sought work there. By 1918, it had a population of over four million and had, as did all the major cities of Europe, definite geographic areas defined by class differences. In Europe, Berlin was second in size only to London and was the fifth largest city in the world. Yet the heart of the city remained centered on the area immediately surrounding the *Brandenburger Tor*.

There are other monuments and buildings in Berlin, which might mean more to many people, but the *Brandenburger Tor*, the *Tiergarten* and *Unter den Linden* are closely woven into my memory. The *Tiergarten* was the park where the Berliners enjoyed leisurely strolls between flowering shrubs and flowerbeds, and well-kept lawns or sat on benches to watch ladies and gentlemen riding on horseback on the nearby bridle paths. Amongst them, in 1930, one could even have admired me, proudly riding side-saddle, elegantly dressed in a black riding outfit, the wide skirt swung over my bent knee and the black, three-pointed hat fastened by a ribbon under my chin.

When we moved to Berlin in the spring of 1918, I was a little girl of only six years and unaware of the events about to unfold. Only much later I realized that, in the years immediately following, Germany was shaken by heavy political storms. The Great War, which had bled Europe for four years and claimed ten million lives, came to an end. Germany's allies, Austria, Turkey, and Bulgaria, had surrendered, and the exhausted nation could not fight on alone. In spite of that, the armistice of November 1918 came as a shock to the German people, who had not been told the full extent of the military situation Germany faced. The victorious allies, France, Britain, Italy, and America, imposed tough conditions and the Germans were not in a position to keep fighting, although parts of the army wanted to continue the struggle. The monarchy collapsed, Kaiser Wilhelm abdicated and went into self-imposed exile in Holland.

Germany was left without government, and opposing political factions in Berlin seized their opportunity. The moderate socialists moved into the Chancellory and proclaimed a German Republic, to be headed by the reluctant Friedrich Ebert. The same day, Karl Liebknecht, the Communist party leader, raised the red flag over the Imperial Palace and proclaimed what some hoped would be a Bolshevik republic. In the absence of leadership by well-known figures like Field Marshal von Hindenburg, who refused to accept the humiliating armistice, and General Ludendorf, who had taken refuge in Sweden, Ebert tried in vain to establish a stable government. The unemployed and the poor were exposed to hunger and cold in the political chaos that followed. Street fights in the historic center of Berlin broke out and thousands were killed. Political assassinations, strikes, and sporadic violence marked the period until order could be restored.

The peace treaty that followed in the summer of 1919 spelled out the nation's fate. The Allies, France in particular, exacted their revenge on Germany. The German Empire was to be dismantled. France was to reclaim Alsace-Lorraine and occupy the rich, coal-mining district of the Rhineland. The Saar would be governed by the League of Nations. Poland would get the industrial region of Upper Silesia and West Prussia, cutting off East Prussia from the rest of Germany. Germany would lose her overseas colonies and most of her army and navy, and, most crushing of all to many Germans, would be forced to accept full blame for starting the war. A reparation commission would be established to determine how much Germany would have to pay to make up for the Allies' losses. The announcement of these terms to the German public set off another wave of resentment in Berlin climaxed by an unsuccessful attempt by factions of the army to seize control of the Chancellory.

To escape the turmoil of Berlin, the National Assembly met in the ancient and politically neutral town of Weimar, where a new and democratic constitution was drafted. In time, the Weimar Republic, as it came to be known, would stabilize Germany and would become a chapter unique in the nation's history.

It would seem that the harsh terms of the Treaty of Versailles would have caused a permanently debilitated Germany and, thus, would have prevented the nation's participation in another war. But, in spite of, or because of, the nature of the Allies' punishing demands of the defeated country, the historic truth is that, in these years, the seeds of Hitler's national socialism were sown.

Marcel Holzer's main concern during these momentous times was seeing that his family was established in their new apartment in Schoeneberg and that his new business, Schenker & Company, Berlin, was established satisfactorily in its quarters *Unter den Linden*.

Schoeneberg

For Erich and me, the world centered on school and home. Our apartment in the *Badenschestrasse*, in Schoeneberg, was not very spacious, but we each had our own room and in the living room was a corner for my mother's grand piano, the Bechstein, to which she was very attached. She had purchased the instrument in part from money she had earned as my father's secretary at Adolf Blum & Popper before their marriage, and it remained with her the rest of her life. My mother had a good alto voice and played the piano to accompany herself. I see my mother at her piano and I hear her singing the romantic songs from Hugo Wolf, one of the most popular song composers of the era, who set his music to poems by Eichendorff, Moericke, and Goethe. When my mother sang, my little white rabbit usually sat under the piano, his red eyes wide open and his long ears popped up. The little fellow seemed to like the music and always came hopping in as soon as he heard it begin. Sometimes he got so wrapped up in the music he forgot his manners.

My parents were outstanding in their hospitality. Just as they had shared a simple *Butterbrot* in the *Abendrots Weg* with their friends, so they showered their guests with every imaginable luxury when they could afford it.

Although my father was not yet a wealthy man, one of his great pleasures was to invite people to our home and to treat them royally. He offered presents, signs of thoughtfulness, and when he entertained them in a restaurant he discreetly paid, and tipped the waiters handsomely, but never in front of his guests. After a day of hard work and tension, my father came home to his family and guests composed and in a mood of leisure; he knew how to leave his worries behind. He worked day after day and never rested, although he often took my mother to dinner, the operas, and theaters. He surrounded us with beautiful things he loved as soon as he could afford them: it was compensation for the meager times when he had to forgo them.

One visitor I will always remember was my father's youngest brother Leon. Actually, he was the only member of my father's family who was a regular guest; just as he had been in Hamburg, so he was in Schoeneberg, and, later in Grunewald. When I was a little girl, I often walked proudly next to him, noticing the admiring glances that followed the handsome, tall, Austrian army officer. He wore the tight, blue-and-red uniform of the "K and K" (*Kaiserliche und Koenigliche) Austrian Army*, the buttons and the belt buckle of shimmering gold. Leon sported a well-groomed moustache befitting his elegant appearance. Those times were probably the happiest days of his life. Later he would have to emigrate with his wife and begin a new existence in New York.

As part of our education, my parents engaged a young Swiss lady who was to be our companion, for a long time as it turned out. My father had never had the opportunity to learn foreign languages, but his travels and business dealings had convinced him how important this was for our future. The presence of Mademoiselle Frieda, "Made" as we called her,(short for Mademoiselle) gave him, as well as my mother and us, a chance to learn French. We were not allowed to speak anything but French with Made. She soon became like a family member and we loved her very much. She was a lighthearted young girl who loved fun and laughter, and over the years we shared many little adventures. Her presence lightened up the otherwise regulated schedule of my youth. After her long tenure with us, she left and married an American.

The most fun we had was when my mother's cousin, Oswald Goetz, came to visit. He was a good-looking fellow and full of good spirits, despite the loss of his leg in the Great War. He was expert in many fields and was an art historian, and later became the director of the art museum in Frankfurt on the Main. During his stays with us, Made would invent all sorts of nonsense and the two of them would play little tricks on one another. Only much later did I realize that Made had been in love with Oswald.

Our favorite times when Ossi visited were when he would sit at my mother's piano and sing to us his own composition, an unending fantasy "The Adventure of Helene." He always created new incidents involving poor Helene and sang with a loud voice while playing on the Bechstein, while Erich and I giggled and laughed and horsed around with the leather contraption serving as his leg. Helene survived a whole generation and evolved into the heroine of countless bedtime stories Oswald sang, years later, for my children.

Even before we moved to Berlin, my parents had enrolled Erich and me in our respective schools, each within walking distance of our apartment. My brother went to the boy's *Gymnasium*, and I to the lyceum for girls, the "Chamisso School," named for the French poet. It was just an ordinary public school and, in my recollection now, seems very old-fashioned, and our little adventures within its four walls, rather amusing. The class photograph shows me—a plump little girl with a large bow in my long, brown hair—wearing an apron tied over a dark dress. All the girls had their shapeless legs stuck in long, probably homemade, woolen stockings. Awkward and shy, embarrassed and "good," we were a bunch of not-too-happy-looking girls. I was not always good, to the annoyance of the elderly teachers, who, on the whole, were rather strict and devoid of understanding of small children. The rules were applied without consideration for the age of the student or for the pleasures and innocence that should be part of childhood. Discipline and uniformity were the important factors. Our class was rather large, a group of thirty girls. At eight o'clock in the morning we sat down at our desks, two girls on each bench, and folded our hands in front of us. There had to be absolute silence after the second bell. When the teacher came into the classroom, we greeted her in a chorus, as one voice. Then we would say a prayer and sing a religious song.

In Germany the church and state were not separated and religious instruction was part of the curriculum. Jewish children were not obliged to participate in Christian religious activities and were excused from class during these times. We sometimes envied them for their "free time." Jewish children, in those pre-Hitler days, meant children of Jewish parents, raised in the Jewish faith. During my first school years these facts were insignificant and not discussed since we considered ourselves Christians. My brother and I were christened in the Lutheran church, and our parents, although never christened, kept in close contact with the Lutheran community.

I don't recall having a "special" friend in those first grades; but I do remember being the *Klassen Aelteste*, the "Class First," which by no means reflected good behavior, but was a certain distinction given to a child with good marks. It entitled the student to supervise the class in the absence of the teacher after the first bell had reassembled the children in the classroom. Silence was supposed to reign. The *Klassen Aelteste* was supposed to write any misbehaving child's name on the blackboard. The teacher, upon her return, would then record the misdeed in the little blue book kept for each student. These marks would eventually be reflected in the student's report card in the column marked "Behavior." I did not enjoy "telling" on my friends, and, one day, the teacher returned to a noisy classroom when I was the *Klassen Aelteste* and saw no names on the blackboard. She was outraged and sent a letter home, saying: "Elisabeth has not yet understood the seriousness of life."

On another occasion during that same year, my grandparents Blum stayed with us when my parents were away. I came home from school and presented a letter from the teacher to my Opi, which stated that I had talked in class and was moved to the back of the room. My grandfather, good-naturedly mocking the teacher, wrote on the note that, in his opinion, all the seats in the classroom were there to be used. The teacher did not smile when she read this.

We were afraid of the teacher, but at least there was a row of windows on one side of the room, through which yearning eyes of tired children could see the freely wandering clouds or the gaily fluttering birds and butterflies.

CHAPTER SIX

GRUNEWALD

By the end of summer 1919, my father had reached his goal of moving his family into a villa before his fortieth birthday. I don't know when he had taken the time to look for a house—one that would meet his family's needs and satisfy his standards—but he found it, in Grunewald, one of Berlin's most beautiful suburbs. It meant much to him, but it was the fulfillment of just *one* of his ambitious dreams. As he built up his shipping and freight-forwarding business, he had fought for recognition in his field at the same time. He excelled in almost all his enterprises: his sound judgment usually brought success even in financially risky ventures that required a great deal of courage. As his business prospered, his income grew until, at last, he had earned enough to purchase a villa.

But during our last months in the *Badenschestrasse* my mother was unhappy. She had a difficult time following my father into his expanding world. She would have preferred to continue a simple and less glamorous life, and often told us she would have been happy married to a man with a fixed but secure income, no matter how modest. I can recall the look on my father's face at such remarks as he smiled at her, expressing pity at her innocence.

My father purchased the villa at *Jagowstrasse* 24 from its original owner, a Mr. Merton, who had just completed it as his dream house. He parted with it reluctantly, but he was obliged to move to Frankfurt. The house, which was to be my home until my marriage, contained twenty-six rooms on three floors and was built of red brick in the Dutch style, with steep gables. The house sat near the front of a large lot on a tree-lined street with other large homes. The wrought-iron fence in front had two pairs of huge wrought-iron gates leading to a semicircle driveway. At both sides, and at the rear of the house, there was a large ornamental garden with trees, shrubs, flowers, and lawns, including a rose garden and some fruit trees. There was also a children's playground and a tennis court. At the far end of the lawn was the greenhouse and the garages, which opened onto a side street. Above the garages was an apartment for the chauffeur and his wife. Since at various times we kept three or more automobiles, we also employed two drivers. Each was required to be on duty every second day. In the apartment over the garage lived Herr Kuehne and his wife. The other driver, Herr Schmidecke, lived elsewhere, not in the villa. My father explained his need of two drivers by saying that he could not expect his chauffeur to drive home late after parties and then be in front of the house with a washed car at eight the next morning, ready for the drive to the office. During most of the day, however, the driver just sat around in the office and waited to take my father to a restaurant for lunch.

The villa was really a dream house. One felt at every turn that it was designed with love and that each detail was planned to give beauty and comfort to the inhabitants. But when my mother first saw the house, she panicked at the thought of the housework involved. What worried her most, though, was the increased social burden that would be hers when we moved into the fashionable neighborhood. More than ever she wished her husband could have been a greengrocer or a simple clerk. And so she was quite relieved when, after signing the contract, Mrs. Merton asked for a delay in moving out. She visited my mother and the two women cried in each other's arms—one because she had to leave the house she had designed so carefully, the other because she was afraid of the change the move would make in her life. It was the second big adjustment my mother had to make in her marriage. This might not seem especially traumatic now, but at that time in Germany people did not change their domiciles as readily as we do today. But she loved her Marci, and she never stood in his way. She dutifully moved into the house and managed to retain her simplicity and her honest, warm relationship with her old friends despite her new, luxurious social life.

It was typical of my parents that their employees were more like their charges: they always considered their human problems and helped whenever they could and, thus, gained their respect and obedience. The Holzer home was the servants' home also. Only once can I remember that there was a problem with a servant, and that resulted from a maid's not quite common love for my mother.

In those years, class difference automatically kept everyone in his or her place, although since my grandparents' generation, the gaps between classes had narrowed. In any case, my father forbade us to ever use the word "servant." He explained to us that they hadn't necessarily chosen to become servants, that the lack of a better education had deprived them of the chance to learn a different profession. He told us that our home had to compensate for their lack of one, and we could help them to feel at home by being kind and considerate. As a result of this attitude towards our employees, we had basically the same staff from 1919 to 1935, when the house was sold.

Before we moved from Schoeneberg to Grunewald, my father ordered furniture and bought paintings for the new house, guided by the advice of Oswald Goetz. Later, when I was old enough to judge, I was not overly impressed with Oswald's taste.

My first encounter with our new home, when I was eight years old, remains vivid in my memory. It was a pleasant, sunny day in August, typical for Berlin, and I wore a pretty dress and short, white socks, ready to run into the garden of which I had already heard so much. Since up to then the public parks had been our playground, the garden was a real sensation: Erich and I raced excitedly over the pebble-covered walkways which surrounded the green, well-kept lawn. We greeted the weeping willows—where we would later suspend our hammock and swing lightly back and forth—the branches studded with light green, slender leaves, the powdery yellow pussy willows dangling before our eyes.

Drunk with pleasure, we ran back to the house across the white stone terrace that separated the lawn from the stately house. Big stone containers of geraniums in full bloom alternated with globular stones marking the edge of the terrace where we would take our meals on sunny days, of which there promised to be many.

Erich and I stopped, breathless, wiped our shoes and entered the house through one of the French doors which opened into the dining room. The walls were covered with a soft shade of blue silk, a color matched by the drapes and oriental rug. Next to the dining room, separated by a large, paneled folding door, was the ladies' salon. We entered it and saw the carved armchairs and inlaid tables and chests in Louis XV style, an Aubusson rug, and, on one wall, a smiling "Portrait of a Lady" by Cornelius de Vos. The room was flooded with light and sun and accented by fresh-cut flowers, which Herr Genrich, the gardener, had brought in by the armful.

Through a heavy, oak door, we reached the living room with its fireplace, its shiny, dark parquet floor covered with a large oriental rug. We were intimidated by this large, rather dark, room with its heavy, leather armchairs and the dark, paneled walls and ceiling. It was called *das Herrenzimmer*, the "gentlemen's room." It was customary in Germany, as in England, for men to retire to such a room after dinner to enjoy cigars and "Schnapps" without the company of the ladies.

Passing through a doorway on the narrow side of the room, we descended three steps and found ourselves in the music room, which overlooked the side garden—a narrow piece of lawn with a small terrace and a narrow, rounded stone bench. In this room, we greeted our old friend, the Bechstein grand piano. It seemed proud of its new place, eager to show off all its gleaming splendor. The French doors of the music room were framed by pale, blue silk drapes and, apart from some Chinese-style chests and comfortable armchairs, a big rug with a dragon pattern commanded the room. Up three steps and through a doorway and we were in the center hall, opening into the library. Bookshelves lined the walls and in the center was a long oak table with large, Gobelin-covered armchairs around it. Two glass-doored cabinets contained a special collection of gold-edged, leatherbound volumes. (These books later became interesting to me after I discovered Eduard, the butler, dustcloth carelessly under his arm, deeply engrossed in reading one of them. Unseen by him, I watched him hide the key to the cabinets after he had replaced the book and, thus, I discovered the kind of literature which one does not let the children see.)

Opposite the main entrance, we now climbed the impressive staircase to the second floor. From the upper hall at the top of the stairs, we explored our playroom and the bedrooms, which were all connected. At the front of the upper hall was a niche with ivy-painted walls and a single window which overlooked the street. It was here that Erich and I, and our governess Made, would take our breakfast, just as the Merton children had done.

After we became more familiar with the house, we discovered other interesting details. Mr. Merton also had installed a balcony off the upstairs hall that overlooked the main entrance hall below. From here the Merton children could observe the arrival of dinner party guests without being seen. We, of course, did the same thing. Also, the playroom had a large, high window opening to the hall through which one could observe the children's activities. Erich and his friend Kurt, who lived nearby, and I with my best friend Helga would share the playroom. Erich and Kurt discovered they could use the window to spy on Helga and me when we performed our veil dances. On these occasions, we draped my mother's shawls and scarfs around our nude bodies and we certainly didn't want to be seen by the boys.

The upstairs, with its many interconnecting rooms was ideal for playing hide and seek. When my parents went out, which happened several times a week, we turned out all the lights and in pitch darkness Kurt, Helga, and I enjoyed our screams as Erich pretended to be a ghost.

I remember very well my parents' bedroom and dressing rooms the way they were then. My parents' dressing rooms adjoined their bedroom. My father had cabinets installed from floor to ceiling in his dressing room. It was typical of him, with his multitude of shirts and ties, shoes, and suits, to keep track of every piece. Not even the butler was allowed to put things away for him. We made much fun of his passion for things and laughed a lot about his everyday habits, his way of dressing according to the weather news, which he carefully followed.

When, as a little girl, I came into his room on Sunday mornings, I often found him sitting there in his pajamas, whistling softly, as he polished his shoes. He would be surrounded by gleaming pairs of shoes and the shoe-polish box. He never wore the same pair two days in a row, and so he needed at least six pairs ready for the coming week. He polished his shoes regularly even though the butler had already done it. His suits were custom-made, and he probably had at least fifty for each season to choose from. Sometimes, he had several suits made from the same material and in the same style, so that my mother would not notice the new ones and scold him. In any case, his gadgets, his wardrobe, and his collection of cars and fine wine made him happy and that was the main thing for us. After all, he had worked hard for all of it and deserved these harmless pleasures.

I don't know when my father's interest in cars started. We never had a car in Hamburg or when we lived in Schoeneberg; but soon after we moved to the Grunewald, he bought his first car, a "Puch." Sometimes we had six cars in the garage, arranged in two rows of three. Among them, over the years, was an "Adler", a "Daimler-Benz", an "Austro-Daimler", a "Mercedes-Benz", a "Graef & Stift," a "Hispano-Suiza", and two American cars—a "Packard" roadster (for my mother) and a "Jordan". The automobiles were an important part of our daily routine. Each new one was exciting; owning them was a sport rather than simply a means of transportation.

Our cars in the 1920s were usually convertibles. My father and the chauffeur sat in front, driving alternately: my mother, Erich, and I sat in the back seats. We were dressed from head to toe in white linen coats and caps to protect us from the dust. We wore goggles to protect our eyes and on rainy or cold days we were wrapped in leather aprons tied around our waists. The wind reddened our cheeks, and the sun burned the skin, but even when it rained, the car remained open. My father, sitting behind the windshield, was quite pitiless in that respect. He was going to "make it" in a certain amount of time, so that he could brag afterwards about beating his own record for the trip across Germany. I remember that we had to plead for a sandwich break or to visit a "toilet," which meant to disappear in the bushes.

In 1921, Berlin completed a public test track for automobiles, called the "AVUS" (*Automobil-Verkehrs Uebungsstrasse*). Here my father could try out his cars at full speed. One day this almost led to an accident. My father, driving a car at high speed, suddenly saw one wheel in front of him, running away quite by itself. He didn't use the brakes for fear of throwing the car of balance. By taking his foot off the gas pedal he slowed the car down and eventually it came to a stop without leaving the track. The incident shocked my mother who tried bravely to accept automobile racing as part of our new life.

Our daily routine after moving into *Jagowstrasse* 24 was dictated by the activities of family and servants. Early in the morning I would wake up hearing the gardener's rake scraping the pebble-covered paths. By the time my father would take his morning walk through the garden, everything had to be in perfect order to the point that the pebbles were not touching the edge of the lawn. He made his rounds in a light, energetic step, "spick and span," as my mother described him, in his dark business suit, his shoes shined, the edge of his neatly folded handkerchief showing just a bit of a corner in his breast pocket. Bending here and there, he removed a weed or inspected the shrubs. Greeted by Herr Genrich, they discussed the work to be done. Then, with a cordial smile, he turned to the terrace, where my mother, fully dressed and coiffed, awaited him seated at the breakfast table. The table was covered with a pretty tablecloth and laid with the chinese breakfast dishes, and Eduard, the butler, stood ready with the steaming coffee. The halved grapefruit, with wedges carefully loosened, was served in a high-footed, metal container, the fruit resting in a glass bowl on crushed ice. To conclude his breakfast, my father gulped down a glass of buttermilk, then quickly kissed my mother good-bye. The chauffeur, waiting for him, cap in hand by the open car door, then whisked him away.

Erich and I, meanwhile, had had our seven o'clock breakfast in the upper hall lobby with Made, and then we were off to school. I had a ten-minute walk to the Bismarck Lyceum in the nearby *Siemensstrasse*, while Erich had a longer distance to the Grunewald *Gymnasium*. Since there were no cafeterias at the schools then, and nothing but water to drink, we each took a package of sandwiches in our satchel to be eaten in the school yard during one of the breaks between classes. In the afternoons, we had sports and games, but, for the most part, school was not much fun. Teaching methods were dry and we had to learn a lot by rote. And we were assigned a considerable amount of homework. School certainly didn't help me to acquire insight into world affairs and the understanding of them as I yearned for. I truly would have liked to comprehend the relationship between cultures, politics, and ideas.

I realized later that we had everything in our youth but intellectual guidance. Neither at home nor in school, nor amongst the people my parents associated with, was there a person who gave direction to our studies. Herr Schiller, one of the directors of Schenker & Company, and Dr. Ruge, my father's lawyer, were both very cultured and intelligent; but we children had no contact with them. Thus, trivial events had more meaning to us than they seem now to warrant. For instance, when we got our first bicycles, it was an event of great importance. We were very happy although we were not even allowed to leave the garden and it was hard to race around on the thickly spread pebbles. But we soon learned to manage and organized competitive games with obstacle courses. Schmidecke, the chauffeur, taught us steering techniques as a preparation for driving. He demonstrated them on miniature toy cars and explained the art of taking curves by considering centrifugal force.

When my father came home at night, he always asked us what we had done that day. On one such an occasion, he told us his adventures as a young man on his bicycle. He had cycled alone across the *Riesengebirge*, a mountainous area of Germany, and he said that he had experienced nature more intensely than in an automobile.

We often attended the popular, six-day bicycle race held annually in Berlin in an indoor arena. Teams raced uninterruptedly for six days and nights, watched by an ever-changing audience. Members of elegant Berlin society visited this spectacle after the theater or on weekends. It was as serious an event then as the Tour de France is for bicycle fans today.

Our whole life was centered around my mother, who now was busy looking after us, my father, and the staff. She also organized the various social obligations which the new life in Grunewald demanded. My father's business depended to a great extent on connections with bankers and railroad executives, so dinner parties were of great importance and very elaborate. When I came home from school, my first question to the butler was, "Where is Mutti?" I usually found her in the dining room where she had helped with the table setting. She used her best embroidered tablecloths from her collection of precious linens. They were handmade by women in the *Erzgebirge* whose lace and embroidery were famous for quality and provided, to a large extent, their families' livelihood. With enough helping hands upstairs and downstairs, the china, silverware and crystal glasses were re-polished before being set on the table. There was a different goblet for each wine that accompanied six or seven courses. The butler taught me to carry several stem glasses in one hand and a way to fold the starched napkins so that they looked like roses or a bishop's hat.

Every harvest, my father bought a great quantity of the most select wines and stored the red and the white wines in two separate cellars, each kept at a different temperature. The bottles were kept separated by vintage, in specially designed wooden casks. Upstairs in a special cabinet, a file card was kept describing each cask. My father would come home from the office, ask the butler about the dinner menu, then select the wines he wanted to be served. The red wines were already at the correct temperature, the white wines were put on ice if necessary. There must have been hundreds of bottles in my father's cellars. He kept buying wine, and although he enjoyed a bottle of the precious stuff at every meal and gave cases to friends and relatives on special occasions, he was never able to consume it all.

While my father devoted his attention to the wine, my mother's pride was the floral decorations, especially the centerpieces of the long table. On party days, everybody was excited and busy and the children were generally ignored. So one day, we decided we would hide under the table to overhear the adults' conversation. We had imagined it would be fun, but we had not accounted for the time it would take to serve the hors d'oeuvres, the soup, the fish, and the roast, followed by a sherbet, a salad, and the dessert. After a while, we felt very uncomfortable between all the legs and skirts and started giggling, which led to our discovery. I don't think that I behaved like the girl in a joke told at that time who lifted her nightgown in front of her blushing face when her mother asked, "Aren't you ashamed?" But I do remember the embarrassment of standing in my nightgown in the midst of all these well-dressed ladies and gentlemen.

My mother used to say teasingly that the butler was the most formal and elegant person in the house, and, indeed, Eduard had served in well-known families and commanded respect. The other help, and even we children, obeyed him without hesitation. The servants so identified with their masters that they spoke of "our house," "our children," and "our guests." They were as proud of the family's possessions as if they were theirs. They also knew what certain guests had given to my parents and made it a point to use those items when these people came to dinner.

Eduard in particular was very aware of protocol for these social occasions. Once Eduard, distinguished-looking in his white tie and white gloves, opened the door for a latecomer, a film star named Maria Paudler. She had informed my mother that she would be late because of a rehearsal so the dinner had started before her arrival, which was, indeed, not according to etiquette. Madame Paudler stood timidly and apologetically at the door as Eduard politely opened it, but she heard him murmur, "The invitation was for seven-thirty, Madam." Later on, when Eduard was out of sight, she reenacted the scene for the amused guests.

When guests arrived, Erich and I stood unseen in our private balcony over the stairs and watched them with great interest. There were some special parties that I remember. My parents knew some members of the movie industry, such as Ernst Correll, president of Phoebus Film, Germany's second largest film company. Another of their film acquaintances, who would one day become my brother-in-law, was Herman Grieving, an executive in the cultural department at UFA, Germany's leading film studio. Other guests included Lil Dagover, Emil Jannings, and Maria Paudler. Lil Dagover was a beautiful woman, elegant and ladylike. My father and she discovered they had at least one thing in common, they each owned a Hispano-Suiza cabriolet. During the party, they exchanged stories about the cars, and my father invited Madame Dagover for a demonstration ride. He "forgot" to tell my mother, his jealous, little wife, of his plan. The next day, a telephone message reached my unsuspecting mother informing her about the open car with two, rather well-known passengers driving above the speed limit down the *Kurfuerstendam*. I assume that one of my mother's lovely jewels is a silent witness of Marcel's remorse.

These parties where not always fun for us children. The wine did not fail to have its normal effect on the guests. Sometimes long after midnight the men would stand, arms around one another, in the hall singing student songs at the top of their lungs. One of those songs, still ringing in my ears, was:

> *Wenn du denkst der Mond geht unter*
> *Der geht nicht unter*
> *Das scheint nur so.*

A silly song, meaning:

> "If you think the moon is setting
> It is not setting
> It just seems that way."

On one of those song-filled evenings, I was tossing and turning in my bed, furious because the noise downstairs prevented me from sleeping. I got out of bed, took my dog's leather leash, and ran down the stairs brandishing the leash like a whip and screaming these strange words, "If you don't stop making this noise I will use my house right!" What a "*Haus Recht*" actually meant I probably did not know. Great surprise and dead silence followed this scene, which, considering an eight-year-old child's position in those days, demonstrated surprising courage on my part.

Children really had no rights, and even adults had a different conception of their own obligations and rights than we have today. My mother, for instance, thought she had no "right" to travel with my father and leave us behind with the staff. Her first duty, she thought, was to her children, and, therefore, she remained home when her Marci traveled. We children did not make our own decisions and did not even participate in our parents' deliberations concerning us. Rules were made by parents and school and obeyed without question. My little nighttime adventure remains in my memory because I probably felt guilty for having told adults, guests at that, what to do. Children did not intrude on adults' lives. They were seen but not heard, and never voiced an opinion without being asked to do so.

Thus I was never asked, and I would not have chosen, to learn to swim. I had a secret fear of the water. Nevertheless, in the summer of 1919, we were taken to the *Wannsee*, a lake near Berlin, for swimming instructions. This large body of water, surrounded by forests and villas, was a favorite recreation area for both Berliners and tourists. It connects through various rivers and channels to the Baltic Sea, to which there was a steamer service. On the *Wannsee* vacationers enjoyed all sorts of water sports. But the water, being close to a densely populated area, was polluted.

The swimming instructor, a husky man, stood on the landing, holding a heavy rod to which a rope was attached. At the end of the rope, a child dangled in the water, kicking and splashing as he "learned" to swim. Soon it was my turn. It was hard to stay afloat, to keep my head above water and balance so I would not tip forward. The sling was tight around my chest and hurt under the armpits as soon as one was hanging in it instead of "swimming" or floating in the water. During the first few lessons I panicked, but I did learn the breaststroke, at least, by submitting to the teacher's discipline.

We had not yet been taught how to submerge, but we soon discovered the teacher's method of teaching the little brats how to dive. Without much ado, I was summoned to the lip of the diving board and the sling was placed around my chest. In spite of his reassuring comments, I was frightened. I hesitated, breathing hard, trying to overcome my inner resistance, when I was suddenly and forcefully pushed in the back, and, in an instant, I was beneath the water. I will never forget the horrible feeling of drowning when the water closed above my head. With a deep, last, choking breath, water entered into all possible openings. Seconds later I was pulled out, seconds which seemed an eternity.

Everyone considered their first try a success except me. Erich and Made claimed I was a coward. It turned out we got infections from the dirty water.

Erich and Made developed sore throats that night, but I was harder hit with an ear infection. In the days that followed, it got progressively worse. The family doctor, who came daily, finally brought a specialist, Dr. Saenger. Without anaesthesia, he pierced my right eardrum, a painful event which simply overwhelmed me. When after a few days he came to repeat the procedure, I clung hysterically to one of the ebony-colored bedposts, vainly trying to escape the treatment. Still, the infection and the pain persisted and the doctor decided to operate. In the absence of penicillin, the usual treatment called for removal of the malleus and the incus, small bones essential to hearing.

So I underwent an operation. The anaesthesia, mostly ether, was a nightmare I have never forgotten. I remember vividly the mask which covered my mouth and nose, the smell, the order to count, the sensation of losing consciousness, and the strange feeling until the drug had taken effect. Awakening was almost as bad, if not worse. My mother's and the nurse's voices seemed as if they came from far, far away, encouraging me to vomit in the futile attempt to overcome nausea and spasms which lingered and caused me agony. The numb feeling and the dreadful pain in my head lasted a long time. When I had to undergo a second operation, my terror was indescribable.

In spite of the nightmarish experience in the clinic, I have some good memories of those weeks. My father came to visit me at night, although he thoroughly disliked every contact with illness and hospitals. I was aware of the strain my healthy and vital father underwent when he came to my sickbed. At home we never dared complain about physical problems because we knew he wanted none of that. My mother, accustomed to his lack of sympathy, would appear in the morning after a night of feeling unwell, and greet her Marci with the words, "Thank you, better." She knew that he would never remember to ask her about her health. My father was just never sick. He once stuck his head out of the window and when my mother asked him what for he did it he said: "I think what I feel is called a headache." His motto was, people are healthy, hypochondriacal, or dead. But here he was sitting next to his daughter Elisabeth—he never called me Liesel—shelling fresh walnuts, which I liked so much. I realized that he must have stopped at Rollenhagen, the fancy delicatessen on the *Kurfuerstendam*, to buy them, and that, again, was unusual because he rarely went into a food store. We were both shy and uneasy. Was he embarrassed or was it me? I was impressed that he took the time to see me.

Several weeks later, I was sent home to continue my recovery. My parents had engaged a private nurse, *Schwester* Margarete Gumpel; I remember her as being a jovial, older woman with whom I shared much laughter. She took good care of me and changed the big bandage on my oozing wound daily. There were no drugs to speed up the healing process and the recovery took months. Eventually I regained my health, but not my hearing in that ear.

During my long convalescence, my brother's friends wrote letters and came to visit me. One visitor was Kurt. A photograph of that time shows him and my brother wearing knickerbockers, smiling for the camera. The photo also shows Molly, my childhood companion. Molly was a little Spitz given to me for my ninth birthday. I still remember my delight when the little white bundle hopped out of a basket straight into my arms. For almost nine years in Grunewald, this little animal lived with us. Erich played with him, often using the dog to tease me. For instance, once after Molliy's bath, he took him to play in the coal cellar, where the white dog quickly turned into a black one. In another mood, Erich wrapped him in newspaper and put him in my doll's carriage over my objections. Once he used scissors to cut a straight line on the dog's shaggy head, saying that Molly needed a part. The hair grew back yellow, and, to my dismay, it stayed like that.

Erich loved to tease and play tricks on me and my friends. Once, I was sitting on the terrace when, all of a sudden, my bedroom window above our heads opened and Erich began tossing out the contents of all my drawers—and those were full of girl's things—followed by pillows, quilts, and blankets, and on and on. Nobody could stop him, and, finally, there was nothing left to do but laugh. I didn't laugh, however, when he refused to pick up my things. He locked himself in his room and claimed he had work to do.

A German Christmas

Christmas was a very special time for us. I planned weeks in advance what to give each family member and made the gifts by hand. With the help of woodworking lessons in school and a handicraft teacher who taught bookbinding, basket weaving, and all sorts of other crafts, I had a pretty good selection of small items that I could make. Birthdays were also occasions to make gifts, but Christmas was more of a challenge.

A warm feeling of excitement gripped me as Christmas approached. The prospect of showing love to my family in this way overcame me like an obsession. I used to watch my parents and others for signs of secret wishes or small needs. Usually, I came up with a surprise, a new and challenging idea for something that I could make and that one could not buy. Making gifts occupied me for months. Secrecy was very important, and I guarded my projects-in-progress carefully. I would lock the door and sit at the large table in the center of the playroom, animated by my inspirations and surrounded by all the materials and tools needed.

The hardest person to please was my father. Each Christmas, I would anxiously search his face for an expression of joy as he unwrapped my gift with an embarrassed smile. Usually he would just bend to kiss me quickly on the mouth with his full lips and put the gift away. But I was well-rewarded years later when I discovered that some of the things I had made as a child, he kept with him and used all his life. My mother was much easier to please, and she showed instantly her gratitude when she received my handmade things. She would exclaim joyfully, "Liesel, it is beautiful," and then she would take me in her arms.

With this part of Christmas preparation behind me, I would concentrate on learning a poem, sometimes a French one to please Made. I also practiced a piece on the piano that would display my progress. We helped my mother prepare Christmas gifts for the poor families in the community whose names she got from the minister, Pfarrer Priebe. We helped sort and pack the gifts—clothing, food, and toys—into laundry baskets which we then would deliver to the families. After the holiday, we read with pleasure and satisfaction the thank-you letters, written in coarse handwriting by stiff fingers visibly unaccustomed to such occupation. Some mothers reported every year on their family's condition, listing names and ages of their numerous children.

With a good conscience, we then turned to our own Christmas, the climax of the year. We celebrated Christmas on the evening of the twenty-fourth of December, the night Christ was born, as the German legend says. A week before Christmas Eve, the gardener brought in a tree, a spruce about three-meters high, tall enough to reach the ceiling of the music room. After he fastened the freshly cut tree in its stand, the doors to the music room, now the "Christmas room," were closed, and no one but my mother was allowed to enter. The curtains were drawn so that no curious child could peek in from the garden. The familiar, but still no less mysterious, Christmas wonder was again hidden under a veil. Soft sounds of Christmas songs found their way into the interior of the house. The maids and the children looked at each other in a special way; everyone seemed to soften his steps, as if noise would disturb the mood. It was Christmas again.

My small, but energetic mother then decorated the tree from a tall wooden ladder the gardener had placed in the room. Silently and completely absorbed, she festooned the tree with countless silver balls, blown by glassmakers in the Sudetenland, where, for centuries, craftsmen had made Christmas decorations and other blown-glass items. Their delicate and pretty ornaments were an essential part of Christmas.

Mutti clipped the metal candleholders with the white candles evenly on the wide branches. This had to be done with care, so that each candle was far enough from the next branch to avoid igniting it. To achieve the appearance as if silver had rained on the tree, Mutti patiently knotted two strands of tinsel together and carefully draped these glittering silver threads separately between the dark green needles. At last, she crowned the tree with a glittering star. Each year—over and over again—it would be the most beautiful tree we had ever seen.

During the weeks of preparation for the family and staff, for friends and the poor people, my mother worked hard. She spent endless hours in the city searching for the appropriate gift for each person and selected every gift with tender care. Each item was something that reflected her taste as well as the recipient's. And she never forgot anyone.

In the "Christmas room," long tables were placed along the walls and draped in white. The gifts were not wrapped but placed on the tables and garnished with pine and silvery ribbons, which enhanced the festive appearance of the room.

As Christmas Eve approached, and Mutti's activities in the "Christmas room" were completed, we waited impatiently. At last the moment arrived. All the members of the household, family and staff, gathered in front of the closed folding doors of the "Christmas room," Erich and I in our Sunday clothes, the members of the staff in their best uniforms. Everyone expectantly lowered his voice and felt his quickening heartbeat.

Inside the room, my mother and father made the last-minute preparations. Outside, we waited impatiently for the silvery tone of a tiny bell announcing the great moment when my father lit the candles and my mother began to play the piano and sing *Silent Night, Holy Night* with her beautiful, warm alto voice. The doors slowly opened, revealing the sparkling Christmas tree: nobody escaped the feeling of wonder and devotion. The children's voices joined with the staff's, and even my father sang the moving words with his sonorous voice while he was opening the doors. An indescribable emotion overcame me and tears welled up in my eyes. It was a feeling of family unity. The candles threw their soft light on the silver decorations and reflected in our eyes; the yellow flames flickered slightly and spread a quiet warmth around us. For several minutes, nothing interrupted the peace that prevailed.

Finally, I would step forward. From my early youth on, I read aloud the second chapter of St. Luke in the New Testament. I was always very moved, and my voice shook as I read: "And it came to pass in those days that there went out a decree from Caesar Augustus that everyone should be taxed . . . ."

The next event was the entrance of Santa Claus. In Germany, there were no "department store" Santas. There was only one Santa, the one you believed in. You could never meet him anywhere except, perhaps, in your own home on that very night. Few were that lucky. After his arrival, my brother and I were asked to recite a poem, and the old man would sit there with his long, white beard. In his hand was a rod made of twigs, and next to him on the floor was a big sack filled with candies, apples, and toys. I was always sick with fear in his presence although he never scolded us. He pretended to know our good and bad deeds and made us promise to be better in the coming year. Sometimes he left the rod behind, which was not a good sign. He said always the same thing, namely that he would leave it for my mother, in case she wanted to spank us.

One year, when I was six-years-old, I discovered that Uncle Hans, my mother's brother, was Santa. I can still feel the stabbing pain in my heart when I recognized Uncle Hans's voice. I screamed "Uncle Hans! It is you!" He had decided that it was time I knew the truth about Santa. There was no Santa Claus: a whole world collapsed for me. That was the only Christmas I remember not having enjoyed. No doll, no toy could have made me happy that year. But, in time, I recovered from the shock.

From then on, it was my brother Erich and I who appeared each Christmas Eve, Erich as Santa, and I, appropriately, as the angel. The photographs show me wearing a long, blonde wig and a floor-length, white chemise with wings fastened to my back and pushing a doll carriage filled with miniature gifts. My mother would read a poem she had composed for the occasion in which each staff member was mentioned. She would recall a funny incident during the year or a special wish symbolized by the token gifts which we then dispensed from the baby carriage.

Then the staff members were led to their tables, and we children to ours. Since the gifts were not wrapped, we pretended to the last moment not to have seen the so-called main present, which was hidden under the table. To our pleasure, and my mother's, it was the last thing we "discovered." Thus, my mother's surprise was not spoiled. Then the cook, called Mamsell; the butler, Eduard; the chauffeur, Herr Kuehne and his wife; Herr Schmidecke and the gardener's family; and the two house maids, Lieschen and Martha, slowly gathered up their gifts in laundry baskets and retired to prepare the Christmas dinner.

We admired our durable and handmade toys. I would especially admire my new Kaethe Kruse doll (I received one each year). These marvelous little, soft-bodied wonders, fashioned after real children's faces, are still made today. The world of dolls was my realm at that age, my fairyland, in which reality and imagination flowed together; and I pretended to be in the center of the doll kingdom.

I had a book called *The Princess Wunderhold*, whose heroine was a doll who could do everything a person can do, and I adored her. I treated my dolls like real children, never forgetting to put them to bed and cover them carefully. I was sure they talked and moved around at night, like the doll *Wunderhold*. For me, dolls have not lost their special charm and are not just decorations or collector's items. Looking at them today, I recall those happy children with the imagination to find a dream in them.

We played with our new toys until dinner was announced, and then we assembled around the candle-lit dining table decorated with pine boughs and silver ribbons. The lights were dimmed and the happy glow of love engulfed us. The traditional dinner on Christmas Eve was bouillon in cups; goose liver pâté on toast; a steamed carp served with boiled potatoes, horseradish, and melted butter; and applesauce with Christmas cookies for dessert. The Christmas cookies were made weeks in advance, using old recipes handed down from preceding generations. After dinner, we munched Christmas chocolates shaped as stars and bells and wrapped in silver or gold foil or sprinkled with colored sugar.

At eleven o'clock, it was time to dress for church. Wrapped in warm coats and caps, we walked through the sparkling snow in biting cold weather to the Grunewald Lutheran Church, where the minister, Pfarrer Priebe, held the traditional service. The church was decorated with pines and lighted only with candles along the aisles and on the tree. The white-robed choir entered in procession, each singer holding a candle. The Christmas story was read, interrupted only by old religious songs. An enchanted spell was cast over all who had come together to worship and to be uplifted in spirit for a short while.

CHAPTER SEVEN

Growing up in the Weimar Republic

> The Weimar Constitution provided a detailed cushion of rights in political, economical, social and religious matters. The statement of rights betrays a warm philosophical understanding of the ideals of 1848 and was comprehensive of American, British and other contributions to the history of freedom. All Germans were declared equal. They had the liberty of travel and emigration. One lived in the greatest sense of security. All in all the constitution reflected the most democratic thought of its period. After its passage by the Weimar Assembly it was promulgated on August eleventh 1919 by President Ebert and became the supreme law of the land.
>
> *Germany*, by Marshall Dill Jr.

These words describe the document that should have brought peace to Germany, a country which had just lost not only the war, but an empire and its crowned leader, Wilhelm II, and which was carrying the burdens imposed by the Treaty of Versailles. The new constitution promised equality, but, in reality, there remained deep class differences in Germany, demonstrated by the violent clashes of the period.

We belonged to a social class that mirrored the confidence expressed by the Weimar Constitution. Industrialists, merchants, and bankers trusted the new system and prospered under it. Members of this class lived well, the kind of life I remember from my childhood days in Grunewald. Actually, they were times of foreboding events which gave Adolf Hitler an opportunity to appear as a savior, somebody who would bring joy to the poor and, most importantly, bread to the hungry, work to the jobless. The German Workers' Party began, as did so many other insignificant, splinter political parties, with a small group of dissatisfied activists. A political unknown in those days, Adolf Hitler became a member of this particular group in Munich, and by 1920, had become its leader. The party's name was changed to broaden its appeal: it became the

National Socialist German Workers' Party. But Hitler was still more than ten years away from establishing a totalitarian state in Germany under the name of National Socialism. The slowly developing conditions which Hitler and others managed to shroud in the name of German Nationalism were ignored by the majority of those people who were fortunate enough to be employed.

All over the country, industries fused into cooperative groups. New German industries, such as radio communications and air transportation, were developed. The first airmail service between German cities and foreign countries created a basis for faster understanding and greater enterprise. Corporate mergers and rapid mechanization of heavy industry brought both progress and increased employment for skilled workers. A great part of the German population was unskilled and also jobless. Poverty and despair spurred opposition to the new government. Those who prospered under the Weimar Constitution supported it; those who suffered, opposed it.

In the years immediately following World War I, Berlin became the center for changes brought about by the new, democratic constitution. Censorship was relaxed, and an attitude of rejection of the old and acceptance of the new prevailed. There was wide experimentation in the arts and sciences and in political and social ideas. Freethinkers, political ideologues, artists, and creative spirits from all over Europe were drawn to Berlin. Along with the cultural diversity and intellectual excitement this created, there was a more sensational side. Berlin became the hottest pleasure town since the days of the Roman Empire. Narcotics, particularly cocaine, were openly sold. Nightclubs, nudist shows, and lesbian and homosexual clubs offered anything and everything to Berliners and tourists. Girls from sixteen on roamed the streets, eager to please.

While perversion prospered, the theaters, cabarets, and music institutions blossomed with unprecedented glamour. Max Reinhardt, called the "great magician" of the theater, took over a new theater building, the interior of which was constructed like a cave with stalactites hanging from the ceiling. The opera in Berlin was directed by Richard Strauss, who had come from Vienna to ensure the transition of the Royal Opera to the State Opera, with Max Schillings as director. The painter Max Liebermann was president of the Academy of Fine Arts. At that time, there were so many talented actors and artists it would be impossible to name them all. Actors like Fritz Kortner, Werner Kraus, Kaethe Dorsch, Elisabeth Bergner, and many others remain unforgotten by theater fans. The operetta blossomed as an art form under the direction of Eric Charrell. These were great shows, performed in luscious style. Entertainment in Berlin was offered in the cabarets and restaurants where dancers, musicians, and comedians performed nightly.

With the collapse of the German mark in 1923, the cabaret became the echo of the public mood. Here the questions, problems, and excesses of the day were ridiculed; members of the government, revolutionary leaders, everybody in public life were objects of animated, inspiring, and sometimes inflammatory chansons. The audiences were rather amused and, at times, shocked. If, what was shamelessly and openly presented as comedy would have aroused the full attention of the spectators, perhaps much tragedy could have been avoided; but the visitors of theaters and cabarets were not inclined to be lectured or shaken from their dreams. They wanted to relax after sumptuous meals and go to sleep with their comfortable illusions.

At the time Ebert became the first president of the Weimar Republic, I was nine years old and I had my first encounter with political reality. My close friend and classmate, Helga Hübner, lived nearby in Grunewald and almost every day after school she came to the *Jagowstrasse* to play with me. Helga was a pretty, blonde girl with a slender, graceful body, which I adored and which destined her for ballet dancing. We went together to Steffi Nossen's dance school, then fashionable in Grunewald. But dancing was not for me at that age because I was a plump child and considered myself unattractive. Helga was my idol.

At school one day, Helga unexpectedly announced to me that she would never come to our house again because we were Jewish. I was stunned. I was totally unprepared for the shock this remark dealt to me. I ran home in tears, rang the doorbell impatiently, passed the butler without a word and raced upstairs straight into my mother's arms. All I could utter between sobs was, "Mutti, what does it mean, to be Jewish?" My anguish prevented me from hearing her answer. She must have felt as helpless as I did. I suspect that she didn't place great importance on the subject. I don't know if my parents ever discussed the incident any further, or if they regarded my pain as mere childhood grief. Losing a friend at that age is not, after all, the end of the world. I'm sure Helga's question was prompted by political events of the time, and political events did not seem to penetrate our family routine.

Unfortunately, their significance becomes painfully evident as one looks back. Political leaders like Streseman, Aristide Briand, and Chamberlain, who contributed one way or another to the shape of our world and our fate, were hardly mentioned in our family. Our daily life was more affected by minor changes: obligatory attendance in public school was reduced by one year. A homework-free afternoon was introduced to allow for organized sports and games at school.

My childhood was generally carefree, but somewhat marred by persistent nightmares. After my encounter with anaesthesia, I had difficulties sleeping. Terrifying floating images sent me screaming into my parents' arms. But there were also other reasons for nightmares. During that time, a mass murderer, named Hamann, was loose in the city, frightening the population. Berliners, mocking their own uneasiness, even composed a little rhyme which, even if it doesn't rhyme in English, expresses the sentiment: "If you wait a little while, Hamann will come to get you and with his ax make mincemeat out of you." Before he was finally caught, Hamann was said to wander around at night doing his gloomy work. I used to look out into the dark garden and imagine that the shadows of the bushes and trees were Hamann. The moonlit garden came alive with all sorts of creeping figures, and I was unable to persuade reality to win over fantasy. I recall the anguish, the struggle between reason and childish fear, that finally made me creep back into bed.

I was also a sleepwalker, like my mother. Events of the day grew in importance in my dreams. I often wandered from room to room, my eyes closed, unaware. I would not wake up until I stood in front of my parents' beds. At least I didn't have the same dream repeatedly as my mother did. She told us that her frightening nightmare was always of a red-bearded man trying to strangle her. My father was a man with strong nerves, and, although he slept next to her, he did not become alarmed by her screams as much as we did. Her nocturnal episodes terrified us. Sometimes she fled into the bathroom; once she tried to jump from the window. After she fell out of bed on one occasion and broke her arm, my father had a guardrail affixed to the edge of her bed.

Mutti also had a remarkable "sixth sense." There was, for instance, the unforgettable night when my father had gone with one of the chauffeurs to Stuttgart to pick up a new Mercedes. About one hour after midnight, my mother jumped out of bed—wide awake this time—ran around the room, then down the stairs to awaken the butler, arousing everyone with her cry: "There is a fire in the house! I smell smoke!" Herr Grenz, the night watchman, came with Lord, the guard dog; the maids appeared in their dressing gowns; and the gardener came running from the third floor, his trousers hastily pulled over his pajamas. There was no smoke and no fire, and after an hour of searching, everyone went back to bed, exhausted. The next morning at seven o'clock, our sleep was again interrupted by the loud ring of the telephone—it was my father calling to say that one hour after midnight the new car had burned in the garage in Stuttgart and was completely destroyed.

Another time, my mother sensed the death of her hungarian dear friend's father, Lenke Urban. Shortly afterwards a letter arrived confirming her premonition.

Mutti seemed to know everything without being told; we could never lie to her, even if we wanted to hide something. She used her "gift" to teach us honesty. Her raised finger and the recital of a poem would bring forth a flood of guilt.

> *Vor allem eins, mein Kind.*
> *Sei treu und wahr.*
> *Lass nie die Luege Deinen Mund*
> *entweih'n.*

> "Principally think of this, my child,
> Be true and faithful.
> Never let a lie blaspheme your mouth."

We had no reason to tell lies, yet an exaggerated system of discipline made us fearful. There was, for instance, the report card. If I got a critical note or remark about behavior in school, I was very upset and even afraid to go home. We were good students and very conscientious; and we were, perhaps slightly reprimanded but never punished if we failed here or there.

Erich was intelligent and ambitious; he excelled in mathematics, and because this was my weak subject, he was often asked to assist me with my homework. I was not pleased with him as a tutor because he could not believe that I really did not understand the problems and he criticized me for being so stupid. Actually, I was so intimidated by physics and mathematics that I never made the *Abitur*, the prerequisite for higher studies. But I had other plans, anyway.

During these years, the threads which weave the cloth of my life became more apparent. There was a similarity between Erich and me: we had one single friend at a time. Shortly after Helga Huebner had renounced our friendship, Rita then conquered my heart. Erich, who used to be friends with Kurt Michalski as long as he went to the Werner Siemens High School, met Friedel Pschorr when he transferred to the Grunewald High School. These two, Rita and Friedel, became our new companions.

Rita was a single child and her parents were of relatively advanced age. In her childhood, Rita had contracted poliomyelitis, which left her with a slightly deformed leg, and her older brother tragically had succumbed to this disease. In my mind's eye, I see Rita just as she appears in our classroom picture when we were about fourteen years old. Taller than I, heavyset, with dark eyes and her blond hair held with a ribbon to one side, she stands next to me, the smaller, chubby, dark-haired girl that I was. The Bismarck Lyceum, our girl's school, had ten grades. We would graduate when we were sixteen. There were only a few girls in my time who chose to continue their formal education beyond that. It was considered quite progressive for women to become professionals in a "man's world," in law or medicine.

Rita came to our house almost daily; I went to hers very seldom. Her mother was a strict and formal person and her father, whose family had a factory in the Rhineland that manufactured garment labels, was always home. We preferred playing records, dancing, and fooling around with the boys at my house. Rita had a very happy disposition. She was easy to get along with, and we never quarreled. Her good heart and her positive view of things and people prevailed into adulthood. Never did she speak a critical word about another person, and I doubt she ever had a critical thought. Rita was not assertive, perhaps not assertive enough, as she became a young woman. Her shyness would, in years to come, give her life a tragic turn. Ours was not just a girlish infatuation: we seemed to be made for each other. We shared every joy and every sorrow for many years.

Erich's new friend, the timid, silent boy in our midst, Friedel Pschorr, used to quietly come and go or sit in Erich's room often unnoticed, regardless of whether Erich was home or not. Rita and I didn't pay much attention to him, we had our own realm just as the boys had theirs.

Robert Pschorr, Friedel's father, was a well-known professor of physics and chemistry and the Rector Magnificus at the Technical High School in Berlin Charlottenburg. Professor Pschorr and his wife were among my parents' large circle of friends and acquaintances. My father believed in meeting new people and stressed constantly the importance of social contacts. Connections, he said, could become stepping stones in a person's life, and if one wanted to get ahead, the right contacts could become decisive. Thus, he didn't approve of our single-friend system. It was one of the few frictions between us. My idea of having an intimate relationship with a loved friend was an important part of my life.

I considered it wasted time to mix with people in a superficial manner, so I associated only with a small group with whom I could discuss serious subjects and exchange opinions. Although I was a lively girl who could have enjoyed a fancy social life, I remained a loner. I loved dancing, but the customary "dancing-teas," held in private homes from five to seven, were rather tedious and formal affairs, with clumsy and embarrassed boys as partners.

In contrast, my parents entertained constantly. Our house was almost like a second home to their large group of friends, or so-called friends, and relatives. Many came almost every Sunday and shared our family life, excursions, and festivities. Our guest rooms were always occupied. Everyone was treated most generously with the best food, drink, and entertainment. However, few of these people returned true friendship to my parents in the harder times which were to follow. Indeed, over time, they were dispersed and only a few stayed faithful. As it turned out, my theory concerning friends was more realistic then my father's.

I had few occasions for group activities or to meet new people. My instructors for piano, gymnastics, and handicrafts came to the house. Exercises under the instruction of Fräulein Schrock were supposed to keep us in shape. She used the popular Mensendieck system that stressed body control. Fräulein Schrock, small and energetic, pushed us forcefully around in the upper hall. Our little group, clad in black bathing costumes, consisted of my mother, Gertrud Stefan, and myself. It was amusing and we laughed a lot during these lessons. Even my father became Fräulein Schrock's obedient pupil and willingly crawled around on the Persian rug obeying her command to keep his "vertebrae lined up."

Fräulein Bamberger came twice a week in an attempt to teach me to play the piano. Her efforts were in vain: her method was not conducive to learning and I lacked talent. But my interest in music was not dampened by this experience, and I enjoyed being a listener. My mother, however, had little patience with me. In between lessons, she sat next to me on the piano bench to observe my progress. She was distressed by my lack of aptitude. In a flash of anger, she would smack me with her beringed hand, which did not help to increase my enthusiasm for the piano.

Fortunately, my mother's anger was easily deflected, at least by Erich. Just as in her maiden days, Mutti loved to laugh and she enjoyed fun. When Erich was the object of her sudden anger, he would distract her with a joke and she would burst out laughing. Occasionally though, even Erich was not so lucky. One of the things my mother could not stand was criticism of food. If, during a meal, Erich would raise one nostril slightly and look at me, it was enough to earn him a slap from my mother. She had been brought up to eat what was on her plate. If she did not eat it, she would be send from the room and nothing more was allowed to pass her lips until the same reheated food was eaten.

Generally, my mother and I had a very good relationship. Occasionally some incidents called for punishment and I understood that I needed it. She used to say, "I am not angry, only very sad." Erich and I were more upset by this attitude than if she had scolded us. Once Mutti did not speak to me for a day or two, and it was absolut hell.

In the afternoon she usually rested, at least that was what I thought she should do. I would take her to my father's dressing room and make her lie down on the grey corduroy sofa. I would cover her with a woolen blanket and tell her, "Now you sleep, till I wake you." I wanted so much to take care of her, but also to control her. Somehow I felt that I was more reasonable than she. I would scold her, "Mutti, when are you finally going to grow up?" In many ways she remained like a child, and I guess this was what made her charming even to her last days.

When we travelled, Mutti admired everything with youthful enthusiasm. She insisted that we voice our enjoyment with true exaltation: unless we raved about a girl's beauty—especially those with blonde hair—glimpsed from our speeding car, she felt her own fun was ruined. She then reprimanded us for being spoiled brats not worthy of being taken along. Her appreciation of life, her sense of value for simple things never changed, although I cannot think of any luxury she did not know. Human qualities, character, honesty, and, mainly, love remained most important to her. When a precious piece of china or glass was broken, a car dented, or something lost, even a jewel, she quietly would say, "Dead things do not count."

Thus sheltered in our peaceful, regulated home, I knew nothing of the clouds accumulating over Germany. Was I too young to understand events or too preoccupied with myself? Or were my parents purposely drawing a curtain around us? For whatever reason, I didn't comprehend the meaning of political assassinations, although two such murders took place in our neighborhood. Maximilian Harden was killed in 1927 directly in front of our garden. He was editor of *Die Zukunft*, a newspaper which instigated rebellion on political issues, and wrote aggressively about well-known personalities. And Walther Rathenau was killed in the *Koenigsallee* in Grunewald in June 1922, victim of an organized plot. Rathenau was a rich, cultured, and rather quiet gentleman—a Jew, who was one of the most distinguished men in Germany. Rathenau had considered the outbreak of the war in 1914 a crisis not only for Germany, but for all of Europe. He participated in the war by organizing a group which controlled the production of metals, chemicals, rubber, cotton, and wool. Thus, he played a vital role by managing the supply of raw products, just as my father worked for the army's food provisions in the *Zentral Einkaufs Gesellschaft*. In 1921, Rathenau was appointed German Minister of Reconstruction and, finally, a year later, Foreign Minister.

Rathenau must have been well aware that his life was in danger, but he refused police protection offered by Chancellor Josef Wirth, who was appalled by the mounting wave of terrorism. Rathenau was murdered in cold blood by a group of young rightists who decided to put him on the list of those responsible for the war and the devastating inflation in Germany, even though they recognized his standing and good qualities. They ambushed his open car, which was driven every morning at the same hour from his house near us in Grunewald at low speed on the way to central Berlin.

Historians' conclusions that Rathenau was not assassinated simply because he was a Jew suggests that anti-Semitism and hostility between Germans and Jews were historically constant. Although there is some truth in this assumption, it is not the whole story. Jews are mentioned in the history of Berlin as early as in 1295. Could they have survived, and even prospered, in Germany throughout so many centuries without enjoying some degree of rights and acceptance? It was a long history of alternating harassment and tolerance, and the Jewish community in Germany attained full equality only in those years after World War I. Numerically, they remained a small minority, about one percent of the population; but because a large number of them congregated in the capital where they were influential, and exceptionally successful, in banking, industry, commerce, and publishing, they were conspicuous and envied. Jews contributed to science and the arts, and the contributions of famous men such as Albert Einstein, Max Reinhardt, and Bruno Walter, is well documented.

In politics, Jews didn't play a vital part because, according to a well-known German rabbi by the name of Prinz, "They are too optimistic and do not understand the enemy." Rabbi Prinz did understand the enemy, however. He became the leader of the Jewish community of Berlin and fought a courageous campaign to save as many Jews as possible from Hitler's actions.

In 1923, the great inflation began to ravage Germany. The steady decline in the mark's value began in 1921, and Germany requested a moratorium on reparation payments to France. The request was not granted and when payments fell behind, France sent troops into the Ruhr, Germany's industrial heartland, and seized German industry. That triggered runaway inflation. The mark's value plummeted downward day by day, hour by hour. In 1921, the mark had been about 75 to the American dollar. By January 1923, it dropped to 7,000 to the dollar. By July, it took one million marks to purchase one dollar. All efforts to stop the slide failed and, by the end of 1923, the exchange rate was in the billions, and finally trillions, of marks to the dollar.

German currency was worthless. The entire German middle class was financially wiped out overnight. People living on pensions, salaries, or other fixed income could barely survive. As the mark's value fell, people hurriedly carried their earnings in suitcases and baskets to the nearest store where they still could buy basic supplies. Only active businessmen in the upper positions in industry and commerce could steer their ships through the storm. Those with foreign investments fared best. Thus, I understand why my family didn't suffer the same fate as millions in Germany, nor did we take particular notice of the desperate situation around us. My father's transportation firm, Schenker & Company, which dealt with other European countries and with the United States, continued to flourish under his leadership.

However, the face of Berlin did change. People lost faith in government and social institutions and lost hope for a decent future. A sort of madness overcame the city. Diversions became obsessions that produced excesses never before seen. Meanwhile, confronted with the suffering of the poor masses—undernourished children, the helpless older generation, and the spread of tuberculosis and other illnesses—workers took recourse in strikes, the unemployed to crime and terrorism. Girls sold their previously carefully guarded virginity and even became prostitutes to survive. Rare, now, were the possibilities of a marriage based on a father's financial strength and a substantial dowry. In an ironic way, women were liberated from the standards of the time, which proscribed virginity as a highly desirable condition for marriage.

Prostitution was legalized and placed under police and medical supervision. Certain streets, like the *Friedrichstrasse*, were set aside for the "girls." The profession soon adopted its own rules, attitudes, and mode of dress. High boots, short skirts, an umbrella, and a large handbag made prostitutes easily recognizable. They lingered in doorways and on street corners whispering to their prospective clients, who could now legally accept their invitations.

I was kept ignorant of these conditions, and I now understand why my parents did not let me go alone to restaurants and dance halls. Instead, I played tennis in a club, went shopping in fashionable salons in the company of my mother, visited museums, concerts, and the opera with Rita, always escorted by our chauffeur. We enjoyed ourselves in spite of these restrictions. We attended the great Charrell revues, the glittering operettas; we giggled a lot and fell in love with stars like Richard Tauber and Harry Liedtke. We were in the happy teenage stage called *Backfisch* in German (literally, "baked fish," not a child, not an adult). We were overly excited and living on a cloud, extremely happy and unhappy at the same time, harmlessly in love.

To my great embarrassment, I matured physically later then other girls. I worried a lot about not being able to marry or have children. Rita and I were actually quite naive. Other girls our age carried on with boys and just laughed at us. We considered our boldest adventure when we shared a bath, in one tub, while wearing dark glasses. We imagined this is what took place in Hollywood.

I don't remember any interest in boys or sex at that period. Instead, I was always inclined toward philosophic thoughts, much more so than Rita. I wrote a diary and engaged in serious and deeply reflective conversations at every opportunity. Unfortunately, I rarely found a partner with whom to share my interests. In school, no one seemed to be interested in literature or philosophy. We read classical plays with lots of pathos. Our teacher interpreted *Don Carlos* by Schiller but it only made us laugh. After graduation I took a private course and studied Goethe's *Faust* with real enthusiasm.

But higher education was not my goal. I wanted to become a kindergarden teacher. This was the only decision in my youth which I made without my father's approval, the only time I managed to carry out my will in spite of him. He had different plans for me than I had for myself. He, having worked his way up from the bottom, knew very well the difference between a life with opportunities in society and a life of poverty. He wanted me to have the kind of education which was denied to him, to know languages that would open the world to me, and sciences, and arts which he had never had an opportunity to study.

During my childhood, our summer vacations were unforgettable. Vacations were among the rare occasions that united our family. We went for four weeks each summer to various resorts, such as the Palace Hotel in Gstaad, Switzerland, or the Hotel Carlton in the mountains at St. Moritz. Vacations were a time to talk, to be close without individual plans or desires. We hiked through woods and up mountain paths, rested near a picturesque lake, or just sat on the hotel terrace reading. My father and Erich wore their knickerbockers, one of the many which we had taken along in our many suitcases. Papi, as I called my father, smoked a pipe instead of his usual cigar. My mother, smiling happily, would admire the views and start a tune in which even my father would join. He had the wonderful talent of leaving his business with all worries behind, sleeping soundly in a chair, and snoring loudly. Now his only interest was how to best match his countless outfits to the weather—the choice of color and style. He made us feel and admire the quality of his woolen garments, and, like a naughty boy, he smiled and confessed to his newest purchases. During vacation my mother looked tenderly at him and said; "Marci has his small-Marci face," in contrast to his usual, businesslike "big-Marci face."

Once we went to Velden on the Woerther Lake in Austria; and drove over the steepest mountain passes, including the dangerous Katschberg, famous for its steep grade. Erich and Papi, considered it a challenge we just had to take. There were hairpin curves on rocky, unpaved roads to master, tests for both car and driver. While Mutti and I trembled in the back seat and anxiously watched the road and the chauffeur's manipulations with gearshift, clutch, and brake, my father was delighted and enjoyed the challenge. Sometimes Erich would run ahead with a camera to photograph the car with its rear wheels resting dangerously near the edge of a cliff. Jubilant, the three male travelers would report to our friends how well the Graef & Stift had managed in the mountains.

Until 1930, we traveled together, a happy family. We spent our last vacation together at the Palace Hotel in Gstaad after Erich had completed his studies in economics and had become "Doctor" Erich Holzer. Erich and I were dancing partners, and I enjoyed the afternoon and evening dances in the elegant hotel immensely. We excelled in tango, the romantic English waltz, and the modern Charleston. Most resort hotels had a pretty dancing teacher and the Palace Hotel was no exception. My father decided to take dancing lessons, and because Mutti thought he would loose weight that way, so she let my father put his arm around the girl's waist, overcoming her usual jealousy.

CHAPTER EIGHT

STEPPING STONES

Within walking distance from our house stood the small Grunewald church I attended regularly. There was nothing grand or remarkable about it as far as its neo-Gothic architecture was concerned: it was typical of old Berlin. It had pretty stained-glass windows, the interior was unpretentious, one felt comfortable in it. It was here that the minister Pfarrer Priebe had acquainted Rita and me, along with other girls my age, with the New Testament in preparation for our confirmation. He had already confirmed my brother Erich and Friedel, who had attended this church ever since he had become a friend of our family. In this church I came closer to worship and adoration of God than ever before or after, but it is impossible for me to determine whether it was the spell Pfarrer Priebe had cast on me or religious elation. When he looked at us with his sparkling blue eyes, speaking about Jesus in his sonorous voice, I was happily transported into my own heaven. I sat in the pew, my eyes fixed on the multi-color images of the windows, the light breaking through them, my heartbeat quickened and I was in touch with the sublime. It really didn't matter why this ecstasy exalted my being, as long as I experienced it.

Confirmation evokes most probably in all girls a mixture of feelings which have little to do with the intention of the church authorities. In any case, I remember being proud to be the center of attention and enjoying the sentimental, mystical atmosphere in church. We were clad from head to toe in black, as if we were attending a funeral. What were we mourning, I wonder, in our black taffeta dresses and black stockings? Was it supposed to be the end of our childhood? Of our innocence?

The white lace handkerchief and a few branches of lilies-of-the-valley were the only light spot in our appearance. We each held a new copy of the New Testament with gold-cut pages and our names engraved on the cover and walked solemnly towards the altar. The great moment came when Pfarrer Priebe blessed us by laying his hand on our heads and gave us a text from the Gospel which would protect us from all evil (so we believed). After the ceremony, relatives celebrated the day with us by giving us precious gifts, books for our basic library, and small jewels meant to accompany us through life. I was now a member of the Christian church, my baptism confirmed, the certificate in a frame. It was the year 1927 and I was sixteen.

It was the year that the National Socialists convened in Nuremburg, where twenty thousand party faithfuls greeted their undisputed leader, Adolf Hitler. Is it possible that nobody in our circles had heard of Adolf Hitler and his violent campaign to impose his ideas? Had we not heard of his twenty-five-point plan? The newspapers had reported his growing popularity and on his ardent hatred of Jews. By 1927, his career had evolved through ups and downs; the party was officially recognized and numbered about fifty thousand. Many had read *Mein Kampf*, and thousands had heard his passionate speeches. Were these people amongst those Germans who would claim later not to have known what was going on?

At that point the wheel which churns out history could perhaps have been stopped, but destiny would have it differently. It is hard to believe that millions of Germans like ourselves were pursuing their own personal goals and ignored the handwriting on the wall. We did not pay attention to the coming deluge which would destroy us. My parents must have thought that draping the mantle of the Lutheran religion around our shoulders would change our identity. Each moment has its uncertainty: the future, even the next minute, is a mystery to the present, and a merciful veil hides the fate humanity creates for itself. No matter how shocking the look back might be—this sudden revelation of our blindness—we cannot return or change the past by regrets.

This realization has led me to believe that there are no wrong decisions: most people try to do the best they can in certain situations and, at that moment, their decisions tend to be the correct ones. This perhaps flawed theory is the only way I can explain (or is it forgive?) my parents and the adults around me for having overlooked the obvious. But in retrospect, I feel reassured that all that happened led to my pre-destined path. I believe there was a profound purpose in a fate that divested me of all help and compelled me to prove myself. I had actually no religion to fall back on in times of distress. I was not trained to meet hardship, I had never been confronted with or heard about hate and terror, I knew nothing about intrigues or politics. There was only God and I.

In this crucial time I was sent to a 'ladies finishing school' in England. My parents meant well and wanted the best for me. Who can blame them for doing what was proper in their eyes? Friends recommended 'Quarry

Court' in Marlow-on-Thames. I looked forward to my first departure from home and was delighted that Rita's parents also had decided to send her to 'Quarry Court'. Unfortunately my stay in 'Quarry Court' added nothing to my education except a better knowledge of the English language. I did not find guidance for my real interests in philosophy and psychology. The two headmistresses, Miss Kathy and Miss Armstrong, were two frail spinsters who had no influence on our sojourn, neither scholastically nor in any other way. My free time I spent either with Rita and Ady Bernstein or busily hooking a rug for my mother. I was homesick and had a great need to show her my affection. I addressed her in my letters as "Liebste Kleine" ("My dearest little One") to express my protective feeling for her.

I remember the miserable food and the chilly days, during which Rita, Ady, and I sat around the fireplace and toasted our afternoon bread on a fork. At least it helped me to improve my figure: I lost twenty pounds, which made me more attractive for my entry into the social world. I also have fond memories of Quarry Court; the communal life with girls of different nationalities, our trip to London to see the opening of Parliament, the church services on Armistice Day.

My relationship with Rita during this time became still closer. We shared a room and had time for the discussions I enjoyed so much. I could hardly bear the idea of returning to our separate homes. I wrote in my diary:

> I will miss Rita's and my conversations about our confirmation. We discussed questions which nobody will be able to answer, but is it not reflection we need instead of solutions? I will find what I seek only in church with Pfarrer Priebe. It is a pity that one devotes only one short year to preparation for confirmation. However, few girls would be interested enough to spend more time with it. I wonder how many of those confirmed with us are still thinking about it?

When the term ended, I went with Rita and the other girls from Quarry Court to the seaside at Bournemouth. One of the girls, Monika, was quite independent, a fact which impressed Rita and me very much. One day on the beach at Bournemouth, a horse and rider approached us at a fast gallop and stopped abruptly in front of our little group of shrieking, bathing-suit-clad girls. The tall young man, Monika's boyfriend, leaped from the horse and embraced Monika. He remounted and pulled Monika up behind him and the horse charged off again. Off they went, laughing and waving to us as they disappeared in the blue distance.

In contrast to Monika's dramatic escape, Rita and I waited nervously to be rescued by my brother and Friedel Pschorr. They had shipped Mutti's Packard roadster to England and were touring Scotland and England. They arrived one day in Bournemouth to take Rita and me for a ride. This was the first time that Rita's feelings for Erich became obvious to me. She blushed frequently and seemed embarrassed. Her tender feelings, her beautiful innocence and purity made her so vulnerable. I wish I could have protected her fragile heart from all the pain which her innocent love would cause her. How can pure love ever be guilty?

While Rita sat next to Erich as he drove, Friedel and I rode in the small, rear rumble seat. Friedel seemed to enjoy himself although he was silent most of the time. It was a pleasant interruption of the routine but not more than that for me.

In the spring of 1929, I found myself in "*Les Roseaux*", a girls' boarding school in Pully, near Lausanne. The school stands five minutes away from the Roman ruins on which the community hall of Pully was erected and overlooks Lake Geneva and the distant mountains on the French coast. I was still a romantic, carefree young girl, an open book with blank pages waiting to be imprinted.

At that time, the older generation of statesmen like Stresemann and Clemenceau slowly vanished from the world stage to make room for those who would give direction to my decade and leave their marks on European history. I knew that Herbert Hoover was President of the United States. But I did not know of Heinrich Himmler or any of the other emerging Nazi leaders. And while political events proceeded, most people in my circle preferred to distract themselves with entertaining works of literature. They didn't listen to the warnings of Erich Maria Remarque in his pacifist novel, "*All Quiet on the Western Front*," or to the voices of Werner Beumelburg in "*Barrage-fire Around Germany*" and Alfred Hein's in "*A Company of Soldiers.*"

In that year of 1929, Thomas Mann, still living in Munich, won the Nobel Prize for literature. Berlin's first television show had been transmitted, and a new era in communications was dawning. People also watched the sky to get a glimpse of the *Graf Zeppelin*, the world's largest airship, launched the year before at Friedrichshafen. When it completed its trip around the world, the airship moored at Staaken, Berlin's airport. Erich was among the hundreds of jubilant people greeting the return of the "big cigar." For leaving school without permission, he had to serve eight hours' detention, but to him the event was worth the punishment.

In physics, medical research, and other sciences, Germany experienced an unprecedented boom, a brilliant light before the darkness to come. I don't recall if I felt left out of all these exciting happenings, but there I was in the garden of *Les Roseaux*, above Lake Geneva, quietly writing in my diary.

I wrote about my grandparents, contemplating my deep attachment to them, and about ideals and goals, completely absorbed in my world.

Les Roseaux, July 21, 1929

I have been here since the fifth of April and I am the happiest girl in the world. Only one person is missing—Rita. It is hard to imagine that we are separated. I cannot share Mutti's opinion that I should get to know another girl. Although in the two months of my stay here I have met some nice girls, I could never feel as close to any of them as I feel to Rita. Rita has written to me every day from Italy, where she went with her parents. Her long letters prove what a sweet person she is. Since I am alone I am even more aware of how much I miss her.

My sojourn is coming to an end. It is unbelievable how much I regret having to leave this house, to turn my back on Les Roseaux. It has been four almost cloudless months. I am so used to it. But why do I complain when an ideal time with Mutti, Papi, and Erich lies ahead? Still, I will miss "lights-out," when pajama or nightgown-clad girls appear at all the windows and on balconies, munching food, whispering, and laughing. Seldom will one find a group in such harmony: there were never any discords or quarrels. But none of them became the "close friend."

There was one exception: Elfriede Stalf, a girl from Munich, more mature than us other eighteen-year-olds. She moved me to confide in her and discuss my deepest emotions in beautiful conversations. I don't know if this is the right thing to do, but if ever I feel sympathy for someone, I open up without reservation and pour out my heart. I always met people who respected my confidence, but some day will I not be disappointed? Is it right to confide without restraint? Or is it better to enclose within oneself one's values and mistakes?

Is it better to disclose self-recognized weaknesses and warn the other person or is it better to hide them? Can concealment possibly help to overcome certain traits in us? I wonder who could answer this for me. If I could find the answer through contemplation and experience, the solution would be of greater value. I need to learn independence, not just outwardly but mentally. But in what measure should we cherish independence if advice from others is also valuable?

I struggled for independence of thought and opinion. But in order to have an objective view one needs knowledge and experience. I felt that I had neither at that point. The problem amounted to a lack of trust in myself. I needed my diary to unburden my heart, but at the same time I reproached myself because I had a mother and Rita and, now, Elfriede—so why did I write a diary?

Elfi had a great influence on me. She was strict with herself and advised me not to give in to every desire but to practice self-denial in everyday things. She thought that privation of even unimportant wishes forms the character and educates the will. Trying to follow her advice, I got up early each morning and took a swim in the cold lake. This self-discipline was supposedly leading us to take responsibility for ourselves and do things without being told. I hoped it would help me to make my own decisions.

The close relationship I had with my mother was in a way the reason why I had to struggle so hard to make my own decisions. Somehow, we must learn to develop our own personalities in spite of love and devotion to parents. Education for self-reliance, for me at least, was put far behind obedience and discipline. We were told what to do and there was no room for choices. On the other hand, parents have to learn to accept the transition from the childrens' role as dependents to their eventual and natural urge to take charge of those who raised them. The ready demonstration of my affection as a child and adolescent explain the difficulty my mother had later on when I became less open towards her. I did not realize how much I had changed, as she often complained tearfully.

> I wish I were strong enough to realize my own shortcomings. It is a blessing that Mutti considers it her duty to remind me of them. At first this criticism might hurt but her admonitions are finally taken to heart.

This was the last entry in my diary in *Les Roseaux*. I had no more time to write because my brother and Friedel came tovisit me. I adored my brother and wanted to please him, but I was also afraid of him. He had an air of superiority that never failed to make me cringe. When the letter came announcing his plans to come for me, I wrote to my mother:

> My heart leaped, I am so happy, so spoiled, my knees tremble. He likes the photographs of me in my riding outfit; he finds my English unchanged

and good. He is concerned about me, reminds me to take my passport, and suggests which dresses to take

I was terribly excited when the two young men arrived. They had driven in Mutti's Packard from Munich, via *Tegernsee*, Bad Kreuth, past the *Achensee* to meet Aunt Mini, who lived in Baernstatt, a small, lakeside village at the foot of the Kaiser *Gebirge*. From there they drove on to Lausanne where I awaited them. We drove to Geneva, to Chamonix at the foot of Mont Blanc, then over the Forclaz Pass, of which we had heard all sorts of frightening things. We had been warned about the road and, indeed, the road was very steep and contained many terrifying curves. In spite of being in a cold sweat, Erich had a lot of fun. In a letter to Mutti, he wrote, "all went very well." I would have enjoyed the trip even more had it not been for our silent travel companion, Friedel. I wrote to my mother:

Erich expressed his enthusiasm in loud exclamations while Friedel did not say a single word the entire time. He annoyed me, to be quite frank. Being taciturn is in order, but one should not exaggerate. Not once did he as much as open his mouth, not even at the sight of Mont Blanc. He is not a pleasant travel companion.

Feelings are usually quickly forgotten unless expressed in writing. They can change so rapidly; buried under new impressions, they sink away. Thus when I read this letter, written so long ago, I was shocked at my own words about the young man I was going to marry. In reality, I did suffer from Friedel's unresponsiveness on occasion. On the other hand, his quiet temperament would pacify everyone around him during a crisis.

My reactions to Friedel's behavior quite naturally changed later on when I fell in love with him. I tried very hard to overlook his sometimes annoying reserve. Like most young people, I had a strong desire to share an experience with another person. However, sometimes sharing an experience could create the inaccurate illusion of having experienced mutual emotions. The development of emotions in two people are comparable to two trees side by side, their branches touching but not entwining. Thus a lover's deepest longing may remain unsatisfied—the longing to fulfill oneself and the other person. Although this became a problem for Friedel and me later on, I did not give much thought to Friedel's problems then. I was selfishly bothered only by his silence.

While we were roaming around in my mother's Packard, we remembered that it was Mutti who had begged my father to let us take this trip. We never took such privilege for granted. We wrote to her on her birthday, which occurred the day we left Lausanne, and mentioned that never before our family had not celebrated her birthday together. This time we would not join the ladies for lunch and enjoy the traditional meal—the first asparagus and the first strawberries from the garden—or smell the sweet fragrance of my mother's favorite lilies-of-the-valley.

Erich and Friedel dropped me off at *Les Roseaux*, then continued on to Berlin. Shortly afterward, I was supposed to leave *Les Roseaux* for Frankfurt, where I would meet my family and go on to Noordwijk in Holland. Madame Perret, the owner of the school *Les Roseaux* had a difficult time persuading my mother to let me take the train unaccompanied. I was very hurt by my mother's lack of trust. Had she read my diary she would have better understood what a mature, eighteen-year-old daughter she had. I really was amused years later to find this letter:

July 11, 1929

Dear Mrs. Holzer,

We are disconsolate to see Liesel depart. You cannot imagine how much we regret it. We fervently hope that she will return for a vacation. I am sure that she will remember whatever she learned here, for she is doing serious work.

You must let her travel alone, Mrs. Holzer, at her age there is really no risk involved, specially since she is so reasonable. There are some trains she could take without traveling by night. I hope you will enjoy your vacation; your daughter will be excellent company for you.

Accept, dear Mrs. Holzer, my best greetings.

Sincerely yours,
J. Perret

I took the train alone to the Hotel Huis ter Duin in Noordwijk where I met my parents. My stay there was unforgettable for several reasons, but mainly because for the first time in my life I was very impressed by an "older" man. It was the hotel's doctor, Dr. Sauvage-Nolting, who was ten years my elder. My father took me to his office because of a minor abscess I had on the inside of my thigh. After the examination, while I was timidly sitting behind my father, the doctor suggested, blinking at me, that I should see him every day for treatment. My father did not notice the doctor's blue eyes resting on his daughter, but the well-brought-up daughter realized the meaning of these glances that made her heart bounce. The next day, I was embarrassed to expose my leg to him, but everything passed in the most correct fashion.

I soon noticed that the doctor showed up wherever we were. He sent white lilies to my room and poems which were addressed to the "Princess Lointaine." I was in a state of constant excitement, unused to the flattery and attention. One day, he caught me in a closed passage between the main house and the annex, took me in his arms, and kissed me. I was bewildered, not knowing if it was the tender kiss that made me feel so strange, or if this was what was called "being" in love. I had so often wondered how it felt to be in love. I had even asked my mother how one knew if it was the "right" man. She laughed and, later, whenever we sat in the hall of a hotel or restaurant, she would ask: "Would you like to marry this one?" Then we would teasingly tear him apart and imagine how awful he would look without his fancy suit or, worse, in his underwear.

Now I could not ask my mother; I had to sort out my feeling and make up my own mind. I felt that I was happy being "loved." Soon the situation was clarified. We took an excursion in the car with some friends of my parents, a Czech couple and their daughter Gerty, who was my age. In the back seat, Dr. Sauvage-Nolting divided his attention between Gerty and me, but I was convinced he loved me. Gerty and I never suspected we were rivals.

The next day, the doctor asked me to marry him and come away to India where he was going to work in a Dutch colony. I knew my answer, of course, and also what my father would say. I went to my room and wrote him that the answer was "no," and that I regretted ending the romance. Before we left the hotel, Gerty confided to me that Dr. Sauvage-Nolting had asked her to marry him!

CHAPTER NINE

Jagowstrasse

Following our summer vacation in 1929 in Holland, where I had encountered Dr. Sauvage-Nolting, we returned to the *Jagowstrasse* in Berlin. I began an interlude prior to my training in the Pestalozzi-Froebel Haus, a school for kindergarten teachers. During this time I tried, as always, to do something useful. I collected books and filled my shelves with volumes of old editions, beautifully bound in leather, with gold-edged pages. Some of these have pencil marks and inscriptions, silent witnesses of my taste and interests, my search for truth. Even in Germany, many of the authors then in fashion are now forgotten. Other authors' works have become classics. It was the year Ernst Barlach, the sculptor, wrote his autobiography; Rudolf Binding, one of my favorite authors, wrote *Erlebtes Leben* ("*The Experience of a Life*,"). There was Paul Eipper, with his *Tiere sehen Dich an,* ("*Animals Look at You*,") and Galsworthy with *Swansong* and many others.

I also had time to go the theater and see Berlin at its best. Rita and I went to many galleries and museums and got acquainted with the works of Georgia O'Keefe, Otto Dix, Barlach, and Braque. Max Beckman attracted the public, but not us. His paintings were not "pretty," and, therefore, we could not share the general admiration for this kind of modern art. There were so many talented men and women and their creativity seemed stimulated as if they sensed that an era was about to end. A short time later, Hitler's henchmen would ban their works and burn books by Jewish authors and other "enemies of the Party."

Almost every week there were new "talking" movies. We were lured to town to admire our favorite film star, Harry Liedtke, just as we would not miss shows with Harald Kreuzberg or concerts of Stravinsky's newest works. We heard Wilhelm Furtwaengler conduct the Berlin Philharmonic Orchestra. We had the choice of four different opera houses, all of them excelled with first-class performances: the State Opera had Erich Kleiber as musical director; the *Volks Oper* ("People's Opera") had Leo Blech; there was the Kroll Opera with

Otto Klemperer; and the City Opera in Charlottenburg with Heinz Tietjen as director and Bruno Walter as conductor. We were thrilled by Gershwin's *An American in Paris* and by Weill's *Three Penny Opera*, and we heard the beautiful and touching voice of Al Jolson in *Sonny Boy*.

First nights were glamorous galas that brought out Berlin's high society in their finery. The ladies' fashions competed with those of the stars on stage. The set designers were at a peak of creativity, inspired by Max Reinhardt and Felix Hollaender. Costumes and the artistry were never matched before or after those years.

On arrival, and during intermissions, the spectators promenaded in the brightly lit foyers to show off their furs and gleaming jewels. A lady could not be, and would not have been, seen twice in the same attire in one season. A lady's appearance was a combined achievement of famous designers like Chanel or Molineux, the craftsmanship of master dressmakers, and many busy hands.

After this interlude, I set aside the pleasures of Berlin. The Pestalozzi-Froebel *Haus* became the theme of my life. I wrote in my diary:

> Children, the dream of my childhood, look at me, their eyes expressing their joy and their sorrow, their disappointments. I see the child, the small person, the future. Is there anything more beautiful than the small face of an innocent child? Into their harmonious world the adult often brings his own conception of life, superimposing it harshly on the tender life just beginning.

> Some of the children were brought to us in a deplorable condition. The eyes of those children already had a suffering expression; they had been abused and had lost trust and joy. Some of the parents, still almost children themselves, had given birth but didn't regard their children as gifts from heaven. With the children more sorrow was born, to the parents and to the little ones. I wrote:

> Young couples living on a bare minimum seem to have older bodies than minds and souls. The children's first tender feelings are suffocated by people and circumstances around them. There are, for instance, the heavily drinking fathers who beat their wives in front of the children. Or the father, impatient and primitive, who punishes the child unjustly, often cruelly enough to inflict permanent damage.

Some parents bring the children to the public nursery to get them out of the way. Sometimes there is a valid reason; the unwed mother needs to go to work; but more often these women want the only room they have to receive their lovers. The children are sad, some are very shy and anxious, others aggressive or dishonest. One searches in vain for the original purity.

I was deeply depressed to find such small children already cruel and hardened. It seemed as if an animal was hidden in them. I asked myself if children from well-to-do parents might have the same fundamental tendencies, perhaps suppressed by education. Was the animal concealed in all of us?

These revelations made me see that reality did not match my ideas. One had to learn to compromise and accept. I tried my best to establish trust between myself and the children. There was one fierce, five-year-old boy with dark hair and dark eyes who surrounded himself regularly with chairs and tables. It was almost impossible to make him join the group. I tried it anyway, aware that he might throw some hard object in my direction. After a while, he began to talk to me and followed me into the yard. It was a proud victory.

When the children arrived in the morning, they were taken by the students to the large bathroom. The children had to be bathed and, if possible, dressed in clean clothes. Some were sick and were taken directly to the nurse. At noon they rested on mattresses spread on the floor. It was difficult to keep the children calm, to prevent them from shouting nasty words in a chorus or running around and starting fights with one another. A strict command by one of the supervising girls was often all the reason needed for a child to raise his hand against her in defense, or even to spit at her.

But there was a positive aspect; it was my consolation and hope that it might be the predominant one. On Christmas, the children sat quietly for once around the lit candles; their eyes shone and all the ugliness which entered their lives was forgotten. The flickering candles cast a veil of dreams over the children and transported them into a better world.

In the same year, 1929, that I attended the Pestalozzi-Froebel *Haus*, my father reached fifty years of age. He was, unlike most people, openly proud of it. He mentioned this fact to whomever was around to hear it. His self-esteem derived from his achievements, which, in fact, were important not only with respect to his age but mostly to his and our future.

Under his leadership, Schenker & Company had developed an international reputation. The company now occupied three floors on one of the impressive buildings *Unter den Linden*. Several able executives managed the different departments. Between them and my father existed an exceptional friendship that stood up against the most crucial test of all: fidelity to him in Hitler's time.

The only exception was Georg Stefan, husband of my mother's cousin Gertrud. Although they had met in my parents' house and had spent every Sunday and holiday in the *Jagowstrasse* with us, and although my father had employed and trained him and taken care of his family, Georg later collaborated with the Nazis and spread untrue and nasty gossip about his benefactor.

One of Schenker's directors was Kurt Schiller, manager of the Eastern Department. His wife was born in Russia and Kurt spoke the language. I remember him as being an exceptional man, extremely cultured and knowledgeable. He was a good friend to Erich, apparently in compensation for a tragedy in his own family which had caused him to cut off all contact with his own two sons. I never heard what had happened, but knowing Kurt Schiller it must have been a matter of honor: Kurt was upright in an exaggerated way, something of a Prussian officer, and extremely stubborn.

He took Erich and Friedel on trips around Germany and introduced them to German art and architecture. They went on bicycles—no luxuries permitted. These "men only" trips filled a void my father left because of lack of time. Neither of the two boys ever forgot these educational journeys through mountain regions, past charming rivers, and through some of the beautiful old German towns.

One other director who became our special friend was Harry Hamacher. Harry and his Rumanian wife, Adela, or "Etelka" as he called her, were frequent guests in our house, and I remember him from childhood through my teen years as a jolly, joking, and laughing man. He was from the Rhineland and was Catholic and very superstitious. When Rita and I were girls, he told us jokes that made us blush and brought him a reprimand from his wife.

Harry's marriage was as unusual as Harry himself; his love and devotion, his sense of responsibility to all his employees, which radiated from his strong and trust-inspiring personality, made him in many ways comparable to my father. He was a friend on whom one could lean, but he didn't approve always of my father's business tactics. There were frictions and disagreements, but I heard about these only long after my father was dead and I, as an adult, became Harry's special friend. He would have married me had I not been Friedel's wife. He was Friedel's friend, too, and thus, our friendship had a flavour of love and flirtation and lasted till Harry died. But just as Emil Karpeles had warned my father when he was a young man not to let his ambition carry him away, so did Harry often try to stop Marcel Holzer from his course of action. But "MM," as he was usually called in the office, was obsessed with expansion, and Harry could not prevent his boss from carrying out his plans. I had to listen more than once to Harry's criticism of my father, usually expressed in his typical forceful way. Only those who knew him as well as I did heard under the rough tone the beating of his warm heart. But I must confess, I disliked these conversations about my father intensely.

The inflation of 1923 had created big problems for the transport business as for every other sector of economy. Harry never really told me how my father managed to weather the storm. And my father kept all business matters, the good ones as well as the bad ones, out of his private life. Thus, we never realized the burden which he must have carried through those years. He was concerned not only with the course of business for its own sake, but as means of producing the enormous sums of money needed to pay his employees during this time when the value of money changed hourly. He had to worry about those families who, according to his philosophy, were entrusted to him.

Daring Enterprises

Early in 1930, Marcel Holzer made his first trip abroad, a business trip to New York. When the American stock market collapsed in the fall of 1929, the New York operation of Schenker's went deeply in debt. My father planned to approach the American railroads and shipping lines in hopes they would invest in the American operation, Schenker, Inc. International Freight Forwarders and Custom House Brokers. Unknowingly, my father's trip also prepared for his and my mother's eventual immigration to the United States.

He sailed on the SS *Bremen* of the Nord Deutsche Lloyd line in February. In his first letter to us, he vividly described life aboard the luxurious liner—the beautifully appointed staterooms, the delicious food, and endless meals. Every night, he said, one was entertained with movies, or one could dance and drink while the orchestra played. It was a relaxing, eight-day Atlantic crossing.

He certainly didn't anticipate the problems he was about to encounter and never would have dreamed how vital the contacts he was about to make would be in the future. On February 18, my father went to Philadelphia to confer with the gentlemen of the Pennsylvania Railroad. It was the first of many trips between the two cities.

Marcel had a very trying time traveling back and forth almost daily between New York and Philadelphia. Although Alfred Ball, president of the railroad's freight department, and others, were doing their best to accommodate Marcel's wishes, the board of directors ultimately turned down his request for a partnership with Schenker & Company. My father's letters to us reflected his frustration and disappointment. Fate, however, would prove that Mr. Ball was a true friend.

During his stay, he did establish a good relationship with American banks and established a two-million-dollar credit line, at four-and-one-half percent interest. (In Berlin, at the time, the interest rate was nine percent and more.) This in itself made the trip worthwhile.

Meanwhile, my father made the most of his visit to New York, meeting with bankers and others in the transportation field. He "wined and dined" with his new acquaintances and saw the night-life on Broadway. During his absence, my mother kept nagging him, as usual, for more reassurance of his love. Her jealousy made her very unhappy even when Papi was right next to her; I can imagine how she felt when he was thousands of miles away. Most probably, she was envious of his evenings out and the dinners, which, he confessed, cost him as much as the large sum of twenty dollars for a single meal. She, no doubt, envisioned girls at Papi's side. And, who knows, perhaps her reasons for feeling jealous were justified.

My father was invited to the exclusive Rittenhouse Club in Philadelphia for a dinner with the executives and important men in the transportation world. The event made a great impression on my father. He listened to a speech in his honor in which Schenker's relationship with the Pennsylvania Railroad was mentioned. Marcel, suddenly realizing it was the custom to respond by speaking to the assembly, felt himself getting pale with excitement. In order to overcome his fear of speaking in public, and in English at that, he rose immediately, thus "mastering his cowardice." He proceeded, going far beyond a personal thank-you address, by using the occasion to talk about his vision of future methods of transportation. He had the necessary figures and arguments at his fingertips, and he impressed the listeners with his wide view and knowledge of world affairs.

But still, he was not able to convince the Pennsylvania Railroad's board of directors. After that, he saw that his plans with the Pennsylvania Railroad were doomed, and he turned to the New York Central Railroad.

When he returned to Germany aboard the SS *Europa* at the end of March, his plan had still not succeeded. But he had established friendships which would last a lifetime.

To overcome the financial difficulties faced by Schenker, my father approached the German State Railroad. In those days before large trucks dominated the roads, most freight in Europe was shipped by rail, and the German State Railroad, being state owned, had a monopoly in Germany. Marcel Holzer proposed an arrangement with them which would give Schenker & Company exclusive rights to ship merchandise from "house-to-house." This meant that all the goods carried by the railroad would be picked up by Schenker at their point of departure, trucked to and from stations, and delivered by Schenker to their final destination. This time he was successful. The ensuing contract took business away from smaller companies and, unfortunately, created much anger and ill-feeling toward my father. Success is always prey to envy.

My father, as always, was looking for creative solutions to problems. He looked at the problem which led to the contract as a business opportunity, just as he had the challenge of overseas shipment of beer when he was still a young employee of Adolf Blum & Popper, in Hamburg.

The "house-to-house" contract with the German State Railroad had both good and bad effects. Schenker had worldwide importance. In Europe it was represented in almost all countries and could, therefore, use an established network of international shipping facilities on land and water. This helped to overcome the problems of import and export of agricultural and industrial products faced by countries on the densely settled continent of Europe. This side of my father's work fascinated him. He felt at last he was a part of the "cog wheel" of world economy, and he tried to explain his passion for his activity and stressed that "being in touch" was the essential, the motor behind his energy.

In spite of the inflation, Berlin had ambitious plans for its ports and was looking for a partner with capital. To answer this need, a subsidiary of Schenker & Company was founded: the *Berliner Hafen-and-Lagerhaus A.G., BEHALA* in short. *BEHALA* was a joint venture combining Schenker with Busch & Company, a large producer of railway cars. In this new enterprise, Schenker owned two-thirds and Busch one-third of the shares; Schenker provided a large part of the necessary funds. Schenker, Berlin, received a lease of all Berlin ports for fifty years and *BEHALA* acted as the managing company. This contract, providing a private company with power over the German capital's ports, was highly unusual.

Berlin's inland port had been expanded in 1914 to accommodate vessels up to 600 tons. This "Western Port" connected the capital with Stettin on the Baltic Sea by way of the Berlin-Stettin Canal. Schenker sent freight, entrusted to them, directly by rail and by water from inland to the sea.

For the next two years, Schenker prospered because of its special relationship with the German State Railroad and the ports. However, at the dawn of national socialism there were undercover intrigues and adversities which could not fail to undermine a Jewish businessman's position. Unaware of the political ramifications, my father steered the company into a highly dangerous area. Resentment grew toward the idea of a private business directing public interests, such as the ports. Marcel felt good and strong, with the rudder in his capable hands and facing right into the storm. Nobody would have been able to hold him back or warn him, and I don't know if anyone tried. He worked almost blindly for the public and German interests, creating income for workers and employees. He reinvested the better part of the firm's earnings in the business and did not, as might have been possible, build his own capital.

Although one was conscious of the importance of this agreement, no one could foresee its personal consequences for my father and his family. The Nazis worked more or less quietly, behind the scenes; but an alert observer could have been aware that they were slowly introducing their members into important positions. Men like my father, leaders in commerce and industry who were ignorant of the goals of national socialism, just could not imagine, even in their worst fantasies, the ultimate direction in which things were going.

CHAPTER TEN

FRIEDEL

A testimony of my thoughts and concerns when I was nineteen are the last pages of my diary. I expressed in them my desire to be understood by another person; I struggled with, what seemed to me, mental isolation. Only many years later did I understand, mainly through the works of Erich Fromm, that the natural human conditions of independence and the need for closeness with another leads to the simultaneous search for both.

At this stage of my emotional development, Friedel Pschorr appeared on my horizon. Although we had shared many casual encounters over the years in my parents' house, they had no specific importance for him or for me. Just as most events in our lives need a special constellation of lesser events and a certain readiness on our part to come to life, it seems that my frame of mind and Friedel's sensibility after the great shock he suffered at his father's sudden death created the right moment for the meeting of our minds.

Thus, while I spent four weeks in a country school in Mellen, near Berlin, as part of my training at the Pestalozzi-Froebel *Haus*, still tossing the thoughts around of which I had written in my diary, an unexpected letter arrived.

Montreux, April 5, 1930

Dear Liesel,

It occurs to me that I mentioned rather thoughtlessly once that I am one of those persons who are nicer when they express themselves in writing rather than orally. This then is a test—how easily one can fail it!

To start with something pleasant, I'd like to say that it is rather a pity that we see each other so seldom. You should definitely forget sometime about the Pestalozzi-Froebel *Haus* and come to visit Erich and me in Munich, or I shall visit you.

I hope you like Mellen. I find Montreux fearfully dull and I am thinking constantly about last year when we spent Whitsuntide

in Glion. Here it is time for the after-dinner dance and the music
is playing a tango, while I turn my pen to the rhythm and find
consolation only in the memory of passed time and hope of the
future. Heartiest wishes.

Your Fiancë

Why Friedel signed his letter as he did I do not know. Was it wishful
thinking? The shy, and often sarcastic, young man was hiding his feelings,
but reaching out to me was a big step for him and a surprise to me. I wrote
back to him:

Mellen, April 9, 1930

Dear Friedel,

I had not dared to hear from you so soon; I rejoiced accordingly.
I should have liked to see the face of one of these funny Pestalozzi-
Froebel *Haus* types would they have seen your signature. Your idea
that I have settled here in Mellen quicker than you in Montreux
goes to show that you have no idea what life is like here. The
dreaded week in the kitchen is behind me, but now I am stuck in
the laundry, busily washing. Then I will be working in the garden
and then again in the house; or trying desperately to get the wood-
burning stoves going. Due to the amount of work, the time is flying
and the day of deliverance is coming closer.

Last Sunday my entire family came to visit. The cows, pigs and
goats turned to look when the Hispano-Suiza appeared, and the
girls . . . ! But, frankly I am not as unhappy as I thought I would
be. To work that hard is obviously new for me, but one gets used
to it quicker than one thinks.

Yes, I agree, Friedel, we should see each other more often. I
must admit, without trying to compliment you, that you have
changed to your advantage in spite of the tragedy. Please do not
let this remark make you a conceited person. I admire the way you
came to terms with your fate.

I feel I am a real "Liesel-on-the-farm."

Affectionately,
Your "Bride"

Thus began our correspondence which was to continue almost daily,
recording the growing pains of our love. I did not know if what I sensed

was the first stirring of love or my need for closeness. My remarks about the tragedy in Friedel's family were made without knowledge of the extent of his suffering over his father's recent death.

This appearance of a man in my life I experienced as if I was standing alone on a stage, when from behind a curtain Friedel stepped out to join me. The rest of the world was hidden behind the scenery surrounding me. From then on, reality had very little meaning for us as we groped to understand each other. Our instinctive attraction was not based on any knowledge of the other's character; the charm of first discovery is the mystery that enshrines a new friend. Actually, Friedel understood this better then I, because he would insist later on that I was too open and too honest in unveiling myself. The problem which had always occupied me—whether one should disclose everything in complete honesty—the problem which I had pondered in my diary, was answered by Friedel this way: one should preserve one's mysteries.

I think all lovers are carried on a cloud of "Hope, Faith and Love, these three . . ." as the Bible says in Thessalonians. Interest is suddenly awakened, and what do we hope to find? Our inborn need for love and companionship guides us into a great adventure. So my eyes, and then my heart, were suddenly drawn to Erich's longtime friend, and I saw him for the first time. Who was he?

—

Friedel was born on June 14, 1907, in Berlin-Grunewald, into an old, Christian German family. He was the third child of Robert Franz Pschorr and Ottilie Scherer and was baptized Fritz Georg Joseph Pschorr. His forefathers had founded the Pschorr Brewery in Munich about 150 years earlier. But while his uncles, August, Georg, and Joseph Pschorr worked actively for the brewery, Robert had decided to study physics and chemistry, which led him to Berlin, where his scientific achievements brought him acclaim. Friedel's mother Ottilie, or Tilla as she was called, was born in 1878 in Frankfurt on the Main.

Friedel's grandmother, who we called Grossmama-Ur, had two other daughters, Carry and Stefanie, besides Friedel's mother, Tilla. All three sisters were very pretty young women. Carry especially caught Robert's fancy, but he proposed to Tilla, who was just seventeen years old. He probably regretted this decision later. They were married in 1899. Tilla did not turn out to be as warmhearted and loving as he had expected, and as soon as she became pregnant and needed assistance, Robert called for Carry, who moved in with them. Carry was sensitive and lovable and always attracted attention from men and women alike. Although she was never favored with a higher education, she made friends with intelligent men of high standards. But since she devoted herself to raising her sister Tilla's children, she never married and had no family of her own. Until her death, Carry assumed her sister's motherly duties and unselfishly served Tilla without expecting reward.

This, then, was the woman who raised Friedel. Of the three children born to Robert and Tilla Pschorr—Carlotta, Herbert, and Friedel—it was Friedel, the last born, who became Carry's favorit. When Friedel was born, Carlotta was already seven; and his brother Herbert, five years old. Although one would not think this an abnormal age difference between siblings, Friedel was treated—and felt—very much the "baby" and grew up like an only child, playing alone in his room much of the time. Carry spoiled and pampered him, this lovely boy with an angelic face. She embraced him with the unspent warmth of her loving nature. And she was proud that Friedel behaved like a little prince, refusing a biscuit if it was broken and eating his cereal only if it was sweetened with raspberry syrup.

Friedel never shared his older brother's and sister's fun and games. He was probably also more or less excluded when his sister Carlotta married Hermann Grieving. Friedel was thirteen at the time, and his new brother-in-law was closer in age to Friedel's father than to his sister. Hermann Grieving was an established businessman, the manager of documentary films for the UFA, the largest motion picture company in Germany.

The atmosphere in the Robert Pschorr home, a villa near us in the *Wangenheimstrasse* in Grunewald, lacked the spirit of family unity. There were no confidences exchanged; the children kept to themselves while their mother took care of her headaches and their father was at the Academy. During Friedel's formative years, his father was absent. Friedel was just seven when Robert Pschorr joined the German army in the summer of 1914. He served at the front for four years as a major in the First Bavarian Artillery Regiment and was decorated with the Iron Cross Second and First Class and the Military Medal with Crown and Swords.

Professor Robert Pschorr was not only a brilliant man, he was a great lover of nature; mountain climbing and hiking in the beautiful Bavarian Alps was his hobby. The only mountain railway in Germany at that time was the *Zugspitz-Bahn* and there were few, if any, funiculars. So the only way to see the full beauty of the mountains was on foot. When Robert was able to be with his boys, Friedel and Herbert, they hiked together in the classical Tyrolian fashion—knee-length, Loden breeches, hiking boots, and knapsacks. The boys enjoyed their father's company. Together, they experienced sunrises and the breathtaking views that were afforded only to those who reached mountain peaks after hours of walking and climbing.

Tilla rarely joined them—she preferred to stay out of the sun—but Hermann Grieving often went along. Professor Pschorr and his son-in-law were great friends. Even after Carlotta's untimely death three years after their marriage, Hermann Grieving, who never remarried, remained close to the family.

Carlotta's illness and subsequent death from cancer spread a mournful gloom on the household. Friedel plunged into a state of melancholy even though he had not been particularly close to his sister. He found consolation through friendship with an older girl, Illy Dax, the daughter of a family friend and neighbor. Her father was the chief surgeon of the *Schwabinger Krankenhaus*, a hospital in Munich that was going to play an important role in my life. Illy tried to help Friedel overcome his depression and loneliness. He, in turn, confided in her and fell in love with her. Unfortunately, he mistook her interest in him for love and suffered great disappointment when he discovered that she meant friendship only.

It was not surprising that Friedel was attracted to our home in the *Jagowstrasse*. Perhaps it was not so much his interest in his classmate, Erich, as the feeling of family closeness in our home. Here my mother was always around, enjoying her children, laughing, and making music. Friedel, known to his parents as a silent, brooding boy, showed his sense of humor and dry sarcasm when he was with us.

Robert Pschorr, aware of the sterile atmosphere in his home, was pleased with the role my parents played in his son's life. He cared very much for Friedel and understood his longing for family closeness. Robert's own search for love had ironically led him away from home and his wife as well. He had found his haven with another woman. Only after his death did the truth about his secret life came to light. His family was shocked to read in his last will and testament that a large part of his small fortune was left to the woman he had loved.

This, and mysterious circumstances surrounding Professor Robert Pschorr's death, contributed a great deal to Friedel's unhappiness and deepened the shadows which had befallen the family. In February 1930, while Friedel was studying law in Munich, Robert Pshcorr went to Munich to chair the General Assembly of the Pschorr Brewery. The next day he visited with friends and relatives and seemed in perfect mental and physical health. That evening he asked Friedel to meet him at the brewery. From there the two men, dressed in evening attire, would go to a carnival ball. When Friedel arrived at the brewery, he discovered his father lying dead on a couch in a small room. Friedel immediately called Professor Dax, Illy Dax's father, who hurried to the scene. After a brief examination of the body, during which Friedel was not present, Professor Dax decided that an autopsy was not necessary. Apparently, as I learned decades later, there were indications that Robert Pschorr's death might have been suicide. He was, after all, a chemist and had access to the means to take his life, but the death certificate listed heart attack as the cause of death. In any case, Friedel was disconsolate.

It was this lonely and disappointed young man who discovered me and who was going to be part of my destiny. Nobody knew the extent of his grief: by nature he talked little and guardedly. But whatever he had buried within himself he revealed, at least partly, in his letters. In them we exchanged thoughts and feelings that in later years we rarely expressed. Life with its overwhelming pressures had different requirements then, this life which would grip us so hard that it almost crushed us.

After my return to Berlin from Mellen, I resumed my studies at the Pestalozzi-Froebel *Haus*. I was saddened to learn that Rita had moved from Berlin. Her parents had sold their house in Grunewald and were moving to Possenhofen, a small colony of private villas in a fishing harbor on the *Starnbergersee*, near Munich. Rita's departure came at a time when I began to shift my attention from her to Friedel; thus, I was pleased to learn that Possenhofen was very near the village of Feldafing and the old Pschorr family villa. Following the death of Robert Pschorr, Friedel's mother had moved from the Grunewald to live in the villa in Feldafing with her two sisters.

In July 1930, my parents invited Friedel to join us in Gstaad for our traditional summer vacation. He readily accepted, and soon we were together in the luxurious Palace Hotel. It was an idyllic romantic setting for Friedel's and my first meeting since our correspondence had begun. At the five o'clock teadances and the after-dinner dances, we held each other close for the first time as we danced. Occasionally, as our heads would brush unintentionally, a spark would shoot through me and my heart would beat faster. Those were days of tender charm, although nothing much was said, no visible indication that our first timid approach would result in a union for life.

As our vacation ended, we went our separate ways, I back to Berlin and Friedel to the university in Munich. Before he left the hotel, he wrote a letter to me and mailed it so it would be at our house in Grunewald when I returned. It was a welcome surprise for I had already gotten used to Friedel's sweet company and I felt lonely after this first separation.

Gstaad, August 8, 1930

Dear good Liesel,

I want you to find these words of welcome upon your return to the *Jagowstrasse*. They shall be the first sign of my thoughts. I enjoy dreaming about the past weeks when we were together. I became very fond of you and from now on I want to create joy for you whenever I can.

As I write this we still have two days together. There are a few things I would like to say to you but I am too shy to express them orally.

I do hope that you will correspond with me. We achieved such perfect understanding during these too swiftly passing weeks. I would be so happy if it would stay like that forever. For your arrival I send you a thousand affectionate greetings.

Yours, Friedel.

I replied immediately, saying I understood his reluctance to speak about his feelings. I also had had the urge to speak to him, but lacked the courage. Perhaps it was just as well that we expressed our thoughts in letters.

Munich, August 11, 1930

My dear little Liesel,

Why do beautiful days pass so quickly? No Soir de Paris perfume, no black and yellow evening dress, no dark-haired head leaning against mine. But these are only the outward remembered signs of the remarkable event when our inner-selves met. This is so rare; but I strongly believe in the supreme importance of this, over the other contact, which is possibly much easier and which I have not experienced as yet . . . .

Blissfully wrapped in a romantic mood after our holiday in Switzerland, I visited Rita in her parent's new house on the *Starnbergersee*. I found her engulfed in romance, too, for she had secretly been in love with my brother for some time. Over the years, Erich and Rita, Friedel and I had spent much time together, and although it seemed a carefree harmonious relationship which we thought would never change, it obviously had changed considerably. Now, Rita was about to experience the first cloud on her horizon.

Her American cousins, daughters of her father's brother who lived in New Jersey, were coming to Munich to study German. Rita had a premonition that the presence of these sophisticated and comparatively uninhibited girls would threaten her relationship with Erich. She decided not to disclose Erich's address in Munich to them, or for that matter, even his existence.

But Alexandra and Thaisa had not come to Munich during the Oktoberfest to mope around, and they already knew about Erich. When, by chance, they discovered the blue-grey Packard with a Berlin license plate, they did not hesitate to fasten a note behind the windshield wiper which said, "If this car belongs to Erich Holzer, please call this number . . . ." Erich found the note and promptly called. He reported this to my family, in Rita's presence, and everybody except Rita found it very amusing.

Soon afterwards, Rita's worst fears were realized. One day, when the two girls were visiting Rita in Possenhofen, Erich drove to the lake from Munich in Mutti's Packard to invite Ty (Thaisa), and not Rita, for a drive and a picnic. I spent the day with Rita, nervously watching her anguish, which seemed to increase with every passing hour. By nightfall, Erich and Rita's cousin had not returned. We sat in our nightgowns on the doorstep while a dramatic, blistering thunderstorm crashed through the trees and sent frightening lightning bolts into the lake and loud thunderclaps echoing off the nearby Alps. Rita cried uncontrollably, and I tried in vain to console her. Her fearful premonitions, which at the time seemed exaggerated, turned out to be tragically true.

When Erich and Ty arrived at a late hour, I exploded and screamed recriminations at them, venting my pent-up frustration and anger. Erich was shocked, perhaps justifiably, at my behavior.

—

The tender beginnings of Friedel's and my relationship so excited me that I still feel their resonance. For the first time, I was lonely in my parents, house. It probably is the experience we all have when we are ready to break loose from our parents, ready to leave the nest. In my case, it would turn out to be a long and painful struggle. At the same time I missed Rita, my companion of so many years. Correspondence with Friedel became the focus of my life. I poured my thoughts and feelings out to him in my letters.

As I outgrew my schoolgirl and teenage stages, children became my primary interest in life. I probably did not connect my passion for children and my first encounter with a possible male partner with the nascent hope a young woman might have to bear children. I was stimulated by my studies at the Pestalozzi-Froebel *Haus* and I was eager to share my excitement and my experiences in the kindergarten with Friedel.

I persisted with enthusiasm to study the theories of famous educators, such as Rousseau, Pestalozzi, Froebel, and in particular, Maria Montessori. I felt a kinship with her: she sensed the needs of children and was able to discover new methods to increase their learning potential. And I admired her. She had been the first woman admitted to an Italian university and the first to receive her M.D. degree. Her work enabled the underprivileged children of her country, and later of the world, to overcome learning disabilities.

My fascination with the kindergarten was not shared by my father. He was worried about his daughter working in the underprivileged section of Berlin, where hunger and unemployment had driven people into the streets. He insisted that I be driven to the school by our chauffeur. I, in turn, persuaded the chauffeur to spare me embarrassment by dropping me at a street corner away from the kindergarten.

I was so engrossed in children that my mother and Friedel called me a fanatic. I suspected, however, that Friedel became jealous of my divided interest. His frequent criticism and low moods began to upset me. He had two roommates now in Munich, my brother and an American psychology student called Schnucki. Erich and Schnucki were dating Ty and Alexandra, and Friedel, although involved emotionally with me, felt isolated and depressed. I tried to cheer him up with reports of my studies and my new sport, horseback riding.

I took riding lessons in the *Tattersaal des Westens* located next to the *Brandenburger Tor*. My father insisted I should ride sidesaddle and be outfitted in the proper manner, so I was sent to an expensive tailor who provided me with the classic, black riding costume—the tightly fitted, long jacket, the black britches, and long skirt. I wore a white stock and the traditional tricorn hat.

Since I showed some talent, the teacher invited me to participate in the evening classes, during which the riders performed figures and "danced," an exercise first introduced and made famous by Lipizzaner stallions of Vienna. As a special treat, I was permitted to ride a beautiful, privately owned white horse from time to time.

Berlin, August 22, 1930

Dear Friedel,

I have just come from my first ride in the Grunewald. I still feel the lovely air and the thrill of riding through the stillness of the forest. An indescribable feeling of liberation and joy pulsed through me as I sensed the warm animal and its eagerness to trot, enjoying the soft ground under its feet with the reins loose.

While out there, close to nature, I contemplated your negative reaction on my comments about children. I tried to understand the deeper meaning of your words which told me that it is your interest in me, and not my fascination with children, which caused them. At first I had not understood why this should upset you, and I am glad you made it clearer so that I can now be sure that I am not alone in this very important matter. My love for children is a part of me and much more than a passing interest.

When you come to Berlin I wish you would let me show you some of Pestalozzi's writings. What he said about life, truth, and mankind is wonderful and worth absorbing. This is the kind of thought I comprehend. I have no mind for politics, political party programs, and current events. The teachers take for granted that we have a certain knowledge of these subjects but I have a hard time following them.

The struggle to overcome timidity and convention and to live up to the promises of our first correspondence began somewhat awkwardly. In the face of Friedel's unpredictable moods, I became anxious and unsure. I was not trained in psychology and knew nothing about the "human condition," as Erich Fromm terms our existence.

An older business friend of my father told me, during a casual encounter while he pretended to be knowledgeable in palm reading, that I was the type of person whose mind would be in constant battle with the heart. Both these regions, he said, were strong in my personal makeup and I was struggling to satisfy emotions and intellect. He was correct. I discussed it with Friedel and told him to deal with his problems without relying on me. Every person, I told him, had to find his own answers. "This is," I wrote, "the reality of life, that we find ways to satisfy our natural needs and fulfill ourselves." I was convinced, as I am today, that only what we achieve through our own struggle is of value in building our character. I rejected help, recognizing that it makes us soft and dependant.

This has remained my silent motto, sometimes unconsciously, throughout my life. I tried to explain it to Friedel—although I was proud he believed I could help him with his emotional problems—that all I could do was try to give him self-confidence. I assured him that I didn't reject his plea for help to avoid responsibility. The situation was difficult because I never knew the reasons for his dissatisfaction, but I made a real effort to console him in his depression.

Actually, we both had similar problems, and perhaps he saw trouble on the horizon. Perhaps he understood what it meant for us to fall in love with each other. He did love me. I struggled to accept his difficult personality and tried to see only those things I loved about him. Friedel found it difficult to accept my impulsiveness. I could not see what was wrong in giving oneself wholly up to love once one had declared it. It was the only way I could be. But from the start, Friedel put up "roadblocks" to his feelings.

I was in love and it would have been simply that. But the dissection of every emotion or thought scared me. I began to doubt that I could enter into such a complicated relationship, in which I could not simply be myself.

Friedel wrote to me:

Our cases are different in as much as you have a happier nature and you overcome whatever disunity you feel. While I am my parents' son. There we are as different from one another as can be. So it is not my fault that I am split. Look at my mother. I know that she is in an extreme condition right now. She is torturing herself with remorse. She thinks about herself, but she has not the will power to overcome her lethargy.

My father, however, was different. He was an idealist; he remained himself and upheld the idea of his completeness. I, the child, witnessed their estrangement. They should never have married. They did not harmonize perfectly. [Friedel considered this essential for a happy union.] My uncle's marriages are similar. The male Pschorrs are difficult gentlemen. Perhaps the younger generation will be better.

All this, combined with my sister's death, my father's death, and my mother's breakdown [his mother attempted to drown herself in the *Starnbergersee*], my bad luck in one examination, financial worries for the future, my disposition to brood about everything—does it all become more understandable?

But I know what can help my state of mind: my willpower. You pointed it out and you were right. No one else can help me, just as no one can help my mother; she too has to apply her willpower. I will have an easier time than she, I am young and I have the intention to better myself.

I made a small beginning. Do I dare tell you? When I did not hear from you this week I became desperate and unhappy. I could not work or sleep. I wrote a pretty ugly letter but with an enormous effort I managed to drag it around with me for twenty-four hours and finally destroyed it, because I did not want to be small-minded. It was one of the few decent things I have done in a long time.

Please tell me: am I more distant from you now since all these stupid things have emerged? Do I mean as much to you as before? If you assist me in my task it will be all right—but if you drop me there will be a catastrophe! Please do not act out of pity. That is what Illy did when my sister died. Then Illy got secretly engaged. I took her friendship for love. We tortured each other. I hope this won't happen again to me. I am afraid of it.

This letter threw me into a panic. It was the threat, no doubt, that I did not have a free choice: unless I stood by him he would not have the courage to live. After this shock, Friedel came to visit and we faced each other. He had appealed to the deepest source of my being, my strongest instinct—motherly compassion, the urge to protect others. Although I sensed the difficulty of guiding a person like Friedel, I was ready to throw my entire being into the battle that confronted me.

I wanted to love and be loved, yet I wanted to be honest with myself. I could not pretend that my state of mind could be called loving. I tried to tell Friedel my thoughts and feelings and offered him friendship instead of love. Where does the difference lie, where does one end and the other begin?

We were in torment, two people obviously meant for each other. I was afraid that Friedel would follow the path of his mother (or his father!) and that it would be my fault. On the other hand, I wanted to fulfill myself in a less complicated way than I envisioned our life together would be.

I could not know then that our problem was but a small one in the face of the political developments in Germany. Wherever I would have turned at that crossroad, it would have been a stony path.

After his return to Munich, Friedel sent me another letter. In it he said, "I love you and I cannot condemn you because you are without fault, but I denounce fate for having nothing but blows for me. How did I deserve this? I don't know what makes me hold on to life—perhaps it is consideration for my mother or sheer cowardice. I am brokenhearted, but nobody ever died of that.

"Peace and tranquility, joy and happiness—why can I find those only in my dreams? In spite of this, I thank you for the experience we have had. It was an illusion, a foundation, which was built for friendship when I wanted to build love. How beautiful it could have been. With your support I would have found the strength to overcome myself, your happiness would have been my goal."

For the first time, Friedel had spoken of love. I had carried my heart in my hand, so to speak, ready to give it to him. Yet I did not want to confuse my readiness to help him as a friend with love. I thought that love, when it overcame me, would be different. My confusion and unhappiness was bottomless, just like Friedel's.

October 1, 1930

Dear, dear Friedel,

That I hurt you so much! I thought for so long about ways to comfort you, to cheer you. Can you believe me that I suffer as you do? I suppose you will think with bitterness of me, and imagine perhaps that I tried to fool you. But I swear that my feelings for you are real and true, even if they are not what you wish for. Always will I maintain and preserve these feelings. I thank you for the words you pronounced for the first time on this detestable day.

Never again should you think that I reject you. It is quite simply not true. Otherwise how could I be so unhappy now? When I look into your eyes I want to close mine, because I do not feel entitled to have inflicted you with so much pain.

Your grateful Liesel.

Although one could have expected a complete break in our relationship after this dramatic exchange of letters, we continued to write and see each other. Whenever I visited Rita's house in Possenhofen, Friedel would come from Munich to stay with his mother in Feldafing. The forest along the lakeshore between Possenhofen and Feldafing offered Friedel and me opportunies to meet without being seen. The physical attraction between us was much more powerful than all our discussions and letters. We gazed into each other's eyes and innocently held hands: yet there it was, the indescribable flame which drives lovers into each other's arms. In our case, however, it remained only a spark for some time to come.

I was young and full of expectations excitable and basically happy, but I defended vehemently my strong convictions.

Reflecting on his own situation, Friedel realized the darkness about himself but did not loose hope that the sun would return to his world. Apparently, I gave him this hope, but I was not able to change his attitude. He remained very private and few people could see behind the curtain he drew around himself. Although we had withstood the storm, Friedel's attitude remained critical and I continued my efforts to please him. He didn't ask for more than my declaration of friendship. Since he was very inexperienced with women, he could not guess how much I wanted him to be more possessive. He said

I had to learn to appreciate his criticism as a sign of interest. His demands, he said, were compliments.

I accepted his criticism and understood it, but, on occasion, his kind of "compliment" prevented me from writing to him. I wanted to please him, but I was fearful of displeasing him. The doubts caused by these mixed feelings prevented me from declaring my love.

Friedel's letters were of various character: sometimes they were letters to a friend, other times to his beloved. I could only guess at the depth of his being. Eventually I realized that one of his virtues was his steadfastness. Before taking a stand or making a statement, he thought about it long enough to be sure of his decision. Friedel's opinions were like rocks, one could build on them. But these qualities came to light mostly in later years when every action and every word was a potential threat to our existence. our relationship was dependent on emotions. Friedel suffered from being away from me and became jealous of my social life. Actually, my social life was that of my parent, in which they demanded that I participate. My father, who still did not encourage my "one person" friendships, sometimes invited young men to accompany me and my parents to the theater or to evening dances. Although I was indifferent to these men, I responded superficially to their attempts at flirtation, all the time wondering in desperation how my latest letter would strike the real man in my life.

The year 1930 drew near its end, but not so the problems that arose from our correspondence. Neither of us was able to change to please the other. Friedel worked toward his baccalaureate and saw almost no one socially.

It would seem that the simple solution to our problem would be to declare our love and marry. Our lengthy courtship by correspondence, which would ultimately stretch over three years, was not our choice, but necessity. My father had always felt that a man should be financially stable and independent before marriage, and Friedel agreed with that view. Although I would have accepted marriage on any terms, I respected Friedel's beliefs more. Thus, we could not marry until Friedel had completed his baccalaureate and his Ph.D. program, which would take at least two more years. In the meantime, we continued to explore our feelings through letters and occasional visits that only added to the test of our patience. The long months of separation saw misunderstandings and self-doubts creep into our correspondence.

In contrast to Friedel's social isolation at the university, my life was filled with activity and complicated by the arrival of Erich back at our house in the *Jagowstrasse*. He had completed his studies in Munich with a brilliant exam and was in the best of moods and up to all sorts of nonsense. Never in later life would I see him like that, lovable and happy, bringing turmoil into our home with his teasing and merrymaking. I was his target as always, and the secrecy with which I covered my state of mind just made him more interested in my letters and telephone calls. He insisted in adding remarks to my letters, which I knew would aggravate Friedel, and he gave me no opportunity for a private telephone conversation with Friedel.

One evening he asked me to go to dinner with him in the city, something he had never done before. I was surprised and flattered. I had always struggled to be friends with him but never really succeeded. We drove off in Mutti's Packard roadster to a Hungarian restaurant in the center of Berlin. The soft, bittersweet music, played by a trio of violinists who hovered over us, set romantic chords vibrating in me. While I only sipped at the sweet Tokay wine Erich had ordered, he emptied the bottle. Thus he was in a "good" mood when he drove zigzag, singing and laughing, back over the silent and empty *Kurfuerstendamm*, while I held on for dear life. I never knew if he did it to impress me or if he was drunk.

When we arrived home, I went straight to bed. Soon afterwards, Erich, still dressed for dinner, came into my room singing in a loud voice. He put on my bra and underwear and then climbed on the top of my wardrobe. My father, attracted by the noise, appeared in his pajamas, took the scene in, shook his head, and retreated quietly.

To me, it was an unforgettable evening: Erich had shared his festive mood with me. It was one of the few times I felt close to him and included in his life. In the years that followed, we would never be as close again.

My father decided that our family would spend Christmas in St. Moritz that year, and Friedel was invited to join us. His mother was still depressed, and he didn't feel he could leave her for the holidays. I worried that he, too, would become seriously depressed in view of the load on his shoulders with his mother and his approaching exam, but I could not relieve him of his major concern, the uncertainty about our mutual future.

After long discussions with his aunts, who were still caring for his mother, he finally decided to put duty behind pleasure and join us in St. Moritz. I suggested to him that we take all our letters to St. Moritz and discuss those matters which seemed important. I felt that letters were no substitute for conversation, and that the opportunity to resolve things would help us mature and grow closer. All went well, and we spent some lovely days in the Swiss Alps in the company of my parents and Erich. But our relationship remained platonic.

After I returned to Berlin and Friedel to Munich, our correspondence began again. I wrote that I was nearing completion of my studies at the Pestalozzi-Froebel *Haus* when I would have a series of examinations "to prove to the authorities that I really understand children." I mentioned how saddened I was that he did not share my enthusiasm for the subject. In January 1931, Friedel passed his junior barrister exam but again I had to find words to help him over his disappointment of not having achieved excellent marks. I reminded him that since he didn't intend to practice law anyway, his marks were of little consequence. Soon he began to see his life in a new light.

"Perhaps now that the exam is behind me, I can trust myself again," Friedel wrote. I was overjoyed by his improved mood. I wrote to him: "You cannot imagine my happiness, hearing the good news. I can hardly believe this oppression is lifted from you. Just think this is the first real joy we have shared. I would love to see you in this condition instead of having just paper to look at."

During another short visit to our home in the *Jagowstrasse*, Friedel overcame his reluctance to talk openly. He revealed his innermost thoughts as he had done before only in his letters. I never thought that I would be capable of confiding in a man as I did in Friedel. Without being aware of it, something had happened between us. Was it friendship or love? I did not care to give it a name.

Friedel didn't experience the transition from friendship to love as I did. From the beginning, his ardent wish was that I would recognize and proclaim my love. Until that moment came, he maintained self-discipline. He could wait, and he respected my honesty. With our first kiss, on the last evening of his stay with us, our lives changed. After he returned to Munich, we again exchanged letters.

> My dearest Friedel,
>   There it is again, the trembling wait for your letter, and then the retreat into the quietest room to read and enjoy every one of your words, let sink in what you write, my beloved. Every sentence makes me want to hold your hand in mine. My relationship with you is new, different. Somehow it is restful to lean on someone—I could send to hell the praised self-reliance so ardently fought for by women.
>   Our last evening in front of the fireplace was a special moment for me. I am happy our first kiss was exchanged in a moment of

great exaltation. It would have been senseless and perhaps even indecent had it not been the expression of our mutual experience. Your restraint causes me to admire you and I am sure that not many in your place would have exercised such willpower. I hope that you are not sorry and that your self-discipline was worth it.

                                                    February 25, 1931

Dearest Liesel,

   It is a pity that you could not see me when I read your letter again and again. It created such a feeling of joy that I did not know how to deal with my happiness. The best would have been to bury my head in your lap to hide my radiant face. But there was the distance separating us.

   Every day I feel the cruel contrast between the beautiful days in Berlin and I have the strong urge to simply return. But I won't complain.

   I know how hard it was for you to kiss me. I know because I understand your healthy, unspoiled opinions (idiots call them old-fashioned). I waited so that you could stay faithful to your standards in spite of your kisses. Now you need not be ashamed of them. I love this feeling of shyness in you and the great restraint, which we respected. It will be like that, even when we approach each other physically. Is it not wonderful how we harmonize body and soul in every important instance?

   With Erich's departure from here my last visible tie to the Holzer family disappeared from sight. Let us hope this interruption will be short. I almost started to cry when I shook Erich's hand which he held out for me from the railway compartment window.

   I confess my jealousy of your friendship with Rita. But now I would find it strange if you had the same reaction to my friendship to your brother, so I suppose I erred in envying Rita. Just as you said there is a difference between a relationship of persons of the same sex and persons of the opposite sex, is there not a difference between the greatest friendship and the smallest love?

   Rita had been removed not only physically from my everyday life but emotionally as well. My girlhood friendship which had occupied my heart so fervently had given way to my first love. Although I still did not admit it to myself or Friedel, our bond had undeniably become a firm union. It was typical of me that I gave myself wholly and completely to him. As the years progressed, Friedel used to say often, "you will have to learn to make concessions." But I think I never did.

After her move from Berlin, Rita was lonely and felt forsaken. I felt ashamed when her letters told me how unhappy she was, that I had forgotten an old friend over a new one. She still needed me. I wrote to Friedel that my feelings toward Rita had changed and I could not pretend otherwise. I felt that I had reached a maturity and outgrown girlish infatuations; "I cannot divide myself and will never belong to anyone the way I belong to you; especially not to another girl or woman."

Although I felt that way at the time, I experienced later love with to a man and friendship with a woman. I also did not want Friedel to be jealous. After all, I was not jealous (or so I thought) of Illy, Friedel's first love, who he still saw from time to time.

In the months that followed, Friedel and I became more and more attuned to each other. Our comments and ideas coincided. Our letters, carried back and forth between Munich and Berlin by express trains, rushing through the night. They carried messages of love, thoughts concerning our expectations and fears of the effect of the passing time on our relationship. Sometimes hot arguments, often taken much too seriously, clouded our romance. In one letter to Friedel in March 1931 I proudly announced that I had passed my kindergarten teacher examination.

Friedel's mother was still treated for depression, and Friedel, in addition to his other worries carried heavily this emotional load. He could not determine whether his mother was really sick or just of weak character. Friedel complained to me about her selfishness and lack of self-discipline. Actually, he explained at length, that his mother had never tried to be close to him. He felt her lack of interest and love had made him silent and withdrawn. He was grateful to his parents, however, for the unintentional warning signals they had given him through the example of their bad marriage. His fear of making the same mistakes was probably the reason why he intensified our dialogue to the extreme and tried to guide me in a certain direction along "the straight line." He wrote, "Now you know why, even at twenty-three, I cannot understand this woman who is my mother, and why I cannot feel love for her as a son normally does. There exists only one woman whose soul I have tried to penetrate. I miss you so very much, but we must be patient and let none of our worries reflect on our inner bond."

At this time, Erich left for the United States on a fateful journey which would confirm Rita's fears and premonitions. While in America, Erich began seriously courting Rita's cousin Ty. Friedel and I knew that Rita considered her feelings for my brother equal to a commitment, if not an actual engagement. Unfortunately and tragically, Erich didn't understand that the code of behaviour for girls just did not permit her to voice her feelings.

I got a letter from Rita that made me feel guilty. She needed my friendship more than ever now. My brother had disappointed her and she was crushed. I explained this to Friedel, and he was angered by my sympathy towards Rita, although I assured him once more that she would not take his place in my heart even if I resumed my close relationship with her. But Friedel was unreasonable. He demanded that I consider his readiness to be fully mine to the exclusion of his work and other people from his life. That, he said, should be reward enough for the small "sacrifice" of letting go of Rita.

He wrote,

"Admittedly it is nice to do something one desires, but there are limits. It is nice to state that one wants no sacrifices, but it seems better if one is prepared to sacrifice certain things. In these matters I will not be neglected, I will not step back either behind Rita or children, even my own should I ever have any. If I were petty, I would ask you to choose between children, Rita, and me. But I am not that way. I let you do as you please. However, in this important question I will not resign till we are of the same opinion, be it yours or mine. I am grateful that you had the courage to tell her I take precedence over her from now on. Surely, it was not easy but, in the name of truth, it was natural. I cannot shake the feeling that there is a difference in your relationship with Rita compared to mine and Erich's. I should explain: my faith in you is limitless. But my trust in Erich is not that unconditional. He is *only* my friend. I expect that your faith in me, like mine in you, is limitless. But do you trust Rita that completely? Are your feelings similar to mine and Erich's? Please think about this and remember, I will not be pushed back by anyone."

I was reminded of Goethe's words in Faust: "*Grau, teurer Freund, ist alle Theory*" ("Grey, my good friend, is all theory"). In spite of all we had said about love and friendship, he could not let go of his jealous and petty attitude. Knowing this normally quiet and good-hearted man, I felt the agitation within him that dictated his letter. I read it decades later with sheer disbelief. The threatening tone could have frightened any girl away.

I was disillusioned to be sure, but I received him with open arms as ever when he came to visit a short while later. The only difference was that this time he had "things to do in town" and did not stay with us. In spite of his letter, I was not shattered as I would have been earlier in our relationship. It is true I didn't argue with him about it in fear of aggravating the situation. In fact, our arguments and the constant hairsplitting of almost everything made me question my willingness to share my life with him, in spite of my feelings. I had more modern ideas than Friedel about a woman's role in married life. I had once before expressed criticism, mixed with a certain admiration, for my mother's life with my father. I had suggested to Friedel that a wife could have her own interests and add to the mutual life with participation in some activity. Friedel thought more commendable, however, the suppression of such desires, and he was happy that my mother had chosen the passive role in her marriage. The entire discussion, and also my wish to do something intellectually fulfilling, was, unfortunately, hypothetical. Our life would be governed by more crucial problems, and no time and strength remained for such idealistic plans.

An issue that had lain dormant and had never before been of particular significance to us was the question of my Jewish ancestry. Friedel was aware of my family's heritage, but we had never discussed it. He decided to bring the "ticklish question," as we called it, out in the open. We agreed to discuss it. Among other considerations, we had to choose between the written and the spoken word as the means to approach this awkward subject. Desiring to soften the harshness of this conversation with physical closeness on one hand, and fearing the difficulty of facing each other in such crucial moments on the other, we changed our opinion constantly.

The decision to talk about our "racial" difference was taken out of our hands. During the Munich Carnival, Erich had met Friedel's uncle, August Pschorr, and some quibble over a reserved table in the ballroom resulted. Erich's behavior seemed disrespectful to the older gentleman. When he encountered his nephew Friedel some time later, August Pschorr singled out the event to bring up the Jewish "origin" of Friedel's friend Erich Holzer. He said, "How can one have anything to do with such people?"—and it was only too obvious what he meant. Friedel thought, "I wonder how he would react if he knew how I feel about Liesel and her family?" It was not cowardice that prevented Friedel from informing his uncle of his love for me. His open struggle with his family over this issue confirmed this soon afterwards.

But now, the subject had come up and occupied a prominent place in our conscious thoughts. I considered the subject a private matter and believed that love would overcome it. In hindsight, I shudder at the thought of the lurking danger, the potential disaster so unbelievably close, and our ignorance of it. Are we, perhaps even now, just as blind to threats against our existence?

With the rising popularity of the Nazis and other nationalistic splinter parties, anti-Semitism had become more openly displayed in Germany. The Nazi's vicious hatred of Jews, made many people, who had given little thought to the issue, aware of who among their friends were Jewish. Thus, Friedel was now in a difficult situation. How he maintained his firm stand not to let anything come between us, God only knows. As an intelligent and aware person, he must have understood the consequences of this battle. Had not his own brother Herbert just married Edda Mueller, the daughter of a Nazi party member? Did not his uncles Pschorr, and many Germans, believe in the righteousness of Hitler's theories which made every descendant of the Jewish "race" an outlaw? In addition, he had to consider my feelings and the naivete with which I regarded the problem. I wrote to him, "I am waiting anxiously to discuss the ticklish question with you, but it seems to me that you overestimate the importance which I attribute to this theme. But, if we must deal with it, let us talk about it!"

Friedel had been coming to our house in Grunewald since 1921 as Erich's friend. He loved and admired my parents; an unusual trust in my mother led him to seek her advice in many critical situations.

I don't know if the thought of my parents' limited participation in any formal religion had ever crossed his mind. But with the rise of National Socialism, his family's "Aryan" social circle became more and more aware of his attachment to a "non-Aryan" family. Even though we considered ourselves Christians, the Nazis did not. I gather from his letters that he was sometimes openly questioned about it and even confronted with choosing between a relationship with us and others. He felt no need to think about his choice. All his life, he had been close to his Uncle August; the day came when Friedel was forbidden ever again to enter August Pschorr's house on account of his friendship with the Holzers—Friedel was hurt, to say the least, but he did not waiver in his conviction. He had no feelings for or against the consideration of religion, he just simply liked or disliked people and would openly come to the defense of his friends when ever the occasion was given. Even his tendencies of doubt and self-criticism did not come into action in this context.

As a student of law, he probably realized that politics were going to be important in everybody's life in Germany, especially in the years just ahead. Among Hitler's most ardent early supporters were university students and those at the university at Munich were no exception. Friedel must have been exposed daily to the recurring themes of Nazi ideology from both students and professors. I think in view of the later crisis between us, Friedel became more occupied with this problem than we both realized.

CHAPTER ELEVEN

CHANGING MOODS

In the spring of 1931, my father took my mother and me to Paris for a brief vacation. In the hotel room, I found red roses and a letter from Friedel to welcome me. His letter was written in a sad and introspective mood, and, in it, he again raised the "ticklish question." The small, gold bracelet on my wrist, which Friedel had given me as a token of his love, seemed reassurance enough that one short letter couldn't be much of a problem. I immediately wrote to him describing in glowing terms my first impressions of Paris. Then, a few days later, I received another letter at the hotel from him that made my world collapse.

Munich, April 4, 1931

Dear Liesel,

It becomes more and more evident that I have to express how I feel about our relationship. Since my return to Munich, I feel uneasy and cannot understand exactly what bothers me. I question and doubt everything. It started with the contemplation, "Do I really love you?" I was alarmed when I could not answer this with a clear and undoubting "Yes!" Neither could I say no, of course. When I last wrote I thought I could avoid this confession. But now I realize it will not do.

It seems that I am now in the same situation you have been in all along. Up till now I was sure of my love and I hope sincerely to return to that frame of mind in a very short time. I have to try to explain my present state, which, I guess, must have to do with the last day we were together in Berlin. Relentless truth is called for at this time as always.

Let me say first that I entertain the thought of being able to marry you some day. I think you know that. Before you left for Paris we discussed for the first time the "ticklish question." Faced with it (and you), I realized how difficult it was to absorb in all depth the implications of your Jewish extraction. I will conquer this question, but it will take time. Perhaps there is something to it after all when people say that Christians have a certain antipathy toward Jews.

I also feel that I compromise you all the time. Illy mentioned, for instance, that she heard we were engaged. I do not care what people say about me, but I cannot stand talk about you. Yesterday I talked to Illy. Now she knows that it is you I have on my mind. She noticed my condition and remarked that I should not start again with doubts, as she had witnessed when she and I were close friends. She thinks that in reality things are often less complicated than they seem and less problematic than I imagine.

I remind you of the other crisis of October, 1930, when you told me that you were not ready for me, and how we overcame it. I am sure we will conquer this one, which is much less important. Be courageous little Liesel, everything will be alright again.

Your Friedel

I sent a quick note to him.

Paris, April 7, 1931

Dear Friedel,

We are returning Wednesday to Berlin. I guess I will be able to write then. Now it would make no sense.

Kindest regards, Liesel.

My curt answer did not mirror the deep distress which Friedel's confession caused me. For the first time, the mention of anti-Semitism touched me with formidable effect. Up to then, talk about it had been an impersonal phenomenon, something that existed but did not really concern me. Being a Christian, and a member of the Lutheran church and completely absorbed in my small world, I had not paid much attention to Hitler's statements about Jews. Friedel's comment that this was only a minor matter shows that even he did not realize the full meaning of what he had put into words. I found myself faced with a problem about which I knew nothing, an onslaught to my pride and my innermost feelings.

I never knew what caused Friedel to consider his uncertainty toward our relationship as a feeling of anti-Semitism. Perhaps his exposure at the university to the daily drumbeat of Nazi propaganda was beginning to have an effect. Perhaps his realization of Germany's inescapable drift toward the abyss was at the root of his thoughts.

Unfortunately, this theme remained my most vulnerable point. It caused me to feel attacked and unsure when nobody, especially Friedel, meant to hurt me. I developed a sensitivity that I learned to cover up by exerting power over others in order to reconfirm myself. At the time, I had, obviously, no broad view of the situation or its effect on my life or character.

Berlin, March 9, 1931

Dear Friedel,

It came out of a clear, blue sky; I felt as if my faculties would leave me. I concentrated on your letter and struggled with it every minute of the day. I don't think you realize the implications and the significance of what you wrote. First, let me tell you, there is no feeling of reproach in me. I understand you and I don't doubt a minute that you felt for me what you said. I completely trust your honesty towards yourself and towards me.

But the moment you begin to question your feelings, you do not love me unconditionally. That is exactly what unconditional love is: acceptance of the other person as she or he is, with all the problems involved. Be courageous and admit it to yourself. I feel more for you than a liking, and less than love. Just because of that fact I am not prepared to deal with your peculiarities as yet. I beg you to imagine my situation . . . a week ago you were certain of your love, now you are not. What am I to believe? Even if I am inexperienced, I am sure that true love does not know this sort of crisis.

You analyze the most beautiful human emotions and with that, you kill them. I believe, as you do, in clarification of our innermost feelings; but we are powerless and cannot direct feelings by thinking about them. They are part of us. Whether love is part of feeling or of mind or perhaps of both, who can tell? If a person loves, both mind and feeling melt into one. That is the mystery, and the beauty.

Two things in your letter hurt me deeply. I am telling you this although I don't want you to regret your honesty.

"Christians have an inborn antipathy for Jews." It could be true, but in our case, it would read as follows: "Friedel has an inborn antipathy for Liesel." This sentence hurt. The other thing was that you, unintentionally, made me jealous, a feeling neither noble nor pleasant. It is hard to hear that Illy, in a moment of so-called crisis, gained influence over you. Anyway I wonder how she heard in Munich that which takes place in Berlin. I do not care what people say and I find her tactless to bring it up when you are down-hearted. I know I should not talk negatively about Illy, especially if she tried to help you.

I want to tell you that your letter sobered me and since you are also talking about a sobering mind, it is surely right to make clear statements. When I read your letter I felt we would lose each other: you always talked about a friendship between us as a dissatisfying relationship. Therefore I don't see how we will continue now. Your love would perhaps have won me. But my entire being revolts against forced attempts to return to your former feelings. Have the courage to admit that this is not the right way. Believe me, it is with a heavy heart that I write this.

In both our interests let us recognize fate, which will have it differently, and that we have to submit to it. Your doubts will torture you. Be calm and reasonable. Be just to yourself and others. We have to carry the same burden now and we will be able to do it because we are young and life is ahead of us. If we should see each other on Whitsuntide let us join hands as two people who understand each other, who shared serious and beautiful hours, who are tied by a spiritual union or call it what you want.

This is my answer on which I reflected a long time. I conquered all feeling to find the best solution for us both. Wait with your answer and try not to torture me with it. Mostly I wonder how we can stay in contact without wearing each other out. I let you be the guide; find a way which will neither separate nor bind us, if there is such a possibility. This I ask you with all my heart.

Yours, Liesel

How many poets have dramatized the age-old pangs of love, and how many composers have set into passionate music those emotions—the pains and joys of our souls, the anguish and bliss of hell and heaven? But few are the hours during which we listen with our hearts to that music, so that we really identify with it, and it becomes truly ours. Only a personal experience enables us to understand more fully, and, suddenly, we might realize that these emotions are a common link between us, our fellow beings, contemporaries as well as predecessors. Although we like to imagine—as they, no doubt, did—that we are unique in experiencing these upheavals, we might as well acknowledge that our feelings are not original, at least not where love is concerned.

Friedel wrote to me, "The belief in our past and the belief in our future is much more important than the momentary confusion. I greet you as your fundamentally unshaken Friedel. I know now more clearly than ever that I love you, and these terrible days of struggle and pain have matured me. It was my trust in your understanding that induced me to reveal my momentary confusion, this unbelievably great feeling of trust I have in you, which tells me that these horrible incidents like the first of October and this Easter are only phases which will evolve someday into a complete union.

"But I am shocked that I could do this to you; I won't beg for forgiveness because you should not forgive this brutality. All I beg of you is understanding and patience for my unhappy tendency to doubt. My willpower lost a battle. Here, I can use my will and not, as I erroneously wrote, in the realm of loving you. I pray that you will have the greatness to understand me, and I trust you will. I feel that these sufferings will be compensated by joys of equal measure."

In this tone Friedel covered many pages, analyzing his thoughts. He tried desperately to reassure me, but he refrained from coming to Berlin. Had he taken me in his arms and kissed our sorrows away, it would undoubtedly have succeeded. Instead, he elaborated on his theory of anti-Semitism. As in all groups of human society, there were, he thought, "wicked" types amongst Jews, who were singled out and their objectionable deeds or character traits were then associated with the entire "race," thus causing an atmosphere of a general antipathy. He was obviously aware of the growing hostility toward Jews in Germany, but insisted that he would come to terms with the problem of loving a girl who was now considered to be Jewish.

There are many examples of racial and religious persecution throughout history, but they seemed to us in the distant past. Now history had caught up with the present. There were thousands in Germany who were Christians, who had never known, or, as in my case, had never cared about their grandparents' religion. But now, as the idea of Jewishness as an immutable racial identity rather than a religious faith gained acceptance, ancestry would become a vital issue in the lives of countless others as well as in mine.

Meanwhile, Rita returned from New York where she and her father had gone to confront Erich and Ty, and I was determined to renew our interrupted friendship. I thought I could help her forget Erich, but I overlooked the fact that deep love becomes part of us and remains forever.

Erich, still in America, had gotten a free railroad ticket—probably through Papi's good connections with the Pennsylvania Railroad—and he traveled happily through the United States, visiting friends in California whom we had met at the Palace Hotel in Gstaad. He, apparently, had no trouble forgetting Rita.

I took automobile driving lessons and went horseback riding in the *Tiergarten*, enjoying my freedom after having finished my kindergarten teacher examination. My parents had our house in the *Jagowstrasse* redecorated with new furniture. I slowly returned to my normal self and looked forward eagerly to a visit by the Stephans and their children.

Wrapped up in these everyday events, we seemed to give only secondary importance to events that should have flashed a warning light, such as a newspaper article that appeared in the anti-Semitic tabloid *Fridericus*. It was an attack against my father over his company's exclusive shipping contract with the German State Railroad. It was the first sign of a rising snake, but it seems that nobody in our house paid much attention to it. I didn't even read the article. Friedel did and suggested suing the paper. But my father, being a busy man and uninterested in politics, dismissed the article as gossip. He did not want to pursue it, and Friedel let the matter drop. It is not likely he would have been successful anyway. Within a few months my father was "persuaded" to sell Schenker, Berlin, and make a contract with the management of the German State Railroad. On January 29, 1931, after endless and complicated conferences with high officials, the sales agreement was concluded. My father would continue as president and keep some of his shares in Schenker & Company, but he no longer would control the company he had built. One day he came home early, sat down at the long table in the library, and asked me to turn the pages as he signed his name on each of 4,000 typewritten sheets.

Soon a gentleman from the German State Railroad, Herr Katter, occupied a desk in my father's office. My father wasn't suspicious or resentful of this person, although Herr Katter was actually supervising every move he made. The sale of Schenker made headlines in the newspapers that attracted unwanted publicity. Nazi propaganda continued to hammer on the theme that Jews in high positions of German commerce were responsible for the miseries of Germany's unemployed workers. Articles appeared about Jews who knew too well how to take leading positions, hinting that their success was the result of plotting, rather than talent and hard work. By thus moving into the limelight, Marcel Holzer created his own downfall.

After the sale of Schenker to the State Railroad in 1931, the main office was transferred from Vienna to Berlin. Now, my father was a state employee at the level of a minister, but he still went every day to the office as he always had. That same year Emil Karpeles, the founder of Schenker whose valuable leadership had guided the firm through difficult times, died.

Erich, occupied with his American travels, apparently was not concerned or had not heard that the Nazis had won 6,500,000 votes in the 1930 *Reichstag* elections. Was it perhaps not reported in the American press? Did no one there believe that Hitler would carry out the program he had openly published in *Mein Kampf?* Erich sent home only glowing reports about the Grand Canyon and the festivities in Ty's parents' home in New Jersey. When he returned, Berlin had become a parade ground for marching SA troops and the Hitler Youth, singing their rousing national songs and venomous anti-Semitic chants. A wave of enthusiasm bordering on hysteria had gripped the country.

The Nazis' activities were not all marching and flag waving: more subtle things were at work. The less pleasant things were at first done undercover. In conversations with a friend or a stranger, one could easily fail to observe the small Nazi party badge engraved with the swastika hidden in the folds of coat lapels. The badge was worn more openly at times, for instance, when the wearer wanted to gain advantage over a partner in business in an adversary situation. The presence of that little lapel pin was intimidating and always created a silent uneasiness in one who might have been a friend just a short time back.

After my mother's birthday in May I went to visit Rita and her parents in Possenhofen on the *Starnbergersee.* I was delighted to learn that Friedel would be visiting his mother in Feldafing. I took the train from Berlin to Munich, where I met Friedel for the twenty-minute train trip to the lake. When our eyes met as he placed roses in my arms, I recognized the "old" Friedel once again and regained my complete trust in him. He succeeded in making me wonder why I had ever doubted his love. I realized the insignificance of the episode surrounding his Paris letter; it became so minimal we did not discuss it again although the "ticklish question" remained.

Friedel and I had a way of making our short visits into real feasts, and this one was no exception. The old German proverb: "Love makes one blind" was most appropriate in our case. We happily ignored the fact that the world around us was not of our opinion concerning differences in "race." All too soon, Friedel returned to Munich.

The morning after Friedel left, still filled with thoughts of him and determined to understand him more fully, I went to the Pschorr villa in

Feldafing. Rita and I rowed a small boat along the lake the short distance from Possenhofen to Feldafing. The boat glided slowly in the quiet water near the shore. The silence was interrupted only by the regular beat of the oars and the gentle sound of rippling water as Rita swung the oars closely over the dark blue surface of the lake. Our thoughts were too personal to be shared. I was dreaming and recalling every precious moment of the previous few days with Friedel. I felt as if the boat was carrying me quietly to another shore where I would finally be ready to commit myself wholly to him.

In spite of Rita's silence, I knew that Erich was the subject of her thoughts. She had buried her sorrow so deeply that no one, not even I, was aware of the extent of her pain, the pain of losing Erich to her cousin Ty. She had tried to pull herself together, but when we were alone at night she had broken down. I spoke to her mother about Rita's condition, but her cold answer was that it was up to Rita to understand that Erich hadn't meant what Rita had hoped. I felt obliged to tell her that love was not that easy to reason with. Nobody, I thought, could judge the depth of another's experience. Everyone has a different capacity of pain and joy, and Rita's pain was deep and, as it turned out, unending.

Rita planned to go to Berlin the following week to confront Erich in the vain hope of regaining his love. Valiantly, she carried her burden, silently and without bitterness, not wanting to hurt anybody. I worried about her forthcoming encounter because there was no longer any real rapport between them and the situation could only get worse. Although Erich had wronged her in carrying on and flirting with her, it was not his fault that he couldn't return her love.

Rita and I guided the rowboat into the small boathouse owned by the Pschorr family, then walked up the road leading to the villa. Feldafing was much like the other settlements along the west shore of the *Starnbergersee*. Like Possenhofen and Tutzing, Feldafing had been a fishing village for centuries before it became a summer enclave for the wealthy Munich bourgeoisie. The village even had a hotel and a golf course for the enjoyment of residents and visitors. In the harsh Bavarian winters, the villas were closed up, and Feldafing returned to the simple existence it had known since before the turn of the century.

From the old Victorian villas one gazed across the lake, through pine forests, on to the shimmering Bavarian Alps in the distance. As we passed the huge houses, their beautifully kept gardens, I imagined past times which were still manifest in Feldafing's streets. Here the grandparents Pschorr had resided summer after summer, when the four sons, including Friedel's father, were young boys. Here the next generation—Carlotta, Herbert, and Friedel—had spent their childhood summers.

I could sense the long history of the Pschorr family in this village, but I had no idea what it would mean for me to be a part of such a long-established family tradition and in what measure this would complicate Friedel's life and his relationship to his family. My curiosity and wish to understand Friedel's background led me to explore what was hidden behind the Victorian walls of the Pschorr villa. I had already an inkling of certain traits in the family tradition, which, I felt, had formed Friedel's views and attitudes and led to subtle differences between us. Although social rules were not openly discussed, they influenced people's behavior and, thereby, had meaning to someone who, like me, was about to become closely connected with a family much removed from mine.

The Pschorr villa is in the *Bahnhofstrasse* 36, surrounded by a lovely garden. From the third floor, one could see the roofs of other villas nearby and the lake in the background. The lawn, surrounded by shrubs and bushes, had a gravel path that led to the vegetable garden and tennis court. The lower end of the garden bordered on the grounds of the Hotel Elisabeth, an old, stone structure with about twenty guest rooms.

Friedel's mother and aunts had gone to Munich for the day, and the house was empty except for Frau Ringenberg who, with her husband, had served with devotion two generations of the Pschorr family. She greeted Rita and me warmly and showed us around. What a strange feeling to be in those old rooms without the family. The house had a special charm, with its old furniture and family photos everywhere. I studied the photos carefully, and Frau Ringenberg explained each of them with much feeling. In photographs, I saw girls from a former generation playing in the garden in their black, wool stockings and long, lacy dresses, with aprons and their hair flying, and boys in short, leather pants and embroidered suspenders. Everywhere, I saw little Friedel with his curls and the dreamy look in his blue eyes. "Here," Frau Ringenberg said, "he wore his little frock," and she told me about him when he was a little boy. I saw the great resemblance Friedel had to his father. I could feel the life of the house, and, for the first time, I tried to comprehend what it meant to be a member of such an old family, one that had built its traditions over so many generations.

I entered the "Palais Grieving," the green room in the center of the third floor where Carlotta and her husband, Hermann Grieving, used to stay. Next to it was the room with the yellow beds where Herbert and Friedel had slept as children. I felt very close to Friedel then.

Friedel had once given me a photograph of the *Starnbergersee*, expressing the hope that I would come to love it, but I had never before seen the lake as I did now. I had not seen Friedel in a white suit in the sailboat bathed in sunlight, and I had not looked over the blue water with Friedel at my side or sat alone with him in the tranquility of the silent boathouse. Now I could look at the picture, and visualize the lake in its changing moods, and share, in a small way, Friedel's *Heimat*—his heritage, his Bavarian roots.

CHAPTER TWELVE

THE FAMILY PSCHORR

During my stay on the *Starnbergersee* I learned much about the Pschorr family. I discovered that in its long history, the family does not have another of its members who, like Friedel, stepped courageously away from the path his forefathers had prepared.

Friedel's great-great-grandfather, Johannes Pschorr, was born December 27, 1731, in the farming region of Bavaria, near Munich. The Pschorr family chronicles trace his antecedents back several generations in the same area. Johannes married Theresia Haberl and settled in the village of Kleinhadern, then consisting of eleven houses (now it is a district in Munich). They lived in the *Spitzweghof,* a prosperous farm, and raised their family there. Their son Joseph, born in 1770, was the only boy of eight children to survive into adulthood. Had he become a farmer, he would have inherited the *Spitzweghof.*

But Joseph had other plans. When he was fifteen years old, he persuaded his disappointed parents to let him become an apprentice in a Munich brewery. It was, and perhaps still is, a great sacrifice for farmers to let their only son and heir learn another trade and, thus, loose a successor. But they were compensated by a strange event that had occurred on a warm summer night in 1773. They had found in their stable an abandoned baby boy. The Pschorrs took this boy in, recorded him in the church register as a "vagabond person's" baby, and adopted him. They named him Johannes Glueck, "Lucky John," and raised him along with their own son. Thus when Joseph left to serve his apprenticeship in a brewery, Johannes Glueck, then a child of twelve years, became the heir of the Pschorr farm. Upon the death of Johannes Pschorr, Johannes Glueck did inherit the farm, which pleased Joseph Pschorr, by then already a brewer.

At the time of Joseph Pschorr's apprenticeship, in1785, Munich was the residence of the Kurfürst—one of the elector—princes entrusted with choosing the Holy Roman Emperor-and had about 35000 inhabitants. Munich was one corner of the "central-European golden triangle" of beer production. The region encompassed Bavaria and the part of the Austro-Hungarian Empire which included Vienna and Pilsen. (The latter is now in Czechoslovakia.) In Munich all trade and commerce was controlled by centuries—old trade guilds. Under the medieval trade system there could be but fifty-two brewing houses in the city, each under strict supervision, and their ownership rights could not be transferred. To be a guildmaster one had to own one of the fifty-two breweries, and in order to own a brewery one had to inherit it or marry the daughter of a brewer.

Joseph Pschorr did the latter in 1793, when he was twenty-three years old. He married Therese Hacker, whose father owned the "Hacker Brewery", which had been in existence since 1417. Even though he was now by marriage a member of the brewery on the Sendlingertor Strasse from the Hacker family he borrowed the money from his sisters' doweries. Ever after he displayed the same kind of self-confidence and courage. To meet his responsibilities and repay his debts to his sisters he had to be resourceful and work hard for it was a time of economic hardship in Bavaria.

By 1806 the Hacker Brewery, owned by Joseph Pschorr was considered the leading Brewery in Munich. Economic conditions had improved in Bavaria due to fundamental changes of medieval regulations which by the early nineteen hundreds century had become burdensome.

Elimination of restrictive trade laws allowed Munich's industrial economy to surpass the historical commercial centers of Nuremberg and Augsburg, Now breweries could produce and sell beer according to free-market demand. Brewers became masters of their enterprises and beer production increased dramatically. To meet the greater production requirements carried a prize. Traditional production methods, brewery equipment and organization had to be modernized. Few brewers were prepared to set a new system into motion. Joseph Pschorr was one of them. It took courage and knowledge to break away from the old principles which the guild had dictated for so many years. While most brewers continued to work in the usual fashion, and live as comfortably as before, Joseph Pschorr took it upon himself to guide his willing colleagues to ways of reforming and modernizing the entire brewing industry. This earned him a lasting place in the history of German beer making.

Joseph Pschorr had created a solid basis for continuing success, and, in time, his output tripled. Never resting Joseph envisioned the need for storage of the precious beer. Far outside of Munich's gates he built for ten long years an underground storage cellar of unprecedented dimensions.

He had envisioned that this would be his final achievement, but in 1820, when an opportunity came along, he could not resist acquiring the "*Bauerhansl Bräu*" a small, mismanaged brewery dating from the 15th century. With it Pschorr bought four adjoining pieces of land, tore down all the old buildings, and erected a new brewery called the *Brauerei zum Pschorr*. This was actually the foundation of the Pschorr Brewery. By now, Joseph Pschorr was sixty-five years old, and he retired from his long and successful work. His son Matthias Pschorr took over the Hacker Brewery and Joseph's second son, Georg the Pschorr Brewery. The storage cellars were shared by both breweries, thus, the affiliation between two of Munich's most important breweries that had begun when Joseph married Maria Theresa Hacker, continued.

In 1864, Georg Pschorr, Friedel's grandfather, gave the brewery to his son Georg, Jr., who also became a leader in the beer industry. He introduced cooled railway cars for shipping beer and bottled beer in a new, modern brewery erected on the site of the summer cellar in the *Bayerstrasse* in 1877. Georg Pschorr, Jr. also created a worldwide network of branch breweries and agencies as far away as Manila, Hong Kong, Cairo, and Mexico City. In Germany, all the major cities had a "Pschorr House", in which pubs and restaurants were managed by lease.

In 1861, Georg Pschorr had married Johanna Fischer-Dick, who came from an artistic family in Frankfurt on the Main. She found in Georg Pschorr a partner equally interested in the arts. Soon their home in Munich, the Villa Saletti, became a well-known meeting place for musicians and painters, who often mingled with the other guests—merchants and civil servants, members of the royal opera and soloists at court.

Amongst the regular guests was the gifted musician Franz Strauss, who soon fell in love with Georg and Johanna's daughter Josepha (Friedel's aunt), who was sixteen years younger than he. Franz Strauss was a thirty-six-year-old widower, whose wife had died of cholera two years after the death of their only child. He had been born out of wedlock to an usher of the court and the daughter of a tower guard. Franz's father, who never married his son's mother, later married another woman and produced seven more children. He died without providing for his illegitimate son.

Franz was raised by his grandparents in a home filled with music. His two cousins became musicians at the royal court in Munich. Franz learned to play the violin by the time he was five years old and soon after that the clarinet and the guitar. When he was seven he played for village dance festivals, and, by the time he was nine years old, he began teaching others to play wind instruments; at twelve, he helped out at the opera by singing small parts. On many occasions, Franz had to play in his uncle's band, which meant long marches to neighbouring towns and hard benches to sleep on.

Franz Strauss courted Josepha Pschorr for seven years before he finally asked respectfully for her hand. After their marriage, they moved into a small apartment in the back of the Pschorr Brewery. On the eleventh of June, 1864, their first son was born, whom they named Richard. Richard Strauss was christened Catholic the same day. The first sounds the baby heard were surely those of Mozart's "Don Giovanni" since the father used to practice at home and that was the opera performed the next day.

Young Richard Strauss did not have an easy time with his father, who was dominating and easily angered by Josepha, his softhearted, patient, and docile wife. Richard was given piano lessons when he was just four years old, but before he could read notes, he began to compose music. His very first composition was the "Schneider Polka." His father wrote the music for instruments and had it performed by the Harbni Orchestra during a private musical evening.

He took Richard often to the *Marienplatz* to listen to the band, and, on the way home, the boy was able to recall every note. From his great-grandmother Pschorr's window, Richard watched the royal guard's band and memorized their melodies as well. He played with his cousins, the Pschorr boys, and composed his first march for them.

Richard Strauss carried his music within himself, and his compositions were like an arch which spans his lifetime. "Opus 10," composed in his twentieth year, harmonizes with his "Four Last Songs," which he wrote just before his death at age eighty-five. Sixty-four years separate these masterfully achieved creations, which express love, tenderness, tranquility, and, finally preparedness for eternal rest.

In 1889, a serious case of bronchitis caused the twenty-five-year-old Strauss to seek rest and recovery in the Pschorr villa in Feldafing on the *Starnbergersee* under Uncle Georg's and Aunt Johanna's care. His godfather, Uncle Georg, then sent Richard on a prolonged vacation to Italy, Greece, and Egypt. He had been in Italy twice before; the first time he composed the symphonic fantasy, "*Aus Italien*". On his next trip he finished *Don Juan*. This time, in 1892, he completed *Guntram*, which proved to be a turning point in his musical creativity. He dedicated his opera, "*Der Rosencavalier*, to his "dear relatives, the family Pschorr in Munich."

Richard Strauss met his future wife, Pauline de Ahna, during a lengthy visit to the Pschorr villa in Feldafing. Her father, General de Ahna, resided with his family in a house nearby. Pauline was a singer and took lessons from Richard's friend who didn't consider her talented and didn't see much point in wasting his time with this pupil.

He told Richard, "Since you live in Feldafing and are not working, I will let you try your luck with "Fräulein Pauline.""

Richard soon had a different interest in the young lady and he believed she had talent waiting to be discovered. He made up his mind to make her an opera singer. When he was called to Weimar as a conductor, Pauline followed him and became the star of the production and later Richard's wife.

When I visited Feldafing with Friedel in 1931, thirty-seven years after Richard Strauss had met his bride-to-be there, the village, and the Pschorr villa, had changed very little. I lost my heart in Feldafing. I liked the old-fashioned way of life. Women got up in the morning and hurried to the milkman with their metal cans to have them filled with foaming, fresh, unpasteurized milk, which was then boiled on the coal stove. I still see Frau Ringenberg, an apron tied over her simple dress as she moved about her small kitchen, servile as all women of her class and time. When I visited the Pschorr villa with Rita that day, I could not foresee that some day I would live there with my children.

Friedel felt that I understood him better because I had visited his family's home. He was pleased that I tried to understand tradition and how it influenced his life. But actually we were unaware of the connection between his tradition and the new term of "race" Hitler had created. Perhaps we believed that differences don't derive from racial or inborn characteristics, but rather from upbringing and traditional customs. In any case, we worked on the theme valiantly. We were convinced that we would come to terms with it, and we regarded the question of our different backgrounds as defined by National Socialism rather unemotionally. As our love unfolded, we were able to disregard the problem as far as our relationship was concerned.

I didn't feel for one instant that the vile words Nazis used against Jews concerned me. I was not anything they described; I remained unconcerned with their speeches, songs, and posters, which one encountered everywhere by 1931. But it beame a different matter when the question arose in connection with our relationship and was discussed with others. Later, when Friedel stood up for his decision to marry me and defended his love, my pride and self-consciousness came into play. As most people do at one time or another in their lives, I encountered the pain of being excluded.

My parents were not pleased by the Pschorr family's concern over my Jewish background, and, most probably, their pride was also hurt. They remembered when Professor Robert Pschorr and Tilla loved to come to our parties and how welcome Friedel had always been in our house.

Tradition and anti-Semitism, I discovered, have a common denominator: in both, hearsay, custom, and myth play a vital role. Tradition and custom, passed on from generation to generation are often based on superstition. People, not unlike sheep at times, often follow blindly the tracks of their forefathers. It takes a strong character and some intelligence to break through that rigid barrier of pattern.

The disciples of tradition and those of anti-Semitism found support and encouragement for their attitudes and convictions. Others, driven by fear, took refuge in these proclaimed "virtues." Therein lies, in my opinion, the answer to the question still asked after all these years. How did it happen? How was it that Hitler could seduce basically decent Germans even in the early years of his rise to power? It is not very encouraging to see that threats and fear direct us in a way which we do not understand ourselves. In addition, the Nazis understood the value of flattering people accustomed to seeing themselves as underdogs. Hitler lifted them to rank and honor which, under normal circumstances, they would never have attained. It was as if the social structure was turned on a wheel that caused the formerly upper society and intelligentsia to rotate to the bottom while the unsophisticated masses rose and became the ruling class.

Friedel and I had to come to an understanding about our personal situation. I wrote to him:

> Today I am able to judge the problem objectively, and agree with you that it will certainly never stand between us. But you should know that the underlying theme has played a certain role in my family, unnoticed and silently perhaps. After all, even though Erich and I were christened and raised as Lutherans, I cannot deny that my parents are from a Jewish background and that many of their friends are Jewish.
>
> When I first became conscious of your family tradition and background I understood that a certain anti-Semitism was a part of it. But you were able to detach yourself, to recognize that, more often than not, prejudice influences tradition and leads to antipathy. You have, thanks to your personal strength, sorted out that which is valuable and that which is not. As you accept me as a person, detached from Jewish or Christian background, so I accept you not as a member of an "old family," but as a person.

I kept this letter for several days to review its contents then decided that my words were well chosen and sent it off.

In that summer of 1931, Friedel joined his family for the marriage of his cousin Hildegard, daughter of Georg Pschorr, to Heinz Guender. His brother Herbert was there as were his uncles, and Friedel knew the "ticklish question" would come up in their conversations. As Friedel had anticipated, Herbert, who had joined a pro-Nazi group, urged him once again to end his relationship with me, and, once again, Friedel resisted. It remains an unresolved question if Herbert had joined the group out of political conviction or just to protect himself and his family against a perceived danger. There were many groups and organizations that sprang up in Germany that were joined by people who wanted to be inactive members. We called such a person a *Mitlaeufer*, or "follower." These are the people who later claimed innocence and pretended not to have had anything to do with the party. They wanted to be treated and judged differently than other party members when the tide turned, although it might have been this "minority" who gave Hitler the votes he needed.

When Friedel and I met following his family gathering and discussed the situation once more, we became convinced our personal harmony was more important than Hitler's "racial" differences. We dreamed, as all lovers do, that we were on a lonely island with no interference, and thus, the "ticklish question" lost significance. My parents did worry about us when I finally confessed my love for Friedel. But neither they nor we saw that it was not only I who was embarking on a dangerous road, but Friedel as well.

Meanwhile Friedel's routine at the university was interrupted by an eventful evening: Friedel attended a meeting at which the speaker was Adolf Hitler. By this time, the leader of the National Socialist Workers Party was a major force in German political life. The Nazi party's gains of the previous year and, in particular, their spectacular gains in the November 1930 *Reichstag* election drew thousands to hear Hitler speak, including many who had never before taken him seriously. On this occasion, he talked for two hours without interruption and without a manuscript or notes in the over crowded hall. Friedel wrote, "As an orator, he is a fascinating figure, and I admit that while listening to him I almost was a national socialist. This man spoke fanatically, using the power of a genius's dialectic, rhetoric, and the art of acting to fascinate. The public was aroused to a storm in their enthusiasm. A terrible hatred against Jews was felt from time to time, as always, partly justified and partly dictated by blind fanaticism. It is sad that he cannot eliminate this. On the whole it was an interesting experience."

Later, Friedel commented often on this one and only time that he saw Hitler. It was a frightening experience for him because he realized the hypnotic power with which Hitler captivated the masses, convincing them that he was their saviour. If a person like Friedel, intelligent, educated, and opposed to the Nazi's program, could not quite escape Hitler's persuasive speech, how should a simpler listener not fall under his spell?

That is the time when I began to have a latent anxiety in my heart, an indistinct feeling of impending danger, a sense of foreboding for Germany and for us. At that time, of course, we didn't know how, and by what methods, this hatred was going to be put into action or whether or not it would enter into our private life. Yet fear was born: it has never left me and is easily aroused, even now.

Germany was now in a state of restless upheaval. For the first time, I began to read the newspapers and worry about the economic problems which affected the country. The depression, which had begun in the United States with the stock market collapse of 1929, had now reached Germany. The worldwide economy was on the brink of collapse. Several important Berlin banks had failed, and unemployment and dissatisfaction with the government was spreading. Schenker suffered financially, although my father remained as calm as ever. One didn't notice any outward sign of his financial losses or the burden of his responsibilities. He worked late every night and appeared in the morning fresh, well-groomed as always. His calm made me forget my worries when I was around him.

But other changes in Germany did not have a calming effect. Hitler's private army of "stormtroopers", the SA, who paraded through Berlin's streets in their brown uniforms, singing and waving their swastika-emblazoned flags, exuded optimism and determination based on a new Germany, a vision of the future promised by Hitler. For those who disagreed with the "new order" that was coming, there were gathering clouds that cast long shadows. Friedel wrote on July 17, 1931:

> While having lunch today I read the newspaper and could not swallow one single bite. Anybody who understands German politics has to be shattered about the events in this country and ought to ask himself whether a catastrophe can be avoided. This is another reason why I am coming to Berlin as soon as possible; a few of your father's words will tell me more than a pile of newspapers.
>
> The times are sad. Will your father be able to travel in August? But even if everything crashes and the entire nation is suspended over an abyss, the undisputed understanding between two small

human beings throws its light on us. So, if the trains are still running in two days and nothing else happens, I will arrive at the Anhalter Bahnhof Friday evening at ten o'clock.

Three days of pure bliss followed, three days of complete happiness before Friedel had to return to Munich. I let Friedel leave, although I was ready to become his. He was scarcely out the door when I wrote to him.

July 21, 1931

Beloved,

How can I tell you what I feel? How can I describe the awful feeling of having to leave you again. This time is worse than all preceding ones. I keep telling myself that it was only yesterday—but one day is an eternity. Never before did I feel that lost. Every time together is more beautiful and different from the time before.

I was happy on Pentecost, but yesterday, sitting next to you in the Packard, I knew the days on the Starnbergersee were not the happiest ones we will experience. I want to enjoy with an open heart and mind the tide of my feelings—but I don't want to let you go, ever. I don't want to be brave either. I rather want you to dry my tears. When I met you a year ago, I was unaware of what you would mean to me. Can you remember what life was like before we knew each other?

The next day, Friedel's response arrived:

"I wondered yesterday if a twenty-four-year-old person can talk about a high point in his life. I think the last three days were just that. There might come a time when even these are overshadowed, but in relation to my past life these days definitely were the high point. Nothing clouded the harmony from the first to the last moment. You were able to make the world appear in a different light. When you enter the room I am electrified. I cannot think of anything that could come between us now. I don't know when we will reach the summit, our goal. It might be happy days such as we just spent, it might be different ones; perhaps we will reach the goal only when one of us dies—but when we reach it, we will reach it together."

Friedel also wrote that he had met with my father during his visit, hoping to raise the question of our determination to marry.

> "It was all over within two minutes. I said I hoped he was not angry that I had not found the opening words; he answered that he, too, could have started the conversation. Thus we parted, both hoping that the next time the ice would be broken. I am almost looking forward to it; nevertheless, the first word will be rather difficult. I have great respect for him, especially when he sits by himself in his armchair, powerful and silent.
>
> "After a good night's sleep I wrote to Herbert and told him about my true feelings for you and your parents. I don't see why I should keep them secret, they guess them anyway. From now on I will confess to everyone who asks me. I will tell them that I will stand by you even if I have to give up my own family. Your mother will be glad to hear it; she is afraid that you will be just tolerated in my family. Oh, if only my father were alive; he would not be as narrow-minded as the others. I imagine he would have looked right into my heart and would have been happy for me that I love you."

Friedel went to Feldafing to inform his mother of our intention to marry. His mother's mental state demanded that her sisters Stefanie and Carry, and everyone in the house, act as if she were normal. She felt persecuted and thought she was secretly being watched and, even, photographed. The slightest move or word could result in a crying spell that would last for hours, but it was impossible to know exactly what to avoid. On the other hand, she was lucid enough to listen to Herbert's comments. The therapist and Stefanie, who took care of her, didn't want Friedel to talk to her about his marriage plans. Herbert, however, frightened his mother by telling her that my presence would endanger the entire family.

Understandably, a mentally disturbed person cannot cope with such illusions. Her whining disagreements with Carry and Stefanie and their mother could have troubled even a stronger person than Friedel. Naively, I asked Friedel to make peace with his brother, but they were worlds apart and had been even before I emerged on the scene. For one thing, Herbert did not fulfill his responsibilities towards his mother and threw the financial and emotional burden for her care into Friedel's lap.

In spite of his agony, Friedel stayed in Feldafing and coped with the problems. His life was dictated by a strong sense of duty, obligation, and compassion. The old gardener, Ringenberg, who had always sided with Friedel, cheered him up by admiring my photograph and telling him I looked like an angel. Friedel tried to stay calm and patient during his stay, and those times when the situation became impossible, he would walk to Possenhofen to visit with Rita and play bridge with her and her parents. He told me that Rita looked beautiful, that she seemed in a good mood, and that Erich's picture was no longer in her room. It troubled me that she no longer wrote to me and that the gulf between us was growing steadily wider. I knew I had lost a friend through no fault of mine.

During this time, a great unrest seized me. Apparently, I was overwhelmed by the alluring aspect of romantic love but also afraid of the problems which awaited me, Friedel's sensitive nature, his changing moods, his often critical attitude—incomprehensible to me—and finally the political situation. Although we assured each other repeatedly that these problems could in no way touch our personal lives, we had a veiled fear and an apprehension of the future. And then there was the constant, if seldom mentioned, threat that I was the mainstay of life for Friedel. I knew that, even if I had wanted, retreat was quite impossible.

CHAPTER THIRTEEN

ANTICIPATION

On the sixteenth of September, 1931, at six o'clock, the train brought Friedel into Berlin's *Anhalter Bahnhof.* He had come to celebrate my twentieth birthday. Our house was crowded with guests for the occasion: Charlie Weilguni, one of my brother's good friends; Gertrud and Georg Stephan, my mother's cousin from England, and others. The setting was not the deserted island we would have preferred, but my heart was full to overflowing. In a quiet moment, I pulled Friedel into my father's study, a small upstairs room with a big desk and a built-in sofa, on which we had sat many times. Here, I finally confessed my unreserved love and my desire to marry him. So the day we had awaited such a long time had finally come. We announced our decision to my parents, who were delighted. The date for our "official" engagement became a matter of endless back and forth discussions. It was finally set for the following Easter, March 23, 1932, a day on which Erich planned also to celebrate his engagement to Ty.

Our time together was too brief, the house too lively, to linger over our happiness. It was so much easier to express our thoughts and feelings in letters, and we were probably too embarrassed to say much anyway. Only our letters reflect what went on in our hearts. A week later I wrote to him:

> Beloved,
>
> The house is quiet and empty without you. Lying in the dark, I look into your eyes. I wish I could do that for a thousand years. This will be the first letter which I can rightfully sign "yours, Liesel." Because only now I really belong to you. I feel a great happiness. I am a thinking, feeling, self-contained person who belongs wholly to another; a human being, complete but incomplete without the other; alone, so senselessly alone without you. Every moment is just a wait for your return.

> Around my neck is the chain with your initials. On my wrist is the bracelet you gave me. But the best is invisible, that is the trace of your kisses. Sleep well and calmly as if I were with you and listen to what I say as often as you want to hear it: I love you eternally.

Thus, we continued as before, exchanging letters, promises, and hope. It is difficult for me now to believe, but we accepted without question the fact that marriage was at least two years away at best. Two years—it seemed an eternity—but at least, we could anticipate it. The reason for this postponement was that Friedel had to finish his studies and my father demanded that he train for an executive position at Schenker & Company. Friedel would not have agreed to accept a salary adequate for our needs without offering equivalent services. He was always haunted by the thought that he would be treated as the boss's son-in-law and not as an ordinary employee. It didn't occur to either my parents or us that there was another way to solve the situation, namely, to let us marry while Friedel was in training.

In any case, Friedel insisted that when we were married we would live on his money. I assured him over and over again that I didn't need the luxuries I was used to in the *Jagowstrasse*, that I was looking forward to a small apartment where I would be my own mistress and do my own housework. But Friedel did not feel quite comfortable taking me away from the life of privilege and luxury I had known. I understood that it disturbed him; it was a matter of pride with him as well.

Some time before these events my father had bought a piece of property not far from the *Jagowstrasse*. He had toyed with the idea of building a small house for me and my future husband on "Elisabeth Ruh," as he called it. I rejected the offer, thinking that this was an unnecessary luxury. Friedel said if we applied my thinking literally, we would have to share all we had with all poor people. I thought of my father's charitable attitude towards all his friends, even distant acquaintances, for whom he had financed a business or regularly sent money if needed, and I was not convinced.

I went to Hamburg to visit my grandmother and tell her my happy news. She remained my ideal, my admired example. I found that she, like many older people who have lost their life's companion, was lonely in spite of many children, grandchildren, nephews, and nieces. Together we went to Opi's grave in Ohlsdorf; my grandmother occupied herself with the flowers and plants surrounding his grave to hide her emotion.

While in Hamburg, I attended a benefit concert for the *Winterhilfe*. This event was organized by party members in order to add funds to the traditional collection on "*Eintopf Sonntag*" (one-pot Sunday); every family was expected to contribute money for the needy on a certain Sunday each month; this money was supposedly saved by making a simple meal, prepared in "one pot." The Nazis had taken over *Eintopf Sonntag* collections to demonstrate their concern for the poor. During this concert, stink bombs were thrown into the crowd by a group opposed to the Nazis. People hurried away as fights broke out between the Nazis and their opponents. It was the first time I had encountered the kind of violence that had become all too common in Germany.

By this time the party was so well organized that its members were responsible for *Eintopf Sonntag* collections in every apartment house—every street in every district of every town in Germany. The collector appeared at each house door, his Nazi party pin with the swastika in his lapel, the house occupants list in his hand. Nobody would have dared not to give a sizable sum since the amount "donated" was marked next to the respective name and the records were filed at party headquarters. This was only one of the things which ultimately could mean the difference between survival and reprisal.

I returned to Berlin. Friedel wrote to me that he felt imprisoned, forced to complete his studies. It was an unbearable existence for him, alone in his rented room with nobody to talk to for days on end, days which turned into weeks and months. He blamed himself for the long wait inflicted on us because of his senseless chasing after a degree instead of working for an income. But running away from his project was not in his nature.

"If only the day would approach quicker which finds us united in the Grunewald church," he wrote, "it will be the overture to a symphony of joy."

Friedel urged me to read the newspapers and educate myself politically. For example there was a pro-Nazi article, in the *Deutsche Allgemeine Zeitung*, called "*Auf die Barrikaden*" ("On the barricades"). It was more important to study everyday events, he told me, than to attend the university.

Friedel's only distractions were the rare occasions when he took a train to Nuremberg to eat a decent meal and go to a movie. He wrote long letters on Sundays, including an important one concerning our future to my father and one to his brother-in-law, Hermann Grieving. Hermann had become the de facto head of the Robert Pschorr family. He was cultured and worldly and well liked and respected, and was, then, still manager of the department for cultural films for *UFA*, the most important German film company. Friedel labored over these letters, worrying about every word he wrote in his clear, beautiful hand. He wrote and rewrote, trying to explain his intention to marry the (spoiled) daughter of Marcel Holzer without revealing the extent of his emotions. He stressed his awareness of the responsibility he took, especially in the position he was in just now, which he considered inferior.

My parents invited Hermann for a visit, and Friedel asked me anxiously to report to him every word spoken on this event. I don't remember any of these conversations, but Hermann had a different attitude then the rest of the Pschorrs, and he probably planned to talk to Herbert about Herbert's antipathy towards me and his continued attempts to dissuade Friedel from marrying me. Friedel was delighted to hear this, and he relied on my personal "charm," as he called it, to win Herman's friendship as the future new member of the family Pschorr. It was the beginning of a very friendly and rewarding relationship between Hermann Grieving, his sister Grete Putsch, and us.

The approach of Christmas put Friedel again in a position to choose between his duty towards his mother and his wish to be with us. His pride made him want to appear before my parents as a future son-in-law only after the official engagement, after his doctorate was complete and after he held a job. To do so, he realized, would mean the end of his visits with us until his goals were accomplished. There was a more subtle complication, too. Erich could not be with us at Christmas, thus, Friedel's presence in our house in Erich's absence could have led to gossip since his friendship with Erich was a convenient cover-up for his visits.

In retrospect, this concern seems petty. The only valid motive for our decisions should have been the foreboding, created by Hitler's emerging schemes. Unfortunately, we never considered this vital point, the only important one as it turned out. If my parents had realized what was happening in Germany, we simply would have married then and there.

We dreaded the big ado planned for our official engagement. We didn't want to face the grinning guests and family members, and even the gifts and the flowers would be unwelcome. We considered all that an intrusion. For us, our exchange of vows in the privacy of Papi's study that September had been sufficient.

Friedel planned to give me a ring for Christmas; my father had the same idea—it was a dilemma. I did not want to offend Papi or Friedel, but the only ring I wanted was the wedding band Friedel would give me. Such stupid and insignificant incidents intruded into the period during which our need for each other's warmth and closeness was as great as it would ever be again. If I regret anything in my life, it was the waste of precious time when our love was blooming without being fulfilled. It was one of those rare times in a person's live that escapes as quickly as time itself. In reality, we were unable to free ourselves from our upbringing and traditional morality, and we pretended it was that which restrained us. I am not even sure my parents would have insisted on all the formalities had we objected. But we did not see this door which might have been open to us at that time—it is probably open only to the courageous.

When my grandmother came to visit, she asked my mother if Friedel would still stay with us during his visits in the *Jagowstrasse*. I had an open discussion with my mother and explained that she had nothing to worry about because Friedel and I had decided on "honorable" behavior. Friedel wrote, "If only you could always be with me, if you could always be in my arms so I could feel your warm, breathing life next to me. Why are we allowed to taste instead of drinking to the fullest? Why do we let "civilization" put us into chains? I wonder if we will feel differently when our blood runs through older veins?"

Our pain and longing grew every day. To control these feelings required almost heroic strength. We considered it a test and knew we could stand it as others had before us. The strain caused by physical separation and our reaction to taboos concerning sex could not fail to influence the future tender moments we had dreamed about for a long time.

The ideas one connected with physical love before marriage were mixed with curiosity, fantasies and fear. Young girls were not informed about any of the different stages and functions of the body At best they gathered whispered and distorted details which caused all sorts of uneasy feelings. To mention any of this to a man was transgression of good behavior and ethical rules. In our letters we dared make allusions to physical desires only in a circumspect manner. Actually we were both completely naïve and inexperienced on the subject.

Our relationship was now such that we could discuss anything without offense. But I was often worried that someone would hurt Friedel, who was so sensitive ; I defended and protected him and became known in my family as Friedel's lawyer. The slightest allusion to Friedel, especially from Erich who loved to tease, made me raise my voice.

At that time my father wrote a long letter to Friedel explaining that due to financial losses in the firm I was not really "a rich girl". As always he wanted to take care of us, but he warned that the future might be a test. While my father wanted to confirm his wish to provide security to us Friedel mistook his comments as a lack of trust to assume responsibility for us. I tried to smooth out all misunderstandings between the two people I loved. Friedel reacted to my father's comments exactly the way which I feared and saw his belief confirmed that he had to "be someone" before he could marry me.

Unconcerned about anything but ourselves, I reported my activities to Friedel. These consisted mainly of parties and getting together with acquaintances. I wrote Friedel about "tea—dances with Hans Meissner—the son of the Secretary of State to Ebert, Hindenburg, and, later, Hitler—and another admirer, Heinz Ksinski, who now lives in New York. I wrote about Ady Leisler, my friend from the days at Quarry Court in England, whose little daughter Christa would two years later reach up to hand me flowers after our marriage ceremony. I told Friedel that I attended a concert by Yehudi Menuhin, who was, then, fourteen years old.

The day came when Friedel finally handed in his doctorial thesis and began work towards the oral examination. Being superstitious, he kept the date of the exam strictly to himself. The uncertainty left me in a state of excitement and anticipation. I told him if he should fail, it would not matter at all to me or to his future success in life.

And then, one morning I awoke and there, in my bedroom, was Friedel! Never will I forget the thrill, the joy which shot through me. He sat on the edge of my bed in his traveling suit, and we threw our arms around each other in sheer delight. He presented himself as "Doctor Fritz-Georg Pschorr": he had successfully completed his examination. I had not imagined what that moment would do to me. My emotions rose gradually, a fire burned within me, and I trembled, overcome with the thought of future bliss, of sharing my life with Friedel.

As usual, Friedel could not stay. He went to Feldafing to be with his mother at Christmas. His sense of duty overruled his desires. With the hope that our love would be strong enough to withstand and conquer the attacks from the Pschorrs and others that were bound to come, I let Friedel go. In Feldafing a letter from his mother's physician awaited him, warning him to postpone any discussion of our marriage plans until after Friedel had consulted with the doctor. Everybody in the household was nervous; sisters Stefanie and Carry worried about Tilla's reaction to the news. Friedel had a two-hour talk with Herbert's wife Edda, hoping that she could convince her husband that besides Jewish and Christian views there were still human considerations which should overrule differences in a family. Friedel met with the doctor, and then went to Munich to ask Hermann Grieving's advice and, as if it would help, went to the family grave at the Wald Friedhof. Here, Hermann had erected a Roman-style memorial, a stone wall inscribed with the names of Robert Pschorr and Carlotta Pschorr, and with room for subsequent dead.

Still undecided on how to approach the subject with his mother, Friedel returned to the Pschorr villa in Feldafing. The manner of living in the old family house was much different than in today's homes where everyone pursues his own activities, and gathering, perhaps, once a day around a dinner table. In the villa, the three sisters spent practically the whole day around the big, oval table in the dining room, the only heated room in the house.

Before mealtimes the discussion focused on who had to lay the table and whose turn it was to help the elderly maid, Fanny, dry the dishes. Tilla, Friedel's mother, would not miss the opportunity to comment on Carry's inability to do anything right, especially dry the dishes. But Carry, who really hated housework, volunteered often enough to do it because then she could sit on the kitchen counter and dangle her legs like a young girl, talk to Fanny, and sneak some food. During meals, Tilla observed Carry with a sharp eye and noted every spoonfull she took on her plate and would comment that she had already had her share. Tilla's concern was not due to frugality, the family had an adequate income and ate well. Tilla simply felt Carry ate too much. But Carry was much too good-hearted to answer or take offense.

Most of the day Friedel's grandmother, whom he called Grossmama-Ur, sat covered with hand-knitted, woolen scarfs around her meager shoulders in an easy chair near the window. From there she overlooked the lake; every time one of the little steamers passed she exclaimed, "*der Dampfer!*" ("The steamer!"); so she would be teasingly called "*Grossmama-der-Dampfer.*" From time to time, she would frantically look for her small handbag, which contained only her handkerchief, and call out for it, "*Mei Taeschche, mei Taeschche,*" in the Frankfurt dialect. Grossmama-Ur would also command someone to close the shutters as soon as dusk fell. She, then, murmured, "I don't want to see the black holes." At night, she called for the ever busy Stefanie and reminded her to fill her zinc hot-water bottle and, every so often after that, to move it around in her bed. Actually, it was cold in the house; someone would stir up the fire in the tiled stove or run in and out with coal, whereupon the ladies would yell to shut the door so the ice-cold draft from the hall would not enter the room.

Friedel's dilemma that Christmas of 1931 was resolved by his mother. In the midst of all the nervous commotion, she abruptly turned to him and asked about me. He told her of our decision to marry, and, to everyone's surprise, she was pleased. Thus, the tension dissolved, but the underlying resentment stirred up by Herbert and other members of the family remained.

In our house in the *Jagowstrasse*, I informed the staff of my engagement to Friedel, and they were delighted. Rosa, the cook, admired this "refined, nice gentleman" and could not understand why the daughter of a rich man like Herr Holzer would have to wait one hour longer. Lieschen offered right away to postpone her own wedding, which she had planned for some time. While I was listening to their comments, I felt quite at home in the basement kitchen and thought how much easier these simple people solved problems than we did upstairs.

This was certainly true for Friedel and his relatives, who continued to make life hard for him. In a way, he asked for it by insisting to know how his uncles would react to our marriage. He visited one after the other and was crushed to hear that he would no longer be received in their homes. When he wrote to me about it, I replied:

> My dear Friedel,
>
> I would prefer not to answer your letter, since it leads to nothing and I do not like to write about this subject anymore. I think, however, that you are right to inform me about the situation which we anticipated. I realize that it hits you harder when it becomes fact. I understand your reaction but did you believe that the lonely paths one chooses would have no rocks? If people gossip, it does not change anything.
>
> Our love is beyond gossip. We have already embarked on our chosen course. I certainly would prefer it if there was no conflict in your family. But let us leave the small things behind and look only ahead. There is so much happiness and greatness in the world, why would people seek to trample it? I will try to the last to go the right way, together with you. I put my arms around you and dream I am with you, then everything else sinks away and I am happy. Ask me as you have in the past if I am yours and I will answer with all my love: I am yours.

CHAPTER FOURTEEN

COLOGNE

"Darling, sweet Liesel, what can I do with my great love while I am constantly away from you? I have only one real wish and that is you, you, and, again, you. A lifetime won't be enough to satisfy my longing. I go mad just thinking I could spend an entire day with you alone."

On a cold, winter day at the end of January 1932, Friedel started his career at Schenker & Company's office in Cologne, where Erich also was serving his apprenticeship; and another period of separation and self-inflicted obstacles to our marriage began.

After arriving in Cologne, Friedel had rented a modern, spotlessly clean furnished room, one of six rooms in the large apartment of Frau von Nordhausen. It meant the inconvenience of sharing one bathroom, but in Germany at that time, one was used to such things. At least, had Friedel wanted, he could have become acquainted with some of his fellow lodgers. His landlady, a somewhat haughty widow about fifty years old, remarked that Friedel behaved like a twenty-nine-year-old but looked like a boy of nineteen.

His daily life soon became an effort to adjust to an unpleasant, and rather tough, job as an apprentice in the shipping and transportation firm under his new boss, Herr Franz. My father had seen to it that Friedel would be given special consideration over an ordinary apprentice. Herr Franz took instructions from Berlin how to train Friedel, the boss's future son-in-law. There was a German saying, "Whoever wants to command has to learn first to obey." The idea was to let Friedel and Erich work in all the departments but to push them through this training rapidly so they could join the executive branch as soon as possible.

Friedel didn't find the system to his liking. He couldn't really get a feeling of accomplishment because he was switched from workplace to workplace quickly. Also, he felt very uneasy about being paid more than his co-workers. "Erich," he wrote, "earns two-hundred and fifty marks, more than older people who have been on their job for years." Friedel started at one-hundred and fifty marks despite his objection. The normal apprenticeship salary was seventy-five marks. The ordinary young apprentices carried their engagement rings for years because marriage was an unaffordable luxury.

Working conditions were not to Friedel's liking either. Sometimes he had to be at the windy, cold harbour to see a cargo arrive or be unloaded. With his tendency for colds and chronic sore throat, he was often sick. He withstood this adversity, but, more importantly, the party's ever-growing influence depressed him. The thought of a wedding band kept him going.

When he moved to Cologne, Friedel had escaped from the pervasive Nazi rhetoric in Munich, the Nazi party's headquarters. But he found, even in Cologne, there were reminders. In March 1932, Friedel wrote to me:

> It seems that Schenker & Company is good enough for the Nazis to transport their party material. Or is Herr Hauttmann, [manager of Schenker, Munich] that eager for every bit of business? Every truck coming from Munich carries the Party paper made up of inflammatory writing. Today, because of the upcoming election, there were 260,000 copies, which amounted to three and a half tons. I was tempted to put a match to the huge pile of newspaper: my temper was at a boiling point. In the office many of the employees are Nazis. I wonder what next Sunday will bring us.

When I asked my father about the shipments of Nazi literature and what he thought about it, he just said, "They pay promptly." I was not proud of my father then. In the April election, which pitted President Hindenburg against Hitler, Duesterburg for the Nationalists, and Thalmann for the Communists, Hindenburg won, although Hitler received one-third of the votes cast in a run-off election between Hindenburg and Hitler. Bavaria cast the most votes for Hindenburg, which was surprising since Bavaria was the center of the Nazis' activities.

Friedel is the only one I know who dared openly say he had not given Hitler his vote. Surely, there were many others as the Bavarian counts prove, but millions did not trust the secrecy of the ballots and, therefore, were afraid to vote according to their conviction. But, in spite of Friedel's political insight, he did not foresee the consequences for our private plans.

He wrote, "I find it revolting that Hitler received an increase in votes of more than two million, and that within two months. It is not difficult to imagine what this will mean for the future and when it will happen." His letters were a little window through which I looked into the world around me. What happened in Germany was a rising tide, slowly mounting to our necks. It is true that Hindenburg was elected for his second term, but he was old and didn't see through Hitler's scheme. Hindenburg, spurred on by the Minister of Defense Von Schleicher, withdrew his support from Chancellor Bruening's government, and Franz von Papen formed a new "Cabinet of National Concentration," as it was called. The ban placed on the Nazi SA and the SS earlier that year under Bruening was rescinded, giving the Nazis renewed vitality. Shortly after, General von Schleicher became the new chancellor. Only then did Adolf Hitler become a German citizen.

Time was heavy on my hands. I was aching to have a planned day-to-day program, the only way to retain my energy and enterprise during this frustrating period of waiting. I thought of going to the university or taking a course in baby care. But, no, Friedel said one can be a good mother without taking such a course, it is a natural instinct. Whereupon I responded angrily:

> One certainly can have children and be a good mother by mere instinct but why not refine the gift of heaven and be knowledgeable about such things? Every animal is a mother by instinct, but we humans should go beyond that. You could not possibly be of the opinion that it suffices to answer to natural instincts only. There are lots of things which one recognizes and appreciates when one has studied them.
>
> I imagine that you do not like this lecture. But your attitude towards this subject is important. I have talked to lots of men about it and found that a man can feel the same way as I in this respect.

Friedel was not impressed and called me a *Kratzbuerste*, "quick-tempered," but let it go at that.

Our cry for each other became louder and louder, but when I asked to be married a year from then, Friedel cautioned me and warned it would be longer than that. His new apprenticeship, he explained, had tied him to our family so, at least, we had that consolation. Since he was going to join the firm anyway, I could not see why he could not do it as my husband. I spoke to my mother about my wish to get married soon. She said as far as she was concerned, I could move in with Friedel in Cologne, but my father disagreed. He made the rule that a married man had to have enough income to provide for the household. However, when Erich finished his apprenticeship and Ty arrived from America, his bride-to-be moved in with us even before their official engagement.

The festivities for Erich and Ty were going to be on Easter—at the same time as ours—a double engagement. Among the subsequent good wishes in response to our invitation was a short, cool note from Friedel's brother Herbert, but it was addressed to my parents and there was no mention of me. Friedel told my mother not to respond with a printed thank-you note, but my mother sent one anyway. Friedel wrote to me, "Now they will laugh and say, they didn't even notice that we do not want Liesel. This kind of people one should not treat with grandeur."

Friedel was right; unfortunately my mother's reaction to Friedel's advice was not an isolated case. As much as my parents loved Friedel, they seldom listened to him; whereas they often disapproved of Erich's decisions but always did as he said. Erich was the more forceful of the two young men.

Friedel swallowed a lot of hurt because of his quiet demeanor. He silently faced his estrangement from his brother and his uncles. He took upon himself his sick mother's financial problems which Herbert had flung at him after their quarrel. Her income, which sustained the household in Feldafing and supported her sisters as well, depended on her late husband's pension and on dividends from Pschorr stock. Under pressure from Joseph Pschorr, who was a major shareholder, the general assembly of the brewery had decided not to pay out any dividends that year. Thus, in spite of careful stewardship of his mother's finances, Friedel had to support her out of his savings, which had been predetermined for our married life. Even the trip to Berlin for our engagement celebration was a luxury his mother could not afford. It was made even more costly when the doctor decided that both Carry and Stefanie should accompany Tilla.

The engagement parties were relatively uneventful. There were two, long tables set up in the upper hall, one for Erich and Ty, and one for us. They were covered with gifts from my father's business friends—silver, porcelain, and crystal—which would adorn our rooms for many years. Friedel's mother was quite calm, and Carry indulged in the sumptuous meals and delighted about the sweets. Our engagement rings, engraved "March 27, 1932," at last were securely on our right ring-fingers. But they didn't ease our situation. On the contrary, our separation seemed even more difficult to take with grace.

Friedel was transferred to a branch of Schenker called "Bartz Paketfahrt," in Cologne. His desk was in a large, cold, and noisy warehouse built of masonry and glass. All day long the brutal noise of rolling cases beat at his eardrums. The standing joke amongst the employees was that one recognized those who worked there by their skeleton like looks and their crutches. And on top of this miserable assignment, we learned that Friedel would stay in Cologne until June 1933.

Everything continued according to my father's program and plans. Although this was a difficult period for the German economy my father bought a new Mercedes, a five-passenger cabriolet, light grey with a narrow blue stripe. At that time all new cars had to be driven slowly for the first 1,500 kilometers. The American "Jordan" was sold for 600 marks, and no one was sorry to see that car go. Some weeks earlier I had an almost deadly accident when I drove it to town. Crossing the Halensee Bridge, under which the railroad tracks ran, one of the front-wheel brakes suddenly locked. The steering wheel was spun from my hands and the car slammed against the bridge's iron rail. Uninjured, but trembling, I called Herr Schmidecke by telephone. When he arrived and saw what had happened, he turned pale.

One evening, Hermann Grieving invited me to dinner at his Berlin apartment where he lived with his sister, Grete Putsch. She had moved in after the death of Carlotta, Hermann's wife (and Friedel's sister). Grete was a wonderful sister to Hermann. She fulfilled every wish and whim her brother could have. He was a gourmet, and she would travel all over town to get just the right kind of meat or an unusual herb for the dishes she prepared with utmost care.

At their apartment, I met Hans Pfuelf, the general manager of the Pschorr Brewery. Hans was married to Georg Pschorr's daughter. He was an able business manager, and he later helped Friedel keep his mother's finances going and defended Friedel during the frequent disagreements within the Pschorr family. That evening I was very impressed with Hans, who treated "Frauelein Holzer" with respect and courtesy and even brought me flowers. He won my heart with his gestures. (As it turned out, Hans, his wife, and children became good and loyal friends to Friedel and me.) After we left Hermann and Grete's apartment, I drove him in the new Mercedes to the *Bahnhof Friedrichstrasse*, where he would catch a train to Munich. We went up to the gates, and I clung to him as if my life depended on him. When I drove home, the streets were bedecked with swastika flags.

I was eager to introduce Hans to my father and had invited him and Hermann to our house. Somehow these three mature men seemed of great importance for our future. That evening, I listened attentively to their comments on politics and their prediction that Germany would become a socialist state. The next day, I reported all this to Friedel, who was pleased that his bride-to-be showed such an interest in politics.

Short Journeys

May 5, 1932

Beloved Friedel,

For some time we both have been on edge. These are not moods but expressions of despair. I cannot bear the thought of next summer, fall, and winter and another spring without you.

But now the week has come during which we will meet in Holland. I will try not to think of the painful separation that must follow. It is cold and wet outside. You will have to give me much warmth to make a real person out of me again.

A week later I was in Heerlen, Holland, following an invitation from my father's friends. I was happy because Cologne was close enough so that Friedel could join me. It was only a weekend, but it was enough to renew my fading courage. Hope, the eternal friend of men, warmed our hearts and cheered our lonely days and nights. I shed bitter tears when I embraced Friedel for the last time before he returned to Cologne and I left for Feldafing to visit my future mother-in-law. I was once more on the *Starnbergersee* without Friedel. The ladies were warm and loving as they took me into their midst. Friedel's mother seemed much better and was relaxed. Yet it seemed strange to sleep in Friedel's room and use his things. Everything reminded me of him, and his childhood became alive. It was as if an illusion took hold of me: I felt his presence everywhere and associated his parents' house with mine.

During my visit, I met Rita halfway between Feldafing and Possenhofen. The encounter was tense and very sad, haunted by memories of the past. We, who once had been inseparable friends, were distant from one another. The rift between us hurt: I wanted to talk to her from my heart as always, but there was an icy, strange feeling I didn't know how to overcome. She told me that Erich had written to her on her birthday and that people thought she was engaged to him because they had read about Erich's imminent engagement. But she reported this as if she spoke about a third person, her soul was far away.

I was received coldly by Rita's parents, and I felt a stranger in their house. I left as soon as I could. It was the second time in my life that I had lost a friend through no fault of mine—Helga as a child, Rita as a young woman. The pain was very real each time.

The next month, I went to visit a girl I had studied with and whose parents lived also in the Grunewald. They had a house in Weningstedt on the island of Sylt, one of a group of islands called Friesland, situated on the North Sea. These small specks of land are separated from the mainland by narrow belts of shallow water. During low tide, the water recedes so that one can walk for miles over the shell-covered sand, into which the waves have drawn ripples. Birds fly low to do their harvesting, while children play and men and women collect shells. The residents of the island, of ancient Germanic ancestry, have preserved their traditions and culture. I recall the flat, sandy, heather-covered land bordering on dunes and the sea with its eternal rushing noise as the waves beat against the beach. I remember the girl I was, wandering with bunches of heather in my hand, longing for the distant Friedel, searching the silent distance. All I saw were scattered dwellings, the low, white-painted houses constructed of coarse stones, their overhanging thatch roofs almost hiding the small windows, ready to withstand the strong winds and driving rain that periodically whip the islands.

I returned to Berlin just before the national election at the end of July 1932. Friedel had reminded me several times not to forget my voting papers, to be sure to cast my ballot. Although I was made aware of the importance and understood the event, I am sure that the implications of the outcome were no clearer to me than to many Germans. In my letter to Friedel, I expressed my surprise to find a Nazi in uniform and a swastika flag posted in front of the voting place. "No other party made any propaganda," I commented, showing my ignorance about the situation.

The Nazis won a stunning victory and became the largest party in the *Reichstag*. Where was I when the bands of uniformed Nazis roamed the streets of Berlin? They were singing loud enough *Deutschland Erwache!* ("Germany awaken!"). This formerly prosperous city had now changed its face. Unemployed people walked the streets or formed lines in front of places offering work; poverty, despair and agitation marked their faces. It was the last year of the Weimar Republic.

I opened one of Friedel's letters, and, into my quiet world, a glimpse of reality penetrated in the form of a newspaper clipping:

—

"FEAR"

by Dr. Max Naumann,
Member of the Union of National Jews

Election time is a time of distinct and honest language. We German Jews address the German public because we are talking about a German, not a Jewish affair. We address this in particular to the German-feeling Jews, those Jews in Germany who belong to Germany according to their heritage, their culture and their feeling. Amongst the other circles of Jews—we call them the in-between circles—circulates a so-called joke: one asks the other if he is already member of the "Nozis." This is supposed to mean; "The organization of trembling Jews." This self-jeering remark stems from the same spirit as the one the enemies of Jews have. The intellectuals who spread this kind of humor are the same who managed to give the German literature and art the reputation of being taken over by Jews. The same people who during many years inhibited growth of the revolutionary spirit and its energy to face the future. These intellectuals who suffocate the Germans with their intellectuality. They are proud of their intellectual freedom, which enables them to jeer themselves as well as others. They have read Ephraim Lessing's *Nathan*, but they forgot the famous quotation: "Not everyone is free who jeers his chains."

The German people judge the Jewish entity after this relatively small group, who are able to interact into almost all parts of public and private life. This is what is generally called the "Jewish spirit." The forces of defense of the German Jews are unfortunately not strong enough to counteract. The weak tolerance with which an important part of German Jews react to these disastrous occurrences seems to justly enforce the German's opinion about the Jews in Germany in general.

The German National Jews, so deeply rooted in German culture and feeling, deny themselves the right to speak openly; this is in the last end a lack of courage. It is not the lack of physical courage of which they are often accused, but of moral courage. There is no greater stupidity than the belief that Jews are more intelligent than others. There are perhaps some specific gifts in some Jews which were educated through the ages because the Jewish people were submitted to work restrictions in certain areas of occupation. They also might have been trained in their heritage of the Talmud, studies which sharpened the mind over generations. But this is not true intelligence, a gift which is as rare amongst Jews as it is amongst the rest of humanity.

The German Jews, behind the intellectual wall of the Ghetto often know only what they read in the *Berliner Tageblatt* or the "Weltbuehne" or the world of Arnold Zweig and Alfred Kerr [a popular critic]. They listen to radio talks by those people who calculate the news they want to spread. They seem to know only that Hitler was a house painter and believe that as soon as the Nazis reign, the Jews are going to be killed. If they won't be killed they will be expelled, is their idea. They believe that the SA will commit these deeds and then accuse the Communists to have done it. Many Jews do not dare to realize that this national movement is by no means built up by stupid youngsters but that wide circles of the population are involved in this fight to revive Germany. The Jews we are talking about do not dare to cross the magic circle because they are afraid, not as much to be persecuted but rather to be refused as intruders or as turncoats.

The real "Organization of trembling Jews" does not exist at all. They are in contrast a herd of people who, lacking personality and courage, should go where they belong and where they don't need to tremble.

All this will be the beginning for the German people and for Germany including the German Jews. It will be possible if the majority of German Jews intend to devote themselves to Germany's future, regardless of the disappointments they might have to suffer. We will see if they will overcome their fears and stop the jeering and if they will stand by their own devotion to German Nationality.

———

This article sheds a rather confusing light on the strange split amongst Jews torn between their Jewish ancestry and their fidelity to the German nation. But I think that it is a testimony of the time which I, as well as millions of others, faced.

Liesel, 1930.
"Amongst the ladies and gentlemen riding horseback in the Tiergarten in 1930, one could even have admired me, proudly riding side-saddle, elegantly dressed in a black riding outfit, the wide skirt swung over my bent knee and the black, three-cornered hat fastened by a ribbon under my chin."

Elise and Adolf Blum, c. 1880.
"I remember my childhood as beautifully enriched by the presence and the compassionate and loving care of my grandparents: I cannot imagine what my life would have been without them."

Marcel Hoizer, c. 1900.
"Shortly after 1900, Marcel came to Hamburg and became a clerk with Adolf Blum & Popper. My mother-to-be was assigned to him as his secretary—an event which would determine their future lives and mine."

Edgar Blum, Liesel's mother's elder brothers 1914. "Edgar became my fathers friend long before he went to work for Adolf Blum & Popper. Edgar was killed in Flanders during one of the first battles of the war."

Trudel and Marcel, 1906. "Trudel and Marcel pledged to stay 'strong and honest' at the very beginning of their relationship, and from then on they supported each other in every situation throughout their life together."

Robert Franz Pschorr, Friedel's father, c. 1890.

Ottilie Scherer, Friedel's mother, 1899.
"All three sisters were very pretty young women.
Carry especially caught Robert s fancy but he
proposed to Ottilie, called Tilla, who was just
seventeen years old. He probably regretted this
decision later. Tilla did not turn out to be as
warm-hearted and loving as he had expected."

Left to right: Josef, Georg, and Robert Pschorr in the service of Kaiser Wilhelm, c. 1890.

Four generations: Friedel's sister Carlotta in front; his mother Tilla, standing; his grandmother (Grossmama—Ur), seated right; and his great-grandmother Scherer, seated left. c. 1903.

Tilla and Robert Pschorr, 1897.

Friedel, c. 1910.
"Friedel was treated, and felt very much the baby, and grew up like an only child, playing alone in his room much of the time. Carry spoiled and pampered him, this lovely boy with an angelic face."

Robert Pschorr at the wheel with fellow officers, 1916. "Friedel was just seven when Robert Pschorr re-joined the German army in the summer of 1914. Robert served at the front for four years as a major in the First Bavarian Artillery Regiment and was decorated with the Iron Cross Second and First Class and the Military Medal with Crown and Swords."

Liesel and Erich, 1913.
'My grandfather took my brother and me regularly on Sunday excursions in Hamburg. Erich and Opi were fascinated by the ships in the harbor; I was probably more concerned about my Sunday coat with its large cape-like collar and my wide brimmed straw hat.'

Marie, c.1914.
"After my mothers midwife left our family, Marie came to take her place as an Allein Maedchen, a maid for everything. When the first air raid alarm sounded in Hamburg in 1914, Erich and I were sitting in the bathtub when Marie grabbed me and my mother grabbed Erich and hurriedly wrapped us in large towels and somehow got us to my grandparents' home in the Aisterchaussee."

Special railway permit for Marcel Hoizer to travel to Bulgaria in 1916.
"My father was called to the War Ministry in Berlin to help direct
transportation of food and clothing to the German Army. Leaving us was
painful for him, but a call to the War Ministry was not only an honor, it
was a lot safer than a call to the army would have been."

Friedel and his brother Herbert, 1914.

Liesel and Erich entertain the family, c. 1919.

*The family Holzer, Marcel, Erich, Trudel, and Liesel,
c. 1919, "By the end of summer 1919, my father had
reached his goal of moving his family into a villa before
his fortieth birthday. It meant much to him, but it was
the fulfillment of just one of his ambitious dreams."*

*Schoolgirls and friends, 1922: Rita, back row, second from left; Liesel, middle row,
left; and Helga, front row, third from left. "Awkward and shy, embarrassed and
good, we were a bunch of not too happy-looking girls. I was not always good, to the
annoyance of the elderly teachers, who, on the whole, were rather strict and devoid
of understanding of small children."*

The Holzer villa in the Grunewald, Jagowstrasse 24, c. 1921;
"Our house sat near the front of a large lot on a tree-lined street with other large homes.
The villa was really a dream house. One felt at every turn that it was designed with love,
and that each detail was planned to give beauty and comfort to the occupants."

"Drunk with pleasure, we ran back to the house across the white stone terrace that separated the lawn from the stately house. Big stone containers of geraniums in full bloom alternated with huge spherical stones marking the edge of the terrace where we would take our meals on sunny days, of which there promised to be many."

The villa's garden, C. 1921.
"Erich and I raced excitedly over the pebble-covered walkways that surrounded the green, well-kept lawn. We greeted the weeping willows (where we would later suspend our hammock and swing lightly back and forth), the branches studded with bright green, slender leaves, the powdery yellow pussy-willows dangling before our eyes."

"*The wrought-iron fence in front had two pairs of huge wrought-iron gates leading to a semi-circle driveway. When my mother first saw the house, she panicked at the thought of the housework involved.*"

The terrace, c. 1920. Left to right, Trudel, Eduard (standing) Trudel's mother, Erich and Liesel. "The table was covered with a pretty tablecloth and laid with the chinese breakfast dishes, and Eduard, the butler, stood ready with the steaming coffee. The halved grapefruit with wedges carefully loosened was served in a high-footed metal container, the fruit resting in a glass bowl on crushed ice."

Marcel's new Mercedez-Benz, c. 1921. Left to right: Trudel, Uncle Leon (Marcel's brother) Mady and the chauffeur's wife, Erich behind the wheel pretending to drive, and Liesel. "I don't know when my father's interest in cars started. Our cars in the 1920s were usually convertibles. When we traveled, my father and the chauffeur sat in front, driving alternately, my mother, Erich, and I sat in the back seats. We were dressed in white linen coats and caps to protect us from the dust."

*Friedel (far left) and Erich (third from left) and friends
in the Grunewald, Berlin, c. 1923.*

*Friedel, Liesel, and Erich's American flirt, July 1930.
"The Palace Hotel in Gstaad was an idyllic, romantic
setting for our first meeting after our correspondence had
begun."*

Liesel, c. 1929.
"My father decided that our family would spend Christmas in St. Moritz in the Swiss Alps. I suggested to Friedel that we take our letters and discuss those matters which seemed important. I felt that this was an opportunity to resolve our problem."

Liesel and Rita, 1928
"Rita and I met on the shore of the Sturnberger See, this lake which I had never seen before through the eyes of a girl in love."

Liesel, 1930.

"At this stage of my emotional development, Friedel Pschorr appeared on my horizon. Although we had shared many casual encounters over the years in my parents house, they had no specific importance for him or for me."

Wedding day, 1933.

"Friedel left to spend the last night before our wedding in the Hotel Esplanade. On his way, he saw the night sky over Berlin glowing red. As he got closer he could see the Reichstag engulfed in flames."

Liesel and Friedel, 1933.
"*The morning after the fire, the 28th of February, I was aroused right after sunrise by singing voices under my window. I jumped up and opened the window to a crisp, beautiful morning, my wedding day!*"
"*Our honeymoon on Mallorca was interrupted by a telephone call from my father. He told us to return immediately to Berlin. The city abounded in rumors in the wake of Hitler's fast moving efforts to destroy political opposition. If we didn't come home at once we might not be able to re-enter Germany.*"

"My reactions to Friedel's behavior quite naturally changed later on when I fell in love with him. I tried very hard to overlook his sometimes annoying reserve. Like most young people, I had a strong desire to share an experience with another person."

Liesel with Rainer, 1938. Nuremburg Laws: "Law for the protection of German Blood and German Honor: Special Legislation for Jews in the National Socialist State: Children from mixed marriages are Mischlinge, half-breed. Such marriages are privileged mixed marriages."

Liesel and Friedel with Rainer, Michael, and Irene, 1941.

Below left: Irene, age two, 1943, before her illness.
"By winter 1943 Irene had been sick for six months, away from home in hospitals. There was no end to the war or her sickness in sight."

Below right: "Michael was a lively youngster, up to nonsense all day long. The little fellow was full of mischief and his pretty little face irresistible."

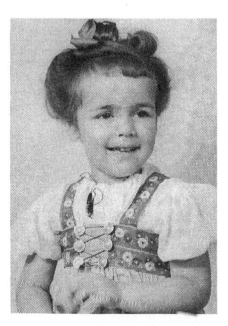

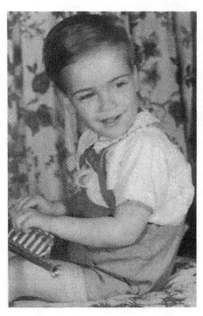

The Pschorr villa in Feldafing, c. 1940. "My presence in the village was ignored by the Ortsgruppenleiter, the local Nazi leader. Was it not thanks to the old family name Pschorr?"

Grossmama—Ur and her daughters, Stefanie, Carry, and Tilla, c. 1943. "I went to my mother-in-law's house in the village as seldom as possible. She ruled over her household and its members, her eighty-five-year old mother, Grossmama—Ur, her sisters Carry and Stefanie, and Fanny, their old cook. Tilla was torn between her older son Herbert's Nazi fidelity and her pet son Friedel's convictions against Hitler: she had no opinion of her own."

Liesel's identity card marked with a "J" and the required middle name "Sara." My soul was split in two. 'Dear God,' I prayed, 'don't let us be hit.' And my other half said, "Send more bombers: make an end of this misery."

*Liesel and Friedel on their second honeymoon,
blissfully reunited in 1946.*

Family Trees
A Selected Geneology
of the Families Blum, Goetz,
Holzer, and Pschorr

Above: left to right, Robert and Titta Pschorr, his brothers Josef, Georg, and August Pschorr and their wives, 1898.

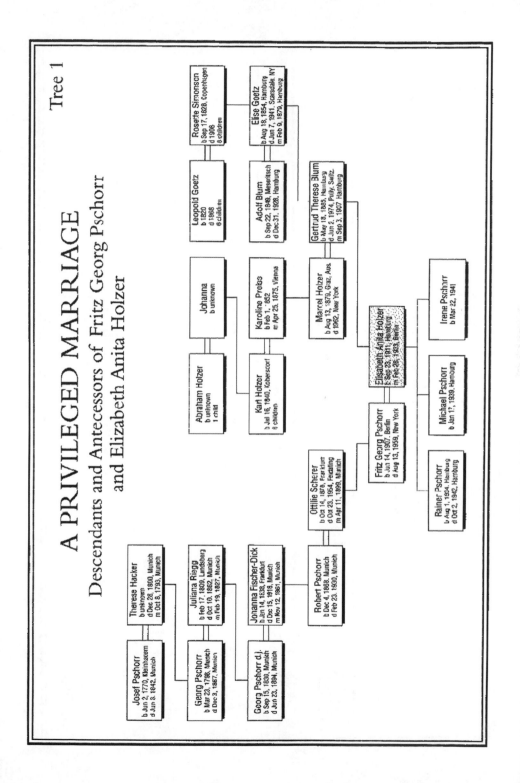

A PRIVILEGED MARRIAGE

Descendants and Antecessors of Fritz Georg Pschorr and Elizabeth Anita Holzer

Tree 1

Josef Pschorr
b Jun 2, 1770, Kleinhaborn
d Jun 3, 1842, Munich

Therese Hacker
b unknown
d Dec 28, 1800, Munich
m Oct 8, 1793, Munich

Georg Pschorr
b Mar 23, 1798, Munich
d Dec 3, 1867, Munich

Julianna Riegg
b Feb 17, 1809, Landsberg
d Oct 10, 1862, Munich
m Feb 19, 1827, Munich

Georg Pschorr d.j.
b Sep 15, 1830, Munich
d Jun 23, 1894, Munich

Johanna Fischer-Dick
b Jan 14, 1838, Frankfurt
d Dec 15, 1918, Munich
m Nov 12, 1861, Munich

Robert Pschorr
b Dec 4, 1868, Munich
d Feb 23, 1900, Munich

Ottilie Scherer
b Aug 14, 1878, Frankfurt
d Oct 23, 1954, Feldafing
m Apr 11, 1899, Munich

Abraham Holzer
b unknown
1 child

Johanna
b unknown

Karl Holzer
b Jul 16, 1840, Koberscorf
6 children

Karoline Preiss
b Feb 1, 852
m Apr 25, 1875, Vienna

Leopold Goetz
b 1820
d 1868
6 children

Roserte Simonson
b Sep 17, 1828, Copenhagen
d 1906
8 children

Adolf Blum
b Sep 22, 1849, Meseritsch
d Dec 31, 1928, Hamburg

Elise Goetz
b Aug 18, 1854, Hamburg
d Jan 7, 1941, Scarsdale, NY
m Feb 9, 1879, Hamburg

Marcel Holzer
b Aug 13, 1879, Graz, Aus.
d 1962, New York

Gertrud Therese Blum
b May 18, 1885, Hamburg
d Jun 2, 1974, Pully, Switz.
m Sep 3, 1907, Hamburg

Fritz Georg Pschorr
b Jun 14, 1907, Berlin
d Aug 13, 1959, New York

Elizabeth Anita Holzer
b Sep 23, 1911, Hamburg
m Feb 26, 1933, Berlin

Rainer Pschorr
b Aug 1, 1934, Hamburg
d Oct 2, 1942, Hamburg

Michael Pschorr
b Jan 17, 1939, Hamburg

Irene Pschorr
b Mar 22, 1941

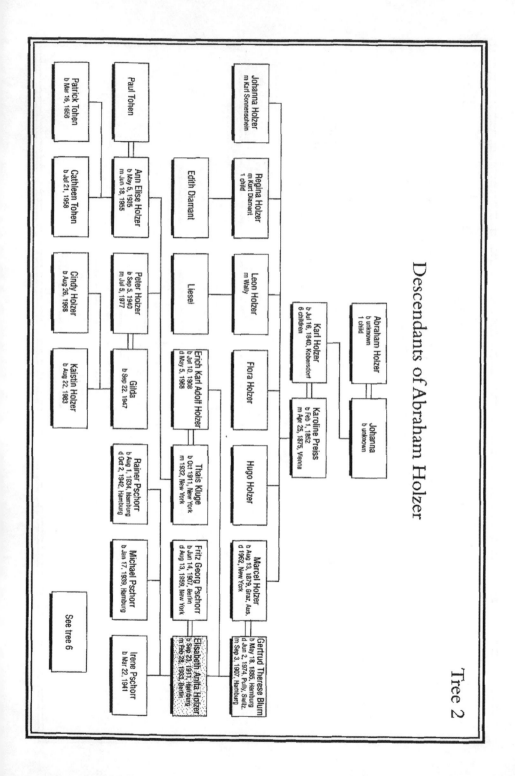

Descendants of Abraham Holzer

Tree 2

Abraham Holzer
b unknown
1 child

Johanna
b unknown

Karl Holzer
b Jul 16, 1840, Kobersdorf
6 children

Karoline Preiss
b Feb 1, 1862
m Apr 25, 1875, Vienna

Johanna Holzer
m Karl Sonnenschein

Regina Holzer
m Kurt Diamant
1 child

Leon Holzer
m Wally

Flora Holzer

Hugo Holzer

Marcel Holzer
b Aug 13, 1879, Graz, Aus.
d 1962, New York

Gertrud Therese Blum
b May 18, 1885, Hamburg
d Jun 2, 1974, Pully, Switz.
m Sep 3, 1907, Hamburg

Paul Tohen

Ann Elise Holzer
b May 5, 1935
m Jun 18, 1955

Edith Diamant

Liesel

Peter Holzer
b Sep 5, 1940
m Jul 5, 1977

Gilda
b Sep 22, 1947

Erich Karl Adolf Holzer
b Jul 10, 1908
d May 5, 1968

Thais Kluge
b Oct 19, 1911, New York
m 1932, New York

Fritz Georg Pschorr
b Jun 14, 1907, Berlin
d Aug 13, 1959, New York

Elisabeth Anita Holzer
b Sep 23, 1911, Hamburg
m Feb 26, 1933, Berlin

Patrick Tohen
b Mar 16, 1956

Cathleen Tohen
b Jul 21, 1958

Cindy Holzer
b Aug 26, 1968

Kaistin Holzer
b Aug 22, 1963

Rainer Pschorr
b Aug 1, 1934, Hamburg
d Oct 2, 1942, Hamburg

Michael Pschorr
b Jan 17, 1939, Hamburg

Irene Pschorr
b Mar 22, 1941

See tree 6

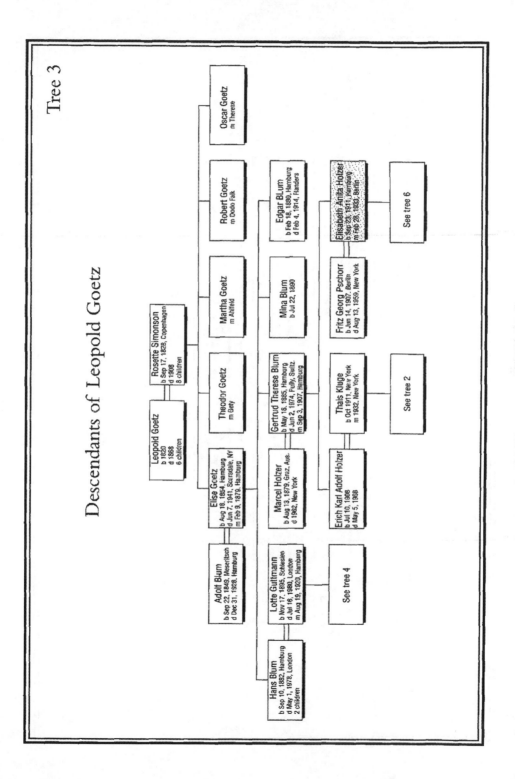

Tree 3

Descendants of Leopold Goetz

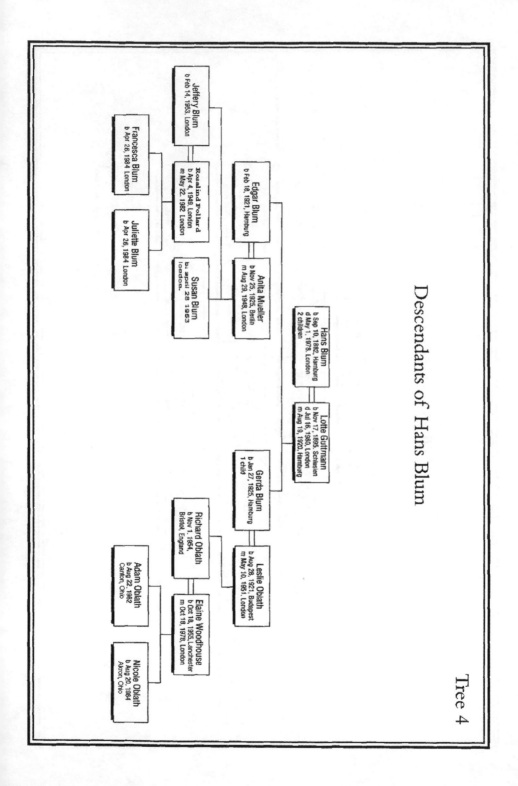

Descendants of Hans Blum

Tree 4

Jeffery Blum
b Feb 14, 1953, London

Francesca Blum
b Apr 26, 1984 London

Edgar Blum
b Feb 18, 1921, Hamburg

Rosalind Pollard
b Apr 4, 1949, London
m May 22, 1982 London

Juliette Blum
b Apr 26, 1984 London

Anita Mueller
b Nov 25, 1925, Berlin
m Aug 29, 1948, London

Susan Blum
b: april 28 1953
london.

Hans Blum
b Sep 10, 1882, Hamburg
d May 1, 1978, London
2 children

Lotte Guttmann
b Nov 17, 1895, Schlesien
d Jul 16, 1980, London
m Aug 19, 1920, Hamburg

Gerda Blum
b Jan 27, 1925, Hamburg
1 child

Richard Oblath
b Nov 1, 1954,
Bristol, England

Leslie Oblath
b Aug 28, 1921, Budapest
m May 10, 1951, London

Adam Oblath
b Aug 22, 1982
Canton, Ohio

Elaine Woodhouse
b Oct 18, 1955, Lanchester
m Oct 18, 1978, London

Nicole Oblath
b Aug 20, 1984
Akron, Ohio

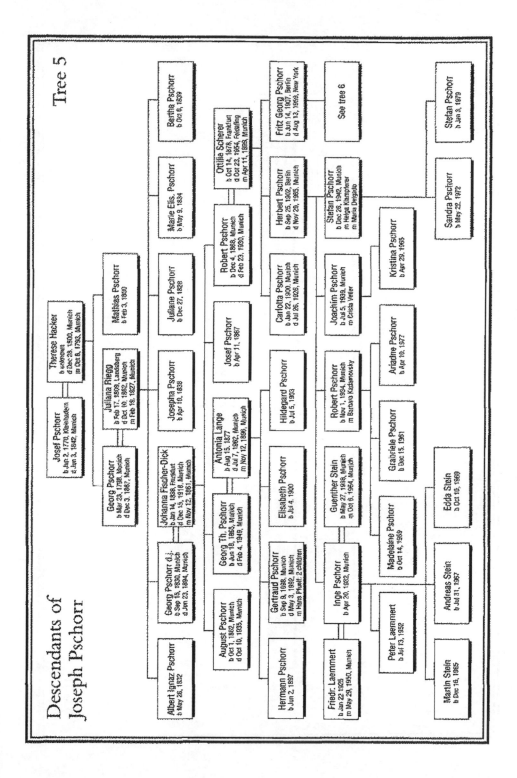

Descendants of Joseph Pschorr

Tree 5

Josef Pschorr
b Jan 2, 1770, Kleinhadern
d Jan 3, 1842, Munich

Therese Hacker
b unknown
d Dec 28, 1800, Munich
m Oct 8, 1793, Munich

Georg Pschorr
b Mar 23, 1798, Munich
d Dec 3, 1867, Munich

Juliana Riegg
b Feb 17, 1809, Landsberg
d Oct 10, 1862, Munich
m Feb 19, 1827, Munich

Mathias Pschorr
b Feb 3, 1800

Bertha Pschorr
b Oct 6, 1839

Marie Elis. Pschorr
b May 9, 1834

Josepha Pschorr
b Apr 16, 1836

Juliane Pschorr
b Dec 27, 1828

Georg Pschorr d.j.
b Sep 15, 1830, Munich
d Jun 23, 1894, Munich

Johanna Fischer-Dick
b Jan 14, 1836, Frankfurt
d Dec 15, 1918, Munich
m Nov 12, 1851, Munich

Josef Pschorr
b Apr 11, 1867

Ottilie Scherer
b Oct 14, 1878, Frankfurt
d Oct 22, 1954, Feldafing
m Apr 11, 1899, Munich

Robert Pschorr
b Dec 4, 1868, Munich
d Feb 23, 1930, Munich

Fritz Georg Pschorr
b Jun 14, 1907, Berlin
d Aug 13, 1969, New York

Albert Ignaz Pschorr
b May 26, 1832

August Pschorr
b Oct 1, 1862, Munich
d Oct 10, 1935, Munich

Georg Th. Pschorr
b Jun 18, 1863, Munich
d Feb 4, 1949, Munich

Antonia Lange
b Aug 15, 1877
d Jul 7, 1962, Munich
m Nov 12, 1896, Munich

Elisabeth Pschorr
b Jul 4, 1900

Hildegard Pschorr
b Jul 5, 1903

Carlotta Pschorr
b Jan 22, 1900, Munich
d Jul 26, 1926, Munich

Herbert Pschorr
b Sep 25, 1902, Berlin
d Nov 29, 1985, Munich

Stefan Pschorr
b Dec 26, 1942, Munich
m Helga Klampferer
m Maria Delgado

See tree 6

Stefan Pschorr
b Jan 3, 1979

Sandra Pschorr
b May 22, 1972

Hermann Pschorr
b Jun 2, 1897

Gertraud Pschorr
b Sep 9, 1898, Munich
d May 3, 1982, Munich
m Hans Pfaehl, 2 children

Guenther Stein
b May 27, 1908, Munich
m Oct 6, 1964, Munich

Robert Pschorr
b Nov 1, 1934, Munich
m Barbara Kazłanowsky

Joachim Pschorr
b Jul 5, 1933, Munich
m Crista Vetter

Kristina Pschorr
b Apr 29, 1965

Ariadne Pschorr
b Apr 16, 1977

Friedr. Laemmert
b Jan 22, 1926
m May 29, 1950, Munich

Inge Pschorr
b Apr 20, 1932, Munich

Madeleine Pschorr
b Oct 14, 1959

Gabriele Pschorr
b Dec 15, 1961

Peter Laemmert
b Jul 13, 1952

Edda Stein
b Oct 16, 1969

Andreas Stein
b Jul 31, 1967

Martin Stein
b Dec 16, 1985

Descendants of Fritz Georg Pschorr

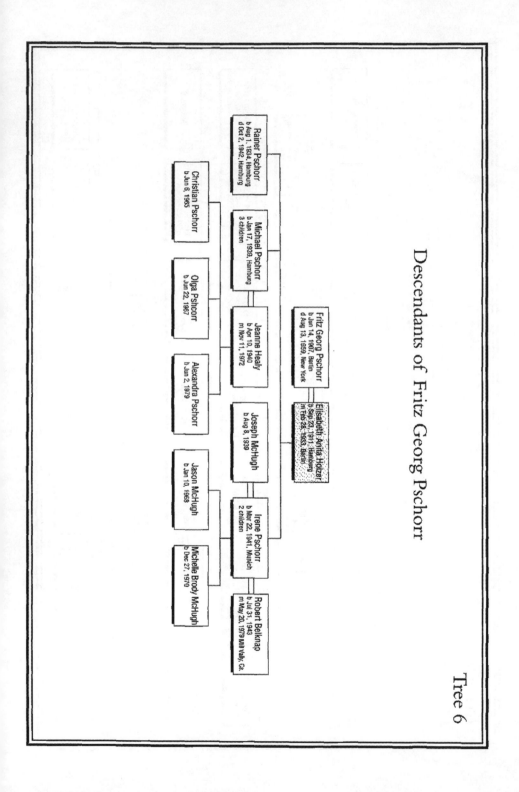

Rainer Pschorr
b Aug 1, 1934, Hamburg
d Oct 2, 1942, Hamburg

Christian Pschorr
b Jun 6, 1965

Michael Pschorr
b Jan 17, 1938, Hamburg
3 children

Olga Pshcorr
b Jun 22, 1967

Fritz Georg Pschorr
b Jan 14, 1907, Berlin
d Aug 13, 1959, New York

Jeanne Healy
b Apr 10, 1940
m Nov 11, 1972

Elisabeth Anita Holzer
b Sep 23, 1911, Hamburg
m Feb 26, 1933, Berlin

Alexandra Pschorr
b Jun 2, 1979

Joseph McHugh
b Aug 8, 1939

Jason McHugh
b Jan 10, 1968

Irene Pschorr
b Mar 22, 1941, Munich
2 children

Michelle Brody McHugh
b Dec 27, 1970

Robert Belknap
b Jul 31, 1943
m May 20, 1979 Mill Vally, Ca.

Tree 6

CHAPTER FIFTEEN

SUNLIGHT AND SHADOWS

Friedel took a respite from his work in Cologne to join me in Hamburg for my parents' twenty-fifth wedding anniversary celebration on the third of September. After several days of happiness together, we parted; I returned to Berlin, Friedel to Cologne. He now worked in the overseas department which handled freight shipments from Antwerp or London to countries overseas. As always when he started working in a new department, Friedel felt inhibited, yet he was encouraged by the thought that it was the way up the corporate ladder. Friedel was not then, or at any time later, enthusiastic about his work, but we never said this to my diligent, ambitious father. Friedel could never make his work the most important part of his life as my father did. We didn't approve of Papi's constant drive for expansion and his fanatic work habits. My mother's tolerance and her unconditional love were the key to their continuous happiness in spite of my father's preoccupation with his business.

After I returned from Hamburg, I was suddenly more aware of the beauty and comfort of our house in the *Jagowstrasse*. Perhaps I realized how privileged we truly were and felt the peace which flows from a settled and structured life.

The season announced its advance towards fall, the gardener brought armfuls of dahlias and asters into the house, and I arranged them in beautiful crystal vases and porcelain containers and placed them in those wide, sun-bathed rooms. We expected house guests, but, being in a philosophical mood and wanting solitude, I was not keen on their arrival. A life long acquaintance had died, and my letters reflect these thoughts:

> The human being's unawareness of tragic or happy events just around the corner seems a terrible and unfortunate impediment which does not equal the intelligence, sensitivity and capability of men in so many other domains. In spite of scientific advancement and technological invention, man still depends on a sixth sense, a foresight, nourished by feelings and uncertainty. He takes refuge

from fear in faith, suspicion, or mysticism. As soon as the reality
of our helplessness strikes us, we react according to our different
nature and some could be driven to despair. I always understood
this and looked upon truly religious people with envy. I am given
more to doubt and I search for so-called reasonable explanations.
Of one thing I am certain: I am in the hands of my God.

A year had gone by since I had finally given my consent to marry Friedel.
It had been an important moment for us. It seems to me that the promise to
marry was more final then than it is today because one did not have an easy
way out once the step was taken. I think even if most people marry without
the thought in mind, the possibility of divorce—an escape from unwanted
obligations—makes a decision for marriage easier. Friedel needed me and my
love, but I was not sure if I was capable then of selfless love, the kind of love
which does not want any compensation.

On that September day in 1932, the anniversary of our commitment to
marry, I waited selfishly and in vain for a telephone call, but Friedel had a
shipment to supervise and could not get to the phone. His best intentions
were already crossed; work did interfere with his private life.

Five days later was my twenty-first birthday. I became of age! Since there
was no hope of seeing Friedel, I decided not to celebrate this day. But the
greatest of all unexpected surprises occured: suddenly I was in Friedel's arms!
He had come to be with me. As before, our encounter gave us strength for
the next separation until we would finally be husband and wife.

Friedel had to set the date. We were completely opposed to my parent's
suggestion to live with them after our marriage until we could afford an
apartment, as Erich and Ty did. Instead, we counted on being financially
independent. And Friedel wanted to be certain he deserved the salary he would
earn. We set the wedding date for February 28, 1933, five months away. By
then, Friedel would have completed his apprenticeship with Schenker &
Company and be working in the Berlin office.

After my birthday in September, 1932, I felt entitled to take the first
steps by myself towards the search for an apartment. Thus, one day I went to
a real estate agency on the *Reichskanzler Platz*. It was the area that bordered
on Dahlem, where several acquaintances and relatives lived, people with less
money than my family but still able to afford a green and pretty suburb.

I told the young man in charge that I was looking for a four-and-a-
half-room apartment, including heat and running hot water. It had to be
in a residential section and could not exceed one hundred twenty marks.

He advised me politely to search in a different part of town, like Steglitz or Lichterfelde, where the rents would be lower. Undaunted, I tried a new apartment house nearby, opposite a park. Eagerly, I rang for the concierge. A sloppily dressed old woman appeared in her slippers and showed me to an apartment in the third floor. Although this place was far from a dream come true, it was a wonderful moment in my life. In my mind's eye, I saw a brass plate on the door with the engraved letters, "Dr. F.G. Pschorr." I wandered through the empty rooms, hardly noticing them. Instead, I saw Friedel and me installed here, and I heard his voice as he called me while I was preparing a meal in the kitchen. But that apartment was also too expensive.

When I returned home, my mother was outraged that I had gone without her and accused me of being ungrateful. She didn't understand the innocent joy I had experienced by going out on my own and the feeling of freedom it gave me. She forgot that some of my friends who were my age were already married and had moved away with their husbands.

I continued to look for a suitable apartment and began other preparations for my married life. I attended a cooking school managed by a lady called Frau Oesterreicher. There were eight girls in the class, along with two older women attending, who, after years of marriage, did not know when water reached the boiling point. I learned cooking and studied nutrition and family budget planning. I loved this new activity and threw myself into it with great enthusiasm and joy. I also taught myself sewing and shorthand, hoping to be able to share Friedel's work and help with his dictation.

My parents still went out often during this time. They took house guests out to the fanciest restaurants and shows, and, on occasion, I accompanied them. One evening, my parents and I visited a nightclub and, when the curtain opened, out came the dance performers. Among them, I was startled to see none other than my childhood friend Helga. She did a modern dance with a partner and looked very pretty in a black velvet dress. I remembered our lessons at Steffi Nossen's dance school and our nightly "shows" in the upper hall of our house, our nude bodies draped in my mother's evening stoles. I was shocked when I saw her then because I imagined the kind of life she must lead behind the scenes. Here she was, Helga, whose taunting had led me to ask, "Mutti, what does it mean to be Jewish?" She didn't notice me in the audience.

As we intensified our search for an apartment, we suddenly found it in the *Duesseldorferstrasse* in Berlin-Wilmersdorf. The six-story, red-brick apartment house was across the street from an open market, but the noises and smells from the market didn't bother us.

Friedel liked the location and the pleasant layout of the four-and-a-half-room, first-floor flat. Here, we would realize our dreams, feel sheltered, and be happy. I think all lovers experience the surge of joy as I did when I saw those empty rooms. Now my imagination could dwell somewhere, the goal was within reach.

For the next two months, I was preoccupied with our future home. The keen rapture of those days is a highlight of my life. Gradually, our apartment took shape. There was the living room and breakfast nook with its bay window. We furnished the nook with two, Queen Ann style chairs and a square table on which I would serve breakfast on blue and white, Nymphenburg china. The long, narrow dining table with six arm chairs, the two glass cabinets and the pretty sideboard invited a well-cooked meal. The living room, with the sofa, eight-cornered table, and the arm chairs, all created such warmth and *Gemuetlichkeit.*

Then there was the bedroom with the off-white, built-in closets with glass doors and the interior designed to house everything in a special drawer or on shelves. It was a wonder of craftsmanship. Everything was custom-made to our needs and to suit Friedel's taste. There were square compartments to store handkerchiefs, rectangular ones for gloves, pull-out shelves for folded shirts, and hooks for shoes. In the basement was a laundry room with modern machines that could wash twenty pounds of laundry at a time, even an electric ironing machine was available. One inserted two marks and eighty pfennig to make them work. The central heat was serviced by the concierge, who lived in the house. Each apartment had a cellar booth for storage.

Every morning upon awakening, I thought about these rooms in which I would live with Friedel and how I wanted them to look. With Mutti, I ordered linens and towels embroidered with our initials "FEP," bed linens, and kitchen towels—and crystal in the Chippendale style. The table silver also belonged to the trousseau which the father of the bride provided.

Actually the bride was poor. My father gave us some stocks, but I had no money of my own. Then I learned for the first time that Papi had established a savings account in my name. I reported to Friedel that it showed the sum of seventeen hundred marks and earned eight percent interest. My father said, "My daughter does not know how to save." I was very hurt by his unjust remark since I never had been given the opportunity to handle money. I decided that I would try to save from the household budget. I worried about the budget and the cost of our honeymoon, which, Friedel had decided, would be spent on the Balearic Islands.

I had heard that the train would cost only 300 marks if we would forego a sleeping compartment. When I mentioned it to Friedel, he laughed and said he could not picture us on our first night sitting up in a regular compartment.

As our wedding date drew nearer, Erich left for New York to be married. He and Ty would return after their wedding to live in my parents' house until they went to London, where Erich would work in the Schenker office there. My mother was very upset that she could not attend the wedding of her favorite child, her *Goldjunge*, her "precious boy." I did my best to console her, but I was unhappy about her order to clear out the playroom next to my bedroom so that Erich and Ty would have a sitting room when they returned. I remember crying bitter tears as I emptied the drawers of the built-in closets in which my childhood treasures had accumulated. My mother looked over my shoulder and pulled out of the mess a wad of aluminum foil chocolate wrappers.

"What is this?" she asked, and I answered, "Don't throw it out, Made collects this." Made, our Swiss governess, had left us years before, and we both burst out laughing.

My parents decided to spend Christmas that year in Garmisch, which is not far from Feldafing. Thus, Friedel could be with his mother and see us as well. My father asked me to join him for Christmas shopping. Places he never went to normally could amuse him; he became like a little boy. We went to the large, and, at the time, only department store, the *Kaufhaus des Westens*, the *KDW*, as the Berliners called it. It was a novelty in 1932, and very popular. He bought a steamer trunk for me, a large, plywood contraption, which was intended for ocean trips. These trunks were like a small cupboard, almost as tall as a person, and opened vertically and had hangers and drawers. Mine was marked with blue and white stripes, the Bavarian colors.

Just before Christmas, I became the proud owner of the apartment key, a token of my dream come true. Friedel prepared to leave Cologne and packed his suitcases with intense joy. He would move to Berlin after I had found him a suitable room to rent.

The last of many letters we exchanged were his instructions to me and my responses. He told me what to do with his belongings, what to pack for the Christmas vacation, and last, but not least, which papers to get for our courthouse marriage ceremony. In Germany, the announcement of the intention to marry had to be posted at the *Standesamt* ("marriage license bureau") six weeks before the wedding and published in the column of a newspaper reserved for such news. One had to submit a birth certificate, proof of residence, and the last former residence. Anybody opposing this marriage had a right to voice his opinion within the six-week period. The marriage certificate was inscribed in a family book, and with that being sealed, the marriage was legally consummated. Since the church and state were separate institutions, a church ceremony was not required and left to free choice. Had Friedel and I not been confirmed in the same church in Grunewald, we would have been obliged to produce membership papers from another church of the Lutheran denomination.

I ran around Berlin to find a room for Friedel. My mother strongly objected to the idea of me going into an apartment house with the sign, "Room for Rent." It could be indecent! My mother, as she often did, lost sight of the real situation.

I hated the thought of Friedel living in a rented room once more while Erich and Ty lived in our beautiful house with its entire floor of empty guest rooms. But I didn't say anything and retreated just a little more from my childhood relationship with my mother. For the rest of our lives, my mother never really forgave me for growing up and moving away from her. She had built her life on us and had no goals other than her family and entertaining friends. But, at that time, I was thinking only of getting away to Friedel.

December 28, 1932

Dearest Friedel

I am so happy when I am with you. I want you to feel the strength of my love which flows through me to you. In all coming struggles we will encounter I want to show you the light side. I feel as though I was born to fulfill this task. The world is beautiful because we met on this earth: we could never have been happy had we not encountered each other. As we wander together, as on the mountain in Garmisch a few days ago, I forget everything which might bother us and feel like spreading my arms to embrace the world. Come soon and embrace your Liesel.

The last letter was written. From then on we thought only of wedding preparations, and time passed more quickly than we had feared. I think we had exhausted our romantic state of mind, and everyday life with its little problems caused friction between us here and there. Friedel sometimes even resented my girlish infatuation, my constant eyeing him, and begging for signs of love. I was so preoccupied with wedding plans and filled with anticipation that I took little notice that on January 30, 1933, Adolf Hitler was appointed Chancellor of Germany.

The night of our *Polterabend*, the "wedding-eve party," February 27, 1933, for which I had waited such a long time, remains vivid in my memory with its frightening contrast between happiness and fear. My mother planned and organized the festive, noisy celebration in keeping with her own family tradition. Friedel and I enjoyed it although, serious and quiet as we were, we could have imagined another type of "last evening" before the wedding. My mother had her uncle Robert Goetz in mind, who was such a good poet and had always produced little shows with rhymes and songs for every occasion. Thus, she surprised us with scenes from our childhood, slides made from drawings. We saw Friedel in the bathtub with earphones transmitting music from his homemade radio; or Friedel with a huge, woolen bandage around his neck, treated by a bearded doctor for his everlasting sore throat; or we admired Friedel, bundled up in furs and gloves while I sat in the background in a bathing suit. Friedel, usually not amenable to teasing, took these allusions to his weaknesses smilingly. I was to be seen sleepwalking or chasing guests in my nightgown, swinging Molly's leash. Songs were performed by young cousins from the next generation—Edgar and Gerda Blum; Hans and Peter Mittler; the Stephan girls, Helga and Ingeborg; and Olga Johanna and Maria Elisabeth Hepner. Erich and Ty were also on stage. I remember Ty as she sang and danced in a slender, bright green dress, a beautiful contrast to her titan-red hair.

The guests had come from all over—Munich, Vienna, Holland, and England. Friedel's family was represented by his mother, Carry Scherer, and Hermann Grieving. Only Rita was absent.

Hans Pfülf, true to his promise, came, but he was not accompanied by his wife, who didn't like to go out or travel. Then there were the friends from the Schenker management, Harry Hamacher and his Rumanian wife, Etelka; Georg and Gertrud Stefan; Kurt Schiller and his wife; and the managers of branch offices, Herr and Frau Hautmann and Herr Engel with his wife.

On that memorable evening, the end of our "bachelor time," my friend Dota, with whom I had attended the Pestalozzi-Froebel *Haus*, recited a sentimental poem composed by her mother and written on parchment in calligraphy, and presented me with the traditional *Jungfernkranz*, or "virginity wreath," made of intertwined sprigs of green myrrh. Supposedly, it has happened that a minister, knowing that the bride in front of the altar was not a virgin, stepped down and loosened the ends of the wreath so they were no longer joined, an embarrassing moment for the young woman. This was certainly not my problem, but I knew the anguish one suffered to make it to the altar as I did.

After much fun and laughter and a sumptuous meal accompanied by exquisite wines from my father's famous wine collection, the guests left the festive house. Cars were driven up to the door and disappeared through the open, wrought-iron gates. Friedel left to spend the last night before our wedding in the Hotel Esplanade. Maids in black and white, the butler, and other help ran back and forth to collect glasses and ashtrays. Soon the downstairs was cleaned up, and preparations for the next day, the wedding day, began. We retired to the upper floor and sat, partially undressed already, in Mutti's sitting room talking about the marvelous evening. The telephone rang. My father walked over and picked up the receiver. From his expression, we knew something terrible had happened:

On his way to the Hotel Esplanade, Friedel saw the night sky over the city glowing red and flames, visible from afar, near the center of the city. As he got closer, he could see the *Reichstag*, the "parliament" building, engulfed in fire. When he reached the hotel, he called my father. Nobody knew how this had happened or why, but we sensed it was not just an accident—it was a disaster with political foreboding.

The history of the *Reichstag* building, a landmark of the German capital in former times, is not very long. The impressive, classical-style parliament building was erected during the reign of Kaiser Wilhelm I, in 1884, on the *Platz der Republik* after long debates about its proposed location. But it was not until ten years later that the first parliamentary session was held in the completed structure. And the last session to be held was in December 1932. Kurt von Schleicher was chancellor then, but the most powerful party was the National Socialist German Workers' Party led by Hitler. On January 30, 1933, when he became chancellor, Hitler cunningly acquired from the aging Hindenburg the power to dismiss parliament and to call for a new election. He had achieved his ambitions up to that point within the law. Later, he changed the law and enacted ordinances as he saw fit. So, at the time of the fire, the *Reichstag* building was somewhat superfluous to the Nazis.

Later the fire was blamed on Marius van der Luebbe, a feeble-minded, half-blind Dutchman. Supposedly, he was caught in the building after the fire started, but nobody was certain who sent him there. Evidence later pointed to Hermann Goering, who probably had used Luebbe as a scapegoat. The defenseless man confessed in a quick trial, was taken to prison, and beheaded. The destruction of the parliament was used by Hitler as a pretext for taking draconian measures against political opponents, particularly those on the left. The fire, so the Nazis claimed, signaled the beginning of a Communist attempt to seize control of Germany, and the next day, the day of our wedding, President Hindenburg signed an emergency decree that suspended all civil rights within Germany and established martial law. Chancellor Hitler soon used his new emergency powers to arrest Communists and other dissidents in the parliament.

In retrospect, one would assume that this portentous event had ruined our private festivity, but this was not so. The morning after the fire, the 28th of February, I was aroused right after sunrise by singing voices under my window, accompanied by a trumpet and violin. I jumped up and opened the window to a crisp, beautiful morning, my wedding day! I saw Schmidecke and Kuehne, the chauffeurs, and Herr Genrich, the gardener, standing there in costumes with artificial paper noses and red hair and funny hats. I was very touched by their singing. Then I opened my bedroom door and a sweet smell of flowers greeted me. Herr Genrich had worked all night winding garlands of lilly of the valley and lacy asparagus greens around the banister and the entry door.

Later, trembling with excitement and dressed in my wedding gown, a light tulle covering my head and serving as a train and a bouquet of white flowers in my hand, I came down this staircase. My knees were soft when I met Friedel at the bottom of the stairs, and we walked slowly out the door and stepped into the waiting carriage, the door held open by a butler dressed in a gold-trimmed uniform. The carriage, laid out inside with white satin, was drawn by two white horses as in a fairy tale. The two attendants in livery put on their top hats, cracked the whip, and out we drove through the open, iron gates under the eyes of the assembled staff and the curious neighbors. The cars with my parents, Erich and Ty, and the guests followed on the short ride along the snow-coated street to the Grunewald church. The ride to the church was much too short. The only time one has this kind of pleasure it should have lasted longer.

We walked into the beautifully decorated church past photographers and a motion picture camera, and, then, accompanied by sweet organ music, we walked dowwn the aisle. I did not see Rita, but she told me twenty years later that she was hiding somewhere in the back just to see us but not to be seen herself.

The wedding party and guests returned to the *Jagowstrasse* where, between the many courses of the dinner that followed, good wishes from far and near were read. The speeches included one by my father who was moved to tears and too excited to say anything more than most. Did he sense perhaps that this was the last time he would preside over a festive table in the beautiful home he had created?

After dinner, the time came for the bride to leave. I changed into a beige and brown traveling outfit, and, then, the sad moment came for my parents when we waved good-bye. I don't think I was sad; I thought, when I return I will have two homes, my old one and my own. Thus, we all dream like little girls. I remember the curious children hiding in corners and behind doors to witness this event. The mystery surrounding a wedding is no more, but children then just did not know what it was all about, and curiosity made them imagine all sorts of things they had heard.

We drove to the Hotel Esplanade. Walking through the lobby clutching my flowers, I felt as though everyone knew we were newlyweds. I was embarrassed and my sense of privacy rebelled.

We left the next day on the train to Barcelona. But not without being surprised by our bridal attendants, hidden behind a kiosk showering us with rice. Other passengers grinned, and, again, Friedel and I blushed.

In Barcelona I got sick. I guess the long train trip, the heat, and the "first night" were all too much. Sitting at the table across from Friedel that evening in the hotelrestaurant I saw him more and more dimly and had I not left the room, I surely would have fainted. The doctor probably had his own thoughts, but he advised us to leave because of the climate. The next day, we tried our luck at Mallorca, where we stayed in the Hotel Formentor, which had just opened. Our room, which overlooked the sea, had Spanish furniture and a four-poster bed with a hand-crocheted spread.

The sea was icy. Friedel, who hated to swim in cold water, stayed on the beach while I tried to be brave. It is a strange time, such a honeymoon. We thought we had known each other so well through our letters, but now it was not apparent. We were caught with a lack of conversation or activity, and somehow embarrassed.

The dilemma was interrupted by a telephone call from my father. He told us to return immediately to Berlin. The city abounded in rumors in the wake of Hitler's fast-moving efforts to destroy political opposition. The situation there was alarming, and my father was afraid if we didn't come at once we might not be able to reenter Germany. If only that would have been so! As shocking as that might have been to us, it would have spared us fifteen years of anguish. It is remarkable that neither I, Friedel, nor my father and mother thought about leaving the country as thousands of others did. At that time,

German citizens, even Jews, could take their possessions and easily obtain visas to enter another country, even the United States.

Friedel was upset over our premature return because he had never been to Paris and had hoped to go there with me. But we didn't dare contradict my father, who most certainly knew what he was talking about. We returned to Berlin only ten days after we left it.

Sonnenburg

I still felt dizzy and weak upon our return. My mother and the doctor met us to determine the cause. The doctor decided it was "*Vasomotorische Stoerungen.*" Nobody was sure what that was, but it was apparently not serious. Friedel and I settled into our new apartment in the *Duesseldorferstrasse*. My mother had hired Agnes, a nice girl from Laegerdorf, to be our maid. It seems to me as if our married life, so fervently awaited, did not materialize—at least not as we had expected, as we had dreamed. Thank God for having had dreams, which, even if unfulfilled, elated us as life probably never can. During our two years of courtship, we had lived what was denied to us in reality. Reality now intruded into our privacy, knocked at our door, and marched right in.

Just three weeks after our return, Friedel opened the newspaper at breakfast time and, growing pale, read that my father was to be arrested. He raced to the telephone and called my parents. My mother, who answered the phone, told him Papi was peacefully sitting in the bathtub. As every morning, he was occupied with his ceremonies of washing and dressing for another business day. We urged him not to go to the office. We begged him to leave the city, the country. My father just could not believe he was in any kind of danger:" the newspaper must be in error." He had a clean conscience and had done nothing which would justify the "captain to leave his ship." Nobody could or would accuse him of something he hadn't done.

That day he kissed my mother good-bye; greeted Schmidecke, who stood, as always, cap in hand at the open Mercedes door; and they drove off to the Schenker offices at *Unter den Linden* 39.

I was not there when they came for him, but I learned of it quickly. I know that the state police (who later became the Gestapo) searched the office, one did not know for what, and arrested Papi. It was the tenth of April, 1933. We had been married exactly forty days. I remember leaning out of the window of the breakfast nook anxiously looking down the street around five o'clock, the time when Friedel usually turned the corner of the *Duesseldorferstrasse*. Behind me were the two chairs and the square table, the pretty setting which was supposed to be the place for our happy breakfast hour. When Friedel finally appeared, slowly walking up the street briefcase in hand, I screamed, "Friedel come quickly, they have arrested Papi!" I will never forget his calm face and the composed manner with which he responded.

Friedel and I insisted that my mother should come and stay with us; we didn't want her to be alone. Erich and Ty were in London, where Erich had begun work for the Schenker London office. After a day or two of frantic inquiries, my mother found out that Papi was behind bars in the state prison of Spandau. No explanation of his arrest was given, but the knowledge of where he was being held was, in itself, a relief. I don't know if it is possible to imagine the shock which such a phrase, "Papi in prison" evokes. It was unthinkable—my father in prison! That was a place for criminals!

From then on, I remember only nightmarish fear for Papi, the helplessness we experienced at being confronted with hate and chaos in contrast to our strictly regulated routine—a life based on order and tradition. Soldiers are trained before they go into battle, nurses and doctors study for years before dealing with patients, but we were faced with conditions and situations for which we were unprepared. We did not understand. Logic, justice, loyalty, courtesy, and compassion had seemingly vanished. None of the familiar attitudes between people counted any more: our world crumbled under our feet.

My father was the first victim of the "New Order" in our circle of friends and acquaintances. Some of them left the country as soon as they could. Our terror was such that we didn't dare turn for help to any of our friends for fear the taint which marked us would spread to them. We were alone without legal advice. It was difficult even to find a lawyer willing to help us, and when we did find such a man, there was little he could do. Since my father had not been formally charged with a crime, a defense could not be prepared for him.

My mother, who had never before confronted authority, mustered her courage and charm to secure a visitor's permit to see her husband. The chauffeur drove her to the prison, where she bravely faced the guards and waited in the crowded corridor until, at last, she was reunited for a brief time with her Marci. Papi consoled her, and said he was sure he would be released in a few days. He reasoned it was all a mistake. This kind of reasoning had gone out of fashion, but he didn't know it.

At that time they called the imprisonment *Schutzhaft*, "protective custody." That meant they pretended to "protect" the prisoner from alleged enemies. My father, who firmly believed in the "right" things of life, like work, honesty, and strength, had been accused of bribery and cheating, but not openly in front of a court or a judge. He was denounced by a dismissed employee. There are always those who have failed who envy the successful. In those days, membership in the Nazi party enabled any individual to denounce others, especially Jewish persons. No trial was necessary. The accusation alone was a tool to imprison the target of one's vengeance. The brutality that slumbers at the bottom of every society had broken loose.

Much of what was occurring never reached our ears, even though we lived in the midst of it. There was no public debate or open discussion, no free press or radio which might have opened this closed book and, possibly, our eyes. For us, the time consisted of day-to-day living, of planning what the immediate next step was going to be in order to free Papi. We lived in fear, fear of the unknown next event, fear of going to sleep or waking up, fear of what might have happened meanwhile to Papi.

Fear of losing life and family can move a nation, can move the world. Unfortunately, this is not a passing phantom; many times in the past this human idiosyncrasy has gripped millions, and in the future fear will again be our master. But we don't like to think about it, we don't like to ask ourselves what we would do in such a situation. We easily condemn those who, out of fear, commit crimes and carry out what they are told to do. I believe almost anybody would succumb if subjected to fear in the right circumstances. We cannot deny that human beings are vulnerable. But I think such a passage in life teaches something as well. I believe the person exposed to fear learns to be humble and to relinquish self-righteousness. Such experience teaches what Christians claim to learn from the example of Christ's life and death. But I think that every human being, no matter of which faith, learns this lesson through a life-threatening experience.

Erich, in London at the time of Papi's arrest, did not come back to help. Was it fear? Friedel tried to solve the problems, give us hope and confidence; he stood behind us like a rock. As always, he said little; he reflected thoroughly before he uttered a word.

The day came, the dreaded day when Mutti arrived at the prison office to ask permission to talk to her husband and was told that he was no longer there. She was thrown into intolerable anguish. We learned that Papi was in a concentration camp called Sonnenburg, near Berlin. Nobody could visit there, of course, and there was no possibility of contacting my father. We had heard stories of starvation, torture, and death at the hands of the state police. I really don't know how we survived the fear and worry and how he survived the camp. But Papi survived and so did we.

After six horrible months, my father was free. Alfred Ball of the Pennsylvania Railroad, with whom my father had done business in Philadelphia, came from the United States in my father's behalf. And it seems that the deputy in charge listened to the American, although I cannot imagine why the ministry should have cared. But the intervention helped; shortly afterwards, on July 13, 1933, my father came home.

When Papi came back to the *Jagowstrasse* he seemed the same, but obviously the experience had been traumatic. He had signed an agreement not to speak about his imprisonment, and, therefore, we could only gather from occasional remarks what he had been through. He probably told my mother things which she did not pass on to us. But his spirit was not broken. As part of the agreement, my father was removed from his position with Schenker & Company and forced to sell his remaining shares. But the most devastating part of the agreement was that he had to leave the country within a certain time and leave his possessions behind. In an ironic twist, the Nazi government also required him to pay a penalty tax, called the *Reichsfluchtsteuer*, which was assessed against everyone leaving the country. The tax was calculated on the value of property left behind; and since everything had to be left behind, the tax was considerable.

Since Nazi law forbade all exportation and transfer of money to foreign countries, my father's sizable life insurance policy went into a barred account with all his other investments. Dr. Ruge, his lawyer, worked on the payment of the *Reichsfluchtsteuer*. My father settled his business affairs, left the house in the *Jagowstrasse* under the care of Friedel and a reduced staff, and arranged his and my mother's journey from their homeland.

My parents left Germany and went to London. It is easy to make this statement as if Mutti and Papi had gone on just another trip, but I knew what it meant for them to leave Germany, the Grunewald, and to leave us behind. In spite of my father's detention and the plain signs of danger for me, Friedel and I never discussed or contemplated leaving the country with my parents. It is hard to leave your country; it is even harder to start a new life in a new country, learn another language, leave everything and everybody behind. True, it is easier to leave under orders, but thousands did it out of free choice. In any case, we never thought about that possibility. Later, I felt bitter about our naivety. We were too young, Friedel said many years later.

Up to this time, my life had been directed exclusively towards personal goals and the fulfillment of my desires. Suddenly, my private wishes and plans were suppressed as political events motivated our actions and thoughts, as they did for everybody in Germany. Civilians had to march in line, symbolically at least, the same as the Nazi storm troops. Obey orders, submit to rules, or face the consequences was the new life.

Looking back on the years of hardship and danger that resulted from our failure to leave Germany, I realize that they were my formative ones. Had we left, our love might have blossomed, our characters would have freely developed as we had dreamed. I cannot judge what a life free of stress would have made of me.

With a certain pride I used to think of the challenges of those years, the confrontations with unknown powers and dangers, the constant demand for decisions, and the way I mastered these situations. I was sure that my character was strengthened through adversity. My example was my father. Consciously or unconsciously, I got my strength from his staunch determination. His unfaltering, firm deportment with which he entered and left the concentration camp—convinced that right could not be made wrong—served as an example in my darkest hours. I was his daughter, placed in a life in which I would stand up to its challenges.

But looking back, I regret that the trials and tribulations had made me hard in certain ways. Feelings rule me which should not be the main consideration in a person's life. Although it is difficult to recall feelings and actions which are long buried under other emotions equally strong and traumatic, I do know that Friedel and I awoke from our romantic dreams and found ourselves different people. My concern was not, as I had expected, Friedel's happiness and comfort. Into the silence of our cozy little apartment came the harsh sounds of marching uniformed men and the sound of revolutionary songs with inflamatory, yet seductive, rhythms. I had heard them before, and now I saw and heard them under our windows, swinging their swastika banners and shouting their fear-inspiring threats against the Jews.

Existence had turned into a bad dream. But, in spite of all, we wanted to continue our lives as we had dreamed. I had only one desire and that was to have a child. Friedel was filled with doubts and fears about the desirability of a baby in these times, but I didn't understand them. He chose not to explain to me the responsibility and the imprudence of one who was considered a Jew bringing a child into Hitler's world. He didn't accept Hitler's laws and refused to reason with me on those terms. Friedel knew the depth of my wish to have children. It was not just a nebulous feeling, a love for children; it was much more to me. I was born to be a mother; a child was vital to my existence.

I was of the opinion that no parent knew what difficulties their child might have to face; everybody had problems and if this would be a reason not to have children then no babies would be born at all. I thought it presumptuous to deny a child life because we were afraid of dangers it might encounter. This opinion caused me many hours of anxiety and doubt; I wondered whether or not it was born of egotism. I was also too innocent to predict what children would have to face. Friedel would not tell me the reasons for his opinion, although he had surely a better idea than I, how things would develop. He wanted to see me happy, and now it was no longer in his power as he had wished and planned. How could he have convinced me, now, at last his wife, young and hungry for fulfillment after the long period of waiting? There were many nights when I cried, muffling the sobs in my pillow, while Friedel pretended to be very tired. I attributed his behavior to all the wrong reasons. Our married life was not unfolding as we had expected.

Then, in the fall of 1933, soon after my father's release from the concentration camp, I found myself pregnant. My excitement merged with continuous worry about my father, so that I could not enjoy my pregnancy as I would have liked. Now his and Mutti's preparations for departure were distracting. As long as I could remember, my parents and the *Jagowstrasse* had been the rock on which I had stood and now this secure foundation of my life suddenly slipped away. Friedel's serious face was a steady reminder of the changes which had taken place; he had retreated into a shell and was just as silent as when we first met. The short period in Friedel's life in which the discovery of love had freed him came to a sudden halt. Unfortunately, great demands would confront him for the rest of his life.

This is the tragedy of Friedel's fate. He chose the difficult course at every crossroad, and his sensitive nature caused him sufferings beyond measure. Nobody, not even I, came to know the full extent of his pain. He faced uncertainties, guided by his own moral standards, and overcame them; but it cost him dearly.

Rainer

It was the hottest time of the year in Berlin when I was heavy with child. My dresses were custom-made and not particularly pretty; no maternity fashions were available. Friedel jokingly thought of starting a rental business for future mother's clothing and all other necessities. I was not apprehensive of the impending event, although I had no idea what was involved and I had never read a book or gotten any instruction about childbirth. Expectant mothers in those days put themselves completely into the hands of doctors and midwives. My ignorance turned out to be the cause of much unexpected and unnecessary anxiety.

Once, when I walked to the market across from our building, I had that first experience of pressure and the sudden thought that I could lose my baby on the street. The feeling of pressure persisted for what seemed an endless time, but Dr. Dorpalen, when I told him about it, was not impressed or willing to give me a plausible explanation. He was the gynecologist who saved my mother's life on two occasions when she had extra-uterine pregnancies. Obviously, I looked up to him as though he was the last word on all that concerned women's problems, and I trusted him completely.

Then the time came. At the small and simple clinic, Dr. Dorpalen decided to induce labor by making me walk up and down the narrow corridor; then I got an enema and a hot bath. The pains became intolerable. The nurse laughed and said sarcastically, "Had you thought that it was that easy?" She put me in a small room and told me to sleep. Perhaps I would do better the next day, she mumbled. I lay in the darkness alone and afraid.

The next day, August 1, 1934, I was taken to the labor room. It was very hot and the table I was lying on was hard; a bright lamp burned overhead. The pains intensified and, then, the baby! A boy! Before they gave me anesthesia, an incredible joy flooded through me. When they brought the child all bundled up, I could not really see or feel him.

After waking up from the anesthesia, the joyous feeling returned and made up for the discomfort of the stitches and pain. I could hardly wait to go to my private room, where I would be attended by a private nurse.

In the hour Rainer was born my life began: my entire being was filled with love. I awoke, and, although I was only twenty-three years old, it seemed as if a circle was complete, a shell was formed, a shell that cloistered my real life and became a permanent part of me. Resting deep within me, it nourished me and became the source out of which everything was born. In the years to come, this source would be put to test. The more adverse the circumstance, the harder became the shell.

Maternity care had changed little since I was born. A new mother was still kept in bed for at least ten days and considered ill for six weeks. During this period, my nurse took care of everything, and I never even had a chance to diaper the baby. All that was asked of a new mother was to nurse and take care of herself so that there would be enough milk. Every four hours, the nurse would bring the baby freshly diapered and bundled in a soft flannel sheet covering the feet and the little body up to the waist. The soft, white batiste shirts I had sewn before Rainer was born and the tiny, knitted cotton jackets were fastened in front so that the baby would not have to lie on a pleat. I nursed alternately with the right and left breast each time; and to remember which side was to provide the next meal, one placed the baby on its right or left side in the crib.

In the morning, before the second meal, the baby was bathed. The nursery was kept as quiet and clean as possible, almost sterile. Few noises reached the baby's ears. One was told that a newborn's nerves were very delicate and that the baby should be kept isolated, as far as possible from bacteria and possible infections.

When the nurse left six weeks later, I was nervous, although she had demonstrated everything I must do. Friedel and I became slaves to the baby's routine. I would not have thought of interrupting the schedule or taking the baby amongst a crowd. Babies were dressed in spotless white, pink, or pale blue, and everything around the crib was washed and even boiled for cleanliness. The first time we gave Rainer a bath, Friedel prepared the water. I followed the prescribed procedure: I tested the temperature with my elbow, then I held Rainer under the left armpit, his head resting on my arm, and let him float in the small baby tub. Babies love water, of course, and he was all joy. Washing his head was another test of courage. There was no "no-tears" soap then. His cries made me panic, and I held him much longer then necessary. That, in turn, made me feel guilty. I had been warned that babies are easily spoiled and can then dominate their parents with their cries.

We insisted the child have time by himself; too much stimulation was not good for the nerves, and a child was expected to learn concentration while playing alone. Our baby was weighed before and after each meal. We wrote dutifully into our little booklet how much milk he had taken, how much he had gained during that meal. Every evening, Friedel checked the book, and we were happy and proud if the results were satisfactory.

My milk production increased over the months. Although I had problems at first I finally, nursed Rainer for six months. When he was a few weeks old, we started to give him raw carrot juice and a fruit puree of a beaten banana and orange juice. I took him on walks every day to the park. He would lie in the beautiful, white baby carriage with white and blue pillows and covers.

During one of my first outings, I proudly pushed my new baby carriage along the nearby streets when several "Stuka Bombers", Hermann Göering's pride, plunged from the sky almost touching the roofs of houses, their shrieking, whistling noise filled the air and panic stricken I fled into the closest house entrance. One had not seen these monstrous bombers before and rumours said that these practice flights were Göring's propaganda. Sometimes I drove in our BMW cabriolet, which was later requisitioned by the army, to our house in the Jagow street and played with Rainer in our lovely garden and tried to ignore the empty house, my lost paradise. I never understood later how I mastered the hurt of separation from my family. After the baby was born I did not even miss my parents; I suppose my motherhood ; I remember my joy to have Rainer; I had "cut my umbilical cord at last. I was Friedel's wife and Rainers mother, and my parents in England faded into oblivion. Life in the Jagow Srasse was no more, but our new life and its demands continued.

CHAPTER SIXTEEN

FOUNDING AMERICAN UNION TRANSPORT

By the time my father and mother arrived in London after leaving Germany, Erich and Ty had already left for New York, where my brother continued to work for Schenker. My parents had decided to emigrate to America also, and, while he was in London, my father arranged for their passage. He had good contacts with the president of the United States Line, and he helped him get the necessary papers for Mutti and himself.

My father was determined to continue his work in his chosen field. But in 1934, nobody could foresee this progress and the future lay pretty dark before us. Although my father was known to be successful in all his past enterprises, he now faced extraordinary conditions. For example, the transfer of goods and money from Germany to a foreign country was extremely difficult, and in this case for a Jew, almost impossible. Every German was required to obey the new regulations whether he was on the side of the party or not. To bypass the restrictions concerning Jews and evade the laws against exportation of valuables of any kind required determination, skill, and courage. Lawyers and others who attempted to assist Jews in this effort placed their lives in jeopardy.

Before he left Germany, he had engaged a professor from the Berlin University to handle his claim. Although the chances for an expelled Jew to receive compensation from a state-controlled company were not good, my father was determined to pursue the matter. (Eventually, he was awarded payment for the broken contract with the *Reichsbahn* and his shares of Schenker and its various subsidiaries. To my knowledge, this was a unique case.)

The executives at Schenker, Berlin, formerly my father's friends, now bowed to the reigning power. Orders from the party were carried out regardless of conflicting personal convictions. The process began of eliminating all Jews from all Schenker branches, including those in London and New York. My father advised Erich to maintain a personal relationship with customers and with Mr. Ball of the Pennsylvania Railroad and to be prepared to work independently should he be forced to leave Schenker, New York, before my father could establish a new Holzer-owned firm there.

An event occurred which hurt my father and Friedel, but they didn't realize the deeper meaning and portent it had. Georg Stephan, who was my mother's cousin's husband, announced one day in the London office that he had fired my brother and he considered doing the same to Friedel. Georg Stephan, who had enjoyed my parents' friendship and help throughout his married life, whose children had been my charges and the object of my love since they were born, threw his newly acquired weight around as if he was the manager of Schenker. He said, among other things about my father, "Nobody goes to a concentration camp without reason." Although Georg Stephan's attitude was typical of many of my father's former "friends," Papi just didn't understand the changes taking place in his homeland.

In New York, my father bought into Roepke & Otto, a Hamburg-based transportation firm which had a subsidiary in New York and was partly owned by the United States Line. After a determined effort, complicated by the fact of his German background, Marcel Holzer was able to become the sole owner of Roepke & Otto. In January 1935, after gaining full control of Roepke & Otto, he created American Union Transport, Inc., a freight-forwarding company in New York. He was the president of the new firm, Erich was executive vice-president, and there were three other executives and five or six employees. From this small beginning, American Union Transport would experience a remarkable development as brokers for the purchase and sale of ships and as brokers for chartering ships for full cargoes, with offices in New York, Brazil, Chicago, and San Francisco.

I have a suspicion that my father was never fully aware of the difficulties and dangers encountered by the people who worked on his behalf. One of these persons was Friedel. There are endless letters and cables exchanged between them which demonstrate that my father would never understand when Friedel told him that most of the things he requested were impossible.

In February 1935 my father wrote a letter to me, the first from America. My parents had settled in Scarsdale, in the apartment above Erich and Ty, who was then expecting her first child. Papi explained that they had made the decision to stay near them so that Mutti could help Ty with the new baby.

He told us of an automobile trip he had taken with Erich and Ty to Florida. He described at length how he had, for the first time, grasped the dimension of the American continent. The distance from New York to Florida, he said, was like driving from Berlin to "Konstantinopel."

He asked us to pack more suitcases and send them through one of Papi's partners who was returning from France by steamer. My father made a list and knew exactly where we could find his three beige tweed coats; the grey, double-breasted one; and the other beige one made from the special material. He wanted the six light-weight suits and just a selection of his socks—twenty pair would suffice. In the left corner of his dressing room closet, we would find his summer undershirts, of which he wanted twelve, and six batiste shirts. My mother, who typed his letter for him, wrote parenthetically, "Oh God!"

Difficulties slowly arose between Papi's business plans and the situation in Germany; neither Papi or Friedel seemed to have any idea of the long-term program the party had for Germany. They acted as if they still could count on the previously valid order to their lives. In their letters, they discussed insurance for the Mercedes and the Hispano-Suiza and the routine maintenance to be done on the *Jagowstrasse* house, where the staff, reduced in number, kept things going until the house could be sold. Friedel, together with Fräulein Hussock, my father's former secretary, took care of routine payments due, and Friedel sold one of the nearby properties my father had acquired.

Friedel urged my father to come to England so that many business matters that required his signature could be resolved. My parents agreed to come after the birth of Ty's baby. One of the conditions of Papi's release from the concentration camp was that he could never again enter Germany, even for a brief visit. Oddly, this restriction did not apply to my mother.

On May 5, Ty and Erich had their first child, Ann Elise. On my mother's fiftieth birthday, May 18, 1935, Ty brought the baby home, and a few days later my mother embarked for Europe aboard the SS *Manhattan*.

Her brother Hans received her in London. Together they went to Hamburg, where they were greeted by their mother, the beloved *Alte*, and Lotte Blum, Hans's wife. Later, there was a joyous family reunion—my grandmother's sisters-in-law, Aunt Dodo and Agnes Goetz, Aunt Tete Goetz, and as many of the cousins as were in Hamburg at the time. It was the last reunion for many family members who would soon be destroyed as if they were weeds.

My mother arrived in Berlin on June 8th. and my joy to embrace her again was indescribable. Like in the olden days, friends came to see her, and for a short time, the political situation seemed like only a bad dream.

In the days that followed my mother enjoyed Rainer, sharing with him her incredible capacity for love and tenderness. Her diary from that visit reads like our earlier days in the *Jagowstrasse*: she received guests, went to movies, and on shopping trips to Clara Schulz, an exclusive fashion house in

Berlin. Only incidentally did she record the sale, for 85,000 *Reichsmark*, of the second house which my father had bought some years previously for my grandparents. Our lawyer, Dr. Ludwig Ruge, tried also to sell the *Jagowstrasse* house and my mother had the sad duty to lead prospective buyers through her beloved home. In the heat of that summer, Mutti packed all Papi's remaining personal belongings, carried on endless conversations with agents and lawyers, and handled a lot of matters she was not at all used to doing.

I felt fortunate that my mother was there in those hot summer days, and I will keep that July in my memory forever. I was pregnant again. We decided under the circumstances that I should not have another baby. Abortion was illegal in Germany at the time and involved considerable risk. Nevertheless, we made arrangements with Dr. Dorpalen, who agreed to perform the operation. Dr. Dorpalen was Jewish and, therefore, having difficulties with his practice at the hospital. We didn't know he was also suffering from deep depression brought on by his situation. The operation was performed in his office and I returned home immediately. That night I suffered a near-fatal hemorrhage. Friedel rushed me to the hospital, where Dr. Dorpalen performed additional surgery to stop the hemorrhage. The surgery, according to Dr. Dorpalen, also would prevent any further pregnancies. Although I did eventually have two more children, I never fully recovered from that episode.

In August, we went to Noordwijk in Holland to meet my father who was coming from New York. I was well enough to travel by train and my mother and Agnes, our young maid, came along to help with the baby so I could rest. Rainer slept in his folding carriage in our narrow sleeping-car compartment. He was just a year old and an adorable baby. I was interested only in him and kept a daily diary about his progress.

In Noordwijk we spent unforgettable days in the Hotel Huis ter Duin, where Dr. Sauvage-Nolting once had asked for my hand. Although everything was very familiar, our impending separation and the uncertainty of our future hung like a cloud above us. We looked like happy vacationers, but it was a sad holiday. My parents received visitors from Germany who came to say farewell to old friends. Stefan Karpeles came, as did our faithful friend Dr. Ruge, who had settled Papi's legal claim. None of us could have guessed what was in Dr. Ruge's mind. He was an exceptionally fine, cultured, and knowledgeable man from an old family from the island of Rügen in the North Sea. His wife was a member of a very well-known Jewish family. Eventually, these two remarkable people were driven to suicide.

Soon, these last days lived in the old style came to an end. My father returned to New York, my mother returned with us to Germany to spend another month before joining her Marci in America. Our parting marked not only the beginning of a long separation, but a new chapter in our lives. Friedel and I had decided to move to Hamburg so that Friedel could work at Roepke & Otto, the firm owned now by my father. Never once at our last meeting in Holland did we consider joining my family in their new adventure in America.

My mother left Germany with a heavy heart because she was leaving me and her beloved "Rainerlein" behind. But on the other side of the ocean was, after all, her second grandchild and Erich and Ty. My father had rented a small apartment on Lee Avenue in Scarsdale by the time my mother arrived in New York. It was a modest home, not even as large as our former gardener's or chauffeur's place. But my mother, having never lost her marvelous enjoyment of simplicity, was not bothered by this drastic change. I suspect that she even enjoyed the return to simpler ways, like those of the early years of their marriage in Hamburg.

My parents had made friends quickly in Scarsdale and had many acquaintances right from the start. So there was no lack of social activities and their rounds to concerts and movies. Their life continued almost in its usual rhythm with its unbroken thrust, the same energy and the same goals. My father pursued his plan to create a successful business and build a grand life such as he had in Germany. I state this with pride—I will always be proud of my valiant father—but a certain bitterness creeps into this remark. That same year, Friedel and I entered into a traumatic phase of our existence, which, intermingled with personal misfortune, would mark us forever.

One can find lots of reasons why we remained in Germany; one could also ask if every other possibility was evaluated before making this decision. While my mother's diary speaks of excursions, parties, and dinner invitations, my recollection of that time is stress, fear, and intolerable and insolvable worries about survival. It seems to me, we were sitting in a net which was drawn closer and closer around us. We were unaware of it at first, as were many others in the same situation. Inside the net, we lost all judgment about our situation and Hitler's plans, as millions of people did. But I should think that viewed from America, the situation ought to have had another aspect, especially for someone like my father who had witnessed the concentration camp from within. Strangely, this experience did not change his outlook, his judgment. As far as other American citizens were concerned, they could not possibly have had an idea about what was going on in Germany. And although it is difficult to believe, most Germans did not realize it until much later.

Return to Hamburg

As Friedel took over the management of Roepke & Otto in Hamburg, we returned to the city where I was born. We were lucky to find a charming, small, two-family brick house in the *Fontenay Allee* 8, part of an estate property. It was one of four houses on a private road lined with trees. The four houses, each for two families, had small fenced gardens and a little terrace. "The Fontenay" was one block away from the Alster and the entire area was traffic restricted. We rented the left half of the building, which had two floors, an attic, and a cellar. Downstairs, the entry hall with a guest powder room led to a dining room, a living room, and a kitchen. From the living room, French doors opened to the terrace and the garden. Really, it was a charming setup. Upstairs was the parents' bedroom, with French doors opening to a small balcony; a children's room; and a "half-room," as one called it. On the top floor next to the attic door was a servant's room. The cellar housed the furnace and the laundry room. From there, a small door led to the cellar of our co-inhabitants, the family Poppenhusen.

Although the move from our first apartment in Berlin to this one was somewhat painful, I think the location, the garden, and the presence of my grandmother and other family members compensated for it. Moreover, the activity of the Nazis was more visible in the streets of Berlin, which was, after all, Germany's capital. Although it was probably an illusion, one felt more out of the way here in our remote quarter of town. Luckily we had chosen small furniture for our apartment in the *Düsseldorferstrasse* and our new quarters could accommodate all of our new things, and we even incorporated the built-in bedroom-cabinets. The cabinetmakers had constructed the intricate interior with countless drawers and shelves in such a way that one could—with some pain and patience—take it apart and reconstruct it.

The living room had built-in bookshelves that formed a cozy corner for easy chairs and a coffee table. Thus, moving in and feeling at home was not difficult. This house is no more. It was not destroyed by bombs or fire which were to devastate so much of Hamburg. It was one of the few houses to survive intact. Decades later, it was torn down, along with the entire neighborhood, to make room for a hotel. It had sheltered us during our hardest times, and, afterwards, it served our good friends Herbert and Ruth Samuel as a warm and cozy home after they lost their apartment in an air raid. But in my mind at least, it still exists and I retain memories of good and bad days connected with the *Fontenay Allee* to which we had moved from Berlin in December 1935.

A new life began for all of us. Friedel, now with Roepke & Otto, had to learn trading in overseas shipments in a small office with new responsibilities and very limited financial means. He got little support and understanding from his boss, my father, who often expected the impossible. Friedel more than once felt frustrated and alone. The great distances overseas, the difficult communication by slow ships, and the lack of prompt responses to his needs made his position very difficult. In those days every step was fraught with problems, restrictions, permits, and taxes. It was almost impossible to please everyone.

Friedel reported faithfully to my father in long letters about his activities. He tried to convey the attitude of the Nazi party, which had begun the process of cutting off Jews from all sources of income. The widespread action concerned all government positions, bankers, teachers, and professors, and the medical profession. One branch after the other fell off the tree on which German Jews had for generations made a living and contributed to German science, culture, and art. Jewish artists soon were banned from the marketplace as were writers. Without the cooperation of the German population these actions could not have been carried out; but my father said in their defense, "Do you know how you would have acted if you had been under threat of losing your freedom?"

Friedel also reported to my father on the investigation by the Gestapo during which every person remotely connected with Marcel Holzer had been interrogated. Amongst them was Papi's longtime secretary *Cläre* Hussock, Harry Hamacher, and even men engaged by the *Reichsbahn*. Every scrap of paper found either in the *Jagowstrasse* or in my father's office was viewed as a possible link to a hypothetical crime or fraud.

Even Hitler's secretary of state, Dr. Otto Meissner, was embarrassed by the search. Dr. Meissner, secretary to presidents Ebert and Hindenburg as well, was my parents' personal friend. My father had once ordered flowers sent to Mrs. Meissner after a party, and the order was found in one of the petty cash records. Dr. Meissner was imprisoned until he could prove the innocence of his relationship with my father.

In addition to Friedel's work at Roepke & Otto, he managed the continuing process of disposing of Papi's assets in Germany. He announced by cable that he had been able to free twenty-five percent of my father's foreign investments despite the fact that these accounts were frozen. He also sold the Mercedes for 2000 *Reichsmark* and shipped the Hispano-Suiza to New York for sale. This car was the sensational light beige roadster in which my father had once chauffeured the film actress Lil Dagover down the *Kurfuerstendam* in Berlin.

Friedel worked hard physically and mentally, and with mixed emotions, to arrange the auction of his father-in-law's possessions. Friedel's theory that my father should have as much cash as possible to start his new life in America, raised by the sale of valued possessions, met with Papi's disapproval. My father wanted everything shipped to America which was, of course, impossible. Friedel sorted out my father's wine collection and the collection of books and packed them to be shipped to New York. Although the household was already legally in the hands of the auction house, Friedel managed to pull out more rare wine and added the bottles to the shipments in the containers, already packed to go; but part of the collection of books and wine were left for the auction. Never did Papi forget or forgive Friedel for that. He also did not fully appreciate our immense good fortune to get two huge containers of his possessions shipped to America. My father's cables directed Friedel to insist on prices for the household goods that were sheer fantasy. It was heartbreaking to let go of the precious oriental rugs, the crystal and china, the paintings, and all the other treasures. But finally the hammer came down. The permits to export the remaining shipment were in our hands and the *Jagowstrasse* chapter of our lives was near its sad end.

After the auction in November 1935, the beautiful house in *Jagowstrasse* 24 in which we had spent so many happy years, waited for its new owner. It was sold for 120,000 *Reichsmark* to Dr. Paul Marx, who was with the Bank of Commerce. His sad work finished, Friedel wrote to my father about the last day when he walked sadly through the empty rooms of the house that had been a second home to him since boyhood.

CHAPTER SEVENTEEN

EDGE OF THE ABYSS

Law for the Protection of German Blood and German
Honor: Special Legislation for Jews in the National Socialist State
1. Marriage between Jews and German citizens is forbidden.
Existing marriages of this kind are nullified. 2. Sexual relationship
between such persons is forbidden. 3. Only persons of German
blood are German citizens. 4. Jews (persons who have three
Jewish grandparents, meaning those who are members of the
Jewish religious community) cannot be German citizens, cannot
vote, and cannot have an official occupation. 5. Children from
mixed marriages are *Mischlinge*, "halfbreeds." Such marriages are
"privileged mixed marriages."

1935 was the year the swastika became the official German flag. And it
was the year of the Nuremberg Laws. Regulations against Jews previously had
been "proclamations," but in 1935 they became law.

Due to the birth of our son, our marriage was now a "privileged mixed
marriage." I was protected (for the moment, at least). Rainer was a "*Mischling* of
the first degree" and also protected. The Nuremberg Laws were just the beginning
of an endless series of restrictions and persecutions of Jews that eventually made
ordinary life impossible. Those who avoided imprisonment were in a hopeless
situation long before the machinery for their destruction was set in motion.

From 1935 on, Friedel and I were between two worlds, Jewish and Aryan.
In that year, it was decreed that all Germans had to work for the state, in the
military or in one of many civilian organizations. To be exempt from this
new order, strict conditions had to be met. The call for universal service to
the State meant that Friedel could be drafted into the army or called to some
other imposed duty. I began to fear these developments and began to worry
about my relatives—my grandmother, and her sister-in-law's families, my
mother's cousins and aunts, and all her friends.

Friedel became the "unproud" owner of three new identity cards. The first was his passport, issued in March 1936, engraved with the Nazi eagle and stamped appropriately for his many business trips to Switzerland, Holland, England, and France. Each time he left the country (he frequently made brief visits to Holland and England on business), he was permitted only ten *Reichsmark*. This law discouraged tourist travel and pleasure trips. Only businessmen who could finance their trips through foreign subsidiaries could leave and enter Germany at will.

The second identification Friedel carried was his *Ahnenpass*, an invention of the Nazi government. All Germans had to prove the purity of their blood back at least two generations on both parents' sides. To do this, one had to research church records and hometown city registers and obtain official copies of appropriate records. Then the documents were submitted for examination and certification to the *Sippenforschung's Institute*, the "Government Board for Research of Kin." The *Ahnenpass* stated that "this ancestry identification . . . is intended for *deutschbluetige* (Germanistic) persons only. Persons of mixed and foreign race receive no confirmation of any kind entered in this book." The booklet contains pages where one's family tree is detailed and text that repeats Nazi ideology and ethical concepts imposed on the Germans.

In essence, Hitler's ideas separated the "pure" German from all other people, while, actually, it is a historical fact that many circumstances in the past have prevented "German blood," and probably all blood, from being "pure" in the Nazi concept. Hitler himself was an Austrian of small stature and with dark hair. Frederick the Great called Germany the *Boulette der Weltgeschichte*, the "hamburger of the world." The truth of that statement is apparent when one studies Germany's geographical position in Europe and the consequences of invasions and wars during which non-Germans left their procreative mark on the German people.

The text continues,

> "This ancestry list shall be proof of German or German-related descent. The list starts therefore at the first (the lowest) person on the ladder, called the 'ancestry bearer,' and reaches upward via the ranks of ancestors from generation to generation, thereby showing the passage of the bloodline carried over the course of centuries to the youngest offspring. It is obvious that in establishing this ancestry passport only physical descendants, that is, blood relations, are considered, and adopted relations and step-relations are excluded. The formula given here enables the detection of a specific ancestor.

The final draft, establishment of which could take a long time, should be done after intensive research and official verification. Once a person has the ancestry table in the aforementioned incontestable form, bolstered by original documents, the first step is complete and there will be no problems to obtain government approval. Sooner or later, this ancestry passport will be required identification for every German comrade (*Volksgenosse*) and there is no doubt that it is advantageous to own such a document. It also helps the already overburdened authorities save time and work if every concerned person provides this paper which documents the qualified ethnic German in the sense of Paragraph 4 of the National Socialist Code. Party membership requires proof of pure German ancestry at least back to the year 1800. There could possibly arise situations in which the establishment of a pure bloodline further back than normal is required. This could be the case if there are several early marriages in former generations so that the year 1800 is not included in three generations."

This rather remarkable text demonstrates the dilemma faced by millions of Germans. Not only Friedel spent time and money on this task, but every German. The instructions contained a veiled threat, and many people working their way back through their forebearers discovered to their horror that they had the "wrong" grandparent. Many thousands of German families thus joined the ranks of Jews and "half-castes" and suffered the deep-reaching consequences. Men lost their jobs, women were shunned, and children excluded from their peers' activities. Often the children suffered the most. The power games of intimidation and bullying common to children are difficult to control even under normal conditions. Added now to that was the element of racial discrimination. It was as if it were sanctioned by the *Fuehrer* to tease or denounce, to isolate and threaten a classmate.

While Friedel was working on his ancestry pass, his anger rose to a dangerous degree. He was able to identify his "pure" blood back to 1800, the year of his great-grandmother's birth. Once completed, his *Ahnenpass* earned him the unwanted military card, in 1939, the third identification he was required to carry. It "entitled" him to wear the German uniform and to swear allegiance to his *Fuehrer*, Adolf Hitler, when the state decided it needed his services.

At the same time that the Nuremberg Laws were enacted, freedom of speech for all Germans was restricted, contributing to our isolation. We were occupied with the unraveling of my father's affairs, which, although we did not realize it then, would be fundamental to our survival. But as far as our life was concerned, we really had no intention of leaving the country.

In the United States, my father, far removed from the German scene, was obsessed with his new business. In her diary, my mother proudly announced his first order from General Motors to handle a shipment of cars. If one imagines how many other firms probably made competitive bids, one realizes how important this was for American Union Transport, a new establishment. This was soon followed by business with Ford Motor Company. My father even received a new Ford as a gift. As in the past, my father's self-confident personality and outstanding knowledge of his field impressed his clients at first encounter.

In March 1935, my parents were able to rent a house large enough to furnish with the precious contents of our beloved Grunewald villa. Friedel had managed to include in the shipment all our oriental rugs and a considerable amount of my father's wine collection. We realized only years later how lucky we were to have rescued so many of our beautiful things, family possessions that made the house as warm as our former home in Berlin. My mother, however, had to get used to many changes in managing a household in America. The hired help, for example, had a much different attitude than their counterparts in Germany. She had to put up with unfamiliar situations, like when her cook quit just before a party or when a cleaning woman would not clean windows or shoes. The woman said, "I do only clean dirt." When my mother found Jim and Frieda, a German couple, all that changed.

Meanwhile, Friedel tried to adjust to his new job and conceal his worries and sad thoughts from me. He related only the news he felt important, and let me enjoy my baby. Only when Friedel joined us at night did I get a glimpse of the world surrounding us. But even Friedel shielded me as much as he could. He related to me only the news he felt was necessary for me to know. God only knows what was going on inside him, behind his serene face.

Rainer occupied almost all my time. I kept him on a regular and quiet schedule in accordance with the child care methods popular at the time. For instance, he was kept on his back as long as possible following the theory that his legs and back had to grow strong enough to sit and stand. Thus he sat up only at nine months. I watched his every new gesture or sound and noted them in my diary. We didn't go anywhere without him.

We enjoyed our home and were happy when nothing disturbed the peace. Theaters, movies, and concerts were still in bloom in Hamburg, and, under normal conditions, we would have had many possibilities for outings. But, following the new restrictive rules for me, we avoided going out. We proudly noticed Rainer's first attempts to walk, his new games and gestures. At night I laid his little hands together and said the prayer to him, "*Ich bin klein, mein Herz ist rein, soll niemand drin wohnen als Jesu allein*" ("I am small, my heart is pure, let nobody but Jesus be inside it"). Soon after he learned to speak he said it every night. I could not imagine life without Rainer. He filled my entire being.

Rainer was a tender and quiet child except for those times when he suddenly erupted in a wild mood. He could sit alone for a long time, looking at a book or listening to his record player, then suddenly change to a happy, lively disposition. His favorite toy was his toy wind-up car. With a serious face, he used to push this little car back and forth, sometimes lying on his belly and imitating the noise of the motor. From an early age on, the tiny car had to come along wherever we took him; he would let the little car crawl up and down his own front, and it seemed as if he forgot everything else around him. In keeping with the belief that the power of concentration was developed by leaving a child to himself, we saw to it that he had little outside distraction. The results were soon noticeable in his play and, later, in his schoolwork. Soon, he recognized the different makes of real cars before he could even speak properly; Opel, Mercedes or BMW, he had their symbols well memorized. When Rainer was two years old, he began to play with Conrad Poppenhusen, our neighbor's little son. Rainer called Conrad "Au," because Conrad once had pinched his cheek, and himself "Eini."

Interlude

One day in the summer of 1936, we were greatly surprised by a letter from my father saying he wanted us to visit them in New York and see how they were installed in their new home. We were eager to go. He had managed to get us free passage on one of the United States Line ships. At that time, German citizens were still able to travel abroad, subject to the currency restrictions, and we had no difficulty obtaining visas. We celebrated Rainer's second birthday, August first, on the ship which carried us to a happy reunion with my family. Shortly before we embarked on our trip, Rainer all of a sudden spoke fluently and not baby language any more. Now Rainer could recite the entire collection of his books; that is to say, I read one line and he added the following without hesitation. If I missed or changed something, he corrected me. By the time we arrived in New York, he knew the names of our stewards, the waiters, every person with whom we had contact.

We disembarked safely on August 8, 1936 and were met by my parents, who were delighted to embrace us once again. Their house in Scarsdale, filled with the Grunewald furniture, made us feel at home immediately, and meeting old friends and new ones was heartwarming after our isolation in Hamburg.

We were overwhelmed by New York—the tall buildings, Wall Street, Fifth Avenue, and Broadway, its wealth in art and music. Also, we were surprised by the beauty of the nearby countryside.

I will never discover the reason for our careless attitude towards the dangerous situation in Germany no matter how often I think about it. Not once during our visit did we discuss with my parents our possible permanent move to America. In hindsight, with the knowledge of the Holocaust and its attendant horrors, it seems unbelievable that we did not discuss emigration. It occurred to me that Friedel and my father did talk about it, but not in my presence. If they did, they, no doubt, concluded that it was not necessary at that time. My father held the conviction that he must provide for his family, and I'm certain he felt he did what he considered best for us. He probably felt guilty that his Jewish heritage had already caused us difficulties and that emigration would cause even greater disruption in our lives. Friedel, in particular, would have to surrender so much: his mother and family, his fatherland, his world. Nobody in their wildest imaginations, their darkest thoughts, could have envisioned what would soon become reality.

We had a leisurely and pleasant stay in Scarsdale. Rainer blossomed in his new surroundings. His vocabulary increased rapidly, he used perfect grammar, and had no trouble with the right prepositions and nouns. He was thoughtful and observing, and his understanding of other people's emotions was exceptional. His temperament was really a mixture of Friedel's quiet and my vivacious features. We called him, laughingly, a "good cocktail." At the end of our holiday, Rainer was sad to leave his Opa. "Poor Opa is all alone in America."

We left New York on September 30th. aboard the SS *Washington* bound for Europe. My mother returned with us to visit her family once again. She and I left the ship in Le Havre to complete the trip by rail. Friedel continued the sea voyage to Hamburg with Rainer, alone with his son for the first time. He proudly announced that he was very capable of changing diapers and taking care of Rainer in every respect. My mother and I went to Brussels, where we were met by my grandmother and Aunt Mini, my mother's sister. We were all in excellent spirits and laughed a lot. As usual, the laughter was triggered by Aunt Mini and my mother. Aunt Mini was intelligent and witty, full of jokes and sarcasm, and my mother and grandmother were an easy audience.

Hans and Lotte Blum were there, too. They lived in London now, where he ran a branch of Adolf Blum & Popper. The original office his father had founded in Hamburg was in the process of being *arisiert*, "Aryanized," according to Nazi law. This meant that all Jews were forcibly removed and replaced by "real Germans."

Actually, it was not a time for laughter. Rapid change was taking place in Europe, and Germany was moving ever closer to the abyss. The army occupied the Rhineland, which had been "demilitarized" since the end of World War I. Hitler also began compulsory military service and forged the Berlin-Rome Axis with Mussolini. But each step that Germany took toward European domination was unchecked by other European countries.

And again, we returned to our home in Hamburg without hesitation. My mother left Europe to return to America with mixed feelings. On Christmas that year we could still talk to each other over the telephone.

1937

The following year the network of restricting laws was pulled tighter. Friedel's position at Roepke & Otto was in jeopardy. Despite being Aryan, Friedel could not be manager of a German company as long as he was a "member of a Jewish family." Because of this crisis and the company's financial difficulties, Friedel urged my father to come once again to Europe to discuss the matter. As usual, Friedel was the buffer between my father and events in Germany. His supportive role in the family was often taken for granted and never fully appreciated by my father and Erich. Given his sensitivity, these tricky situations had a negative influence on him. Friedel just never seemed happy, and that, in return, made me unhappy.

In our marriage, my health continued to play a negative role as well. In the summer of 1937, I discovered that I was pregnant again. In June of that year I had a miscarriage. Afterward, I felt miserable. My doctor diagnosed my general tiredness as low blood sugar, and I swallowed tablets of *Traubenzucker*, "sugar made from raisins." He recommended that I take a rest to overcome the disappointment of a lost baby. So I went to the *Eibsee* at the foot of the *Zugspitze*, the highest mountain in the Bavarian Alps. I took along Rainer and a young girl, Lotte, to take care of Rainer while I was supposed to rest. Friedel stayed in Hamburg because of his work. He had once described himself in a letter to my parents as "a moody husband." That adjective he gave himself probably explains my most vivid recollection of my stay at the *Eibsee*. Friedel came to visit me, and I had a fit of jealousy because he certainly was not moody or silent when he met Lotte, who was a very pretty young girl.

In a photograph taken then, Rainer, in his *Lederhosen* and Tyrolian hat, is self-assured and smiling. I recall no instance of naughtiness or disobedience. He usually occupied himself in his own way, his fantasies replacing toys or people. But he had one great wish and that was to have a brother. When he was just a toddler himself, he looked at every baby and expressed his wish to have one, too. By this time, I wanted another child as well, but mostly I wanted to fulfill Rainer's wish. I also thought of the future and of the blessing to have a brother or sister of one's own. I had this illusion although my own brother often disappointed me, but then, as today, I was a romantic.

It was not surprising that Friedel who had had many misgivings about my first pregnancy had even more now. In spite of that, I became pregnant again and carried the baby for almost six months. I had a very wonderful doctor in Hamburg, Dr. Glaevecke. I simply adored him. He was almost middle-aged and had excellent "bedside manners." During the entire pregnancy, I had been confident but anxious. I knew that something was not the same as it had been carrying Rainer, and I trembled constantly that I would lose the baby.

I called Dr. Glaevecke in panic when I started to hemorrhage again. I hoped that, despite my fears, I would not miscarry. He looked me over and wondered that I was not in pain. He got me to the hospital just in time, but the baby was not ready to live and did not survive. Leaving me in tears, he promised to look at me "from inside" as soon as I was well again. And so he did a few months later. I still had my deep fear of surgery ever since my childhood experience with anesthesia. Things had not much improved since then. I was twenty-six years old, and this was to be my second major operation. But it was inevitable if ever I was going to have another child, so I fought my fear and consented to the operation. Dr. Glaevecke found during the surgery that my uterus had grown attached to the bladder as a result of the earlier surgery by Dr. Dorpalen. Dr. Glaevecke was able to correct the problem, and I soon returned home to Friedel and Rainer. Rainer! In the foreground of my existence was always Rainer. I had to explain to him that the expected baby was not going to be with us.

Dr. Dorpalen had, meanwhile, taken his own life. His son and Dr. Ruge's son both died of polio that summer. Thus, my problem seemed insignificant in the midst of their families' tragedies. It was at this time that I became aware of the possibility that Rainer could contract polio, and, strangely, this fear never left me. It was only one of the fears which I tried to bury within.

Fear

To some people it might seem strange to write about fear. But in my life fear has played an important role. I am not proud of it.

As a child in the Grunewald, I remember the fear of burglars who threatened to break into houses like ours and other fears common to children. There were bigger fears, too, like my traumatic experience with surgery. Then it occurred to me that fearful incidents seemed to happen around me just because I was afraid of them. Because of my fear of surgery, I seemed destined to have repeated surgeries. Years after having seen an airplane crash as a child while walking with my grandfather in the park, Friedel and I witnessed an air crash during an exhibition in Staken near Berlin. The plane crashed not far from our car on the road. Then the *Stukas* did their share to frighten me forever of planes. And after that the air raids! I sometimes felt they were sent to punish me for my cowardice; or they were, like all fateful incidents, God's way to test my strength.

I developed a theory in which I was convinced that every fear attracted the very thing I was afraid of. Thus, the news in 1937 of the polio epidemic in America stayed like a dark cloud above me. Nobody talked about it, but I know the other mothers around me worried about it, too. The changes within Germany also began to build fear within me.

I was so involved with my life and my fears that it seemed strange to realize that, after all, there was another dimension apart from our personal experience and my personal suffering. The people of Germany began to feel the effect of Nazi policy. The party's fight against communism increased, and thousands of citizens disappeared in prisons and concentration camps. In Spain, where General Franco had become chief of state, the civil war attracted many Germans. The Nazi government supported Franco's Fascists against the anti-Fascists, who included Communists. Secret shipments of arms for Spain passed through Hamburg. Amongst those who helped organize and protect these dealings were many German communists, who, driven by fear for their lives and the lives of their families, had abandoned the communist party. They now wore the brown shirts of the Nazis. These people were called "beefsteaks" (brown on the outside and red in the inside).

Because of hidden identities and hidden loyalties, mistrust between Germans grew from day to day. In time, nobody trusted their friends or their friends' children. One did not confide opinions or feelings to anyone. One just simply went about one's business. Within families walls arose between its members. Often husband and wife were on different sides, and the children, forced to be members of the Hitler Youth organizations, were the worst danger to families. Sometimes, they brought inadvertent trouble to a family by repeating remarks someone had made at home, innocent remarks, like doubting the wisdom of a law. Thus any opinion expressed in private could bring the Gestapo to the door.

Men in uniform were not the same as before. They were no longer primarily husbands and fathers: they had sworn by their honor to serve Hitler to their last breath. Within groups of children reigned a new spirit of false ambition to be the best of Hitler's disciples. Hitler became Germany's god. He demanded blind obedience, complete submission, and suppression of personal opinions. We stayed away from the new line of orders like many other Germans and did not realize the extent of the changes which took place than! I can only speak about it now because of what I have learned years later after Germany began its deviate course.

Two Short Holidays

In the fall of 1937, we decided to go on a week's holiday. We drove in our open, two-tone BMW from Hamburg south through Germany to Feldafing, where we left Rainer in Carry's care. From there, we went over several high mountain passes to the Dolomites in Italy. We had hoped to forget our troubles, but we found we could not relax. Rainer was on our minds constantly. So we made a hasty return trip, driving through the night. Friedel got tired, so I took the wheel and promptly got lost. Dead tired we arrived in Feldafing long after midnight and although we were afraid to wake the ladies at such late hour, we rang the old cowbell; when I held Rainer in my arms once again the spooky night drive was worth all my fears. We realized that one can not run away from one's troubles.

In January of 1938, my parents, answering Friedel's urgent pleas, came once again, to Europe. After a stormy trip across the Atlantic, we met in Holland. There, my father's good friends, the Honigmans, received us and we spent several wonderful days in their home in Heerlen. Their daughters, Hertha and Trix, had been my bridesmaids, and we had maintained our friendship. Friedel was able to discuss business with my father and obtain his signature on several important documents. From there, we went briefly to Brussels; then my parents returned, again without us, to New York. My mother wrote naively in her diary about this last visit before the war, "It is heavenly, everything is so harmonious." But she added, "Farewell, forever?"

This was the year Hitler declared himself Minister of War and promptly invaded Austria. He then occupied the Sudetenland. He was riding high from one triumph to another, drunk with the joy of easy victory. Nobody could stop him now, and nobody tried. The air seemed to vibrate with chants, every street of every town echoed the Nazi hymn:

> *Die Fahne hoch, die Reihen dicht geschlossen,*
> *SA marschiert in ruhig festem Schritt.*
> "Lift up the flag, march closely together,
> in a quiet determined step."

When the soldiers marched, the people in the streets were intoxicated; men, women, and children shouting and laughing, ran alongside the ranks of uniformed, blond young men. Those who were damned witnessed the spectacle and crept deeper into their corners, paralyzed with fear. It seemed as if every word was directed against those who were not and could not be with those who marched. Those young, blonde and brown-haired Germans were the lucky, selected ones. I turned away from the window; I told myself, "they cannot mean me," and took Rainer in my arms. My parents were safely in New York. Could they have failed to see the danger surrounding us, the wave which would roll over Germany? It was never discussed, even at this late date, in the steady stream of correspondence between my parents and us.

Friedel wrote to my father in September 1938:

> I fail to see what to do with this firm [Roepke & Otto]. All your well-meant advice provides no solution. Even the best ideas are of no help if the existing laws leave very small margin to move in any direction. If we continue without a feasible plan, I shall have to liquidate. With as little cooperation from your side as I have received, I will be forced to take this step. Again and again I have asked New York to send money in time to pay employees and settle with the banks, but again there was no mail on the ship which just arrived.

> Even when Friedel was able to write from London, thus avoiding the German censors, he was unable to overcome his frustration with his position and my father's incomprehension of it. He felt guilty and inadequate and became more and more silent and depressed, adding to the already existing strain we endured.

Crystal Night

On the tenth of November 1938, Friedel returned from town early, white as a sheet and almost crying. During the previous night, the Nazis had begun their biggest feast so far. Friedel was deeply shocked when he saw the result in Hamburg. The Nazis had destroyed the Jewish shops, smashed the windows, leaving the streets strewn with shards of glass. Because the Nazis tried to hide the scope of their brutality from the German population, we did not learn the full extent of "Crystal Night" until later.

Synagogues were burned, Jewish cemeteries destroyed, Jews dragged from their homes in the middle of the night and arrested. The authorities ordered local police not to arrest more than the city prisons would hold so as to hide this action from the general populace. The SA and SS were cautioned not to endanger "German" life and property. As always, the action was carefully orchestrated by the Nazis. The pretext for this night of unprecedented violence was the murder by a Jewish youth of Ernst von Rath, a relatively unimportant German civil servant in the Paris Embassy.

"Crystal Night" was the start of the Nazis determined effort to eradicate all the Jews in Europe. More "regulations" and repressions, designed to strip Jews of their very existence, followed in rapid succession. One new regulation compelled Jews to hand over to the Gestapo all metal in their possession, including gold, silver, steel, and aluminum. Included were military medals and, especially, pistols and rifles. My grandmother went to the collection site nearest her home and surrendered her memorabilia, amongst them the rifle and military decorations of her eldest son, Edgar, who had given his life for the fatherland in one of the first battles of World War I.

CHAPTER EIGHTEEN

DECISION

Following "Crystal Night," Friedel made a momentous decision. He decided to emigrate to America. The frightening and revolting episode of "Crystal Night" had caused a deep psychological rift between Friedel and his country. He was ashamed to be a German. He immediately went to the American Consulate and applied for a visa for the three of us to emigrate to America. But, tragically, his decision was made too late. He was told that the German quota was filled. Nevertheless, the prospect of leaving his home country was a jolting turn for a man with his traditional upbringing and deep attachment to the fatherland. It meant he was willing to accept separation from his family, his financial security, and all that was familiar. The Nazis sickened him to the deepest roots of his soul. We did not know how long it would take until our emigration would become a reality.

We were put on a waiting list, three names amongst an untold number of applicants waiting to emigrate. Little did we know that the waiting list was nothing more than a farce, that in reality there was no longer emigration from Germany. Our situation in the years just ahead would become increasingly dangerous as the deadly threat of persecution by fanatic executors and defenders of Hitler's policy increased. But day-to-day problems were too demanding to allow time and energy for regrets. In our ignorance, we were confident that, in time, we would be permitted to emigrate.

Had Friedel and I known the forces at work in America, the visionary country, we would probably have despaired and lost all faith. Perhaps, we might have even fled from Germany. The United States of America and its principles of right and freedom was a glistening star of hope to millions. Actually, the immigration laws, which limited the number of immigrants by nationalities, were mishandled by Secretary of State Hull in 1938. Instead of meeting the needs of the emergency situation, the existing quotas were not filled although the American government knew that Hitler was carrying out his program of suppression and murder. In 1938, heads of states had met in Evian, France and had formed a committee for refugees. Unfortunately, many small-minded intriguers who had their own agendas prevented the execution of their resolution. Britain was the first to take action in favor of Jewish refugees. The United States did not act.

The tragedy ultimately ran its course, although thousands of persecuted Jews had friends and relatives in the United States who would have gladly provided the necessary guarantees for financial security. The formality of providing affidavits for prospective immigrants was not the problem. The real reason for stalling immigration in this crucial time is merely speculation and cannot be proven. Intrigues prevented good intentions from being realized. However Mrs. Roosevelt's intervention helped, to admit one refugee ship. If she could have drawn her husband, the president, out of his inactive attitude, perhaps millions could have been saved from the gas chambers.

In Germany, the break with the past had come silently and slowly. We were not aware of being at the beginning of a new era. The party's work was efficiently planned and thoroughly carried out. Contrary to the testimony of many Germans made in self-defense after the war, the party program could not have been accomplished without the cooperation of the people. The mystical and emotional tendencies in the German's inherited culture allowed him to be seduced, to accept, and, more than that, to adore Hitler's ideas. The enthusiasm bordering on hysteria at mass reunions, the singing and shouting in the streets and during assemblies was real. People seemed not to notice the disappearance of their Jewish fellow citizens amidst all the uproar. The German Jews, although recognized as gifted and industrious fellow beings, had obstructed the ambitions of many. Their places were gladly occupied by those who had enviously waited in line to climb up the ladder.

The Nuremberg Laws were the "legal" tools used to eliminate Jews from civil life and leading positions in economy and industry. Jews had to wear the yellow Star of David on their outer garment. Their drivers' licenses were confiscated. They had to step off the sidewalk if they met a German. Jews were not allowed to sit on public benches in city parks. They were not allowed to participate in public assemblies and could not leave their houses after dark or go to movies or to theaters. They could not own a radio or pets, and they could not have any relationship with a non-Jewish person. Jewish lawyers and physicians lost their licenses; teachers and professors were dismissed. Hospitals and doctors could not treat Jewish patients.

It is impossible for me to say if we knew about the hundreds of restrictions imposed on Jews. I heard of them years later: Jewish children were excluded from lessons during which "national socialistic ideas" were taught; medicines produced by Jewish firms were not to be prescribed if there were substitutes available; members of the party were not to enter restaurants in which Jews were served; all city employees were asked not to enter Jewish shops; Jewish sport groups were not allowed to participate in Sunday programs for German youth (they could, however, hike in the woods).

Unfortunately, I became aware of some other restrictions. In 1939, I was given a new identity card which was stamped with a large "J" for *Juden*. All Jews who did not bear one of the Jewish forenames listed in an Interior Ministry circular had to adopt a new, additional name: Jewish women had to adopt the middle name, "Sara" and Jewish men the middle name "Israel." New identification cards were issued to all Germans, and, in the case of Jews, the new middle-names were added. Jews could not leave their houses after eight o'clock in the evening. Jews and *Mischlinge* (children from mixed marriages) could not own radios. This interdiction was also true for Aryans who lived in "Jewish houses." Later on, of course, there were no Jewish houses or, for that matter, any Jews who would have to be concerned with this and other restrictions.

Although our household was considered Aryan and our marriage was a "privileged mixed marriage, second degree" because of our child and because Friedel was "pure Aryan," fear never left us. There could have been a new regulation any day which would bring disaster. I was in a vacuum: I shared neither the fate of Jews or Germans. German women had to work in factories or serve in other forced labor. Because of my Jewish identity, I was exempt from that. Because my marriage protected me, I was spared the fate of Jewish women.

Actually, I didn't even know any Orthodox Jews amongst our many German Jewish friends. I knew nothing of Jewish custom, tradition, or religion. I had never been in a synagogue. Friedel's opinion was that anti-Semitism in Germany would have been eliminated in one more generation. The assimilation of Jews through intermarriages and their contribution and sharing of cultur had made Jews part of the German people. Now anti-Semitism was planted and advanced in such a cunning manner that the population accepted the distorted images of Jews presented to them: Jews were evil and directly responsible for all Germany's problems.

In spite of the Nazi's efforts to spread anti-Semitism, some people still were not all that conscious of Jews. They didn't identify a person by religion or culture when they met them. My mother's cousin Elsbet Goetz once met a young German on a train who was taken by her beauty. He sat next to her, and they had a pleasant conversation. As they parted, he asked her if he could see her again, but she explained smilingly that it was not a good idea. She told him that she had the "wrong grandmother," a discreet way of saying, "I am Jewish." The young man was confused. He admitted that he had no idea what a Jew was or why there were laws to avoid them. Unfortunately, this attitude was not prevalent enough to prevent the fate which awaited Elsbet.

CHAPTER NINETEEN

MICHAEL

In the summer of 1938, I was pregnant again and in a state of anxiety. Would I be able to carry this child through nine months after my previous experiences? I had the first scare in the *Lüneburger Heide*. That Sunday we had intended a nice outing with Rainer. The *Lüneburger Heide* is a nature preserve, a flat region, about seventy square miles, near Hamburg. It is sandy, dry farm country, covered with brush and heather. Later, it gained some notoriety as the place where General Montgomery accepted the unconditional surrender of the German High Command to the Allies. In 1938 it was a pleasant place, where we wandered through the sea of blooming purple heather that moved gently in the mild breeze. Friedel and I enjoyed the stillness and beauty surrounding us, we felt as if we were on a remote island. Rainer marched gaily ahead of us. Suddenly I felt the all too familiar trouble come upon me. I sat down and buried my face in my hands. We were far away from any living soul—what were we to do? Friedel persuaded me to walk slowly back to a lonely farmhouse where, fortunately, the farmer had an automobile. He drove us to our car, and Friedel then rushed me to the hospital and Dr. Glaevecke. I still consider it a miracle that he was able to save the baby. The hemorrhage was stopped and the pregnancy continued.

Three months later I stood with Rainer in front of the town hall, reading a notice containing alarming news. Was it Hitler's rejection of President Roosevelt's plea for a peaceful settlement of European problems? Or was it Hitler's cancellation of the Navy Pact with England? Or perhaps Germany's termination of the Peace Pact with Poland? Whatever it was, I remember that the words cut through me and I realized that war would be unavoidable. I went into labor, two months before the baby was due.

After I was installed in a hospital bed, the nurse informed me of Dr. Glaevecke's absence. This was another blow. He had told me of his plans to visit Japan, but he had assured me he would return in time for my confinement. He had established a fatherly, warm relationship with me, and I trusted him, and only him. He had made this pregnancy possible by his skillful surgery: without him I was lost. I felt deserted and desperate beyond expression. Day after day, I lay motionless; the doctor in charge gave me injections hoping to somehow prevent premature birth.

Elsbet Goetz, my grandmother's niece, who later died in Auschwitz, sat next to me and tried to console me. She stayed with me for a long time, perhaps ten days. Then, one day, I heard Dr. Glaevecke's voice in the corridor, and in he came, saying, "What stupid things are we doing here?" A feeling of relief washed over me, and I broke into tears.

He made me get up immediately and walk to the delivery room. Only minutes after I was on the table, my second son was born. It was the seventeenth of January, 1939. But if I had thought that the worst was over, I had a bitter surprise awaiting me. The tiny baby weighed only three pounds and his life was in danger. His survival would depend on expert care and God's will. Only later, after I had been allowed to see the baby, did I understand Friedel's pessimistic attitude when he first visited me. It was, indeed, a mystery how such a tiny being could survive. In the days that followed I sank into depression, with tears and uncontrollable sobbing. Physical weakness had shattered my usual courage. Nobody dared raise my hopes. The most difficult times were when other new mothers in the maternity ward nursed their babies. The nurses went back and forth carrying the freshly bundled babies to their happy mothers. I lay alone with my fear for my baby's life.

The infant had been immediately taken to Dr. Gmelin's clinic for premature babies, where he was bundled in cotton cloth and surrounded by warm water bottles. He was placed in a small crib covered with a fine-mesh net. Dr. Gmelin did not believe in incubators for premature babies. At the time, mechanical incubators were still imperfect, and many babies placed in them were blinded by excess oxygen. Dr. Gmelin believed that the babies should breathe normal air and be fed with drops of their mother's milk. Only if necessary were they fed intravenously.

After a seemingly endless time, I was finally allowed to get up. I walked the long corridor with shaky legs to the nursery and peeked in through the window. There, the healthy normal babies peacefully sleeping in their cribs were lined up in the spotless room. My baby was not amongst them. Finally, I was released from the hospital, and Friedel drove me to Dr. Gmelin's clinic. There, I was clad like the nurses, in a white gown, cap, and mask. A nurse placed the tiny bundle in my arms, and I saw for the first time the small face, the perfectly shaped, tiny hands, the frail fingers equipped with faultless nails. Was there hope? Was there really a chance for this tender creature to withstand the dangers surrounding him? I lifted my entire being up to God, realizing that only a higher power could protect this child. It was one of those rare times when I had no difficulty summoning the Divine into my consciousness. I uttered from the depth of my being, "Thy will be done."

In charge of my baby was *Schwester* Grete, a nurse totally absorbed in her difficult work. I will never forget her. Several times over the first critical months, her diligence saved Michael's life. One day when she was off duty, she happened by Michael's crib and found him turning blue. Her quick action with an injection saved his life. Her care and intuitive reactions could never be replaced by modern machines.

It was the end of March before we told Rainer that he had a little brother. We wanted to spare him from the possibility that the baby might not survive, but by then, Michael, although far below normal size, had gained weight. Rainer was radiant with joy. He easily accepted the idea that small babies do not come home right away. After Rainer had seen his brother through the glass window at the clinic, Michael became a reality for him. "He is so cute, so tiny," he exclaimed. Rainer was then four and one-half years old, and he assumed a protective attitude toward Michael. Although he had never been around a small baby, he shared our fears and little joys.

It was up to me to get the flow of milk started by using a breast pump. In addition to supplying the small amount needed each day for Michael, I had to stimulate a flow sufficient to nurse normally someday. As soon as I was out of the hospital, I had to perform this emotionally and physically trying task; often I cried because I was never certain if this small quantity of milk would reach the baby in time to sustain his life. I would take Rainer by the hand and walk to the clinic to deliver the small bottle, telling Rainer stories about his baby brother.

We were told Michael could come home when he weighed six pounds. Our daily visits to the clinic continued. Rainer would peddle his little red car in front of our house, up and down the *Fontenay Allee*, and when people passed, he told them the latest news about "his" baby. "My little brother has gained five grams today"; or, more often, "My baby lost ten grams today."

The news varied every day, and anxiety became our constant state. Before Michael had reached four pounds and was not yet three months old, he underwent surgery to correct hernias. The surgeon, a specialist in premature babies, performed miracles with the help of a new kind of anesthesia for fragile infants. All went astonishingly well.

I tried to be optimistic. Each day when I delivered the milk to the clinic, I would search *Schwester* Grete's eyes for a sign, good news or bad. Often enough, she reported a crisis, but she never let me leave without hope. One day she said she was sure the "rascal" would make it because he had stamped his foot when she was a minute late with his meager meal. "You will think of me someday when you have problems with that stubborn little fellow," she joked. It made me smile.

In April, we brought Michael home. I had prepared the small upstairs room with the little bed and dresser, the linens starched and everything spotless. For Rainer, I had sewn a white smock that made him look like a doctor. He would enter the room, his washed hands folded behind his back, knowing that he could watch but not touch the baby. From time to time, he tiptoed into the room to see if the baby was sleeping.

When Michael was seven months old and weighed little more than eight pounds, he was christened in the Johannes Kirche by Pastor Dittman. There was good reason to place this child in a special ceremony into God's hands. It had been a hard fight for him to reach normal birth weight. Clad in the traditional long, white Pschorr christening gown, he looked adorable with his blue eyes and long eyelashes. A few days later, he had a coughing spell, and I thought he would suffocate. At first I thought something had lodged in his throat, but the rasping sounds in his chest turned out to be bronchitis, and we had to rush him back to the clinic. A nurse carried him upright day and night until he recovered.

The children were my entire focus, they made me happy. Whatever the problems were, I tried to find solutions. I didn't rely on Friedel or friends, and I drew a curtain around myself and the children. My newfound self-reliance gave me feelings of strength and confidence, and it shielded me from the outside world.

The task was manifold. I had to learn to care for a baby who needed everything surrounding him to be sterile, and I had a lot of difficulty nursing. Rainer would stand next to me wondering how the milk came into the breast. He asked, "Can gentlemen do it, too?"

"No," I said, "only mothers."

"But what do fathers do when they are alone with a baby?" And after a thoughtful pause, "*Schwester* Grete, what did she do?"

Rainer became livelier, sometimes even wild. He was not as obedient as before and wanted to be with us all the time. Now he didn't play in his room as he had before the baby arrived, but happiness showed all over his face. He wanted to share all his toys with his brother and carried them to his crib. A mother could not have watched more carefully over a baby than Rainer. He allowed nobody into the nursery when Michael slept, and any visitor, even his father, was told to wash his hands and not to touch Michael. Then Rainer would take the visitor's hand and show him "his" baby.

He loved Michael so much that he wanted the crib placed next to his bed. Rainer's interest in the baby never tired. It was touching to hear him call the baby all sorts of tender names when he was alone with him. He wondered if Michael would become a good boy or a naughty one. I told Rainer it depended on his example. Rainer caught me by surprise, saying, "How come I am such a naughty boy when you are such a good example?" Actually, Rainer was a little whiny at times and that he called being "naughty."

Once, when Rainer was five, I rewarded him with some pennies for dressing by himself. With this money, he bought a toy duck for his little brother. His enthusiasm was very touching.

While I was tending the children, trying to keep up the modest household, Friedel did his best to run Roepke & Otto. Throughout Germany, business, especially international shipping, was increasingly difficult to conduct. Since Jewish businesses were transferred to Aryan owners who were often inexperienced, new management was often incompetent. Friedel did his utmost to disguise the true owner of Roepke & Otto and, thus, keep control of the firm. Dealing with my father by correspondence required skill and tact.

Friedel's position as a son-in-law often required tact, too. For instance, he tried to convince my father that I could under no circumstances be an heiress of American-Jewish property. My father, as much as he wanted to help us, couldn't know the pitfalls of the situation. Friedel wrote to him:

> I will herewith try to spell out my thoughts for you to consider in a quiet moment at home, although you will find it an unpleasant task. You should immediately establish a last will in favor of Mama. If anything should happen to you, it would be a terrible blow. Privately, and from the materialistic point of view, the consequences could be unthinkable. You must avoid leaving anything of value in the United States to your daughter. Under the present law she would have to surrender everything to the authorities, and would be prevented from ever emigrating. She cannot own any foreign property. It is an unpleasant topic, but I implore you to do whatever is necessary under strictest observation of American law.

Friedel carried the burden of concern for the family on both sides of the ocean. He was apprehensive over my father's health, knowing what a hard worker he was. He implored him to take a vacation. He felt a deep sense of joy when he learned my father had taken his advice.

> "Dear Papa, with great joy I acknowledge your telegram which brings us the good news that you finally are taking a vacation. I found White Sulphur Springs on the map and we are following you and Mama in spirit."

At the same time, our chances to emigrate faded. Our situation was reduced to survival with no chance of escape. My father made attempts to get us out of Germany using whatever connections and influence he had. His efforts were futile.

Department of State
The Foreign Service
of the
United States of America

American Consulate General
Hamburg, Germany, May 4, 1939

Mr. William Cleason O'Brien
27 Ave. Champs Elysces,
Paris, France

Sir: The Consulate General at Berlin, Germany, has requested this office to inform you regarding the immigration visa cases of "Mr. Joseph," his wife and two children.

The records of the Consulate General show that Mr. J. who is well known to some of its officers, his wife and their minor child R., were registered at this office on November 15, 1938 as prospective immigrants to the United States under the German quota with non preference status and with the waiting list number 10992/94. Mr. Joseph's other child could be added to his registration number any time before the visa is actually granted to him if he is found qualified to receive one.

The basis of the quota system, prescribed by the immigration laws is that as quota numbers become available they are used for, and immigration visas are issued to, qualified applicants under a particular quota in strict order of their priority as established by the dates of their registration. Unfortunately, it now seems probable, because of the large number of prior registrations and the limited quota as of November 15, 1938, will not be reached for several years.

Since the members of this family seem not to be entitled to preference or non-quota status under any of the pertinent provisions of the immigration laws, there is no way in which consideration of their case can be expedited. Mr. J. called at this office recently and in my conversation with him it was clearly explained why he must wait until his turn is reached on the German waiting list before his visa application can be considered. He will be notified sufficiently ahead of time when his turn is approaching so that he will be able to secure the necessary papers.

You may be assured that when his turn is reached their application will be given every consideration and attention consistent with immigration laws and regulations.

Very truly yours
Wibur Keblinger
American Consul General

CHAPTER TWENTY

WAR

Even though we were unsuccessful in our efforts to leave Germany, my grandmother was more fortunate. After the horrifying events of "Crystal Night" and the intensified efforts by the Nazis to eliminate Jews from German soil, our family decided that my grandmother must leave. Her son Hans and his family were already safely in England, and he managed to secure a visa for his mother. On the twenty-second of November, 1938, *die Alte* left her homeland where she had been happy during her long life. England seemed a safe place at the time. But by the summer of 1939, war between England and Germany seemed inevitable and my parents, who feared for my grandmother's safety in London, decided to bring her to America. In August 1939, my parents ventured back to Europe again. They boarded the Holland America liner SS *New Amsterdam* in New York bound for England with the intention of returning with my grandmother. They had just arrived in London when the news of Hitler's invasion of Poland on September 1, 1939 left no doubt about the situation. In quick succession Britain and France declared war on Germany and America declared its neutrality. A German submarine sank the British passenger ship SS *Athenia* off the coast of Ireland, with the loss of 110 lives.

My parents, who were still German citizens, faced the possibility of being interned as enemy aliens in England. They had no choice but to return to America without my grandmother; they scrambled for a passage. They went from London to Brussels and quickly to Holland in a desperate effort to book passage on a ship. By sheer luck, my father's friends got them tickets on the SS *Volendam*, due to sail on the ninth of September. They made it to the ship and got safely on board, uncertain what would happen next.

The ship, under military orders and in complete darkness, was guided into the English Channel, past the Isle of Wight, and out to sea. My parents were relieved to be on the seemingly quiet open ocean, but the presence of British officers, who checked the passenger's passports, was a reminder that this was not an ordinary crossing. After two days at sea, the ship was stopped by a British cruiser and searched. The rest of the voyage was uneventful, and my parents arrived safely in New York where they were greeted by Erich and Ty and their American friends with understandable joy. My father, however, was still determined to bring *die Alte* to America.

On September 20 1939 Poland surrendered to Germany, and a strange "peace" settled over Europe. Tensions remained high that fall and winter throughout Europe as everybody waited to see what would happen next. My parents in America continued their lives as usual, but they were, naturally, anxious about us. Our correspondence, subject to Nazi censorship and restricted in length became very sketchy; although our news was limited to everyday occurrences we hoped that they would get clues of the real situation. Friedel's Christmas letter to them that year contained mostly trivialities. He wrote, "Liesel looks very tired, which is not surprising with all the work she has with children and household chores. On the other hand she is fully occupied, an advantage when there is nothing else to do. Although we would like better to have other distractions at times." This meant that, by law, I was practically tied to the house and that we could engage no help. He continued, saying that we shared the house with Poppenhusen but that we had to "restrict our acquaintances, as you can imagine."

Friedel had a lot of questions concerning the business but, since he never got answers, he assumed Papi had his reasons. This left him responsible for the salaries of seven employees, in a declining business situation. They continued to work for a while anyway, but when business did not pick up, Friedel had to decide between a merger with another firm or liquidation. In late 1940, he chose to liquidate.

1940

On Christmas, 1939, we still had hope that there would be no war with the United States, so that I would be able to reunite with my family, or we hoped that conditions in Germany would get better for us. But the year 1940 began with the ominous prospect of Europe plunging deeper into war. The passive period of the war which had lasted through the winter was shattered when Germany invaded neutral Norway and Denmark in April. In May, Germany invaded and quickly conquered Holland and Belgium. Then the German army attacked France. By summer, France had surrendered to Germany and the British army was driven off the continent at Dunkirk.

Even though the German army was victorious at every turn, the cost of the war began to be felt within Germany as food and other essentials for daily life became scarce.

We had decided not to go to Feldafing that winter. During his last visit there, Friedel had found the house where his mother and aunts lived very cold and the food even more scarce than in Hamburg. As the war intensified in the spring, black markets followed on the heels of the shortages. At that time, black market supplies still stemmed from hidden German sources. Farmers who didn't deliver all their produce to the trade asked ever-mounting prices for their goods or traded them for merchandise such as linens, woolens, and shoes, which were already in short supply. In Hamburg, Friedel had connections with some old friends who purchased things on the black market. Farmers who smuggled butter and eggs into cities to sell on the black market risked imprisonment but found the high profits irresistible. Our small savings quickly melted away, but we thought it worthwhile to acquire nourishment for the children, even if a pound of butter cost hundreds of marks.

There were no vegetables or fruit available since most farmers had been drafted into the army, and the women worked in factories or substituted for men as letter carriers, drivers, and did other essential jobs. Meat never reached the markets but was canned and went with other supplies to the army. The soldiers had to be fed, Europe had to be conquered. Civilians just did not count: they were not useful except for labor.

One of the few bright spots for us that spring was the news of my parents' new status as American citizens. On May 16, 1940, they stood in front of a judge in White Plains, New York, and, having successfully passed the required examination, pledged allegiance to the American flag. They had journeyed together for thirty-three years, and they now passed over the threshold of a new homeland as devoted to each other as on their wedding day. They opened the door to a new future for their children, grandchildren, and great-grandchildren.

Thus, the unhappy events that had forced them to leave Germany were transformed into a blessing, but the difficulties of emigration cannot be diminished. Only those who have left their homeland can quite understand the deep implications such an event has on a person's life and being. Even those who are not overly sentimental or nationalistic experience the shock of leaving the familiar, the native country, and facing the difficulties in the new land. My father, helped by his powerful character and energy, was challenged rather than frightened. My mother, leaning on her Marci, overcame the loss of her country but never the pain of leaving us behind.

While they established their new life, we watched the development around us with ever mounting anguish. Everybody was focused on the war news. It became obvious that all civilians were included in Hitler's war plan. Every German became a soldier in some form. The entire population was to take part in the production of necessary material or in one of the many organizations designed to ration and distribute the *Volksgut*, the "people's possessions."

In August 1940, German bombers began the assault on Britain. Every night swarms of bombers crossed the English Channel to bomb military targets in England. Everybody was certain that the nightly raids would soon bring England to her knees. The British attempted retaliation and bombed Berlin for the first time. The damage was minor, but it stirred the wrath of the Nazi leaders who then began the bombardment of London. The raids continued for months, bringing death and destruction to the citizens of London and other English cities.

In New York, where the news of London's ordeal was described in detail, my father became very concerned for my grandmother's safety. As an American citizen, he felt he now had a good chance to get an immigration visa for her to enter the United States. This time he was successful, and in November 1940 my grandmother undertook the first sea voyage of her life. She had always had a fear of water, saying, "the water has no beams." Despite this, she found herself, now over eighty years old, a seafaring lady.

In a letter written on board ship to her son in London, she describes her adventurous trip:

> November 15, 1940
>
> God Poseidon is throwing the ship around in an unkind manner. After we stood in freezing weather in Liverpool the tender finally took us aboard. This procedure at night was really terrible: we climbed over a shaky bridge.

> November 16
>
> Excuse me for not continuing yesterday, it was impossible to write. Suitcases were sliding through the cabin, bottles fell off the dresser, the rug went on a ride and broke the mirror. In short, *Ein Vernuegen eig'ner Art ist doch so'ne Wasserfahrt.* ("Pleasure of a special kind is a trip on the water.")
>
> "I am afraid to go up on deck because I don't want to fall. But I have a gentleman friend who is so very kind, he takes me

upstairs and wraps me in a blanket. With the help of Vasano I can
stay there all day.

The next day *die Alte* was still full of laughter and wrote of her roommate's
problems in her usual humorous way. As they came closer to the American
continent it got warmer, and foggy. The constant sounding of the foghorn
caused her, the girl from Hamburg, some alarm. But the old lady ventured
up on deck every day until she was startled by a hailstorm. She took refuge in
her bed ; that, for her, was a first. She had never been in bed in the daytime
except at the times of the birth of her four children. On the rare occasions
when she had felt sick, she would say, "It will all come out in the wash."

Although the crossing she experienced was during one of the worst
November storms in memory, Elise Blum ended her letter with a grateful
acknowledgement to her children who had taken care of her in her time of
need. And it was, indeed, a reason for rejoicing.

My grandmother, uprooted but safe, continued to enjoy life in Scarsdale
just as she had in Hamburg. Until her death a year later, she played bridge
and found amusement on each day. And she enjoyed the company of her
daughter and favorite son-in-law and her darling, eldest grandson, Erich, and
his family. She wrote one last letter to me, recalling the times we had shared
and of her worry about tiny baby Michael. When the news of her death
reached me, I burst into tears, my lonely misery overwhelmed me. Rainer
climbed on my lap, put both arms around me and said, "Don't cry Mami,
you still have me."

My father bought a family grave at a cemetery near White Plains, New York.
During the funeral, Oswald Goetz, Elise Blum's nephew, spoke moving words
and noted that we had now buried the first family member in American earth.

The year 1940 ended with the biggest bombing raid yet on London,
on the nights of December 29th and 30th. So far the British air raids on
Germany had been small and scattered. But that was about to change. there
were no bomb shelters in German cities at the beginning of the war. "They
were unnecessary", we were assured. Germany was so well protected by the
Luftwaffe that there was no danger from enemy bombers. Only by the end of
1940, it became apparent that air raids were a real possibility and construction
of shelters began. Most houses in Europe have cellars, and in Germany they
were almost universal. They had to function as air-raid shelters until public
bunkers were ready, but basements designed for heating and plumbing
installations offered very limited protection against bombs. Still, they were
for a long time the only refuge for the general population.

Sirens were installed all over Hamburg, and we were instructed to seek immediate shelter when they sounded. The shrieking noise is unforgettable, even after all these years. In every part of the city was an air-raid commissioner who, in turn, assigned an overseer. These men were of course party members and were feared especially by those persons who were not party members. Disobedience or detrimental remarks had serious consequences. The mere presence of these men was a successful means of spreading fear and suspicion into every household. The system worked amazingly well. Pleasant neighbors became spies. The little, round swastika insignia in the buttonhole had become a source of the power over life and death wielded by otherwise insignificant persons. As long as these badges were visible, the wearer was easily identified; but if they were hidden under the lapel, one careless word could lead into a trap. Thus, everybody was treated with suspicion.

There was little we could say which could not be used against us. A single careless remark could be the basis for denunciation. We learned to be silent; dialogue and expression of thought became crippled. By the war's end I was so unaccustomed to free speech, I could not carry on a simple conversation with strangers.

Blackouts were a great concern. Every ray of light had to be blotted out at night, a difficult task with children in the house. Light bulbs were blackened or removed. Black curtains shrouded every window. Before opening a door after dark, all lights were turned off. Obviously it was in everybody's interest to keep the city dark in order not to be a target for enemy bombers, but how much the blackouts actually prevented attacks on cities remains questionable. In every household, sandbags and pails filled with water were kept in preparation for fire.

When the first scare came in Hamburg, it was bright daylight and most people were not in their homes. Friedel was at his office at Roepke & Otto. It was around noon when the sirens howled for the first time. The sound which soon would become our steady companion for years, scared me to death when I first heard it. Panic shot through me; I ran out into the *Fontenay Allee* where Rainer played as always in his red peddle-car. I tried hard not to convey my fear to him as I led him to the cellar, explaining that he had to go there every time he heard the siren. With baby Michael in my arm, we sat in the cold cellar for a long time. I strained to detect the sound of approaching airplanes. I discovered that silence can be terrifying. During an alarm, the streets were deserted, one was utterly alone. All life seemed to cease. I felt as if the entire city was holding its breath.

We sat there for a long time listening for anything from the world above. Suddenly, I heard a key turning in the front door, and, to my great relief,

Friedel called to me and came down the cellar stairs. I had not heard the "all-clear" signal, which had sounded long enough before to give Friedel time to walk home. He took me in his arms, and we stood there silently gathering strength from each other for the ordeal to come, strength to face our special problems and those we shared with everybody.

Although that first alarm had proven false, we realized, perhaps for the first time, the terrifying danger an air attack brought right into our very home. Anti-aircraft gun emplacements were built throughout Hamburg. The guns, called Flak (*Flieger Abwehr Kanone*) were directed against the high-flying bombers. Directly behind our house was one of the anti-aircraft stations. When the air raids became a regular feature of our lives, we would also hear the brutal thunder of the heavy guns, and our house would shake with each blast. Although this emplacement offered a certain protection for us, it also was a target. I wonder if Friedel's father could have imagined that one of the instruments designed by him and used to direct the anti-aircraft guns towards their moving targets would be so close to us.

Friedel and I didn't admit our thoughts and fears to each other. On the contrary, I grew to be very firm and unmoved, conscious of my role as a mother. Rainer watched me and copied my example for his big-brother role towards Michael. Such self-discipline came intuitively to me. I closed my eyes to all the dangers around me. Large-scale events taking place in Europe no longer registered with me; I became unaware of national or foreign policy or of important changes in other countries.

This ignorance was caused by my instinctive need for self-preservation and by restrictions imposed on us by the Nazi government. Newspapers could print only whatever passed the censors and were fitting to the national socialist policy. Listening to foreign radio broadcasts was punishable with imprisonment. Friedel defied the law and tried to listen to BBC's daily news, but listening was not the only danger. Knowledge of the forbidden news was also dangerous since as much as a careless word spoken to another person was often traced to the source. So Friedel didn't tell me what he had heard.

Irene

In July 1940, I had discovered that I was pregnant again. Two years earlier my greatest wish had been to be able to bear a brother or a sister for Rainer. Now I was scared to death at the prospect of another baby in such times. We thought that Friedel would be called for military duty at anytime and that the war would bring untold hardships, not to mention my fear of being taken away to an unknown destiny. Michael had just reached a near normal weight for his eighteen months. Lack of sleep and the heavy work during the days began to tell on me.

After Friedel was forced to liquidate the Hamburg office of Roepke & Otto, he formed a partnership with Rolf Sommer, who, with "Aryan" capital, was ready to open a business in Hamburg. They started a small manufacturing firm producing baking aromas and soap substitutes. This new enterprise occupied almost all of Friedel's time, and he found the work suited to his talents. When the factory was bombed, they were forced to move to another city, and a suitable site was found in Marktredwitz, a small Bavarian village that was unlikely to become a target. Friedel had to be in Marktredwitz much of the time, and, as travel between the factory and Hamburg became more difficult, I was often alone. His absence caused a strain on our relationship.

We, then, decided to leave Hamburg and go to Feldafing, which was much closer to Marktredwitz. We went back to Feldafing that winter because the daily and nightly air raids were very hard, especially for me because I was pregnant.

Friedel announced our intention to return to Feldafing, and Aunt Carry offered spontaneously to speak to the *Ortsgruppenleiter*, the person in charge of the local Nazi party office. She went to him and asked his official permission to let me stay in Feldafing. She asked for his promise not to harm me, and, apparently, he agreed. How she managed to extract this from him Carry never told us. She urged us to come and said that it would be all right. Later, however, she saw the fate of one of her best friends, an elderly, wealthy Jewish lady in Feldafing who was paralyzed and had been confined to her bed for many years. The *Ortsgruppenleiter* did not hesitate to have her dragged from her bed and transported away. I think she died on the way to the concentration camp and, thus, was spared further suffering.

We didn't want to move into the Pschorr villa, where my presence could cause an awkward situation for Friedel's mother. Friedel found a small house owned by a family named Hecht that stands near the old church in the heart of the village. The house was rented to several people, room by room and had space available. We were installed in the first floor, sharing the kitchen and the bathroom with the other lodgers. The house was simple, almost primitive, but we were happy to have been accepted and were not in a position to voice objections.

We also had help at the time, a simple Austrian country girl named Mitzi. She was exactly what I needed. Later she was joined by Sister Mary, a nurse for the baby. It was certainly a stroke of luck, since household help was considered unnecessary. And a Jewish woman had no right to have help. Food was very scarce at that time, and it took inventiveness to get a meal on the table. Sister Mary was a down-to-earth, practical person, who was able to bake and cook with our inadequate rations. Both girls were of incredible help to me. Michael was a lively youngster, up to nonsense all day long. Thank God, there was no lingering evidence of his difficult start in life. The little fellow was full of mischief and his pretty little face irresistible. Rainer, who now attended the small village school, adored his little brother as he had from the first day. When he was home, he often sat with him in the playpen reading to him and showing him the pictures in the books.

In spring and summer the place was comfortable enough, and the country life was very pleasurable, but in winter it was another story. Each room had a stove which needed to be heated and wood had to be found for cooking. Winters in Bavaria are very cold and the little house was really not made to shelter people from snow and ice. The walls were not insulated, and frequently they were covered with ice crystals. The laundry, washed in cold water without soap some of the time, was hung outside, where it froze stiff. But since everybody had similar problems, they were just taken in stride and not talked about. "Shared hardships are half-hardships" goes the old saying.

During this time, I went to my mother-in-law's house in the village as little as possible. Although her nervous condition was not resolved, she ruled over her household and its members. Her eighty-five-year-old mother, Grossmama-Ur, her two sisters, Carry and Stefanie; and Fanny, their old cook. "Oma Tilla," as Rainer called his grandmother, was more than uncertain about my presence in Feldafing. Torn between her older son Herbert's Nazi fidelity and her pet son Friedel's convictions against Hitler, she had no opinion of her own. Every time Herbert left her after one of his infrequent visits, she became more fearful and doubting than before.

Friedel, who still managed all her financial affairs, felt that she should believe and trust him. And he took charge of his mother's psychological balance as well as mine. While Herbert was no help in the task of keeping her calm, Friedel spent a lot of time trying to convince his mother that no harm would come to her because of my presence in Feldafing. It was hard on him. He realized that my mother-in-law might become a danger for me, since she gossiped with all her many, idle friends. Herbert had warned Friedel time and time again in no uncertain terms of the risk he ran for the family and had suggested Friedel should divorce me. Friedel found the suggestion offensive for many reasons, not the least of which was the knowledge that divorce would mean a concentration camp for me. Friedel broke off all contact with his brother. Friedel never forgave him.

Later on, after the war, I was more inclined to forgive and forget. I attributed Herbert's attitude to fear. I have learned about fear and the power with which it drives people.

Contrary to Oma Tilla's and Herbert's behavior was that of Aunt Carry. She, who had raised Friedel, adored him as well as me and our children. Seeing her, one would not have expected her courageous acts. Spurred on by her convictions and political opinions, she went fearlessly to the commander of the Hitler Youth training school which had just been installed on the former golf course between Feldafing and the neighboring village of Tutzing. She walked to the camp, her head held high, and looked disdainfully at the uniformed boys and their swastika flags. Carry demanded to see the officer in charge, who turned out to be a member of the SS. She responded to his greeting "Heil Hitler," the prescribed *Deutscher Gruess*, with a rather unfriendly "*Gruess Gott*," which was and is the common greeting in Southern, Catholic Germany. She told the officer she thought the songs the Hitler youth shouted while marching through Feldafing's streets were shocking. They made vulgar and vile allusions to Jews and made people sick, especially if one had Jewish friends as she did. It is hard to imagine the SS man's reaction or his facial expression. Needless to say, the Hitler Youth did not change its ways, but no action was taken against Carry.

Carry is the only person I know who dared oppose the authorities. In this small village everybody knew everybody. The population was a mixture of villagers, merchants, and occupants of the villas. The villa residents stemmed from the upper class members of Munich's old families, like the Pschorrs. With the rise of national socialism, the traditional social structure in Germany was dissolved. There was no "upper class" any more. Many villagers, like their working class counterparts throughout Germany, had joined the Nazi party and greeted the opportunities which now lay open to them. Our tailor, Herr Steidl, became a policeman, the butcher was the mayor, and the most important job had been given to Herr Brubacher. He was now *Ortsgruppenleiter*, the local party leader. He had unlimited power, and his ambition was, as that of many men in such a position, to make his village *Judenfrei*, "free of Jews."

With the rise of the Nazis and men like Brubacher, and the fall of the class structure, the relationship between citizens became very uneasy. The formerly devout servants of the upper class were inexperienced at handling their newly acquired power, and it made them dangerous. It was interesting to see people with whom I thought I had warm human contact turn against me, although I felt they did it more for self-protection and did not really mean it.

The transformation from the previous way of life to the present one reached into every niche of every little village. There was no privacy, not even in one's own house. "The walls have ears" was the warning in everybody's mind. Don't trust anybody, do not discuss politics, the war, or the shortages. Pretend you believe the war will be won and the Third Reich will last forever. Do not make remarks in presence of the children; they might, in their innocence, repeat them. This was particularly true in the Hecht house where our fellow tenants were unknown to us.

One day, I carried a laundry basket up the stairs with Mitzi, our maid. In the middle of the staircase Rainer came running and in a loud voice asked, "Mami, what are Jews?" My heart stood still. I cautioned him to be quiet, I would talk to him later, but he insisted. I reached out and slapped his face. It was the first and only time I had ever done that. One did not have to strike this boy; I will never forgive myself for this uncontrolled act. Had I not asked my mother the same question when I was eight years old? At that moment on the staircase, I felt as if the whole world would point a finger at me and say, "There she is, she is Jewish."

Shortly after our arrival in Feldafing, I went to talk to my mother-in-law about finding a gynecologist or obstetrician. An abortion was on my mind, although I realized the illegality of it and didn't mention it to Oma Tilla. She gave me the name of her old doctor in Munich, and I paid him a visit. The doctor was shocked when I told him what I wanted, and he refused to follow my demand. I was so ashamed that I could have crept into a mouse hole. My guilt was overshadowed with terror when he said, "You have two sons now, but you never can tell whether you will lose one. Then you will be happy to have another child."

I resented his remark so much that I never forgave him. If it is true that babies are influenced in the womb by their mother's mood and psychological state, my new baby would have been a fretful child, for these months were not happy ones for me. My history of difficult pregnancies, operations, abortion, miscarriages, and hemorrhages were reasons enough to upset a pregnant mother. Still, my natural strength assisted me as it always did.

One day I took the train to Munich and went to the university clinic to consult the famous Professor Eimer, head of the obstetrics department. I passed through many doors, filled out many forms, and, finally, I confronted him. I don't recall the exact conversation, but most probably my "non-Aryan" ancestry had become apparent. The great professor regretted very much not to be able to treat me, or admit me in his clinic. He wished me best of luck just the same and out I went.

With the birth coming closer, I had only one possibility and that was the old doctor who agreed to take me on account of his years with my mother-in-law. His clinic was installed in an old apartment in the *Werneckstrasse* in Munich. The next problem was to find a bed in the city where I would be near the clinic. That created a problem because I did not want to embarrass or endanger anyone with my unwanted presence. Finally, Friedel located some acquaintances in Munich who invited me to stay in their home while awaiting my time.

When the first pain started, Friedel rushed from Marktredwitz to take me to the clinic; but the nurse just laughed and sent me away, saying I should appear only when the pains came in very short intervals. Since we couldn't wander around the streets, we went to a movie theater. I felt cramped and hot. I had no idea what the screen presented, instead, I anxiously observed my pains, restless and afraid in the middle of the crowded theater. Finally, we could wait no longer: Friedel had to return to Feldafing before nightfall to look after the children. We returned to the clinic and begged for a bed.

I was admitted and was told to walk up and down the hall and had the usual doses of castor oil jammed down my throat, followed by a hot bath. Then, I was installed in a small bed and asked to sleep. I slept little that night, and all sorts of nightmares haunted me, mostly fear of what was to come and a feeling of being abandoned. One or perhaps two days passed, and still I had not given birth. During that third night, I lay on a table and the labor had not advanced. I wondered if I would ever give birth at all. The midwife and the doctor did not seem concerned. Their casual conversation in the back of the room about the new law that prohibited all birth control did little to ease my discomfort.

On March 22nd around three o'clock, my little girl was finally born. She was taken away immediately according to custom, and I fell into an exhausted sleep. There was nothing of today's loving first contact between mother or father and child. The father was always absent anyway, pacing the hall or drinking to the event. The mother didn't get to see the baby until the next day, and, if she was not as bold as I was and did not unwrap her bundled child, she did not get to see the little body at all. Thank God the baby was healthy and well formed, which was, of course, my first concern.

I became anxious because my little girl was covered with black, soft hair. Although I was sure that it would disappear in a few days, I was concerned that somehow the dark hair would reveal her Jewish background and we would be asked to leave, or worse. Amongst all the blond, "pure" German babies in the nursery, this dark-haired baby was conspicuous so I clipped some strands of hair from her head and neck. I was glad when Friedel came to take us back to Feldafing.

Before going home, Friedel had brought me Rainer's letter: "Dear Mama, I am glad I have a little sister. Michael helps Mitzi to empty the stoves, he takes the ashes out. We went to the Zoo. Love, Rainer."

Now we had three children. I forgot all my worries and felt incredibly happy, rich, and blessed. Although things were quite difficult at first, there followed months which I will never forget. I thought having three children was really the glory of motherhood. I was proud to go out with them and show them off in the village. Rainer and I loved to play with Michael and baby Irene. She was baptized on June 14, Friedel's birthday, in Oma Tilla's house. Oma Tilla was the baby's godmother. Under a painting by Zumbusch of Friedel as a baby, the minister blessed the little girl who was clad in the traditional Pschorr christening gown. She was given the name Irene for peace and Angelika for angel. We considered the English translation because we had not forgotten our plan to join my American family someday.

We continued to live in the Hecht house in Feldafing, now made a bit more crowded with the arrival of Irene. Irene cried a lot, and for weeks we were afraid we would be evicted because the other tenants were annoyed by it. Eventually, though, we settled into a routine. I often nursed Irene in the only comfortable chair we had. I sat near a window which overlooked the path leading to the village church. One day as I sat there, holding the baby against me and, as always, enjoying her peaceful sucking noises, I heard male voices and footsteps. Friedel was in Munich to have his tonsils removed, so I knew it couldn't be him. Mitzi came running to me. Her face was pale with fright as she whispered that *Ordsgruppenleiter* Brubacher and Herr Steidl, the policeman (our former tailor), and two SS men had come to search the house. Even now, as I write it, the fear and panic of that moment makes my heart beat faster. Outwardly calm, I closed my blouse and, with the baby on my arm, met the four men. I took Michael's hand and followed them into our small bedroom. They looked around, for what, I didn't know and they didn't say. Then Herr Steidl was ordered to watch me while the others searched the house. When they finally left, they took what little money I had and some of our provisions—but not me!

Not long after that I developed a breast infection. I had not much milk to give anyway because of my undernourished and nervous state, so I switched Baby Irene to powdered milk, called "*Alete* milk." Babies were entitled to whole milk according to their ration cards, but in our village, as elsewhere, the farmer who was in charge of milk collection skimmed off the fat for his butter. Adults had a weekly ration of skimmed milk, but even that was subject to cheating, which had become widespread throughout the entire food distribution system. One had to have friends amongst the farmers and merchants or else.

I visited the local doctor, and he performed minor, but very painful surgery to cure my infection. Then he ordered me to nurse baby Irene to relieve the pressure caused by the milk. Soon afterwards, I weaned the baby.

My parent's letters continued to reach us since Germany was not yet at war with America. It was then that I learned of my grandmother's death on June 6, 1941. My father seldom mentioned his feelings in his letters. But in a letter that September, he spoke of his love for his grandchildren. He said of Peter, Erich and Ty's son, what a charming fellow he was, with "very light blond hair and many teeth." Ann, their daughter, he said, had darker hair but light blue eyes and was an unusually intelligent six year-old. He bitterly regretted not being able to enjoy Rainer, Michael, and Irene as they grew.

> Dear Liesel,
>
> It is the most beautiful experience for grandparents to live and see their grandchildren grow up, a true resurrection. They are uplifted by the hope that the new generation might live in a better and lovelier world than they.
>
> Here my thoughts stop. We know and feel with you what you are going through and might have yet to face. We can do nothing to make it easier for you to carry on. But I know and trust you have everything within you, everything you need to withstand this ordeal. Although nobody can tell, I know that it will come to a good ending.
>
> We are far away. You have Friedel and your children. For them, especially for Rainer, many difficulties will arise, dramatic problems. I am aware of it, but I remind you that we chose, with open eyes, a path which might lead into "the freedom" perhaps not even for you but for future generations. This is not a sacrifice, but it is the clear recognition of a necessary and useful development.

Take our fondest wishes and kisses as our only present for your birthday. Do you remember your birthday table as it used to look? You will be thirty! And we know you as a twenty-six year-old girl. We are celebrating our thirty-fourth wedding anniversary. How quickly the time passes and how hard it is. I embrace you as yours,

Papi

My mother's letters, faithfully reporting their lives' events without mentioning those things which would be censored, served as a family contact and record. As in earlier and happier days, my parents were surrounded by friends, or, at least, those who seemed like friends. My mother dreamed of the time when she could be with our children, when she could help Rainer with his homework, play with Michael and Irene, whom she had never seen.

Her tender thoughts usually brought tears to my eyes, a weakness I knew I could not afford. The discipline that I imposed on myself excluded emotional outbursts. It changed me from a romantic, warm-hearted girl to a serious and determined woman.

CHAPTER TWENTY-ONE

DUTY

On September 20, 1940, Friedel had been called to military duty and reported to *Kaltenkirchen*, a military training camp. This evoked not only adverse feelings in Friedel and me but also left us in increased danger. Friedel was drawn into a war in which he might lose his life for an unjust cause. I was alone with the children and my Jewish identity card and without my Aryan husband.

Friedel spent six weeks in Holstein, training and drilling; then he was assigned to an ammunition supply camp, well removed from the front, where he supervised transportation of bombs and ammunition. Friedel found he enjoyed the company of men from Hamburg assigned to the same unit. The British bombed the area almost every night, but he felt relatively safe since the bombs never fell near the camp.

Six months later Friedel unexpectedly returned to Feldafing. What had happened? The commander of his unit wanted Friedel to become an officer and ordered him to take the officer training course. There were more papers to be filled out and, lo and behold, he had to specify his wife's origin. He was dismissed on the third of March, 1941. His commanding officer, who was a soldier but not a Nazi, was surprisingly sympathetic. He personally drove Friedel to the train.

At first we didn't know the implications of Friedel's dismissal. Soon it became clear that this was not a favor bestowed on us but, on the contrary, an imminent danger. Friedel, spared from military duty, had to serve Germany nonetheless, and in a less honorable way than as a soldier. To be killed in uniform was too good for someone so lowly as the husband of a Jewess. Friedel was drafted into the *Arbeitsdienst*, the compulsory labor force known as the "Organization Todt" in recognition of its administrator, Fritz Todt, the autobahn builder.

This unit was in charge of highway defense and construction. In other words, it was hardest labor, almost as bad as concentration camp work. Men in this unit were degraded for one reason or another and considered politically undesirable. They were deported from their hometowns and held in special barracks out of the public eye, where the food and general conditions were terrible. They were assigned to compulsory labor projects to aid the war machine and treated like slave labor. Sickness and death were commonplace in the Organization Todt. We knew Friedel would never be able to stand up to these conditions. Day by day, and week by week, we waited in dread for the order assigning Friedel to a labor camp.

At the time the order arrived for him to report to Hamburg (which was still our official residence) for assignment, we were still in Feldafing. Never will I forget the last walk from the Pschorr villa to the little railway station. Herr Ringenberg walked along with us, and we were all three crying. A funeral march could not have been more heartbreaking. Friedel, white as a sheet, managed to get on the train. Herr Ringenberg and I waved as the puffing, old steam engine pulled away, certain we would never see Friedel again. We did not pretend—we just wept. But God held his hand over us. On the train, Friedel became very sick. When he reached Hamburg, he was immediately taken to the hospital, and the doctor found he had contracted hepatitis.

Although Friedel was very ill, we rejoiced—nothing better could have happened. After a hospital stay in Hamburg, he was sent home, and, as he slowly recovered, he was examined periodically by army doctors. Each time he had to report, he succeeded in fostering a new outbreak of jaundice or persuading the doctor in Feldafing to grant him a "sick leave." Thus, he remained a civilian with a work unit identification card for the duration of the war. But, as we would discover, the Organization Todt was not yet finished with him.

Friedel had come back from the military camp in March 1941, just in time for Irene's birth, and had received the call to Todt's work force a short time later. When he was in the hospital with hepatitis in Hamburg, I left the Hecht house in Feldafing with the children, dismissed Mitzi and Sister Mary, and moved back to Hamburg to be with Friedel.

Our little house in the *Fontenay Allee* 8 in Hamburg was like an island amidst the roaring ocean of war and disaster. After the bombing of German cities by the British began in ernest in May of 1942, the raids on Hamburg increased. Night after night, we climbed out of our beds, grabbed the clothes carefully prepared the night before, ran to the children's rooms, and carried them down to our small, dingy cellar. There, we had established a refuge with beds, food, and water. In those terror-filled moments before the bombs fell, there were many things to worry about in spite of careful preparations. Are the bathtubs filled with water? Is the gas turned off? Are there candles and lamps, food, and a fire extinguisher downstairs?

The cellar was not much of a protection, but one felt safer there. We had broken through the wall to the cellar of our neighbors, the Poppenhusens, to enlarge the small doorway between cellars. Thus, we could console each other, and the men could work together in case of fire. On several occasions the house was struck by fire bombs, small, cigar-shaped incendiary bombs dropped by the thousands on German cities. They were sometimes hard to detect because they entered with their sharp noses into roofs and sometimes penetrated to the next floor. They could lodge in mattresses or furniture where they could smoulder away for hours before setting the house afire. In that way, many houses were destroyed while the unhappy inhabitants were huddled in their basement shelters. One such bomb, in an air raid near the end of the war, killed our pediatrician, Dr. Gmelin, who had saved Michael's life as a baby. He was crouched in his cellar, holding his small son on his lap, when the bomb entered the wall sideways and struck him.

As soon as the explosions stopped and the sound of the planes began to fade, Friedel would rush upstairs not knowing what to expect. He would quickly search each room, looking for fires and smoldering incendiary bombs. Fortunately, when those penetrated through the roof, we managed to discover the glowing sticks before they started to burn the house. When we were certain that our house was safe, we would rush to our neighbors to offer assistance.

After an air raid there were always more questions; what happened elsewhere in town, who was killed, wounded, or made homeless? I remember one such night in particular when the entire street seemed to be aflame. Practically every house was burning. The men climbed on the roofs dragging hoses, trying to spray water on the houses, particularly those which had not yet caught fire. During such air raids, the water pressure was inadequate, and everything depended on the direction of the wind. Garden hoses are not very effective, but there was no other means of fighting the fires and the men worked out of desperation. While the men did what they could to slow the fires, the women who were fortunate enough to still have homes turned to another task.

The small fires caused by the incendiaries left an incredible mess in the house. I tried to clean up the broken glass and the sand and water that had been tracked through the house. Broken windows were covered over with cardboard. Sandbags were refilled and preparations made for the next onslaught. Often this work took until morning.

Neighbors were the only people one saw during these terrible nights. We were cut off from the city of Hamburg and from the outside world. I felt a deep loneliness in the midst of the chaos. The sizzling sound of fire, the smell of smoke, and nearby flames leaping against the sky linger long after the enemy's planes have disappeared and their engines' roar has subsided.

One unforgettable, dreadful night the little wooden house across the street from us burned like a pyre. Luckily, the old lady who lived there was not in it. There was no possibility of saving the house, one could only stand and watch. I had never before heard the howling wind caused by uncontrolled fire, and I was stunned and terrified. Suddenly, Rainer and Michael appeared in our doorway, Rainer held Michael's hand tightly. The frightened children, left alone in the cellar while Friedel and I checked for fires in the house, had ventured upstairs to find out what the terrible noise was. We huddled together in the doorway and just stared helplessly into the fiery night.

What happens to mothers in such moments? I thought of the millions of mothers who clutched their children's hands and realized the awful truth that they could not protect them. The God-given instinct to protect one's children is so powerful that even today I feel Rainer's little hand in mine, his questioning eyes upon me. Perhaps I reassured him by saying what I fervently felt: "God will help us."

In the spring of 1941, we learned Germany had invaded Yugoslavia and Greece with great success. Hitler abandoned his aerial siege of England and turned toward Russia. And then in December, war with America was unchained through Japan's attack on Pearl Harbor. Hitler used the opportunity to declare war on America. Now the separation from my parents was complete; we were at war with America. Until then, we believed emigration was still possible.

American consulates in Germany were closed. In the *Fontenay Allee*, one of our neighbors was an American consul and, when he left, he gave us his iron ration of yellow dried beans; some green, unroasted coffee; and rice. Although these were welcome gifts, one had to be concerned that the smell of roasting coffee, a scarce commodity, could raise suspicions and lead to serious consequences. Our Jewish friends, the Blumanns, had given us before they left the country a case of *Kernseife*, a simple soap which Ernst Blumann had produced in his former business. It was also a lifesaver in the complete absence of any other washing material. Near the end of the war, soap again became available—made from the ashes of human bones!

ELIZABETH PSCHORR

After Germany declared war on America, correspondence with my parents became increasingly difficult. We usually sent two copies of each letter, each on different routes, via friends in other countries; RCA radiograms from my father, however, were still reaching us. Before long, we could communicate only through the Red Cross in Switzerland. Each message was limited to twenty-five words and had to be "strictly personal in character." Also, the following rules had to be observed:

1. Preferably the reply should be typewritten and an English translation should be attached if the answer is in a foreign language. 2. Erasures, deletions, and crossed-out words are not acceptable. 3. Use or mention of the following is not permitted by censorship: abbreviations, Biblical quotations or references, business matters, codes in place of customary references, defense matters, descriptions of persons, including babies, employment in defense or government work, firm names, geographic names, legal documents, unusual phrases, military or naval subjects, money or requests for money, nicknames, poetry or text in block formation, politics, radio broadcasts, radiograms, airmail, telegrams, cablegrams, shipping information, weather conditions.

Needless to say, our brief letters required careful thought and composition to avoid censorship.

Friedel spent much time working on my father's tax and business matters and legal affairs. His devotion went far beyond the call of duty. He tried to get "blocked marks," money that couldn't be sent overseas, to send to my father's brother Hugo and his sister Flora in Austria, who my father had always supported before he left Germany. Shortly afterward, these two went the path of the rest of my father's family, to the extermination camps. Only one brother, Leon, his wife Wally, and their daughter, and one of my father's nieces, escaped the Holocaust.

Thus, it was Friedel, over and over again, who carried the burden of worries. To the very last, he accompanied the condemned in our family and tried to make their departure easier. It was he who helped keep my father's private affairs in order in Germany and get the most possible out for him. Every step was a complicated struggle with government regulations that exposed Friedel to personal danger. I remember very little of his activities because Friedel, in order to spare me, didn't share them with me. In retrospect, a sense of guilt haunts me because of my own behavior towards Friedel later on and shame for my father and brother who showed little comprehension for Friedel's steadfast loyalty. Friedel did not have the gift of easy communication, therefore he had few friends. But his deeds remain the source of our love.

In Hamburg, in the fall of 1942, we reluctantly sent Rainer to school. Even with the war and its privations and hardships, a semblance of normal life continued, and all children of suitable age were required to attend school. Also in September of that year, the Americans began regular daylight bombing of German cities and military targets, adding to the British nighttime attacks. We wondered if reading and writing was worth the danger. I was worried also that Rainer might be exposed to an unfriendly, anti-Semitic encounter as I had been at almost the same age so many years ago. But we couldn't keep him home, of course. So, that fall Rainer and Conrad Poppenhusen, our neighbors' son and Rainer's playmate, went to class and sat side by side on the same bench.

On the first of October, I went to awaken Rainer and found him complaining of a strong headache and a sore throat. I opened the window to call out to Mrs. Poppenhusen, who happened to be in front of the house, that Rainer was not going to school that day, that he had a sore throat and a headache. Since he had both symptoms often enough, I did not think of calling the doctor and said lightly to her that it probably would blow over soon. Mrs. Poppenhusen gave me a strange look and advised me to call the doctor at once. I learned later that Conrad had been home for several days and apparently had a light case of polio. Rainer had brought Conrad his homework the day before, and nobody had prevented Rainer from entering Conrad's room. Mrs. Poppenhusen disappeared into the house, and I called Dr. Gmelin.

I watched anxiously as the doctor tried to raise Rainer's head and found his neck stiff. He ushered me from the room and took my hand. He told me not to panic but that he feared Rainer had meningitis, which, he said, was contagious. I should keep Michael and Irene out of Rainer's room. Had I been struck by lightning, the shock could not have been worse. (As it turned out, the other two children did get mild cases of polio.)

Professor Pette, head of pediatrics of the *Eppendorfer Krankenhaus* came that afternoon. I had called Nelly Goetz, my grandmother's niece, to come and take care of the two children. Lieschen Oelkers came as well. It was evening when Friedel and I rode in the professor's car through the darkened streets to the hospital. Rainer, wrapped in a blanket, lay across my knees, rather stiff and still. He said, "The stars are very shiny." I cannot remember anything else he said. At the hospital, he was taken directly to an isolation ward. The doctor took a spinal tap and asked us to leave. We could not stay with Rainer; it was too dangerous for the other children.

No sooner had we returned home and fallen asleep than the air raid siren sounded. As always, I raced to drag Michael and Irene to the cellar, where I dressed them and put them in the beds we had prepared. I was sick with fear and worry: I could not stop thinking of how they would carry the hot and sick child into the cold hospital shelter. Was he covered properly? Was he frightened about his condition? Was he frightened to be away from us and with strangers?

When the "all clear" sounded toward morning, we went back to our bedroom and fell into an exhausted sleep. At eight a.m. the telephone rang. Friedel reached over to my night table where the telephone was, I saw his face from very close. He did not have to say anything, his expression told me. My boy had died all alone while I was asleep.

It is impossible to describe our despair. I hit my head against the wall and sank to the floor. The world had collapsed around me. I did not want to talk to anybody, to see my children. I did not want to live. I was struck at my weakest point: a mother who had lost her son. To the last minute Rainer had been radiant as if a light was shining from him, a light that was now extinguished. I refused to believe that this had happened. Only two nights before he had climbed out of bed and, standing on the stairs, spoke to me. I don't remember his words, but I do see him thus, with a gloriously happy smile.

I did not want to see my Rainerlein in his state of glory. My entire being resisted, but Friedel thought it best and he led me to Rainer's bed in the hospital. There he lay, pale and still, and the glory of God was visibly shining about him. Pastor Spieker came into the room and said, "God is calling him back and, through him, He is calling you." His words shocked me. He explained that we need these shocks to hear God's voice.

God is seeking me? I had refused to listen, and Rainer had died for my sake. I should be glad that I was chosen. It was a hard lesson, but, in spite of myself, I never forgot that to be thus selected is obliging.

My consolation was that Rainer was spared from the hard future during which he would have had to realize that he, his brother and sister, and his mother were unwanted in their own country. I clung to the thought that now the ugliness of our time could not tarnish his purity. I was relieved that I did not have to teach him to conceal and lie, that he died as clean and honest as he was born. Over and over, I had to rethink this. The only way to bear such excruciating pain was, and is, to imagine the suffering which death spared him. Suddenly, I felt heroic because I, and not my child, was the one to carry the burden for the rest of my life. My sense of protectiveness grew, and I was able to take Rainer back into my heart from whence he had come: I closed him in, like in a shell. Like a precious pearl protected in a shell, he has been there, safe from danger, ever since. Thus, it is true that nothing dies which the power of love preserves.

We found a special place for him in the cemetery of Hamburg *Bahrenfeld*. There, amidst the pines and other trees, stands the wooden cross which once marked the grave of Friedel's sister, Carlotta Grieving. A wreath of carved leaves and flowers and two birds embellish the names:

Rainer Pschorr
Geboren am 1.8.1934
Gestorben am 2.10.1942

Blinded by tears and torn by pain, we sat and watched the coffin disappear behind a curtain in the crematorium. In this terrible moment, as we knew what was taking place behind the curtain, the pain was almost unbearable. The ceremony at his grave I do not remember.

By then, correspondence with my parents in New York was possible only through Red Cross messages limited to twenty-five words. If the messages got through at all, they would take three to five months. Thus, our painful message of October 5, 1942, informing them of Rainer's death, did not reach them until January 8, 1943. (*Am 2. Oktober starb ploetzlich unser geliebter Rainer trotz Serum nach eintaegiger Krankheit an Kinderlaehmung ohne zu leiden. Wir sind untroestlich. Michael und Irene gesund.*) "On October second, our beloved Rainer died suddenly. In spite of serum, he died after one day of illness without suffering. We are unable to console ourselves. Michael and Irene are healthy."

A month later, they learned the tragic tale of Rainer's one-day illness from Lieschen Stravenhagen, Mutti's childhood friend who was in Switzerland and who had learned the details from a letter written by Friedel. She wrote my parents that meningitis had been the beginning of polio, and that paralysis of the lungs had ended Rainer's young life. Lieschen's letter arrived in New York at the same time as one of our earlier Red Cross letters happily describing Rainer's first days in school. This coincidence illustrates how great and confused the time lapse was between my parents and Friedel and me. One can easily imagine the strain on my mother, who shared our fate in absence and uncertainty. But at least a thread of communication was left unbroken.

Our good friend, Herbert Samuel, wrote of Rainer's death,

Er ging voran; ein Mittler userer Liebe
Trug er sein reines Herz in Gottes Vaterhaus
Schoepft nun mit unbefleckten Haenden
Tiefstes Geheimis, spielend, laechelnd aus.
Und Gott, der Vater nimmt sein heftig Draengen
Der guten Augen strahlend Wunder ganz.
Wir, die wir leided glauben unter Traehnen
Erblicken ihn im hohen Lichterglanz.
Nichts stirbt, was Liebe's ganze Kraft getragen.
Ein Weilchen waehrt's, schon sind wir neu vereint.
Und ueber uns'ern Mueh'n und Plagen
Ist es sein Stern, der unsern Ziele scheint.

"He led the way; the messenger of our love
He carried his pure heart home to God above.
Dispersing with his pure, unblemished hands
playfully smiling God's deepest mystery,
"And God, the Father, receives his urgent plea
His blessed eyes, his radiant wonder. But we,
through despairing tears do perceive
Him in his glorious light—and we believe.
"But nothing dies, enshrined in our love.
The time is short and soon we meet above.
It is his star that sheds his glorious light
on paths to higher goals through toil and plight."

It was a terrible time in our lives. The air raids, the sleepless nights, and daily fear added to our deep sorrow and strained our nerves beyond endurance. The feeling of helpless frustration that takes hold of even the bravest person in the air raid shelter takes a heavy toll. It is, as a soldier on leave expressed it, worse to await the house crashing down upon one's head than to face battle directly. My soul was split in two. "Dear God," I prayed, "don't let us be hit." And my other half said, "Send more bombers: make an end to this misery."

CHAPTER TWENTY-TWO

IRENE

As the war entered its fourth year, our hopes for an Allied victory sank lower, although there had been a significant turning point in January 1943 when General Paulus' Sixth Army was destroyed in Stalingrad. But could one rejoice at the news that 146,000 soldiers had died and 90,000 more were taken prisoners and would probably die in Russian camps? We were surrounded by mourning families, and the odor of death seemed to lie like a cloud over Germany. In April, we learned that 56,000 Jews had been killed in the Warsaw Ghetto to put down an "uprising," and in May, that the last of the German troops had capitulated in North Africa.

After we had buried Rainer, we left Hamburg and our house in the *Fontenay Allee*, for the relative security and calm of Feldafing. The Hecht house in the village was fully occupied, and Friedel insisted we move into the Pschorr villa with his mother, Carry, and Stefanie. Friedel continued to travel between Feldafing and his business in Marktredwitz, although rail travel in Germany had become increasingly difficult.

On one hot, beautiful summer day in 1943 an unusual event occurred: the trains were running. I decided to take advantage of the situation and go to Munich. Perhaps there, I could find some food items for the children that were unavailable in Feldafing, but it would be a perilous adventure for me to leave the village. At least there people knew me and had great respect for the Pschorr family. Outside of this relative sanctuary, I would risk immediate arrest. Since every one had to carry an identification card and present it on demand, I could easily have been caught with mine, the one stamped with a large, red "J" identifying me as "Elisabet *Sara* Pschorr." My identity card made no mention of my "privileged marriage," and I'm certain there would be little time for explanations. It was a crime punishable by death for a Jew to appear in public without the Star of David. Ironically, if I displayed the yellow star, I would be arrested even before I got on the train since Jews were not permitted to use public transit.

I left the children with Carry and walked to the train station, where I was able to board with no difficulty and without being asked for my identity card. Fortunately, the train was crowded with passengers pushing and shoving in the aisles as uniformed railway guards moved back and forth through the train to check identity cards. The thirty-minute trip to the center of Munich was a cat-and-mouse game. I used the crowd to move from car to car, from toilet to toilet, successfully evading the guards. Luckily, the entire excursion went without incident, although I returned with little to show for my efforts. Still, I returned home safely, and greatly relieved, to join my children again.

Carry and the children, Michael and two-year-old little Irene, were at the station to meet me, and we slowly walked along the *Bahnhofstrasse* back to the villa. Irene, suntanned and healthy looking in her red-and-white-striped sunsuit, which once had been Rainer's, lagged behind. At first, I thought she was just dawdling and didn't pay any attention to it, but as I noticed she was unable to keep up, I became alarmed. I questioned Carry—was something wrong with Irene? She told me that while Irene had played in the lower part of the garden near the vegetable patch she had suddenly cried desperately; Carry had calmed her quickly but found nothing wrong.

Down in that part of the garden was an old beer barrel filled with rainwater and right behind it, the fence that separated the Pschorr property from the yard of the former Hotel Elisabeth. The old hotel had been transformed into an army hospital. Everything there was very makeshift, and the hotel grounds were untended; that part of the yard was used as garbage pile. I did not know this at the time, but the discarded bandages that were heaped there in decaying mounds attracted thousands of insects. One of these had stung my baby.

At first I didn't see the tiny red mark just above her knee. That evening she remained lethargic and irritable so I took her to bed beside me in the third floor "green room" that had become our apartment. This had been, in former years, the bedroom of Friedel's sister, Carlotta, and her husband, Herman Grieving. I always sensed that Friedel's mother hated to see me in it now. When the night closed in, my little girl was restless. She threw herself violently from one side to another and obviously had intense pain in her leg. Still, I did not discover the small, red, swollen blotch where she had been stung.

During that hot August night I didn't sleep. Friedel was still in Marktredwitz, I was alone with my fears. I watched Irene and became more and more concerned. Thoughts of Rainer's short illness and his sudden death just a few months before filled me with agony. The thought that now Irene might fall victim to the dreaded illness was devastating.

Irene tossed and turned, she moved her legs back and forth without stopping hour after hour. At last morning came and I could safely seek assistance. I telephoned Dr. Strupler, the eighty-year-old family physician in the village, and he came immediately to examine her. His conclusion after the examination was that Irene was suffering from sunstroke. I was somewhat skeptical of his diagnosis, but I agreed to follow his suggestions. He advised me to move her bed to a cool room and keep her quiet. Since our "apartment" was just under the roof and very hot, I went downstairs and began to move Irene's bed into my mother-in-law's "music room."

Furnished with a piano and Biedermeier chairs and table, the room had not been used for music for many years. In those days it was not used at all, a situation that was soon to change.

Oma Tilla was very upset about our desecration of her "music room," but I paid no attention to her senseless whining and installed Irene's bed behind drawn curtains in this cool corner of the old villa. I stayed with Irene throughout the day and with mounting anxiety I watched her condition worsen. Clearly, she needed medical attention, more than Dr. Strupler could provide. I suffered with my child through another night of sleeplessness and a growing sense of panic: it was an unbearable situation.

There was no possibility for me to take Irene to Munich to a decent hospital. I would need an ambulance and official permission, and both were practically unavailable for civilians. If we went by train, I was certain to be questioned. In desperation I thought of Illy Dax, Friedel's former friend with whom I had been out of touch for several years. Her father, Professor Dax, who had been associated with Munich's finest hospital for years, was now dead, but, perhaps, Illy still had contacts there. Illy was married now to the son of the Wolf family, who owned a perfume and soap factory, and their summer house was next to Josef Pschorr's property in Munich. I decided to take a chance.

Setting aside all scruples, which otherwise forbade any contact with those who could be embarrassed (or worse) by knowing a "non-Aryan" like me, I managed to reach Illy in Munich by telephone and implored her to help me. She promised to do what she could. I will never forget my tears of relief when the next morning an automobile arrived at the villa. The driver took me with Irene on my lap to Munich, to the *Schwabinger Krankenhaus* in the heart of Schwabing, where Illy's father had served so many years.

The driver stopped in front of the hospital, and a young doctor appeared immediately and opened the car door. He climbed in and examined Irene right there, to determine if she had a contagious disease—like polio—before admitting her to the hospital. When we got out after his examination, the car was driven away, leaving me stranded with Irene in the center of Munich. The doctor carried Irene inside and placed her in the care of one of the Catholic nuns, clad in the usual long, black dress and huge, white, starched linen headdress. The doctor told me to go home and inquire in two days.

I didn't want to leave my child in this city that was being bombed by day and night so I considered staying nearby. But, although I knew many people in Munich, some of whom I counted as friends, I dared not compromise them. By good fortune the trains were running that day too, or I would have had to walk the thirty kilometers back to Feldafing. Again, the overcrowded cars enabled me to avoid identity checks. At the villa I called Friedel in Marktredwitz. He said he would try to get to Munich.

The next two days were agonizing. I didn't dare call the hospital, and considering how busy the doctors were with bombing victims, I could not expect them to contact me. Miraculously, the trains were still running two days later, and I returned to the hospital. I found Irene's room number at the admittance desk and walked as hurriedly as I dared through the long quiet corridors. Irene's bed was empty! My heart sank, my legs nearly buckled. Filled with panic and uncertain what to do next, I paced the hallway outside the room. After several minutes that seemed an eternity, a nurse came and looked at me with sad eyes: Irene had been transferred to surgery. The dreaded word! There it was, and this time it concerned my baby.

"Whatever for is she in *surgery*?" I cried out. The nurse shrugged and said Professor Bronner would explain. As I rushed in tears along an endless corridor to the operating room, I saw Friedel coming towards me—I fell into his arms. We stood there at the moment when Professor Bronner stepped out of the operating room, still in surgery garb, his gloved hands bloody. I was afraid to hear his words. He told us that an insect sting had become infected, but he had located the site of the infection, deep in the bone marrow just above the knee. He had made an incision in her leg and drilled a passage through the bone so that the pus could drain out. Soon, we would know if we were lucky. He explained that osteomyelitis was either a chronic disease, lasting between one and fifteen years and crippling, or it was acute, which meant death.

"Go home and pray for either of the two destinies. We cannot do more for the moment," were his unforgettable words.

Friedel and I returned to Feldafing and endured what I considered to be one of God's tests. We waited helplessly and prayed. We prayed for more courage and faith in the "good" ending. Irene survived the next day, and the next. Friedel had to return to Marktredwitz, leaving me with Michael in Feldafing. In the following days, it became apparent that Professor Bronner had saved Irene's life by his quick action and skill. But I also believed in her protecting angel. She was spared, but her suffering was going to last years.

She was confined to the surgery ward, which would be her home for the next five months—an only and lonely child in a huge room with old and sick people around her. I tried as often as possible to visit her, but the unreliable trains were my only means of reaching Munich. Her leg was thickly bandaged, and from underneath the bandages a rubber tube, a drain, protruded. The bandages had to be changed every day and the drain kept open.

Soon she began to improve, to gain strength. She sat up in her bed and became not only Professor Bronner's darling but also a favorite with every patient in the ward. Those who could walk, most of them on crutches, came to her bed to see her. Some of them read her stories, which she learned by heart. Professor Bronner was actually concerned that her mental development would far surpass her age if this situation would continue too long.

When the air raid sirens howled, and they did almost every day, one of the nurses or Professor Bronner himself carried her downstairs to the huge cellar which served as shelter for all the patients and the staff. Sister Landibertha was the nurse in charge, and no one could have taken better care of Irene than this exceptional woman. She was one of those persons whose heroic deeds are not inscribed into the books of history. Her devotion was without end.

She and the other nurses at the hospital faced those frequent evacuation signals with great moral courage. Their bravery gave consolation and fortitude to the men and women who were strapped to their beds in casts, attached to bottles and tubes. The beds had to be rolled to elevators which were not designed for these occasions and held only one bed at the time. Often, the elevators did not function because of lack of electricity. Then the nurses, some of them quite elderly and all of them undernourished, ran back and forth, rushed up and down, grabbed the patients in their arms, and carried them down stairs, trying to get everybody in the cellar before the frightening roar of the oncoming planes was heard.

At that sound, the huddled patients, doctors, and nurses fell silent, everybody anxiously listening in the dark, trying to determine which direction the planes were taking. The noise of the explosions which followed and, then, the departing sound of the bombers gave the breathless group relief. This time the building had not been hit and they were safe. Each of them was, then, left with the fear for their homes and relatives "out there."

One day I was visiting Irene when the alarm sounded, and I carried her to the basement. As the planes approached, I sat next to her and looked up at the big steam pipes which ran across the ceiling—and quickly looked away. That day, too, the hospital was spared.

The separation from my baby was as hard for her as for me. Each time when I managed to make the difficult trip to visit her, she cried at my departure. I finally had to ask myself if it did any good at all. But I had no other way to find out what her condition was and which course the illness was taking.

As winter approached, the trains ran more infrequently. The city of Munich continued to suffer under the bombs, and many locomotives and railway cars had been destroyed. When I managed to board one of the trains that passed through Feldafing, the cars were dirty and cold; often they were windowless freight cars converted to passenger use. And I continued to have more problems than my co-travellers. The Gestapo had intensified its search for "non-Aryans," and one never knew if agents would be aboard the train or not. In any case, the uniformed guards continued to examine identity cards. Fortunately, the trains continued to be crowded. Passengers carried their rucksacks, suitcases, and packages loaded with food for which they had illegally traded; they were tired and unwashed, exhausted and hungry. Everyone was concerned with his own problems and not those of the person next to him. Fortunately for me, few people talked, nobody cared to exchange words, words which could lead to a concentration camp. I continued to slip from car to car, inwardly on the verge of panic, but outwardly calm. Once in the bombed-out city, I would climb over the rubble and debris at the train station and fight to get onto an overloaded tram which would take me to the *Schwabinger Krankenhaus*. To return to Feldafing, I would leave the hospital and retrace my steps. The erratic train schedule created an additional problem. At times I would stand with the crowd on the station platform, hoping that a train would come before the ever-present guards had time to check the identity cards of those waiting.

During her hospital stay, Irene had undergone several more operations. Each time, her rising temperature had indicated that the infection was spreading, and each time she was rushed to the x-ray room and, subsequently, to surgery. The recurring problem was caused by pus eating away the bone, creating a dangerous pocket of streptococci. A bone splinter then had to be removed from the space, which the professor called a "death chamber."

Without modern drugs, such as penicillin, there was no way to kill the infection. We had to watch and wait to see if our little girl was strong enough to conquer the infection on her own. Thus she was confined to her hospital bed and got thinner and thinner all the time.

I felt very discouraged and very lonely. I sometimes asked myself if Friedel really needed to be in Marktredwitz since making baking powder and soap at such a critical time didn't seem worthwhile to me. There were other dangers too; in the villa, the three elderly women and, in the village, any number of people who could, by a simple word, seal my fate. In nights without sleep, I listened to the bombers pass high above Feldafing on their way to Munich. And then from the villa windows I could see the sky over Munich glow from countless fires burning uncontrollably through the city where Irene lay helpless in her bed.

"Dear God," I prayed, "help us out of this darkest hour." It is hard to believe in the "good end," as my father had called it, when one feels so utterly helpless and forlorn. I asked myself, with so many dying around us, why should we be spared? Surely they were not less than we, surely they did not deserve death any more than we.

Then, things got even worse. One day I arrived at the hospital after the usual struggle through Munich's dangerous streets to find the wards empty, the halls quiet, not a soul around. Irene, like all the others, was gone! In the frightening emptiness, I ran around looking for a doctor, a nurse, anyone. Finally I found one of the sisters who told me that the administration had decided to evacuate the patients to a safer location. The huge, white cross painted on the roof was no longer a guarantee of safety during air raids. Bombs had fallen all around and could hit the hospital any moment.

Hurriedly and without a real plan, they had split the patients into small groups and placed them in the few vehicles available and taken them to various locations outside of Munich. There were no lists, and the doctors would have to search some time to find their patients. Irene, the nurse told me, had been placed on the lap of a woman who was able to sit up, seconds before the driver had closed the door of an overcrowded bus. She had no idea where the bus had gone.

Speechless and stunned, I returned to Feldafing and waited. Days later Professor Bronner called me and said that Irene was safe. She had been taken to the *Post Erholungs-Heim*, a small vacation center for post office employees in Rosenheim, away from the center of Munich. I learned later that the bus had arrived there unannounced, and the hospital administrators had had a tough time persuading the post office officials to open their doors to the evacuated patients. Consequently, the bus was forced to park for some time in front of the building until, finally, the refugees were transported inside.

Unattended for hours, strapped to their beds and stretchers, they had suffered in the freezing cold.

The building was hardly equipped for their needs, and there were not enough nurses and medical supplies. But nobody complained; they all realized that they were lucky to have escaped Munich. Rosenheim, as it turned out, was an important railroad junction and was, therefore, also a target for Allied bombers. Fortunately, the recreation center was situated in a small village several kilometers away from the tracks.

The next day, carrying a small package of food for Irene, I managed to get a train from Feldafing to Munich. To reach Rosenheim I had to change to a mainline *D-Zug* interurban train, and that required a bit of waiting. As the bombings had become more frequent, it had become even more dangerous to linger at the Munich train station, but I had no choice. I noticed, however, that the threat of an air raid did not deter the Nazi guards from their usual activities on the platforms. The station was crowded with refugees, mostly frightened women and children, from all over Germany. Piles of their quickly amassed belongings, suitcases, boxes, and cartons filled the spaces between them. The atmosphere was tense.

By the time the train got to Rosenheim, it was evening and I knew I would not be able to return to Feldafing that night. From the train station, I walked several kilometers to the village and arrived after dark, stumbling around till I found the sparsely lit building. I had no right to enter it, but in the apparent confusion and disorder, I hoped to be unnoticed. Inside, I managed to find Irene in one of two beds in a small room asleep. Without waking her, I returned to the narrow corridor where patients on crutches were milling about. There I stayed until the patients returned to their rooms and the lights were turned out. Fearful of discovery, I slipped back into Irene's room—she was still asleep. I quickly crawled under the second bed. Hardly breathing, I lay against the wall all night, worrying that Irene might awaken and notice me. Every three or four hours, the night nurse flashed her light into the room to check on my baby. It was a long night.

The next morning I pretended to have just arrived and visited with Irene; she was thin and pale and obviously not any better. There was not much food around for anyone and the kind of nourishment she needed—butter, eggs and milk—were hard to come by. I left the food I had brought on the floor beside her and asked a nurse to see that she got it. Deeply distraught, I had to leave Irene.

Two weeks later I undertook the journey again. I saw that no one had given her the food I had brought on my first visit. She had lost weight and strength.

By winter 1943 Irene had been sick for six months, away from home in hospitals. There was no end to the war or her sickness in sight. Uncertainty about this illness tormented me day and night. Professor Bronner saw my agony and was sympathetic and understanding. I thought about consulting with another specialist, Professor Oberniedermeyer, chief surgeon of the Hauen'sche Children's clinic. Professor Bronner called me and asked me to come to his office in Munich. He as much as took me in his arms and said he knew the problems I had as Friedel Pschorr's Jewish wife and that I must trust him and not risk seeing someone else. Since seeking a scond opinion would have only added to the danger of Irene's and my situation, I decided to trust him. Professor Bronner advised me that Irene could be sick an undetermined time and no hospital in Germany could provide the necessary care. He had serious misgivings that a further and prolonged hospital stay might impair her psychological development.

"And you are a courageous woman and able to learn to treat her yourself! We will go to Rosenheim and get Irene in my car and I will teach you to care for the wound. Then you will take her home and feed her as best as you can and lead her back to the normal life of a three-year-old child."

So we brought Irene, wrapped in blankets, back to the *Schwabinger Krankenhaus*. When her bandages were removed, I was confronted for the first time with the bloody and deep wound in the leg of her otherwise tender, sweet body, and I was profoundly shocked. Her leg was pierced and the rubber drain inserted vertically. Other incisions to remove diseased flesh and loose bone splinters had not yet healed. I shivered at the sight, but I knew I could stand it and that I was able to do what nurses did. Professor Bronner had made a special instrument, essentially a thin, long tweezers, which he inserted through the open wound and grabbed the rubber tube when it slipped out of position. Unfortunately, the tool, quite indispensable for our case, was the only one of its kind. That would prove to be a problem when the drain slipped out of its place.

Professor Bronner said to watch carefully and to keep the wound open at all times so that the infecting pus could be drained off. Wrapping the knee bandage required a certain skill so much more when Irene began to stand up and move around more. At the time, I was given only one wide, long bandage. Like everything else, medical equipment was dreadfully scarce.

A driver took us back to Feldafing. I carried Irene upstairs to the green room and put her in the crib, wondering how I would master the new problems, caring for her and Michael, who had become a lively little boy. In Friedel's absence, I also had to provide food and wood for the oven in addition to the other household chores. But I was happy to have Irene back and the opportunity to care for her. Every morning I washed and dressed her leg, after diligently boiling the only bandage we had. It was a long procedure to straighten out the gauze and roll it up tightly. Soon, Irene learned to hold one end while I rolled the other. With her returning strength, she stood up in the crib and after a while learned to walk again. Then, even the best wrapped bandage would not stay in place and the drain fell out of its place on several occasions. Professor Bronner had said that when the drain was displaced, it must be repositioned within twenty-four hours. On one such occasion when the trains to Munich were not running, Professor Bronner sent a driver to the villa with the instrument; a local doctor performed the little intervention. But according to the child's screams it was not easy and very painful. I held her steady during the treatment and was horrified.

Another time when I couldn't get the instrument, in desperation I carried Irene to the army hospital below the villa, the former Hotel Elisabeth. An orderly led us through the corridors, passing the wounded and sick soldiers. They lay in beds in all imaginable stages to my horror and embarrassment; but even though they were suffering, my appearance with a little girl caused laughter. I felt very much out of place. The chief surgeon managed to replace the drain tube, but not without causing Irene a great deal of pain.

In spite of these emergencies, Irene slowly recovered from her hospital stay. Michael and I were always with her, and I tended to all her needs. I often washed her long, brown hair. Then I brushed it around the handle of a wooden cooking spoon to make her curls. I took her out for fresh air in a baby carriage and, later, in a stroller, and Michael walked beside me. I used available material to sew clothes for the two children. Irene needed a warm winter outfit, so I used a wine-red jacket and skirt I had and made a sort of snow suit and cap. I lined it with white sheepskin and it looked darling on her.

When it came to the children, I stopped at nothing—flannel that formerly was used under bedsheets became trousers for Michael and other warm articles of clothing. By that time, there was a cold wind blowing between my mother-in-law and myself. She would not yield to the desperate needs the war had brought upon us. For her, manners and social customs remained the highest priority. She did not assist me in any way and had no comprehension of the children's needs.

The largest, most efficient wood stove was in the dining room. For the children's baths, I heated water on that stove in a big, heavy pot, then carried the hot water up three flights of stairs to our "apartment." After a while, I could no longer carry the pot, so I brought the big, oval laundry tub used for their baths downstairs and placed it in front of the heated stove. Oma Tilla almost fainted from the shock to see her naked grandson being scrubbed from head to toe in her dining room.

The silent war in the house made my life even more difficult. Time crept from one such day to another. Little changed, and there was no progress towards a normal existence. At night I sat in my tiny *Wohnkueche*, our small kitchen, my feet in the oven to capture the last bit of warmth from the evening meal, usually *Griesbrei*, "thick semilina." The bedroom was cold, the sheets damp, and I could not sleep with my feet cold.

On those occasions when Friedel was able to travel from Marktredwitz to Feldafing, his mother took him aside to complain about my "unacceptable" ideas. The sad truth is that I do not remember Friedel playing any role in our life at all during this difficult time although he was working to help us and was subjected to danger himself. He was far removed, both physically and emotionally, from our life in Feldafing. This feeling must have transformed me and was, surely, leading towards our estrangement.

In the face of what was happening in Germany and all over Europe, however, with the destruction of cities and the death of millions, the suffering and hunger in my little world was insignificant. By comparison to millions around us, we lived in a sheltered paradise. Feldafing and the nearby villages had not been bombed.

The beautiful city of Hamburg was destroyed during a weeklong air raid at the end of July, 1943. Over 40,000 citizens of the city were killed in the firestorms. So extensive was the destruction that it was impossible to bury all the dead. Parts of the city were simply walled off, leaving the unfortunate victims entombed in the shattered ruins of their homes. I was fortunate to be spared the sight of the destroyed city, the sight of her terrified citizens running as living flames through the streets, the homeless struggling in the darkened rubble. I learned about the horrors of those days and nights from Lieschen Oelkers, who had been staying in our house. Just before the big raid, she had gone to look after her mother in Laegerdorf. When she returned to the *Fontenay Allee* she found our house untouched, except for a few broken windows. So Herbert and Ruth Samuel, whose Hamburg home had been destroyed, moved into our apartment.

I was happy to be able to help these dear friends, whose words and deeds had meant so much to us when Rainer died, but I was not able to see them; travel to Hamburg was now almost impossible. We continued our day-by-day life in Feldafing. The war had now entered its fifth year, and Germany was aching with the burden of wars on all borders. Children and women were drafted to maintain the home air defense. But despite the slaughter, nothing seemed to be able to stop the madman Hitler. Even his generals could not distract him from pursuing his hopeless goal, his dream of a thousand-year Reich.

At the end of 1943, Germany held its breath.

CHAPTER TWENTY-THREE

REFUGEES

As the war continued, Germany was bombed at night by the British and by day by the Americans. One by one, German cities were reduced to ruins, and many thousands of Germans were left homeless. The government was forced to relocate civilians to areas that had not been bombed, and following the destruction of Hamburg in 1943, thousands of homeless people were sent south to Bavaria to be quartered in every town and village. Almost overnight, the population of Feldafing increased from about eight hundred people to about eight thousand, mainly mothers with small children from northern Germany. Every house had to shelter as many families as it had rooms. For us, living in the Pschorr villa, it meant one room for me and the children and one for Oma Tilla and her two sisters. Of course, I was already living with Michael and Irene in one room, but the new order meant that the ground-floor kitchen, with its old-fashioned coal stove, and the bathrooms were shared with the new families. In the months that followed, more refugees crowded into Feldafing and the surrounding villages.

The confusion was overwhelming. Refugees poured into Feldafing with their belongings in packages and suitcases. Some had lost everything. The family who moved into the upstairs Green Room, which I had occupied, consisted of a mother with several small children. Soon after she arrived, she gave birth prematurely to a baby who died. I saw them walking downstairs with the little carton containing the baby's body. The dead child was taken to the cemetery. It was a blessing for them.

The Bavarians and the northern Germans had never seen eye to eye. Now that they had to share the already insufficient necessities, women became like wildcats. In the kitchens, the homeowners fought with the newcomers for every scrap of food, every drop of milk. Understandably, all these undernourished women had justifiable reason to be on edge. They feared for their absent husband's lives, they faced an uncertain present and an even dimmer future. Conditions were tough; water and food were scarce. There was no firewood available. Although there were trees around Feldafing, the forests were state property and one was not allowed to cut trees. Also there were the constant political disagreements, fear of spying ears, and mourning over losses. But my impression is that even in less precarious circumstances people tend to be extremely jealous of each other when the walls of privacy fall. And when survival is in question, all that counts is self-interest.

I continued to cope with my own problems. Friedel came to Feldafing infrequently as travel became more difficult; he stayed in a small hotel in Marktredwitz. Occasionally I got away from the house in the *Bahnhofstrasse* and its unpleasant inhabitants to pick berries in the woods or to gather pinecones for the daily cooking fire in my small stove. When the Bavarian winter set in, I would hang the laundry in the garden and take it down when it was frozen stiff. Then, I lay these boardlike things near the stove during the night so they could melt and dry. From time to time, Carry stayed with the children, and I rode my precious bicycle to a nearby village or an isolated farm in search of butter and eggs. I carried woolen underwear or bed linens or whatever I could spare or "find" in the old attic to trade. Sometimes it worked, but too often a peasant woman would look me up and down and, while beating ten eggs into a bowl for her pancakes, would coldly refuse me. Carry, too, would go from farm to farm to beg for food for the two children.

Because of Irene's chronic illness and Michael's frail condition, I was determined not to let their nutritional needs suffer. Michael was jealous of the time and attention I gave Irene, and he tried to capture my interest by annoying me. Too often I lost patience and unjustly punished him. I yielded to pressure, fear of discovery, fear that the children might talk about our extra food, fear of being denounced. At times I broke down and retreated to the only private place left, the toilet. I would close my eyes and pray from the bottom of my heart, "Dear God, do not let them take me away from the children, help and protect us!" I knew that millions of others were also suffering and that millions uttered the same prayer. To this day, I have not found the answer to the eternal question: why some people's prayers are heard and others are not.

Those days in Feldafing marked me. Ever since, I have not found pleasure in things most people enjoy. Laughter became more precious and rare. I cannot forgive those who pass judgment without ever having experienced such tragedies. Because of these experiences, I cannot make concessions. I feel, however, that my values were formed through these hardships, and I do not regret having lived through them.

This period of my life is mainly in my memory. At that time one did not speak to others or write anything down. A mental picture emerges from my memory: I walked one day on the road between Feldafing and Tutzing. I saw coming toward me a group of grayish, downtrodden beings, moving along in a slow, sluggish step. They were being herded by armed guards. Sensing danger, I returned home immediately. Only later did I realize that they had been prisoners from the nearby concentration camp at Dachau being forced to some unknown destination.

The fate of Germany was removed from my existence. I knew that the country was now in the Allies' grip. Chaos and disorder surrounding us announced the approaching end of the war, but into our isolation no sound entered from the outside world. I just lived from day to day with no radio, no news, and no communication with friends and even Friedel. But, as I learned later, those of us in the south of Germany were cut off from the north. All means of transportation and communication were being used in Hitler's last desperate efforts to resist the Allied invasion. And tremendous energies were being focused on the accelerated machinery needed to destroy millions of Jews and other prisoners in concentration camps. Millions had already been murdered, but the program for their complete destruction in Europe continued and even became more intense as Germany collapsed.

My own survival, I believed, was based on our "privileged marriage." Official notices concerning my status were sent to our residence in Hamburg from time to time, and when Friedel received them on one of his periodic visits to Hamburg, they only increased our anxiety. One such notice that came in 1943 translates as follows:

Office for Northern Germany of the
National Society for Jews in Germany
Central Registry, Hamburg

Mrs. Elisabeth Sara Pschorr, Hamburg, Fontenay Allee 8

In comparing our files we notice that we do not have your identification. We are obliged to carry an exact file of all persons who are Jews in the sense of the law and live in Hamburg, including all your descendants.

Also we need certificates to find out if you, according to law, have to be a member of the Jewish congregation in Germany. We send you herewith forms which you must fill out and return as quickly as possible. You are obliged on the order of our supervising administration to fill out these forms.

It is in your interest and in those of your relatives to fill out the questionnaire completely so that we are in a position to answer any official demands.

Should you need any assistance, especially concerning any laws and regulations concerning you, we are able to answer on weekdays during office hours.

Central Registry of the National Organization
for Jews in Germany.
Arthur Israel Ballin.

I had not learned that the "privilege" had ended for many of the mixed marriages in Germany. Even the children of Jews married to Aryans were now targets of persecution. I didn't know when a notice from the Hamburg Gestapo commanding me to appear on a certain day at a certain place arrived in the *Fontenay Allee* in Hamburg. Because the mail service was no longer functioning, the notice never reached me in Feldafing. We learned later that several notices were sent to that address, and, finally, the Gestapo came in person to the house. Frau Poppenhusen, who still lived next door, told them we had moved; she pretended not to know what had become of us.

In October 1944, Friedel received two orders to report for duty to the Organization Todt, one from Hamburg and one from Marktredwitz. He had managed for months, with the help of others, to stall his assignment to forced labor. Now he had to choose between Hamburg where the work seemed the lesser evil and an underground hydraulic plant near Marktredwitz which was known as the worst assignment of all. But by this time, Friedel had become skilled at using the Nazi bureaucracy to delay his fate and was able to prevail once again. His partner, Herr Sommer, knew a person in the Organization Todt who was in charge of personnel files, and he managed to have Friedel's records disappear. Thus, Friedel remained in Marktredwitz.

All our hopes were directed toward the United States. I see myself in the Pschorr garden, old Herr Ringenberg beside me, looking at the bomber squadrons in the distance as they approached Munich. I cannot forget the contradictory feelings of fear and of hope for more, and heavier, attacks. We just could not understand why the Allies could not bring Hitler to his knees. The uncertainty was unbearable. How much longer would it last? Was Hitler perhaps unbeatable? Would we survive? What, in God's name, was in store for us? These tormenting thoughts the old gardener and I exchanged as we stood in the garden. I felt very close to this old, faithful man, who remembered Friedel and Herbert when they were children, and their father, who was long dead then. It seemed like a bad dream that, year after year, the Germans conquered and destroyed (at least according to German propaganda) and were not stopped by the combined forces of the other countries.

After the July 20, 1944 attempt by German army officers to assassinate Hitler, the nation had learned the horrible consequences. The Nazis, who kept the general public uninformed, were quick to publicize the aftermath of the failed attempt on Hitler's life. Over five thousand men—generals, officers, and ordinary soldiers—had been executed, including many, it turned out, who had not participated or even known of the attempt. Human life had no meaning to the Nazis. If that was the way they treated German soldiers, what could one expect if one was, like me, among the persecuted?

The feeling of being insignificant in this ever-increasing tempest took hold of me. Often I crouched with throbbing heart in my cold and lonely bed. My sense of isolation was increased by publicized orders from Hermann Goering that the police were not required to protect "enemies of the Reich." His order jeopardized anybody that was even suspected of being against the party. I felt like creeping into a hole with my children in order to avoid any dangerous confrontation.

We could only wait and hope that war would end soon. In spite of the hardships we suffered, we were far better off than most Germans. Feldafing was in little danger of being bombed, and we were all together. Even Friedel came back during the last weeks of the war. He had decided the end was near, and he risked the journey to Feldafing, bringing with him his small radio, a link to the outside world.

Many families fled from their homes, trying not to be caught in territory expected to be invaded by the Russians. Gossip and scary tales circulated ahead of the advancing armies. Nobody knew if the Russians would really rape the women and murder the men, but the fear was real. Unfortunately, it turned out to be the truth in some instances. The same behavior was predicted by the American black soldiers, but I cannot say if those gruesome tales were realistic. At that time, we didn't know the exact position of the Americans or the Russians, but we felt we were better off in the south of Germany. Even with the radio, we didn't know that Hitler was holding out in Berlin. When the end came for him, on April 30, we didn't hear of it for days. We didn't know that by then the Americans had reached Munich. We were just sitting together, shivering, awaiting our fate. And Friedel, his ear pinned to the Swiss radio station, was as calm as ever.

CHAPTER TWENTY-FOUR

THIRD OF MAY

One morning while Friedel was still in bed, I walked down the village street as always to get the children's milk. The distribution dairy was in the center of the village and the local women regularly met and gossiped there. Usually they ignored me, perhaps they were embarrassed. On that particular morning, May 3, 1945, as I took my place in the milk line, I was greeted to my amazement with a rather friendly, "Guten Morgen, Frau Doktor," from several of the women (In Germany, the husband's degrees and titles are used for the wives as well). When I reached the head of the line, I heard someone say that the American army had reached Tutzing, the next village south of Feldafing. I quickly handed my milk can to the owner of the store and waited impatiently as he filled it. I ran home with the raw milk almost turning sour from being shaken around. I ran up the stairs shouting out to Friedel in his bed, "The war is over!"

Friedel stayed calm. Actually, he was right, we had no real reason to rejoice because we didn't know what the news meant exactly. Apart from the fact that Germany was beaten and there would be no more air raids, we still were Germans and would have to share the fate of other Germans. We realized, I perhaps a little slower than Friedel, that the country was destroyed, and those responsible would be punished, and again, we were in the middle of it. All sorts of steps could be taken by the invading Americans. We wondered if their commanders would differentiate between good and evil or, perhaps, take the laws into their own hands and dispense punishment right on the spot!

After that day passed with no sign of the Americans, our anxiety increased. The great silence that fell around us while we waited for the Americans was as frightening as the noise of the war. There was no confirmation of the news. We had no contact with outsiders and nobody left the village. Was it days or weeks? Was it eternity? No author could have imagined the drama which was about to unfold before our eyes, nor could we have imagined what the little village of Feldafing was about to endure.

Unexpectedly and without warning, the village was transformed overnight into a place of chaos and fear. After the silence and anticipation of the arrival of the Americans, one day the main street was filled with sick and dying people in rags who stumbled and dragged themselves along, evidently with their last strength. They were apparitions, unspeaking, like walking dead. At first, nobody knew where they came from and who they were. They were not Germans, but some of them spoke enough German to identify themselves as inmates from the concentration camp at Dachau.

It is hard to describe the horrible state of these people, their appearance has been etched in the world's consciousness since 1945. Photographs of those from Dachau and the other camps portray better than words their abject condition. Those in our village had been locked up in stifling cattle cars in which most of their comrades had died. The Nazi commander of the camp had attempted to remove the surviving witnesses of his crimes. He had herded them onto the train which headed south from Dachau in the vain effort to escape the Allied army. When the train crew realized the Americans were nearby, they abandoned the train and ran for their lives. The train remained where it had stopped near Feldafing for several days, the trapped victims too weak to break out or even cry out. By some miracle, the cattle cars were noticed by passing Red Cross workers and the doors were opened. Corpses came tumbling out. The living crawled out and scattered despite the efforts of their rescuers to help them. Some, their legs barely carrying their skeletal bodies, made it to the nearest village, which was Feldafing. They went from house to house seeking food and shelter.

Most of the local residents opened their doors to them, more out of shock and fear than compassion. The former prisoners showed understandable hostility toward the German residents, but that did not dissuade the residents from feeding them and giving them spare clothing. No one considered the diseases these prisoners might have brought with them. I never had occasion to ask any of the German residents about their reactions to the appearance of these victims of the Nazi regime. Did those who never had resisted the Nazis, or had agreed with them, have any remorse?

I did observe deep astonishment and guilt and shame in some citizens. But there were also those who turned in disgust from the gruesome evidence of suffering and degradation, among them my mother-in-law. She would have nothing to do with people on the doorstep who "eat like animals and have no manners." These men had not seen knives and spoons in a long time and ate with their hands from old cans. I cooked soup and gave them what I could, but I did not let them enter.

Soon enough, the American commander of the region and the Red Cross made public their rules and regulations. The first order was to bring beds and mattresses to the nearby barracks of the abandoned Hitler Youth training camp located between Feldafing and Tutzing. Under penalty of arrest, every woman had to help restore the camp for the newly arrived former inmates of Dachau. Next, every person had to be vaccinated against typhoid. It was a painful treatment, given in one shot, which caused swelling and made work and even walking difficult. But we were grateful for this protection anyway.

Within twenty-four hours Feldafing was transformed into a refugee camp for concentration camp survivors and the already present refugees from Hamburg. Now there were white and black Americans, North Germans, Bavarians, and Jews from Poland, Lithuania, and other Eastern countries. If the villagers had never met Eastern Jews they had their chance now. They were going to share life with these displaced persons for a long time to come.

We had feared the arrival of American troops. There was no doubt in our mind that the reprisals against the population would be carried out by men who would act under orders and under the stress of personal reaction to Dachau. These American soldiers were thousands of miles away from home, and had lost an untold number of comrades in battle, and had risked their lives to liberate a country which had not been able to liberate itself of its elected Fuehrer. They had seen with their own eyes the concentration camps and witnessed the horrible sight of mountains of corpses. Now they would see German civilians who claimed ignorance of those horrors. One could not expect them to sort out those who had never joined the party or claimed to have had no choice.

The first, probably unofficial, action that gave us a sample of what might be in store for Nazis was the quick "trial" of *Ortsgruppenleiter* Brubacher. The American commander had him hung by the feet in the forest. Although we welcomed this action in principal, this first signal of the mood of the Americans caused us fear. The men in American uniform felt sure of themselves, the masters of the village. The uniform can change, but the men inside it are subject to the same human imperfections. They were our liberators, but, at the same time, avengers. Therefore, we again had reason to be cautious.

But our fears were unfounded. The Americans were disciplined and organized and apparently not interested in reprisals against ordinary people, at least in Feldafing. It is difficult to describe this period objectively. One likes to forget that human beings are basically selfish and brutal. One hates to accept that compassion is rare amongst them. One does not like to remind others of these dark hours in history, especially since many Germans had a tendency to either completely deny their involvement or try to hide this period of their past from following generations.

Often, I have encountered the opinion that it serves no purpose to bring out into the open the "forgotten" past. But it would not make sense to write of that time at all if one will not speak about what one experienced. Without passing judgment, I will only relate my personal impressions, which by their nature are, in spite of all good intentions, probably tinted by my emotions.

I am convinced that there is a latent potential amongst all ordinary men and women to succumb to pressure under dictatorships, that every person can be morally seduced by personal hardship to commit acts he or she would never have thought possible under comfortable circumstances. Consequently, I never felt bitter against Germans or Germany for what had happened to me. If ever my feelings were tested, it was during the tough first days of occupation.

Since there was not enough room in the barracks for housing, kitchen, and office facilities, the American commander took a map of Feldafing and with a pencil drew a line extending the camp limits into the residential section of the village. The owners and inhabitants of the villas within that area were ordered to evacuate all their belongings and furnishings and find other quarters for themselves within twenty-four hours. Our house, the Pschorr villa, was not within the area to be evacuated. The request was, I thought, a reasonable one, but it caused understandably a lot of hardships. The order contained an implied threat of punishment for failure to act, and everyone concerned responded promptly. I don't know how others solved the difficulties of relocation: I was busy enough helping Lulu Pschorr, whose villa was within the new refugee camp limits, move into our house. Aunt Lulu was Joseph Pschorr's wife, Friedel's uncle who was a member of the Nazi party and against Jews in general. Nevertheless, I engaged in packing and moving her things into our garage. Instead of following the orders to clean the camp, I helped empty Lulu's villa, which could be considered as following the other order to evacuate the villas. The three-story house was filled from cellar to attic with furnishings, linens, silver, and crystal, probably originating from several generations. I don't know how we managed to stuff it all away in the garage. I took one tablecloth and spread it on my kitchen table. Sometime later, Lulu discovered it and was not pleased, but I did not feel guilty. Most of her things were stolen later anyway.

When the DPs (Displaced Persons) moved into the vacant, cold houses they thought it only right that they should have some furniture and heat. The former inhabitants had left nothing. The DPs began to make fires in the middle of rooms on the parquet floors, burning whatever they could lay hands on. It was done for reasons of self-preservation, but the owners of the villas took it for maliciousness.

This situation made me feel, once again, as being between two extremes. I felt sympathy for the former prisoners and understanding for the house owners who saw their homes being ravaged. The villagers had not suffered hardship that could compare to the mental and physical agonies the DPs had undergone. They really had no comprehension of the survivors' state of mind. They could not be expected to know about their nightmares. Until that moment, we had been subjected to years of racial hatred but had not been directly confronted with the victims of it. Nobody but these strangers in our midst knew for certain what had happened behind the electrified, barbed-wire fences of the concentration camps. Could these villagers have imagined the unimaginable, the tortures our compatriots had invented behind the wire? Their ignorance of the suffering endured by the DPs does not excuse their lack of pity at the sight of these men and women.

The situation was tense. Had the owners of the houses provided beds, mattresses, kitchen utensils, and some food, I think it would not have come to looting, stealing, and begging. On the other hand, they had been ordered to remove all their possessions. They were accustomed to obeying orders. As soon as the DPs were able, they came to the village demanding clothing, shoes, even watches. They felt they had a right to these things, and the Red Cross was not in a position to provide more than bare necessities.

I tried to understand my mother-in-law's and Lulu's attitude, but their hardness even towards us was inexplicable. Lulu, thanks to her connections, had enough to eat, but she did not share the apples hidden under her bed or the honey and marmalade with anyone, including us. At teatime, Irene stood with hungry eyes watching Aunt Lulu munch her bread covered with marmalade without being offered even a crumb. If, within my own family, selfishness and greed could raise such walls between us, one can easily imagine what happened between the prisoners, who were on the verge of starvation.

There were, however, occasions to restore my trust in the superior ethics of some of the DPs, men and women, our brothers and sisters, who through their steadfastness preserved courage and pride. I met two of these exceptional persons, two brothers from Lithuania who had come the first day to our door. I had offered them something to eat. Despite the ordeal they had endured and the rags they wore, they were proud and dignified, clearly they had not been reduced to the level the Nazis had intended. They reappeared after several days and asked me to help them get some men's clothing. I managed to get some unused suits and shoes from other families for them, and they were happy. They did not beg or steal, and they were eager to restore their outward appearance. It so happened that their quarters were in Aunt Lulu's villa. I felt very bad about those large, empty rooms which I had helped to evacuate, but I found no response when I mentioned this state of affairs to Lulu. She refused to yield anything which might aid the DPs in their desire to return to normal lives. I felt ashamed in front of these men, but I could do little about it.

Friedel remained in Feldafing caught in the dilemma of whether to return to Marktredwitz or attempt to work for the military government. He went to the nearby American headquarters and offered himself as an interpreter. We thought it was the best way to cooperate with the "Amis," as they were called, and we hoped to gain some privileges for the family and ourselves. But although we made friends with some American officers, these first days and weeks were not without tough moments. An order was issued that all Germans must surrender precious things, watches, and cameras. This carried the usual implied threat that failure to comply would result in a trip to Dachau. Friedel absolutely refused to give up his radio and decided to hide it in the garden. Ringenberg and he found some loose boards in the old tool shed, which seemed safe enough to conceal the last of our treasures. A radio was, after all, our only contact with the outside world. One night, two American soldiers began to search the premises, each with a flashlight in one hand and a gun in the other. I was terrified and wondered if the risk had been worth it. We watched them from the house and had no idea what they were looking for, but they did not find the radio and soon left.

Friedel's situation was now more delicate than mine. I was simply a German Jewess, overlooked somehow by the Nazi killers, a survivor of the pogrom, while he was, in the eyes of the liberators, a blond, Aryan, typical German. Who would believe him any more than all the others who claimed they were not members of the Nazi party? In a small village like ours, it was difficult to go unnoticed, but we tried to be as inconspicuous as possible.

The behavior of the village population resembled a stage tragicomedy. Their superior manner had turned quickly to that of docile underdogs. Within days the badges, the emblems, flags, and uniforms, the Hitler portraits, had all disappeared. I was greeted politely by everyone: they seemed to ask silently for me to vouch for them. They knew that, sooner or later, everyone was going to be questioned about their party activities. Later, when the official trials began and people from the village were either punished or "de-Nazified," we had requests to testify in their behalf.

After a few weeks, the American invasion troops were replaced with occupation troops, and the small town hall became the local headquarters. The International Red Cross was in charge of the DPs. Scarcity became widespread. If we thought there had not been much to eat during the war, we now learned real hunger. The Americans had regular food rations as did the DPs, who were better fed than the villagers. Until a ration system was established, the villagers had to make do with what food they had stored and what they could obtain by any other means. The fruit trees in the village were stripped, there were no eggs or milk, no meat. In no time, a black market began. After some weeks, the DPs began to want money and were willing to sell their food rations. It was a bitter but fitting irony, I thought, the Germans dependent on displaced Jews.

I did not observe any anti-Semitic behavior in these black-market transactions, although for fifteen years Hitler had tried to hammer it into peoples' heads that Jews were the source of all evil in the world and, especially, in Germany. In Feldafing, at least, Jews traded with the villagers, they made friends, and, later, there were even one or two marriages. The same phenomenon occurred with the American soldiers. Once the occupation army replaced the invasion troops, the American military government forbade fraternization between soldiers and civilians. In spite of this, German women and girls—most having been away from their men for a long time—did not mind at all the attention the Americans offered them. One could say it was just their hunger for cigarettes, coffee, and nylon stockings which drove women of the "master race" into the arms of the former enemy, but there was more to it than that. Villagers mixed freely with both Jewish DPs and black American soldiers. Black men were a new sensation for Bavarian village girls. The old talk of rape and brutality had changed into a different tune. Apparently, the black soldiers were not used to this lack of hostility toward their race and were very generous to the German women. The next year there were thousands of babies born in Germany who were the product of "fraternization" between American soldiers and local girls. Unfortunately for the children whose fathers were black, they were born into a society which did not accept them as readily as their mothers had accepted the attentions of the black soldiers. In many cases the fathers returned to America soon enough, and the German women were left to cope with this problem alone.

Spring was here, everything began blooming. From day to day, in spite of the difficulties, the atmosphere became less strained. Somehow everything fell in its place, people tried to adjust to the new situation and find the most favorable path for their survival, just as everyone had learned to accept the necessities of the Hitler regime and the war. Slowly, I became aware of how absorbed I had been in the isolated little world of Feldafing and our struggle to survive. I was only dimly aware of the monumental events that had swept the world. Hiroshima and Nagasaki were only vague names. Only now did we learn the fate of Hitler and Goebbels and Goering and of the last days of the Nazi Reich.

In those first few months after liberation, several events stand out in my memory. For instance, in my mind's eye I see myself running downstairs in my nightgown one dark night to answer the loud and impatient banging against the front door. There stood before me a soldier, a black man, so I thought, demanding that I prepare quarters for his men. He was an officer in a French armored division. It turned out that he was not black at all, only dirty from his ride on an open tank from Berchtesgarden, Hitler's country house. The man scared me to death because of his threatening tone, his commanding voice, and his hateful attitude. Later, Friedel and I learned why he was so outraged by this German woman in her nightgown: his entire family had been murdered before his eyes by the German invaders in Paris. At dawn I awakened everybody in the house, and we cleared the lower floor by evicting the family from northern Germany which had been occupying it. We prepared as many beds as we could find. Soon the tired, dirty soldiers stormed in and fell exhausted—on the white linen with their dirty shoes and uniforms.

This invasion into the crowded house turned out to be a blessing in disguise. Since I spoke both English and French, I began to construct a careful relationship with these French officers as well as the Americans despite the rule against fraternization. I suggested that we trade our fresh bread for the dry stale bread they carried with them, and they eagerly accepted. I offered to cook for them since we had to share the kitchen anyway. Again they accepted. Their used coffee grounds I carried upstairs to my family, and at last we tasted real coffee again. I also cleaned up their rooms and made their disgusting beds which they had shared with girls the night before. The soldiers became very casual about leaving their food rations ripped open and lying about. They were sick of the dried and canned food anyway but to us it was an almost unreal delicacy. I could easily help myself to food items which we had forgotten even existed. There were round, tall cans with fatty slices of bacon rolled into them, and real coffee and chocolate, cigars and cigarettes.

Most important to me was the opportunity to explain our situation to them, that we, too, were victims of the Nazi regime. I thought I had established something like a human relationship with them and that they had some understanding of our plight. Then, one of the French officers made the remark that my husband was probably a Gestapo spy since I was Jewish and had not been interned in a concentration camp. After they left, I realized that an enemy is an enemy: they had stolen our radio.

American tanks had been driven through the village, carelessly running over fences and streets, and had been stationed parallel above the golf course. The tank crews were bivouacked nearby, and the tanks left in the care of guards. One day it occurred to me that these friendly-looking Americans might be able to help me with something that had troubled me since the day the war ended.

I walked with the children to the golf course where the men in charge of the tanks stood leisurely around. My heart was beating in my throat when I approached one of the soldiers and started up a conversation. He was friendly and seemed eager to talk. I told him about my parents in New York and that they had not heard from us in years, probably worried to death, not knowing whether we were alive. Reluctantly, I disclosed my Jewish background to him. It was difficult for me to openly admit being Jewish after years of hiding the fact. He was understanding and listened sympathetically to my story. Then he offered to mail a letter to my parents on his own PX number. I was overwhelmed with joy: tears sprang into my eyes. It was the first good thing that happened to me in years. I had forgotten what joy was, this lovely feeling when the heart tightens and one feels elated, this rare happiness of a fleeting moment. I thanked him and ran home to tell Friedel and write my first letter to Mutti and Papi. It was as if a wall had parted.

May 12, 1945

My dearest beloved Mutti and Papi,

What a moment! To be able to address you directly after these long, difficult years! It is still hard to believe that war, fear of bombs and Nazi terror are over, that one has reason for hope that we will, after all, see each other again, if that is God's will.

Well, we are alive, healthy, and all four together in Feldafing. That I can make this statement and that we were at least relatively well the whole time is in itself an unbelievable miracle, an exceptional occurrence for which we are thankful to merciful God, who guided us through such untold dangers and shielded us from the gravest disaster.

What our fate could have been we see and hear only now, the inconceivable, awe-inspiring horror, of which we were spared. Many survivors from Dachau are right here in a transition camp and illustrate with their own appearance all one has heard. It is true. We have terrible years behind us, but what was that compared to these people's fate and condition. For us it was panic and fear, and constant, cautious, maneuvering to avoid dangers. Often one did not know where to turn, what to do and there was nothing to pull one together but iron will and laying one's fate into God's hand, saying, "Now come as God will."

The children are well. Irene, who for almost two years now has had osteomyelitis, has developed well anyway. But the illness is now, we hope, in its last stage. Michael is frail, but resistant and actually less frequently sick than our poor, beloved Rainerlein used to be.

Rainer's death remains an open wound, especially now that the other nightmares are behind us. One of them came after Friedel was expelled from army officer training on account of my Jewish background. He was consequently drafted for heavy labor but was rescued with the help of his partner and many manipulations. It would surely have been his end if he would have been forced to work as a member of the Organization Todt, a unit in charge of building Hitler's Autobahnen.

I am very run down and overworked. One does not get younger under the stress of great demands. I have to learn laughing again. I long desperately for your loving, helping hands, for rest, which I can do only near you. Will this day ever come? If you can please send news as soon as possible. We need food items urgently. This must be all for now. We hope you get this letter, we will try everything to reach you again.

With much longing and love, yours,
Liesel

This letter, forwarded by the American soldier, reached my parents weeks later. In the months to come before the regular mail service was restored, we were able to communicate thanks to the efforts of American soldiers who mailed and received our letters. After what seemed like a very long time, I received a reply to my first letter. I can imagine my father in his faraway home in Scarsdale fighting back tears and with a trembling hand as he wrote:

My beloved only daughter,
What a great moment indeed to hold your letter in our hands, to see your handwriting again after years of terror, fears, doubts,

questions, and prayers. Thank God for that. I cannot tell you now and perhaps shall never be able to tell you what we went through all these years of separation, war, and terrible news from everywhere. Even during my time in the concentration camp I didn't know how much a soul can cry and anguish. Our hearts are burdened by the thought that perhaps we did not use enough influence or pressure on Friedel in 1938 that last time we were together (also with little Rainer!) for you to come over then. Especially since only nine months later Friedel decided to take that step and it was too late.

I am deeply moved by the thought that you have had nobody with whom to confide your innermost feelings. And I always realized the difficult position Friedel was in too. I hoped and prayed he would stand by you, be firm and grow more firm as the difficulties arose. Deep in my heart I had a sincere and humble confidence that you would pull through full of faith in your fate, in spite of agony and pain, and would master your life.

My poor Liesel, when you lost Rainer, when this hardest blow struck you so mercilessly, when through tears again and again I read your letter, I felt amidst the nameless pain and sorrow your strong soul and I thank God for that.

But you have come through! It is not over yet, many things must still be overcome, I know. But I am proud of you nonetheless. Your letter of May 19th shows the same greatness of soul you have demonstrated after your little son's death, whose loss will cause eternal suffering for you and us. Keep that strength and we shall master all difficulties and be reunited in the end.

My father explained in his letter that he could not say when we would be allowed to leave Germany. With Alfred Ball's assistance he had pursued our case at the State Department. But the situation had been complicated by the war. There was little he could do but reassure us that the worst was over and the "end will be good."

He told Friedel that his business, which had prospered during the war and now had fifty employees, had a place for him. He was confident that once we were in America our life would begin anew. "We can help you and Friedel build a better life, which you deserve so much. These first twelve years of your married life have been suffering only from the very day of your wedding."

Friedel wrote to my father that our American soldier friend was being send home, and therefore our special mail service might be interrupted. He didn't know if we would be lucky enough to find new friends who would help us (as it turned out, we were). He weighed the possibility of moving back to Hamburg. Our home there had survived intact and had not been requisitioned by the British. Conditions there might be better than those in Feldafing, but Hamburg was in the British sector and that might complicate our chances of immigration to America. If we stayed in Feldafing, which was in the American sector, our chances of immigration might be better, and our fragile communication link to my parents might also have a better chance. I doubt we would have been able to leave Feldafing at that time in any case.

Friedel wrote that nobody could tell when trains would run again and when mail service would be restored. The Pschorr brewery in Munich started up again in spite of severe damage, using the Hacker facilities to produce beer. Friedel announced that he was leaving for Marktredwitz to attempt to start up his factory there.

I added a note to Friedel's letter expressing my impatience with the situation. I could not understand why, now that the Nazis were gone, we could not see any real change, why we could not communicate freely with my parents. Whatever inner strength had enabled me to endure the previous nine years was crumbling fast.

With this first exchange of letters, a barrier was broken behind which I had suppressed my feelings. Determination and courage in the face of hardship gave way to self-pity. Years of pain and fear and mourning of Rainer's death overcame me, and I felt utterly alone and miserable. My illusion of a quick reunion with my parents was shattered, my misery seemed now endless. I changed into a different person of which I am not proud. Soon after Friedel returned to his factory in Marktredwitz, I learned that he had found a girl there who could give him more than I had to give.

In a complete state of devastation, I turned to another man, a man in Feldafing who had survived the concentration camps. I was feverish to be with him, and I ignored all the common and, formerly to me, natural rules of restraint and whatever consequences this relationship might bring. All I knew was that I was wanted, and this made me happy.

Thus, Friedel and I went through a strange period in our lives that caused us both a great deal of pain. In letters to my parents, I struggled to let them know my marriage was on the brink of disaster, something so foreign to them, as it once had been to Friedel and me.

CHAPTER TWENTY-FIVE

OCCUPIED

By August I had lost all hope of seeing my parents in the near future. Life in my mother-in-law's house, the daily routine, Irene's continuing illness, and Friedel's absence all weighed heavily upon me. Irene needed another operation to remove a bone splinter from the two-year-old open wound in her leg. All this time, I had continued to wrap her leg to hold the drain in place. She was now a lively child and the drain had a tendency to slip out no matter how well I wrapped the bandage.

Irene's latest complication coincided with a visit from an old friend. One day an army jeep pulled up in front of Oma Tilla's house, and a man in an American officer's uniform got out. It was Rolf Bie, an old friend of Erich and Friedel. Rolf was Jewish but he had left Germany in time, and now had returned as an American soldier. I couldn't believe my eyes when I saw him, and I burst into tears. He carried with him all sorts of gifts; chocolate, soap, coffee, and innumerable other treasures. He spread it all on the table in my tiny *Wohnkueche*, and the children thought he was Santa.

I asked Rolf to drive Irene and me to Murnau, near Garmish, where Professor Oberniedermeier was waiting to operate on Irene. The professor had established his children's hospital there in a hotel after he had been bombed out of Munich. As we got in Rolf's jeep, poor little Michael had a tantrum. He screamed and rolled around on the driveway; he wanted also a ride in a jeep. Again, I had to leave Irene in the care of nurses and doctors, and have her encounter the trauma of yet another operation.

After an anxious week, I was determined to see her and to find out if the operation had gone well. Murnau was sixty kilometers away and I didn't have a travel pass and, under occupation law, no one without a pass was allowed to leave his "place of domicile." So I decided to attempt the trip on my bicycle. I had to sneak out of the village and avoid the roads. I pedaled along pathways and across fields and through forests as best I could, driven by the urge to see my little girl. After a long way through unfamiliar territory,

I found myself in a dense forest. In a distant clearing I saw two parked jeeps and I immediately became apprehensive. There was no way to avoid the jeeps; they were blocking the path. I got off the bicycle and pushed it forward slowly while I was wondering what to do. As I drew closer, I saw a pair of uniformed and booted legs dangling from the back seat of each jeep. Obviously the Americans were sleeping or drunk. I approached as quietly as I could, hoping to get past them without being heard. They evidently did hear my approach because they both sat upright and, as I drew nearer, they jumped out and looked at me. I felt sweat break out and I stood paralyzed by fear. One of the soldiers, an officer who appeared to be drunk, asked me what I was doing there. I told them in my best English, which was not that good, about my little baby, sick in a hospital, and my urgent wish to look after her. The officer, an older man, came close and said he would let me pass if I would first "stay a little" with him. I thought this time I am going to learn what rape is like, and I felt panic well up inside me. But hoping the man's drunkenness made him good natured, I promised him to return and stay with him if only he would allow me to visit my baby first, since visiting hours were strict. To my surprise, he was sympathetic and was willing to let me pass. I assured him of my return. The other soldier, who was apparently also drunk, said nothing. I got on my bicycle and pedaled away as fast as I could.

With trembling knees, I finally reached Murnau and found the hospital. Inside, in a large hall, I saw Irene playing with many children. A nurse told me Irene was recovering normally and that soon, in several days, I could take her home. I left the hospital and considered what to do next. It was late in the day and I knew I couldn't make it back to Feldafing before nightfall and I was fearful of the American soldiers. I had no place to go in town, so I left Murnau and found a hayloft at a nearby farm and climbed up. That night I did not sleep much.

The next morning was cloudy and cold, with thunderclouds already forming. I set out on my bicycle early and did my best to find another way back to Feldafing, crossing over fields and meadows. In the distance I saw the jeeps, but the soldiers were different men and they ignored me. I went as fast as I could across the fields, noticing the gathering black clouds above. Suddenly the thunderstorm broke and I was drenched. The rain streaked over my face and mixed with my tears of exhaustion as I pedaled on to Feldafing.

On the twenty-first of August, I wrote to my parents:

> Irenchen looks very well; she had an intestinal anesthesia
> during the surgery and did not notice anything. It seems as if the

infection has finally been stopped. She was quite happy in the big room with many children, nice nurses, and a charming doctor. She is so very accommodating; everyone was delighted and loved her, and praised her reasonable behavior. The difficulties of having my child more than sixty kilometers away without telephones or trains created some minor problems. I made the trip on a bicycle which could be a great pleasure with the gorgeous Alps before me. But with rain and other difficulties, it was a minor pleasure.

While Irene and Friedel were away, I tried to have some distraction. I went swimming in the lake and even made it to the destroyed city [Munich], where, believe it or not, concerts had started again. After those years of isolation, one has to try to start a new life. Although the old weights are hanging on each limb, I want to feel once more that I am still young and that I was not born only to work or look after the children. Much love to you Liesel.

I wonder if my parents sensed the revolt in this letter. In Friedel's absence, I had found a friend. After returning from the ruins of Munich, the sight of which is hard to imagine and hard to describe, specially if one has never seen a city made unrecognizable by years of steady bombing, I greeted with joy the relative calm of Feldafing, its green trees and meadows. And I found a letter awaiting me! The first mail delivery! It was from Aunt Dodo! It was an unbelievable surprise, a shock—Aunt Dodo Goetz, Oswald's and Elsbeth's mother, had returned from the concentration camp after three years of detention. She wrote that she was without news from Elsbeth, who had been sent to Theresienstadt with her in 1944. She knew that Elsbeth had married in the camp, a surprising fact to us, but that, afterward, she had been separated from her daughter and had not seen her again. I later discussed this with one of the DP's, who told me that Elsbeth had been taken to Auschwitz where Jews were gassed by the thousands. It was the first time I had heard of the death camp at Auschwitz! Aunt Dodo didn't know about it either and for the rest of her life, she kept hoping to see her daughter again. It was not until then that I got an understanding what Theresienstadt and the other camps had been like. Theresienstadt was sort of a showplace, where elderly Jews were kept. Representatives of international organizations, from foreign embassies, the Red Cross, and journalists were supposed to get the impression that the interned people lived normal lives, as in a ghetto, with all sorts of comforts and distractions. The facade streets were built for this purpose by the starved and elderly prisoners. There was a library, schools, and even public swimming pools. The inmates decorated, planted, and polished up the scenery with their last strength. During the time that this work was going on, they had a somewhat better life than those in other camps.

It appears that people in Theresienstadt didn't realize until the end that death awaited them. The intention of Himmler was, however, to work the older Jews to their last breath and have them die from exhaustion or illness without the necessity of costly gas chambers and the use of German manpower. After all, the war effort was not supposed to be hindered by the campaign within the country against the Jews, communists, and other state enemies.

In fact, the huge enterprise of killing Jews did weaken the war effort. It involved railroads, soldiers, and many essential war materials. Extermination of millions required an unbelievable number of "staff" on every level, but Hitler's fanaticism pushed Germany relentlessly towards the abyss. The madness of those years has meanwhile, become part of European history. Everyone who witnessed it carries with him or her haunting memories and visions.

For me, one of those moments had occured one day on the *Mittelweg* in Hamburg, a main street near the *Fontenay Allee* where we lived. I saw an open truck pass by driven by a soldier. In it, seated on benches, were a dozen or more people on their way to an inevitable destiny. One of them was Aunt Agnes, my grandmother's sister-in-law.

Aunt Dodo said in her letter that she had heard twice already from Oswald, who had emigrated to the United States before the war. That made it more difficult for me to understand why I had received no letters directly from my parents. At that time, the only letters we had received were through the courtesy of an American soldier. Friedel was right, nothing much had changed for us. The house was still filled with refugees. At least there were playmates for Michael among the seven children living with us.

There followed weeks of hoping for letters, news, anything which would have been a welcome change. I kept writing as often as there was an opportunity to send the letters through our American friend. In these letters, I expressed my desperation and impatience and tried to let my mother know about my state of mind without bluntly stating the facts. I wanted to prepare her for the shock of my shattered relations with Friedel and my adventures with another man.

Friedel came seldom now to Feldafing and, when he did, I noticed his preoccupation; his mind was elsewhere. I couldn't understand how he remained as calm and quiet as ever while I seethed inside. He seemed not to notice any change in me, that I, too, had a secret. I finally could stand it no longer and I declared my infidelity. And he confessed his. We decided to separate.

I was filled with deep despair and I could not reach Friedel emotionally now; a barrier was between us and I could not understand it. We continued to plan our emigration and discussed it coolly. Friedel felt he had too much to finish before leaving Germany and that I should consider leaving with the children and without him. It was a terrible time for both of us. We were torn apart and our thirteen-year marriage, a bond of love which had withstood the hardest tests and the greatest dangers and mutual tragedies, was in ruins.

I met a Swiss-American army officer who suggested that I visit the Swiss Consulate General in Munich, and to try to go to Switzerland with the children. Nothing came of that visit; however, the consul did agree to send a letter for me. I wrote to my mother, squeezing in between the important news requests for every day items such as a comb, a pair of slips, and other necessities. I was anxious to convey it all; desperation, problems, and needs, not knowing when I would have the next possibility to mail a letter. I wrote in tears:

> You have no idea how hungry for love the soil is on which fall your tender words. Only now I realize that I have been in a polar climate and that my homeland is in the warm south. Do you understand? Do you really understand without any further explanation? Friedel is not here and does not have the slightest idea which turn my life has taken. I live in two worlds . . . a terrible problem. But I, and only I, can find a solution.
>
> How can you possibly speed up my departure? My longing for you and a new life is hard for me to bear. I suffer from the narrowness of this atmosphere more than before. I want to let blossom that which has been dormant all these years. Of all these tribulations, the hardest is that I am without your warm, motherly advice.
>
> I feel I should have been more open with you. If one is young, one has often wrong ideas concerning pride. Now, although I am still young, I think I have matured in many respects.
>
> Friedel returned from Hamburg after a seven weeks absence, and, then, he left immediately for Marktredwitz. You want to know about him? He is always the same. He is tranquility in person; quiet and calm. A sweet, good guy, the way you knew him. Surely my impulsiveness is too much for him. But I am a lively creature and not ready to resign. I long to live again in my own home, but I am holding out here till you rescue me.

Finally, on November 26, a letter from my parents arrived! I read it quickly and wrote a response.

> Your long awaited letter finally arrived. I had no news for a long time. Rolf was here three times now. Why did you not send him a letter and packages? He is in constant touch with his mother in New York.
>
> We just spent an evening near my tiny stove. I usually sleep in the kitchen on a sofa, then I don't have to go into the ice-cold bedroom. The children's room I heat a little bit from afternoon on.
>
> Munich has receded into the distance for us but I did manage to get to a movie there. It must be incomprehensible for you that a simple movie is a major event for me. It was a welcome relief from the constant reminder of the deep needs of the Germans in their destroyed cities.
>
> Irene is such a good girl; she is already like a little mother to Michael. She speaks for hours about all the things she wants, dolls and oranges, and, then, "Mama, what else is there that's good?" My God, they don't know what they are missing, the fruits they don't know, and all the other beautiful things which make children's hearts rejoice. Still they find things to do although they have no toys.
>
> And again Christmas is coming. I wish so fervently there would not be a Christmas this year when everything, but everything, is so hard. There remains only hope. One should never lose hope.

Before that letter from my parents arrived, almost two months had passed without news. But I did get seven packages during that time so that the children enjoyed many good things they had never known before. They ate breakfast with cacao and honey, and praised good Mutti, who by now was very real to them although they had never seen her.

Michael went to the same school and had the same teacher as Rainer, but he had difficulty trying sit still and concentrate. I imagine he had not yet recovered from the loss of Rainer, his brother, his friend, and his protector. I am sure that his death did not leave Michael undisturbed, but I was too occupied with my own sorrow to notice it.

And then Irene commanded all attention, all care, and, probably, all admiration for those years. She was a pretty, lively, and well-behaved, little girl, so that one was quickly drawn to her. And because of her illness, people felt sorry for her. By this time, she was normally developed, tall and healthy-looking in spite of it all.

My parents had no real insight into our condition because of the years of separation between us. Thus they could not understand why I emphasized over and over again that, because I was Jewish, my chances of leaving Germany were greater then Friedel's. It hurt them to think that I actually should feel Jewish now. In reality, of course, I did not. I was disappointed that my parents thought it necessary to remind me of my Christian faith, which I thought had shown through all my letters. This faith had carried me through long years of hardship and deepest sorrow.

My parents had not really studied Hitler's doctrine and therefore didn't comprehend the difference between religion and race that the Nazis had stressed. Few people had, in fact, given these themes enough thought, either before or after the Nazi era. It so happened that I had often contemplated why religious denomination should make a difference at all. To me, faith was then and is today a fundamental attitude not bound to any church.

But I knew the hard reality that displaced persons and Jews had greater chances for emigration than ordinary Germans. Some of them had already gotten affidavits promising financial support from American relations, and had left for Sweden or Switzerland. From Sweden, we heard, they were able to travel to the United States aboard American military vessels. I was desperate and pleaded with my parents to do something. I gave them several addresses of people in positions of authority and asked them urgently to pursue the matter. I told them about Hans Blum, my mother's brother, now in Denmark, and in touch with many people. My cries were lost in the night. When I finally got news from my mother, it turned out that she had written to many soldiers, but the addressee was invariably on leave or had been sent to a new post.

My mother saw everything from her naive and idealistic standpoint. She had heard about difficult times but never lived through them. I tried to explain, but in vain, that every human being had different reactions to experiences. I wrote many pages of detailed description of life in Feldafing, the conditions in the house, my non-relationship with my mother-in-law, the tension between Friedel and me, his moods, and my desire to be well dressed and pretty again, but I don't think she ever really understood.

Meanwhile, the German postal service was reestablished: letters and packages within Germany were forwarded. I read in a newspaper that the former manager of American war production service, Donald Nelson, announced the foundation of an organization called "Packages to Germany."

Thus, it became possible to send packages directly to private persons in Germany. I asked my mother to enquire about this possibility.

In December, Friedel wrote a short letter to my parents in which all private matters were avoided. He mentions me only in connection with our sleeping arrangements, namely, that he sleeps with the children because of the slight heating possibility, and "Liesel sleeps in the living room-kitchen."

Friedel then wrote a long letter to my parents summarizing, from his viewpoint, much of what had happened to us during the preceding seven years.

Christmas, 1945

Dearest Mapas,

You are absolutely right: I should have set to work much before this to write a detailed letter. There are no excuses, only extenuating circumstances, such as uncertainty of the arrival of letters and the abundance of subjects to be treated. I do not know where to begin and end, and I would prefer to discuss everything face to face. Often, there are external circumstances that make letter-writing difficult and, in this case, the somewhat primitive conditions here, especially now in winter when one is confined to narrow spaces, makes it difficult.

Thus, even now at the beginning of this letter, which will be written over several days, the noise of my typewriter bothers the children who are supposed to be asleep in the adjoining room, and disturbs Liesel, who writes at the same table.

I would prefer to write in English, but it would not go that smoothly and many things should be expressed as well as possible. Therefore, I choose my paternal language. Papa's compliment that my English is better than his is very charming but, unfortunately, it falls short of reality.

It seems inconceivable that eight years have passed since our mutual winter vacation in 1938. I look back on ten rather ruined years of my life and it does not feel good. You are, even though young at heart, now in an advanced age, and we show some greying hair. Liesel does not like to hear such resigned statements, but if one is, like I, of a melancholic character and disposition, one has a hard time looking at things otherwise. Basically, we survived. Obviously, you cannot imagine how we lived and still live here. One improvised, became indifferent, or depressed. One thought perhaps of tomorrow, but the day after that was in the foggy distance. Year after year, we lived in fear of the terrible power of a malevolent state until we became resigned to it and almost looked at it as a sport to evade these guys.

With the passing years, materialistic problems became more and more important. Food and drink, clothes, and a roof over one's head were the daily problems. We made out very well in comparison to others. Minor things like a pair of children's shoes or half a pound of butter were of the same importance as a nobleman's estate or a Mercedes in former times. Listening to the foreign radio in fear, the actual events of the war, the air raids, the howling sirens, the bomb shelters—all were part of our daily lives.

But let's return once more to 1938. Then we thought we had time, and as far as I remember, you didn't even raise the subject. Furthermore, your future was unsettled and everything a little uncertain. Nobody could guess that things would accelerate the way they did. In short, we cannot reproach one another for our decisions.

It will be more and more difficult to let the thread run through this letter to give it the inner structure intended. One theme will follow the next, with slight aberrations. [Here Friedel gave a lengthy, detailed account of our circumstances during the war years.]

Looking back, I could say that actually nothing much happened to us in comparison to other families. Things always turned out well, but those years cost us frayed nerves and grey hair. Year-in and year-out, the pressure was constant, the anguished question was always present: what the next day would have in store, what will the postman bring? One was afraid of the papers, radio news, and telephone calls; disaster could lurk anywhere. One must add to that the rumors and the tragedies that struck friends and acquaintances, the constant manipulating and living as one's own prisoner in order not to arouse attention or cause the slightest reason for annoyances.

All this is quickly written down, but each of these examples is a long story. For example, can you imagine the sweat it cost to be a German in civilian clothes traveling by rail as I did? Not only were the trains always packed, but one had to face the ever-present controllers, who checked every male's identification for his status with the army or the labor force.

Rainer's sudden death was our only real loss in these years. The death of this child who we both, perhaps, somewhat unjustly, loved the most seemed senseless, even in a time during which human life became cheap. But a child, this child, so unprepared! It remains a wound which will never close. And then came the hard thing—to inform you! Was he not the only one of our children you knew?

Michael, a child who gave us so many worries the first weeks and months of his life, was closer to death than to life. Today he is a valiant little fellow, but a bit difficult. His arms and legs are thin, his premature birth might always bother him. He weighs only 37 German pounds, the same as Irene, although we stuff him with all imaginable things to eat.

Liesel has reported to you about Irene. After having overcome her leg illness, she is plump and well, an especially good child, with a resemblance to Rainer. She would be easy, if she would not imitate the rascal Michael at times. The children are always tip-top in spite of all problems and, because of it, Liesel deserves highest praise. She needs rest and relaxation. She weighs 104 pounds, against 110 before the war. And I, 123 against 135.

Now I want to look back once more. I ask myself why I did not start my own business as I have now done right after finishing my studies? I had already my own money and, if it would not have been enough, my father-in-law certainly would have helped. Instead, I became a small man in Schenker, with the odor of a privileged son-in-law, in a small job with a small income and an uninteresting occupation. And what was it later at Roepke & Otto in Hamburg? An unpleasant and unsatisfying drudgery, going downhill all the time no matter what one did. It was not my type of work. I say it honestly.

A small or medium production affair, such as I have in Marktredwitz, seems to be more for me than a large commercial one. But this short review is not a reproach. It is just a statement, which is always easier to make after the fact.

Concerning our house in Hamburg, and whether we shall return to it: what makes Papa think that our house there is empty? There are five people in it; the three Samuels, and two women. During the last air attack on Hamburg, the house was almost destroyed. Two bombs exploded so close that the pressure took off half of the roof and blew out windows and doors. Now it is repaired as much as possible, but there is no heat. There is no wood for the stove and, for ten weeks now, potatoes have been unavailable. Electricity is minimal, gas was recently restored, but it is rationed. So, life there is very hard.

It was one of our best ideas to stay here in winter. Even if it is not ideal by any means, at least we are better off than in Hamburg. We have some wood from last year, and a small amount of coal from the brewery, which is, of course, worth gold. We keep it in reserve for the freezing days to come.

But the question of our Hamburg domicile also calls for a decision. In September, I told Samuels that we would come back on the first of April, 1946. We would be entitled to return, although securing the needed permission is difficult. But that plan is now revoked although the Samuels don't know it yet. If I let them have the apartment, I am rid of it for good, but if they find another apartment, strangers will move in whom one cannot evict ever (because of the housing shortage in the destroyed city). Besides all that, there is always the danger that the British will requisition the houses in the Fontenay because of their lovely location. The remaining neighborhood has fallen under this hammer already. I hope you, in your six-room apartment in America, have understanding for such dilemmas.

And now we hear your call: "come into the New World." Evidently your call is a clarion trumpet for Liesel; for me, the sound is somewhat dimmer. This may sound strange, I know millions would envy us for our situation. I do realize that life in Europe will be difficult. To you, I may even sound ungrateful, so I must try to explain, even if it is hard and some words will sound clumsy.

In spite of everything that has happened, I have my roots in this country. In the course of years, my anchor has gone to the depth of the ocean. The imperative of 1938 to leave following Crystal Night is gone. If Germans are permitted to enter America at all, they will always have a certain *au gout* on the other side of the world (I myself would not give a visa to a member of this politically immature nation). I would arrive with nothing in my pocket, and would have reservations vis-à-vis the bed prepared for me without my effort. Difficulties with the language and—don't let's pretend—a completely new field of activity certainly won't be without problems for me. Add to this the thought that some day we might be exposed to ventures in a foreign country without your help and support.

These are not heroic thoughts, I admit. Liesel will, while reading this letter, smile a little, thinking that it is somewhat bourgeois and behind the times. But everybody has to live with his own skin, which one cannot change like a shirt.

Actually, prospects for emigration, which we have contemplated for seven years now, are still not in sight. There are no consulates as yet; mail to foreign countries within the reduced Germany functions between the three Western zones, but within the Russian zone, only as far as the Oder. We had hoped for news (and even for help) from our former neighbor in Hamburg, Consul Chase. It was, presumably, announced on the radio that things will get going soon, but we did not hear it because we no longer have a radio. One has to wait.

The idea of an interim Swiss sojourn is in the dark as well. It could work for Liesel and the children, just as they could eventually leave for America without me. The matter of Switzerland has other sides as well. First, there is the financial question: it would cost a lot of money. Beyond the German border, we are penniless. Your financial situation and ability to help us is not clear to me. Rumors and some of your remarks give the impression that you are people out of a fairy tale: sometimes money does not seem to be of any concern to you. Then, again, Mama mentions savings on christmas gifts while Papa writes about having fifty employees, which seems a remarkable expenditure. Yet he says, "Hardest work, which does not mean that we make a lot of money." (I will not deny that my ideas of the relationship between work and money have shifted somewhat and that they are probably in need of revision.)

Discussing the matter of money is not very polite and perhaps somewhat indiscreet, but since I am honest about myself, I took the liberty of discussing it.

Then, in the matter of Switzerland, there is also the question of transportation. In Germany, it is still a problem, at least for Germans. A journey of fifty Kilometers is difficult, 100 Kilometers is easily a small torture. More than that resembles an expedition. Anyway, one cannot wander away with children, household, and a knapsack on one's back—or are these also old ideas, long obsolete? Do I hobble behind my time?

In order to go to Switzerland, one would have to cross the French occupation zone which would be, at least for a male German, not without difficulties.

Speaking of zones: the British is the favorite, perhaps because the English have the greatest experience with the administration of foreign countries, then follows the American zone, favored because of the somewhat better food supply. The Americans were welcomed here in Bavaria at first by the reasonable part of the population, which is a considerable group of people. Since then, some water has run into the wine. The French Zone is third in popularity, if one can call it that; and last, a distant fourth, is the Russian zone.

My own situation is, as I tried to describe, somewhat difficult. At the moment, I am standing on four legs: Feldafing, Marktredwitz, Hamburg, and USA. That is not very satisfying. Marktredwitz is difficult to maintain, that leg is uncertain. One decision always depends on the other and I have no idea of how the sequence of events will unfold. My partner, Rolf Sommer, also wants to know what my plans are. I would like to know too. I would like to feel solid ground under my feet again. But working in Hamburg while everything else takes place in Feldafing, is not ideal considering the difficulty of travel and the problems arising from changing zones. Perhaps the idea of having a Bavarian branch of my firm can be realized. It should be decided soon.

Every letter has to end at some point, and this should be the last page. I tried to say a lot, I am sure I have not always succeeded. Many things are missing, many things sound wrong, too. And, also, I wrote with the distraction of playing children or Liesel cooking, or the older generation appearing at our door, drawn by our warm kitchen.

I return once more to the subject of 1938, so that the circle closes. Eight years have passed and we thought we would be with you on Papa's sixtieth birthday. Miserable time! Lost time! We have changed: we are not the same as we were in many ways. There is much between then and now. For you we will always remain the "children." At home one remains a child even if there are grandchildren or even great-grandchildren, even if one's head shakes and his hair is gray.

Mama's letters move me to tears, and I don't mean that disrespectfully. For her, we are like Hansel and Gretel, who wander through a dark forest hand in hand, and who have now reached a clearing. In the distance, we see the good fairy waving to us from the doorway of the gingerbread house. It is Mama.

This could be the theme of our marriage which, after twelve years, offers a lot of material for the fairy tale. It is true that we have emerged into the lighter part of the forest, but the gingerbread house and the cookies are hopes for the future which is always veiled in the present, a future which men always hope for, and are afraid of, and which they can never change.

Just now my mother has entered into my final apotheosis. Mama, with the emphasis on the first syllable, was always closer to me than my own mother. And if this letter speaks understandably more about us than you, I want to say in the end that I lived in constant thoughts of unity with you. I embrace and kiss you.

Yours, Friedel.

I cannot help but read between these lines and see the bitterness in his words. Remembering the glow of our love and Friedel's determination to create a heaven for us, his patience to win me over and lead me into this paradise, I recognized that the years had destroyed all that, and forever changed us. We did not understand what had happened. I had no sympathy for Friedel's hesitation and arguments, his fears and reasons. I was like a drowning person; I wanted to reach the other side of the ocean in the hope of finding there what I had missed.

After Christmas, I wrote another long letter describing our holiday festivities. We had a roasted chicken and canned Belgian peas, saved from before the war, and the last can of sardines on toasted, white bread, made from a ration of white flour—a special event for Christmas. On Christmas day, the ladies invited us to share their rabbit dinner. Some of the residents of Feldafing had begun raising rabbits. I enjoyed not cooking for once. At night, we had sausage on bread, and Swiss cheese—also a special ration for the holidays. The next day, I made a good broth from chicken bones, and we even had a piece of meat to fry. That day a package from my mother arrived containing bacon, breast of chicken, chocolate, and garters.

"Oh, delight," I wrote, thanking her. Michael got a scooter for Christmas, and Irene, a little wooden carriage, which a carpenter in the village had made. I redressed Irene's doll and, thus, they were happy since they did not know any different and could not compare this Christmas with better ones.

Finally, even my father's letters arrived, written in August! My mother sent many, many things, only it took almost six months to receive them.

Eventually, we heard news about relatives and friends. I told my mother that I would try to have the children photographed, and I described the clothes I sewed for them out of material which I obtained through *Kleiderkarten*, "stamps for clothing." Irene looked lovely and was warm in wine-red pants and a white jacket which I had made from an ironing board cover. I said that I had her hair cut so that the curls I made by brushing her hair over the handle of a wooden cooking spoon framed her face.

For Michael, I had a trunk full of Rainer's beautiful clothes, most of them still too big for Michael. One can always use drapes and blankets to make coats, I told her. Only shoes and stockings were a problem. But I was very proud that Irene always looked the prettiest in the dresses I had made for her. A sweet little girl as she is should only wear light colors, I thought.

"Please send cocao, which Michael likes best for breakfast. If you would see his little face, his thin arms, and hear me say, 'eat your bread without butter, I have none, and stop asking me for more sugar,' you would understand how hard it is.

"When they are cuddling against me in bed, I tell them about Oma and Opa, then Irene asks if you can get mad on occasion. I say, only very seldom. 'And Opa?' Opa gets mad only at certain things, for instance, if one talks with his mouth full or bangs a door, or if one puts his feet on a chair. I think to myself, 'If only he would have the opportunity to get mad at them.'

"America is a vision of paradise for them and me. It is hard to think of all the months which have come and gone since the end of the war and still none of our dreams have come true! My dear brother, how smart he was to find a new fatherland in time. Does he know how much he was spared? I was destined for a long apprenticeship—I am ready to pass my finals."

CHAPTER TWENTY-SIX

FREIMANN

The new year found us still in Feldafing, in our same situation. In America, however, my father's life continued to be marked by change. His firm, which now counted sixty employees, moved to bigger and better quarters at 17 Battery Place, on the tip of Manhattan. Sitting at his desk, my father had a good view of incoming and outgoing ships and the Statue of Liberty. This would be American Union Transport's home for many years to come. Marcel M. Holzer, president of his new company, had not changed in one important respect since he had managed Schenker & Company in Berlin. He still was filled with ideas, and his energetic, enterprising leadership was inspirational, and, as before, he maintained a warm relationship with his employees. If anything, his success had given him greater courage and he took greater risks. Although I did not realize it then, his constant drive for expansion had made him a materialist. But he also had other sides to his character.

Although we tried to renew our relationship with my parents through correspondence—now made easier through friends, relatives and Jerry Rosner, our faithful American *postillon d'amour*—it became evident that not only the ocean but worlds separated us, the Germans, from them, the Americans.

On January first, my father wrote two letters, one to each of us with the same news, in case one was lost in transit. And the news was really important: the American immigration laws had been reestablished. Visas again were going to be based on national quotas; the German quota was 26,000, of which ten percent could be used each month. My father had heard that officials were leaving for Germany to set the machinery in motion. Amongst those was Howard K. Travers, chief of the State Department's Passport Division. He happened to be the successor of my father's attorney, Mr. Schoffield, who in turn was a friend of Mr. Ball of the Pennsylvania Railroad, our friend whose efforts had freed my father from the concentration camp.

Papi's letter gave me renewed hope that soon we would be reunited. A passion now possessed me. My wish to flee was actually a desire to escape from myself. I erroneously thought that America or my parents would solve my problems. Running away from the past, from Friedel, my only love, was all I could think about. Our daily struggle for food was greatly relieved by the packages sent by my parents via our soldier friends. We never ceased to appreciate the generous help of Jerry Rosner and the other soldiers who were our bridge between worlds.

My mother responded to a letter by sending pralines, puddings, canned milk, and fruit juice, butter, and sugar. Her gifts arrived about the time Michael got the measles, which was very serious in those days. He became delirious and developed a high fever which I treated with cold compresses around his legs. It was hard for me to watch over another sick child, and it brought on sad thoughts of Rainer and Irene's illnesses. But Michael, although frail, overcame the measles in three days, and I claimed his quick recovery was due to the vitamins and fruit juices my mother had sent.

On February 21 our affidavits arrived, one for me and the children and a separate one for Friedel. These important documents stated that my father vouched for our support and financial security. It was the first sign of a possibility that our emigration would become a reality. We also learned that the American Consulate soon would open its doors in Munich. At the same time, American consulates started to function in Frankfurt and Stuttgart, but were not yet open to the public.

Our buoyant optimism was deflated when we learned that although the immigration laws were essentially the same as before the war, the former waiting lists and numbers had no bearing anymore because all the records had been destroyed. We also understood that preferential treatment was unlikely unless one had friends in the highest places in Washington who were willing to intervene. There were too many Germans waiting to emigrate to America, and the technical difficulties, including a shortage of available ships, were too great to accommodate everyone anxious to make the journey.

Friedel wrote these facts to my father in a stern and factual manner, and I mentioned that he should be more grateful for my father's help, whereupon we quarrelled and he threw the letter away. It was typical of our growing emotional conflict. In the end, Friedel rewrote the letter and stated that I could not understand his reluctance to leave his fatherland in spite of all that had happened. And it was true, I could not understand. It seemed natural to me that I looked to my parents for support and understanding of my emotional condition, which to a great extent was caused by the strain of thirteen hard years.

I wrote to my father:

My beloved Papi, the concern and love which flows from your and Mutti's letters arouse a dangerous agitation in me. I have forgotten what it was like when, as a child, I placed my life into your care, but I am longing for it again and pray that this good luck may once more be allotted to me. At the moment I don't dare to even think of such happiness and I cannot share your optimism.

My letters revealed my conflicting tensions: hope and uncertainty alternated with impatience and despair. It was like having one foot in the door and fearing the door would be shut. We exchanged news about relatives and friends on both sides of the ocean, people we had been close to at one time but had not heard from during our isolation. For a few months, we exchanged a flurry of letters.

My father wrote a response to Friedel's long letter in which he expressed his opinion of the situation in Germany, an opinion probably shared by many. There emerges the picture of a man I had not known before, a passionate American denouncing his land of origin. He seemed like a strong bird who all of a sudden had stretched his wings in the land of liberty. I felt that with his strength he tried to lift Friedel out of his passive and somewhat negative attitude, to induce him to muster his courage and leave Germany.

January 30, 1946

Dear Friedel,

To receive your letter from Christmas was a special event. It is so terribly long ago since we lived close to each other. Twelve years: part of a lifetime packed with the most shocking personal and historical events. During this time Germany lived through a period in which it believed itself capable of more than other peoples. It believed itself close to victory yet it is now destroyed. Only madmen can believe in success when it comes at the destruction of others. Only madmen call success that which is built on disregard of laws, ideas, and sentiments which most people consider civilization.

The most dreadful part is not that the Nazis committed abominable deeds, it is that the German people as a whole thought themselves powerless and let it happen. Thus, in the eyes of the rest of the world, they became accomplices. Germany destroyed itself, the Herrenvolk thought themselves empowered to crush others, to be the only ones with a right to live and exist.

It seems that people in Germany, and I mean the good sort of which there are millions, don't understand now what is happening to them and why they are treated the way they are, and why one does not "make peace" and shake hands and forget the past, and begin to work with each other. One could have taken this attitude if Germany would have risen in the decisive moment and cleansed their own ranks, to free the innocent and decent people amongst them.

What happened, and is still happening in Germany, prevents this. Suspicion remains and no trust can grow because Hitler destroyed other nations' faith in Germany's "word" by breaking promises and contracts. The result seems to be the widespread wish to disable Germany! Other nations think, what matters the destroyed lives, homes, and cities in Germany? Didn't the Germans start the destruction?

The Germans thought the Americans came as liberators to help and rebuild. But one can help only those who make an effort themselves. Unfortunately this has not happened. Also Americans don't understand other nations, they don't know how to colonize and therefore it is not surprising that our [he now considers himself an American] occupation and administration is not exactly a success. One can build trust only with trust and for that the German people as a whole are not ready—yet. Until one day recognition might come. But till then many years will pass, many, many years, and during that time Germany cannot expect good things.

We read so many articles about what our observers see and hear, believe, and predict and from their conclusions one can gather what Germans think of Americans and what they had expected of them. Just as the Americans don't understand other nations, so the others don't understand the Americans. We are a mixture of European nations. We are in a small way what Europe should be in a big way: A community of people from all races, Nordic and Southern Europeans of all countries.

Americans are not invincible, physically or mentally, but their country is like no other. Nobody in the world can compare with the achievement of production which comes from this community of men. Therefore I say there is no greater or better country and it still is the country of unlimited possibilities. I don't regret that I was not born here, that way I can compare better. But I do regret that I didn't come earlier, much earlier.

Nobody who has lived in America for some time can ever again feel secure in the narrow and miserable conditions in Europe. This will not change, the so-called leaders of Europe have ruined it in the past and in the present. And the future? There is none.

After this outburst, which comes naturally because we have not talked to each other in such a long time, one realizes that our personal circumstances depend on the general conditions surrounding us. You have now told us about all those things which confirm my worries of these past years for Liesel, you, and the children; persecution, fears, dangers, and needs.

We are grateful to you for having done your part in saving Liesel, your wife, and mother of your children, those with whom you share the unforgettable memory of Rainer in a time which brought you great dangers as well and much anguish. But who knows what it was good for? I am convinced, looking back, that I was saved by experiencing in 1933 what others experienced later, others who perished. You say it yourself when you talk about soldiers' graves in Russia.

I deplore all militarism no matter whether organized by knights of an order, mercenaries or modern armies. It always teaches and glorifies killing and conquest rather than preparing men by intellectual means for the advancement of all mankind.

As you know, I am a believer of predestination. Is it not strange that Jagowstrasse 24 and the Fontenay Allee 8 remained intact amidst the ruins? And that you left Hamburg one week before its destruction, and that you got sick and were saved from the Organization Todt? But in spite of all that it is important not to let things glide and leave it to fate. We have to work for this end.

It is possible that we did not have the right arguments in 1938 to bring you over here. You mention yourself some reasons for not leaving then, you did not consider yourselves in danger. Whatever the reasons, they were the wrong considerations. One can be helped but in the end everyone creates his own life. When you talk about your apprenticeship are you sure that you see things in their right light? You had to learn fundamentals just as Erich did, and he too had to work as a small employee in Manchester in order to climb into management.

I still believe in this order of training. Protection alone does not keep business going. But, of course, work should bring satisfaction and should be carried forward by courage. We experienced this again here. First there was no money, then never enough, then we created again something which brought satisfaction from our work. And not only me; Erich, Otto, Hirschfeld and Hermann—each has his own field of action.

There is room for others. We are making big, international business, not mere customs or storage. Rather we are shipping worldwide, chartering and selling ships, financing customer's shipments and collecting at destinations. Great turn-over and lots of interesting work.

We have more than 1,000 shipments per month, many customers in South America, Iran, Iraq and Turkey. We just shipped fifty locomotives to the Brazilian government, insured in London. We now have an order for 120 more. We shipped an entire factory installation to Brazil. We charter full loads of coffee from Brazil to Suez, coal from here to Africa, cotton to Shanghai.

He went on for pages with glowing reports of his booming new business, hoping his success story would encourage Friedel to leave with me as soon as the visas were established. I wonder if Friedel was not rather overwhelmed instead of encouraged. Papi explained that he understood Friedel's hesitation to leave the country of his roots, but he corrected Friedel's idea about the position of German immigrants in America. The war, he said, had not diminished their status. He named the German brewers like Anheuser-Busch, Schlitz, and Pabst and the many well-respected scientists and industrialists of German birth.

He was effusive with advice to Friedel about how to run his little business in Marktredwitz, what to do with our rented house in Hamburg and the furnishings, even why he should choose between his duty towards his mother and his obligation to his small family. But Papi's suggestions could not help to solve Friedel's fundamental problem: leaving Germany, his mother, and, now, even his newly found girl in Marktredwitz. It was a terribly difficult step for a man like Friedel. He was understandably torn apart.

Emigration was much easier for me. I had my parents and my brother to go to, and practically a home in Scarsdale. Thus Friedel and I struggled. After reading Papi's letter, which took until March to reach us, I wrote to my mother:

May 11, 1946

My beloved, my only Muttilein,

Papi's wonderful, dear letter to Friedel from January 30th arrived last week while Friedel was still away (and he has not yet returned). I think he will come tomorrow and I wonder what he will say when he reads it. Papi's letter opened again a whole new world that intoxicates me and I will bring to it everything that is alive in me. Papi puts into his lines his mind and his clear intellect and those together make him my idol by which I compare all others. In him there is much wisdom and nothing that is small-minded. I have a very special vision of him and he gives me strength.

I feel so enormously rich, Mutti, that I have you both and your understanding and love. Who else has such luck? I learned the hard way to appreciate values and I know now that it isn't your financial help or your position as American citizens that I value, but rather other things that many with greater wealth never get to know.

We began to get letters from friends in Germany. Also, Friedel got requests from all sorts of people who needed desperately his confirmation of their "anti-Nazi" attitude during those past years. He could confirm those requests only in rare cases, like, for instance, for the man who had removed Friedel's file when the Organization Todt was trying to conscript him. But turning down all those people who claimed to be only cowards following orders and not really Nazis was hard for someone who had learned to fear a powerful government. We were not bitter or full of hatred against Germans. Even my father's harsh judgment of Germans did not convince me that one could have avoided the catastrophe by standing up against the Nazi government. Lack of concern over the fate of Jews had been part of the general desperation. Non-Jews had seemed indifferent to the elimination of Jews, as long as they themselves gained their vacant places in the long food lines in front of empty stores.

I was sensitive to the plight of many "old friends" who now reappeared, especially those who now eagerly corresponded with my parents in Scarsdale. My parents did not understand my attitude. I wrote to my mother that these "old friends" would not contact her during the war because they feared (correctly) that the mail was censored and they would became targets of suspicion in Germany.

My father had set opinions concerning Germans and Jews. He did not want to admit his and, therefore, my "racial" origin. Admittedly the "fine art" of determining who was Jewish and who was not was created by Hitler.

But at sometime my father must have remembered that he, in his youth, had decided that it was best to leave the Jewish community and have his children baptized and raised in the Lutheran church. He steadfastly refused to understand that this step did not count under the Nazi "philosophy" and that I was even better off after the war to be considered a persecuted Jew.

Friedel attempted to explain these fine differences to my father during this crucial time. He wrote from Hamburg where he had gone on a business trip:

April 7, 1946

Now I would like to talk about the events surrounding our chances for emigration. Although I was not in Munich these past two weeks and therefore don't know if Liesel heard anything in that connection, I go by what I hear which is definitely negative and nowhere is there a light on the horizon. Just listen to one case that was brought to my attention: a woman living in Coburg and who is not even German, but Lithuanian, tried to go to America. Her deceased husband was a Russian Jew. Her son-in-law is an undersecretary in Washington. She has not succeeded and not even in this case is there any hope in sight.

I don't say that it will never happen for us, but I believe it will take a very long time. Perhaps I am by nature too pessimistic, but it seems to me that things will be as I predicted: perhaps we will see a new morning about two years after the end of the war.

In the Third Reich Liesel and I were people of the lowest class and now as Germans we are exactly the same in the eyes of the Allies. In both instances we were not at fault for the conditions surrounding us. As soon as an American consul hears the words, "German nationality," all is lost. One hears about this attitude here in the British zone as well as in Munich in the American sector. It is bitter, but one cannot change it.

This attitude on the part of the Allies has caused resentment and discouragement amongst the "good" Germans who had looked forward, as we had, to liberation from the Nazis. A better understanding and sorting out of the differences in Germans would have been beneficial to both sides, the losers and the winners.

At first, the Hamburg population would have strewn flowers before the victorious English army, even though the British had destroyed almost eighty percent of this city. Now there seems to be, if not hatred, not nearly the good feelings of last year. But these people are still disciplined. A London newspaper supposedly reported that plunderers of bakeries in Hamburg take only one loaf each.

But I was going to speak of emigration. In several respects it is not helpful to get optimistic reports from Scarsdale while the reality here is very different. First, Liesel already lives in that other world and after all these sorrowful years she is somewhat imbalanced anyway. Your optimistic reports versus the reality here cause her a constant up and down, torn between hope and disappointment.

Secondly, don't forget, our entire future and existence is at stake after all. Somehow this situation resembles the one in 1939: we had decided to leave and from overseas came the optimistic report that the waiting list and quota were not to be taken seriously. We got our hopes up and then it didn't work.

Please don't take this as a reproach. It is just a statement. I don't want to have more misunderstandings enter into our correspondence. But it seems right to me, in contrast to Liesel, to keep both feet on the ground. I prefer to be pleasantly surprised rather than have the ground slowly eroded from beneath my feet by acting prematurely. Actually I see very little chance for me to emigrate in the near future, and little chance for Liesel and the children unless you can do something over there or if she gets a "Displaced Person" status.

My situation might be further influenced unfavorably by the fact that I was in the army, although only for six months. Even though I never fired a shot, we were at war with the United States and I was therefore an enemy soldier. Did you think of that when you sent separate affidavits?

By the way, in order to avoid further misunderstandings, I didn't regret my expulsion from the army (as Papa seems to think). However, nobody should believe that I liked this activity or the shabby uniform! I thought, as did many others, that playing soldier would be beneficial to my wife. As long as her husband was in the army, logically, nothing would happen to her. Therefore, my expulsion because of Liesel's "racial" origin was another injustice and degradation, and placed her in greater danger. So you see, my trend of thought was not that wrong.

Let me summarize: Please write about emigration frankly and don't arouse false hope and illusions. I will continue what I am doing now and hope someday to be pleasantly surprised.

On April 1, 1946 the great day came—the American Consulate opened its doors to the public and direct mail to America began to function. But I could not rejoice because the same day I learned some devastating news. It appeared our hopes for emigration were forever destined to be raised—then shattered. We were told only those people who had been in concentration camps were going to be considered for emigration. I thought this was the greatest possible injustice to many persecuted people.

As a German, my application for a visa through the consulate was turned down. So I went to the displaced persons' camp in Tutzing and applied to "Unnra," the organization in charge of emigration of displaced persons. I showed my identification card marked with a "J" and the prescribed middle name "Sara." Since I had been in "hiding" in Feldafing away from my official residence in Hamburg, I was accepted as a displaced person as well as a Jew. My case was forwarded to the consulate in Munich and since there were few German Jews left applying for emigration, the quota was not filled.

Miraculously, within three weeks I received the long-awaited notice to present myself and the children in Freimann, the emigration camp near Munich. The door opened, and the fulfillment of a dream ended a chapter of my life.

Easter Sunday, April 11, 1946

My dear Mutti,

Only a quick note to you and Papi to inform you of the latest events. It is three weeks ago that I registered us with Unnra while Friedel was still in Hamburg. I thought that it would not make any difference if his request for a visa would be made a little later. But suddenly everything happened much faster than anybody thought and already I got an invitation to appear with the children in the emigration camp in Freimann.

It arrived the day on which Stefanie Scherer [my mother-in-law's sister] died of a heart attack. I had to organize the funeral and arrange for the transportation of Stefanie from another town, where she had been on that fateful day. I succeeded after endless running around to have our appearance at the camp postponed to the following Sunday, the 13th of April (Papi's lucky date!)

I sent a telegram to Friedel and impatiently awaited his return. He arrived late Saturday night and we went to the refugee barracks at Freimann with our sixty kilograms of luggage late Sunday night.

Everybody who emigrates has to go there. The camp contains 3,000 to 4,000 displaced persons, mostly former concentration camp inmates from all parts of Europe. The barracks were once used by the army. You probably can't imagine what it is like, but it is the life of soldiers in camp, or worse.

We have a small room with six wooden double-decker bunks with straw mats. The children lack nothing. They have their bedding, good food in a kindergarten, and they are free to roam within the huge building. Myself? As you know I can adjust to anything if necessary. I have a lot of work with Essen fassen, pick up food, clean the room, wash and run to straighten out paperwork formalities.

When the sun is shining the primitive conditions are bearable. In our barracks are mostly German Jews from Theresienstadt. They are mostly old people between 70 and 80 years who now, after liberation from their terrible experiences, go to their children in America. Surprisingly, quite a few of them knew Elsbet and her husband and told me about her tragic end.

Some days ago we were asked to appear before the consul, but we had to postpone our appointment because Friedel's request for a visa had not yet been approved. Now we are hoping to have our turn Tuesday or Wednesday after Easter. We are now considered Displaced Persons because we fled the Gestapo and can prove it. We hope that everything will be all right because it is our only chance. The first train leaves Munich the 26th of April and should reach Bremerhafen on the first of May, where the refugees will again be in a camp until the first ship leaves for America.

But I don't think we will be with the first contingent because all the others have already been processed and officially "dispatched." But everything is supposed to run continuously. Actually, if we both get our visas, we are going to request that Friedel be allowed to stay and sort out his business affairs before leaving. But it will be difficult.

Although the rule is to stay in camp, we procured a leave of absence for Easter but we have to be back in camp on Monday. I am using the two Easter days to organize everything we will leave behind. I could take only the most important things. Those things I hope to get later I will pack into cases. The rest I will give away.

So next week we have to decide everything. Although I am not convinced yet that it will really happen, what else can I do but count on our departure? I have no time to answer your letters. Now, farewell and cross your fingers and get information about the first incoming transports. Perhaps you can pick us up from Ellis Island. I embrace you,

Liesel.

CHAPTER TWENTY-SEVEN

THE NEW WORLD

My letter of April 11 was the last I sent to my parents. We still were literally oceans apart, and the tension was unbearable. I was like a racehorse in the starting gate, ready to go at any cost. Friedel was still undecided, even though he had followed me to the camp at Freimann. Our relationship was lying like broken glass between us. The children experienced everything in the camp as a terrific adventure. For the first time in their lives, they met strangers and saw the world outside Feldafing and experienced our strictly maintained routine.

My reports to my parents don't reflect the emotions which ebbed and flowed within Friedel and me during that time. The expectations, intensified through almost fifteen years of hope, and those feelings evoked by anticipation of the desired but cruel break with the fatherland made us increasingly tense. I didn't stop to think or reconsider my decision and, regrettably, didn't give much thought to Friedel's views on emigration. I presumed he wanted as much as I to leave Germany. I was simply chasing after my lost youth.

Two agonizing months passed. Refugees left the camp at Freimann and more arrived, and we waited for our final "dispatch" documents. I lived in the small room with the children. I bathed myself and the children in a large communal washroom with open toilets and showers. There, I encountered suspicion and even hatred from the Jewish women who had suffered at the hands of the Nazis when they discovered I was not one of them. Although I was Jewish, I had not shared their common experience. Their nakedness and shamelessness was a bitter experience for me who was, by nature and upbringing, reserved and accustomed to privacy. But I didn't flinch. The goal was all that mattered.

And then, finally, in the first days of June, we were called. Friedel had decided at the last moment to come with us. He would not have the ocean between himself and us. But he let nobody know how hard the decision was for him.

The departure from Freimann was my first disillusion. We were marched from our barracks to the railroad siding and herded—and that is the correct word for it—herded into freight cars by American soldiers. The American officer in charge was actually pushing people and directing them with a horsewhip in his hand. Those among our group who had been in concentration camps and who looked upon the Americans as liberators must have experienced a horrible moment as we shuffled into the cars. The sliding doors were left open and we began a two-day, bumpy, noisy rail trip to Bremerhaven. There were many stops and delays. At station stops along the way, the men would jump out to try to get food and water. I was mainly concerned with preventing the children from falling out of the open doors.

We arrived in Bremerhaven on June 8, 1946 and disembarked from the train at dockside. And there it was—the *Marine Flasher*, the troop transport that would take us to the land of liberty. Alongside our ship lay the SS *Europa*, Nord Deutscher Lloyd's famous luxury liner, which had just passed into French possession. I was overcome with emotion when the moment came to board the ship. Once on board, I learned that my father had managed to get us special treatment. The passengers were separated by sex and taken below to dormitories, while the children and I were directed to a cabin with one other lady, a cabin normally assigned to officers. Friedel, however, was assigned to a dormitory below deck. He was immediately singled out because of his German nationality and blond hair, about the worst combination one could have among the Jewish displaced persons. He was relieved from his awkward situation by the ship's captain, who then assigned him to a cabin with a rabbi.

Life on board was exciting and unforgettable. Although it was hardly a luxury ship, the *Marine Flasher* seemed like paradise to us. Once at sea, tensions relaxed, and the passengers were allowed to move about the ship. The children quickly became darlings of the crew. Irene, with her brown curls, came running to me the first day proudly and excitedly holding up a cherry, shouting, "Look Mami, I have a plum!" She knew plums from pictures, but had never seen a cherry. Her naiveté caused amusement, and I didn't fare much better. We were invited by the captain to visit the officer's mess, where I was offered a Coca Cola. "What is that?" I asked. My ignorance caused a ripple of laughter amongst the crew.

We also visited the ship's bridge, where the captain explained the radar system to Friedel and said proudly that the ship was making eighteen knots, a good speed for a troop ship.

We steamed south to avoid the stormy North Atlantic and passed by the Azores and Bermuda. Even so far south, the sea was rough and most of the passengers became seasick. I lay in my bunk with Irene by my side and became so unconcerned with life that I did not care to even wash Irene or myself. We were soon joined by Friedel, who, in his misery, crept in with Michael.

Thank God we were in full form nine days later on June 18 when we sailed into New York Harbor. We were right up on the sun deck, the sky was gloriously blue, and the sun shone on the Statue of Liberty as she stood there to greet us quite personally. Sirens howled, and the tugboats blew shrill whistles, flags fluttered in the wind to welcome us.

There it was—the gorgeous Manhattan skyline. Slowly the tugs nudged the ship toward the pier, the ship and us! We were safe, our hearts raced as we waved and searched for familiar faces amongst the crowd on the pier. And there was Erich! As the ship docked, people on the pier ran and shouted and cried and screamed as the pasengers pressed against the ship's rail—never has a ship received such a welcome!

Suddenly, there was Papi on board—and I was in his arms. The children clung to their Opa. For a precious moment all the terrible past slipped away.

We had to tear ourselves away from this long-awaited, wonderful, warm embrace. We had not quite made it yet. In the belly of the ship were the immigration officers awaiting the newcomers. Standing in line to confront the uniformed, stern-faced men evoked in me an anxious feeling, a feeling that has welled up in me ever since when I face uniformed men in authority.

But soon it was over, and Friedel and I and the children were free to leave the ship, finally, to set foot on American soil. As we moved with Papi down the gangway, I searched the sea of faces behind the steel barrier until I found my little Mutti. I ran to her and lifted the children over the barrier. They embraced her and cried, "Oma, Mutti, we are here!" They had never seen their grandmother, but I had painted her picture so well they knew her well enough.

A reporter with a camera saw Irene as she was standing there in her homemade blue lodencoat with the red-lined hood, clutching her "Karlchen," a Kaethe Kruse doll. He handed her a huge sandwich, and as she took it, he snapped her picture. The photograph appeared the next day in the newspaper with a story about newly arrived immigrants from Europe.

We collected our meager luggage and were guided through the huge customs building and out onto the streets of New York. My parent's Cadillac was waiting. Was this real? Air conditioning, electric windows, a radio in a car? Off we drove to Scarsdale. The house on Rutland Road seemed like home. There were our furnishings from Grunewald and all the wonderful ordinary things Americans were accustomed to but which we had forgotten—the bathrooms, the refrigerators, the radios. Rose, my parents' German maid, served food that was at once familiar yet strange. Everything seemed a dream.

When I entered the room that was going to be ours, I found a letter lying on the bed. It was addressed to "Mrs. Liesel Pschorr." Out of the distant past came the voice of Heinz, a friend from Grunewald when I was a young and frivolous girl. He welcomed me and my family in a very formal manner. He had gone to England with his parents when the Nazis came to power and had lost track of me, but he had not forgotten his Liesel. He and his parents had moved to New York, and when the war ended, he ran a classified ad in a New York newspaper read by most Germans in New York. It read: "If anyone knows the whereabouts of Liesel Holzer please contact Heinz K. under this address." The ad was called to my father's attention, and he wrote to Heinz and thanked him for his offer to help us.

Holding his letter in my hands at the very moment of my arrival surprised me, and I realized at that moment that the war had overshadowed most of my memories of earlier times.

America

The new world had many more surprises in store for me. There were everyday events like my first trip with Mutti to a food market. Never could I have imagined this amount of food stacked in endless rows—so much precious food everywhere, and all one had to do was pick it up. Everything was there, and I was stunned by how casually the people walked around, apparently unimpressed by this wealth. It would be a long time before I could be indifferent in the face of abundance.

The hot, humid summer passed quickly. Many months Friedel and I had lived in this new world, and still I felt lost. Friedel went to work for my father at the American Union Transport offices in Manhattan. For about six weeks in the fall, the children had attended their first classes. Suddenly, they spoke English fluently. Their Uncle Erich encouraged them and told them they should convert to Americans as quickly as possible. They reprimanded me when I spoke German. The children had quickly understood that, to Americans, Germans were Nazis. Although I did not realize that these terms meant anything to them, I respected their feelings and their desire to join their new peer group.

For Friedel and me, the transition had not been without problems. My brother's attitude seemed to us one of shame that we were German, and,

perhaps, also that we were "almost" Jewish. Along with the wonders that
flowed out of the horn of plenty came the realization that we had to overcome
the effects of years on the edge. We also had to reestablish our relationship with
my family. The experience of life under dictatorshhip as second-class citizens,
the fight for survival, and dealing with hardship had changed our outlook
and our values. Confronted with ways of life we had known before the war,
and which the Americans still practiced, our "homecoming" was complicated.
It seemed as if well-meaning family and friends thought we should simply
forget all that had happened as quickly as possible. Accordingly, they did
not ask questions about our ordeal or express sympathy. Their attitude,
unfortunately, was felt by Friedel and me as lack of interest. We would have
welcomed the question: How did you manage to survive? Once more I felt
isolated, as though I were on an island.

Truely, I was on an island. The stormy sea which had raged around us for
so many years had receded and left us for a second time stranded. Friedel and
I had been married at the peak of our passion only to find ourselves thrown
into the chaos of the Nazi nightmare. We were isolated, and everything seemed
to vanish under the onrushing waves. Now, as the struggle for survival was
over, as the anxious waiting for liberation shrank away, we were faced with
our shattered marriage. We were victims, yet we were responsible.

I used to think of personal problems as if they were tests. My otherwise
concealed belief in a higher power emerged again. God was testing my
strength, I thought. And I was certain I had failed: our vows to be man and
wife and love one another exclusively and completely had not withstood the
test. Under no circumstances could we remain together. Naturally my parents
were devastated to learn of my decision, and they could not understand my
stubborn attitude. They tried to change my mind, but I was resolute: I fled
from our marriage as I had fled from Germany. I buried love deep within
myself.

I was at the lowest point in my life, driven by a primitive, instinctual,
and irresistible force. I went to Nevada, where, after six weeks' residency, I
got a divorce. Friedel moved into an apartment in New York and continued
to work at my father's firm. I returned to Scarsdale and remained with the
children at my parents' home.

I had left Friedel at a time when he needed me most. He had little support
from Erich, his former friend and brother-in-law. It seemed to me that he
suffered more than I. Determined to begin an independent life for myself and
the children, I took a job as a saleslady in a department store. In this way, I
felt, I could meet Americans and master the language. Babies were still my

passion, and I enjoyed selling layettes to the women with new babies. Later, I got a job at a fancy children's shop in New York. I remember the exquisite and expensive little outfits and wondered how anyone could enjoy squeezing a child into such very unchildlike clothing.

It was during this time that I encountered some surprising attitudes in my new homeland. My mother and I went to visit an old friend, a woman who once had lived in Hamburg and who now lived in New York. She and her five brothers had escaped from Germany and immigrated to America in good time and had established themselves comfortably; but they had been unable to get their elderly mother out of Germany. The old woman had gone into hiding as the Jews were relentlessly arrested and sent to concentration camps. The only person who dared maintain contact with her in Hamburg was Friedel. As often as he could, he visited her after dark and brought food and clothing. She assured Friedel that she would not be taken. If the time came, she would use poison she had procured, at great difficulty, to end her life. A few days later while walking with the children in the *Mittelweg*, I saw her amongst many others, in the back of an open truck on her way out of town.

Sick with agony as I remembered the disgraceful event, I went that day in New York to her daughter's house to convey my sympathy and tell her about her mother's last moments. I was shocked when she, while serving a fancy punch, asked me never to speak of her mother in her house. Her daughters, she explained, did not know about their Jewish origin. It would ruin their social standing in the community and hurt the eldest daughter's chances of marriage into an "American and very Christian" family.

Several encounters of this sort changed my idealistic views of my new compatriots. I felt even more isolated and made no new friends.

One day just before Christmas, Mutti and I took the children to the city. In the late afternoon we arrived in Grand Central Station. It was rush hour, people were hurrying about, flickering advertising light blinding them. The vendors and beggars trying to catch our attention caused me to hold the childrens' hands a little tighter. We got on the subway, and when we emerged at Times Square, night had fallen. The square was bathed in light from the glittering advertising signs. Irene, who had never seen such lights and was used to blackouts, exclaimed, "Are we now in heaven?" Indeed, that's what it seemed like as we walked along the street admiring the store windows with their Christmas decorations, the electric candles on countless Christmas trees and the kindly, nodding Santa Clauses. We stopped to see the moving toy trains in winter scenes and the figures out of fairy tales. Christmas songs came from every direction. People carrying huge packages were pushing about with rather strained faces. Had they noticed that a war had torn the world apart?

Reunion

I didn't see Friedel much after my return from Reno. He would come on weekends to visit the children and take them out for the day, but we exchanged little conversation. One evening the telephone rang. It was Friedel, who asked me in a timid voice if I would like to have dinner in the city and, perhaps, go to a movie. I hesitated—his invitation came as a complete surprise.

We met in Greenwich Village in a small restaurant. The old street was lit with gas lamps, and their glow created an intimate, and almost European atmosphere. Inside, the tables were decked with white linen and candles. Friedel shyly presented me with red roses, and the two of us acted embarrassed and awkward—we who had lived through years of more strain and anguish than most people experience in a lifetime.

Soon the darkness of a movie theater cast a veil around us. I think neither of us saw or heard the film. Our hands met and at the touch a long-forgotten feeling flooded through me. Never will I forget this moment of coming home. I wished it would last forever and I would never again be without it.

In the car on the way home, Friedel pulled over on a parkway, and, silently, we embraced. This exquisite moment was rudely interrupted by a loud knock on the car window. A policeman on his motorcycle leaned over and shouted through the glass, "Move on, folks, move on!"

Friedel managed to say, "Officer, we have been married for thirteen years!"

"Move on, or you'll have a ticket for illegal parking."

Thus ended our adventure of losing and finding one another again. Our bond had survived after all. Soon after, our little girl, Irene, answered the doorbell and there she faced the old mailman. She announced joyously, "Today my Mami marries my Daddy!" We were, indeed, privileged to be given a second chance.

EPILOGUE

The reunion of Friedel and myself brought great happiness to us and our children at last. Together, we mastered our new assignments and created for the first time a real home for the children under normal circumstances. We moved into a small house near enough to my parents so that they could enjoy their grandchildren, and we warmed ourselves on their devotion and love.

Thirteen years of marriage were behind us. Thirteen years more were given to us. But then, abruptly, this life ended with Friedel's heart ailment. After a first warning he recovered, but his life was in danger. The omnipresent fear of separation enclosed the two of us, and we experienced happiness as never before. We were clinging to each other, and, again, we were on an island and in God's hands.

But, then, on my father's eightieth birthday, in the midst of a garden celebration, suddenly Friedel lay dead in the grass before me. Moments before, his last speech honoring my father had revealed to the assembled guests and me a transfiguration that seems to eminate from us just before death. Then, silently as he had been in life, he slipped into eternal sleep, but he left behind his love for me and his children.

Irene and Michael grew to adulthood, married, and had children of their own. When I first started to write about our very personal history, set within the history of Germany in a turbulent time, I had in mind to relive the memory for them and my grandchildren. But, inescapably, I was caught up by those peoples' times and customs, which seem to have marked our present lives. As a matter of fact, the change of these societies became more and more obvious as the different personalities came to life. My memory of them blended with their own words through their letters and diaries, all I had to do was let them emerge by quoting them.

As I began my journey into my own past, the many letters that provided insights into my parents' and grandparents' lives came to me by a strange coincidence. The son of one of my mother's dearest friends, Lenke Urban, came to visit me in California. I had not seen Gabi Urban in forty years, and we had much to talk about. We sat near the fireplace and I showed him a sealed wooden box my mother had always kept in her closet. My mother had told me it contained her love letters, and she made me promise not to look at them. I knew my father had written many letters to my mother and assumed that these were all the box contained. Over the many tumultous years, the box had survived and I had kept my promise. I had never looked inside it. But that night, with Gabi present, I decided to open it.

Inside were two leather-bound books inscribed with gold lettering in German: "Letters Nov. 1902 to Dec. 1903" and "Jan. 1903 to Dec. 1904." When I opened one of these volumes and looked at the letters, I exclaimed, "This is not my father's handwriting." "No," Gabi said, "it is *my* mother's." As we examined the letters more closely, we were stunned. The invisible threads of our lives had intertwined two generations of friends. In the letters, written in the finest Gothic script, two romantic girls documented their Victorian, rather harmless, flirtations and ideas. And we, their children, seventy-two years later had now discovered them.

After removing the bound volumes, we saw at the bottom of the box carefully bundled letters in my mother's sharply pointed, straight writing and also others in my father's strong, determined hand. This correspondence between my parents testified to their sudden, budding love which was to last a lifetime. These expressions of their feelings confirmed my mother's description of my father, her Marcel. It was through these letters, and my parents correspondence before and after their marriage, that I finally came to know my mother as a young girl. What I discovered I wanted to hand down to my children and to theirs.

One of the letters from my father to my mother, written before their marriage, contained the lines: My love, Do you love me? Say it always, let me hear the sweet, wonderful words always. Say it again when I should die.

These words are especially moving to me, for when Marcel died in 1962 at the age of eighty-three, in Lenox Hill Hospital in New York, my mother was not able to be with him to fulfill his plea by saying the precious words: "I love you, my Marci". Marcel had suffered a small stroke and was taken to the hospital a few days before. Trudel never left his side. But on this one day, she went to lunch with her friend Kaethe Schlesinger, and on the way, she suffered an attack of Meniere's disease, an event of the inner ear that caused her to lose equilibrium. She was almost unconscious when she was carried into the hospital and placed, not next to her beloved Marci, but in a separate room on a different floor. There she lay, anguished by her ever-present premonitions, helpless and unhappy.

I came to the hospital to see her, then went to my father's room. I went to the window to close it; as I turned, I saw my father raise himself to the edge of bed, his gaze broke, his head fell back, and he was gone. I ran into the hall calling for doctors and nurses, but Papi was lifeless and no one could help.

I was so used to seeing my parents together, strong and healthy, that I was not prepared to carry the burden of the loss of a beloved father and also carry the tragic message to my very sick mother. I spent no time at the deathbed— instead, I escaped, suppressing the realization of what had happened, and went to face my mother. I opened her door softly, in the darkened room where she lay, her glaucoma-stricken eyes closed. I perceived her small frame and a heartbreaking pity seized me. She felt my presence. Her lips formed one word: "Marci?" she whispered. And I nodded.

In spite of the doctor's warnings, we raised her up into a wheelchair and reunited this couple for their last farewell. After having read my parents' letters, I am convinced that in spite of this dramatic separation at the moment of Marcel's death, he heard her say the words she had promised him sixty-six years earlier.

These letters and the connecting stories span three generations and two continents. It may be up to the reader to discern between traits and traditions particular to my family and those of different cultures and customs in different places. Times have changed in all of them. The forward motion of science and technology has an inescapable influence on us. But has man preserved his human nature in spite of it all?

Germany and the Germans is an endless theme. We are showered with literature and documentation about its recent history. I tried to tell the rather simple truth about people one finds everywhere in all countries. I feel the events in the period of history I witnessed could happen anywhere, if the stage is set similarly and the actors are different people but the same characters. That is to say, we humans are fallible.

Get Published, Inc!
Thorofare, NJ 08086
08 September 2009
BA2009251